Beginning Game Graphics

Harry J. Evry

Professional ■ Trade ■ Reference

ISBN: 1-59200-430-X
Library of Congress Catalog Card Number: 2004091913
Printed in the United States of America

04 05 06 07 08 BH 10 9 8 7 6 5 4 3 2 1

Professional ■ Trade ■ Reference

Thomson Course Technology PTR, a division of
Thomson Course Technology
25 Thomson Place
Boston, MA 02210
http://www.courseptr.com

SVP, Thomson Course Technology PTR:
Andy Shafran

Publisher:
Stacy L. Hiquet

Senior Marketing Manager:
Sarah O'Donnell

Marketing Manager:
Heather Hurley

Manager of Editorial Services:
Heather Talbot

Senior Acquisitions Editor:
Emi Smith

Senior Editor:
Mark Garvey

Associate Marketing Manager:
Kristin Eisenzopf

Marketing Coordinator:
Jordan Casey

Project Editor:
Tarida Anantachai,
Argosy Publishing

Technical Reviewer:
Norm Fortier

Thomson Course Technology PTR Market Coordinator:
Elizabeth Furbish

Copy Editor:
Ginny Kaczmarek

Interior Layout Tech:
Susan Honeywell,
LJ Graphics

Cover Designer:
Mike Tanamachi

CD-ROM Producer:
Brandon Penticuff

Indexer:
Peggy Holloway

Proofreaders:
Jan Cocker and Steve Honeywell

I proudly dedicate this book to the loving memory of my mother, Phyllis Evry, and my father-in-law, John H. Prince.

Phyllis Evry

John H. Prince

Without their endless love, limitless support, and profound inspiration, this book would not exist.

They made learning fun. They made life rich, and they gave boundless gifts of joy, music, kindness, love, and laughter, to touch the heart, lift the soul, and brighten the world.

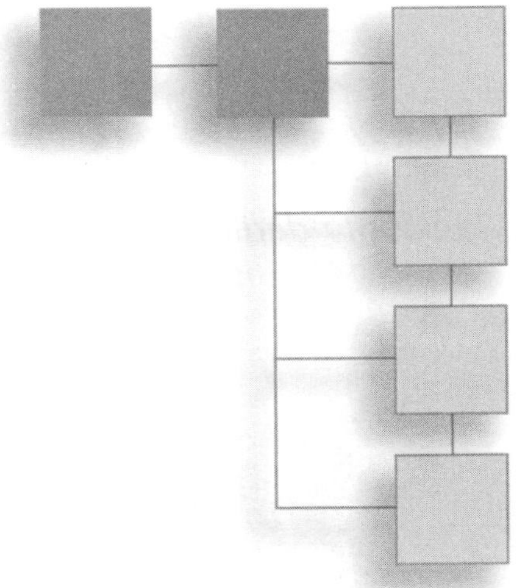

Foreword

In the distant past, almost all great games were born and bred in the back bedroom. Creativity, and sometimes outright wackiness, reigned supreme. Then, not so long ago, the game business began to look a little more like Hollywood each year. If you couldn't afford a high-end machine with high-end hardware, speak C like a second language, and put out mega-bucks for a marketing campaign, you couldn't get a game on the market.

Fast-forward to the current decade: The tools are back in your hands! The average budget computer today beats the pants off of the first Pentiums, and advanced, but easy-to-use, tools are widely available and inexpensive. For a song (OK, relatively cheaply) you can fully outfit a one- or two-person development studio capable of creating some pretty advanced games—and, because of the Internet, you actually have a fighting chance of getting someone to take notice of them.

Whether you choose to put your creations on phones, handheld computers, or PCs, 3-D graphics are the mainstay of modern games. Knowing the tools and techniques to create this stunning and compelling imagery could be a key factor in the success of your gaming opus. With this book and your very own copy of gameSpace Light, you can develop your 3-D modeling skills as you create your own video-game models.

All it takes to create great games today is a little creativity, a handful of low-cost tools, a lot of time, and a whole bunch of motivation. I'm guessing that, because you are reading this book, you have most of these requirements well in hand. Now, let's see what you can do. Good luck.

Michael E. Arrington
Director/Marketing
Caligari Corporation

Acknowledgments

It takes an enormous effort to create a book like this, and I am very grateful to have had the privilege of working with so many talented and dedicated professionals.

I gratefully acknowledge the contributions of all of my friends, partners, co-workers, clients, students, mentors, colleagues, and associates, whose stories, ideas, vision, guidance, art, and insight have directly or indirectly helped to shape the content of this book.

Special Thanks

Special thanks to Jackie for being there; to my father, Arthur Evry, for countless examples and opportunities; to Coralie and all our friends and family for their generous support and encouragement along every step of the way.

I would like to offer a special note of gratitude to my good friend and trusted illustrator, Steve Mutz, who has never failed to bring life and magic to even my oddest visions and craziest ideas. More than merely adding visual interest to the pages of this book, his outstanding artwork served as a powerful inspiration to help keep the book focused and move the book along.

Thank you, Emi Smith, Heather Talbot, and Michael Arrington for your faith and support.

Thank you, Tarida Anantachai, for your tireless effort, assistance, and dedication.

Thank you, Ginny Kaczmarek, Norm Fortier, Sue Honeywell, Jan Cocker, Steve Honeywell, and Peggy Holloway, for your patient guidance and many contributions to the book.

Thanks to Heather Hurley, Mike Tanamachi, and Brandon Penticuff, for pulling it all together in a beautiful package.

I can't possibly list everyone who contributed to the book, so in conclusion, let me thank the entire editorial, layout, marketing, sales, distribution, business, and production teams, who have worked countless hours to make this book a success.

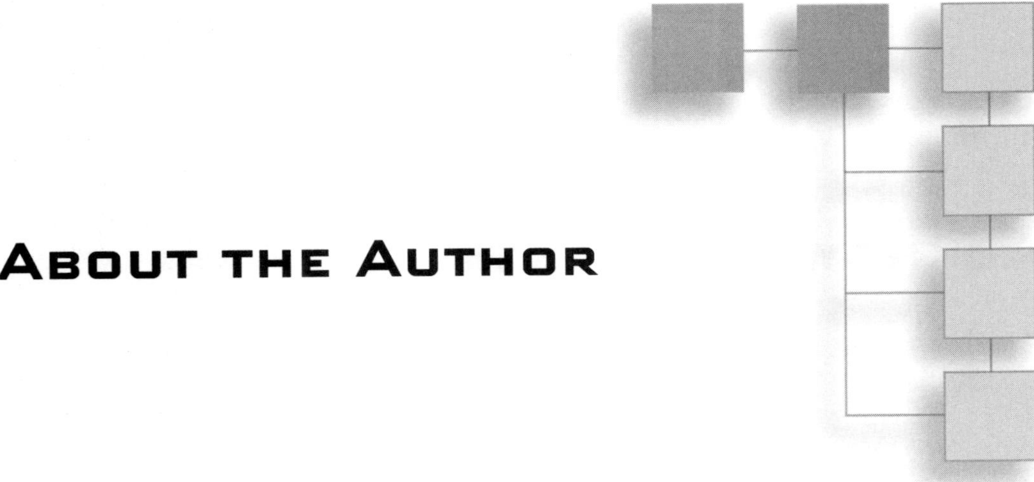

About the Author

Harry Evry is a programmer, designer, artist, composer, and producer. He has taught and presented numerous classes and seminars on subjects ranging from game scripting, programming, and media development to environmental theming, architectural simulation, and level design. He is the founder and president of Gamescapers, and is the program director responsible for the development of "The Gamescapers Workshops."

Harry has been responsible for a wide range of commercial projects ranging from video games, theme-park attractions, and television shows, to game shows, casino systems, flight controls, and consoles and displays for Paramount's Academy Award-winning Star Trek Art Department.

Harry co-authored and sold his first commercial video game while still in junior high school, and has won numerous awards from the California State and Ventura County Science Fairs for his pioneering efforts in Computer Animation, Network Rendering, Voice Synthesis, and Virtual Machines. At the age of 13, Harry became the youngest fully matriculated student ever admitted into California State University Northridge.

Harry considers himself very fortunate to have had the opportunity to work, consult, and subcontract with such innovative and respected companies as Aristocrat Gaming Systems, Bechtel, Cooksey Design Associates, DBI, International Magic Factory, Landmark Entertainment, Lorimar Television, Mattel, Paramount Pictures, PowerMag, SmartSound Software, Sony, SpectraFX, The Technology Arts and Magic Company, The Walt Disney Company, Thomson Learning, Universal Studios, Virtual Horizons, Vista Electronics, Walt Disney Imagineering, and Warner Communications.

Contents

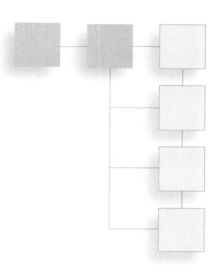

Introduction

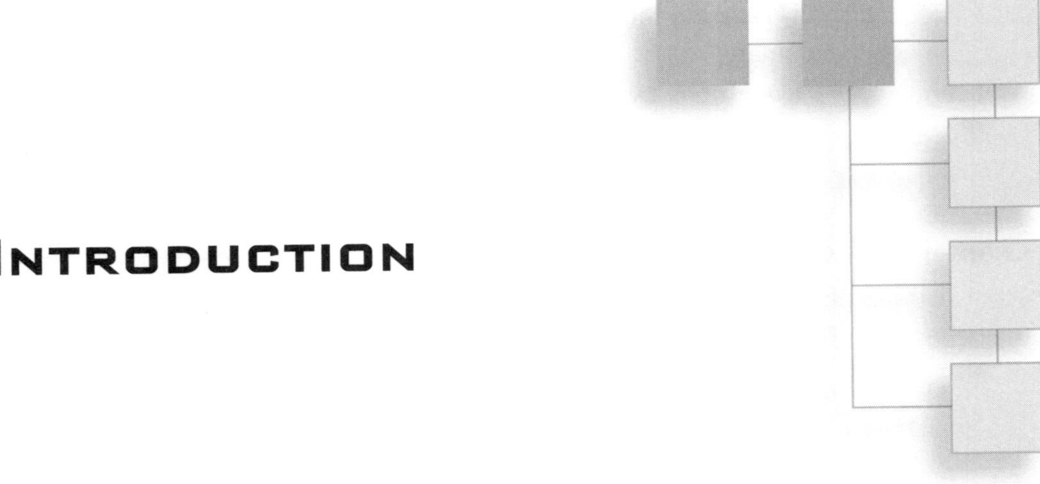

The video-game and interactive entertainment industry is the fastest growing segment of the world economy. New game studios are appearing each year, and as technology continues to improve, new opportunities are constantly emerging.

This book provides an introduction to the exciting world of the video-game artist. It offers powerful and easy-to-use tools to get you started, and covers many of the methods, philosophies, and proven techniques that can improve your game demos and help separate you from the crowd.

What You'll Find in This Book

This book contains everything you need to build your own video-game models. It comes with a full, working version of gameSpace Light, as well as an exclusive 3-D video game that you can use to test the new models you build.

By the time you reach Chapter 4, you will already know how to build a model and import it into a game. By the end of Chapter 11, you will be building sophisticated models like a professional. Chapter 12 is a bonus chapter where you will build your own game vehicle and take it for a test drive.

Who This Book Is For

This book is intended for four types of readers:

Video-Game Enthusiasts

Whatever your age or level of experience, if you love video games, this book is for you.

Whether you are an avid gamer or just want to learn more about the industry, *Beginning Game Graphics* will introduce you to the most fundamental concepts of game development. It will walk you through your first simple models, help you build your first game, and help you develop the skills to create sophisticated game models of your own.

Experienced Artists Looking to Enter the Video-Game Industry

Game artists use much of the same tools and technology used by today's digital animators and special effects artists, but the needs and methods of video-game art and film art are far from the same.

If you are an experienced digital artist or a 3-D animator with a background in design, film, or animation, this book will give you the knowledge and insight to tune your skills in the direction of video games.

Students and Teachers

I have been teaching professional game development classes for over four years. This book is designed to serve as an accompaniment to a 10 to 15 week class. The depth and the subject matter presented are strong enough for a university, college, or post-secondary class on game graphics, but I have tried to keep the tone light-hearted and easily digestible.

I have tried to keep this book fun, friendly, and easily readable, in the hopes that it will motivate and inspire college students and professionals, while still holding the attention of much younger audiences. I have successfully taught many high-school and elementary school students to create their own games, and several classes of elementary school students actually helped to test some of the lessons in this book.

Game Programmers, Producers, and Level Designers

This book is ideal for programmers, producers, level designers, and any independent video-game developers who would like to model their own props, sets, and characters. Whether you need to build models for your own demos, or just want to impress the art department, this book offers a crash course in 3-D modeling, with the specific needs of video games in mind.

How This Book Is Organized

Chapters 1 and 2 introduce the fundamental concepts of video games and video-game graphics. They are written from the perspective of the professional game artist, but their content is equally useful for game designers, level designers, game programmers, and producers.

Chapter 3 shows you how to install gameSpace and the Adventure Explorer video game.

Chapters 4 through 11 guide you on a step-by-step path from the most basic primitive modeling techniques to some of the advanced workflows used by professional game artists.

Chapter 12 is a bonus chapter that shows you how use your new modeling skills to model your own vehicles, which you can actually ride in the game.

The enclosed CD contains a full version of gameSpace Light that is free to use and will never expire. It also contains the Adventure Explore video game, a utility called ObjectImporter, several video-tutorials, and a directory of Textures that you will use in projects throughout the book.

Chapter 1

Fundamentals

Game artists create the characters, backgrounds, objects, textures, and visual assets that create the appearance of a game. The video game industry is relatively young, but games have had a place in our society for a very long time.

The Origin of Gaming

Games have been around since the beginning of civilization. Before the first child learned to walk on two feet, games were already a proven technique of natural education.

Animals use games as a way to prove their strengths and develop their skills. If you have ever had a pet dog, cat, or bird, you have undoubtedly found that even pets invent games to occupy their time. It is no wonder, then, that the allure of games has a universal appeal. Games are instinctual for animals, as well as for humanity.

What Is a Game?

A game is an activity of intelligent creatures. These could be people, animals, or automated robots with artificial intelligence.

> **A game is any contest between two or more intelligent entities that is governed by a complete set of mutually accepted rules.**

A game must have a comprehensive set of rules. When you buy a card game or a board game, you are not just buying printed cards and a colorfully painted board. The key components that define any game are the official rules and the step-by-step directions that make the game unique. The biggest difference between dodgeball and baseball is not the shape of the ball, but how the games are played.

The rules of a game must be complete. They must cover all possibilities, or the game could easily disintegrate into confusion and chaos. Imagine playing a game of football if there was no rule for what should happen to continue the game after a field goal. The goal would be complete, and the game would erupt into complete confusion because none of the players would know what was coming next.

The rules must be understood and accepted by all of the players. If one player doesn't know it is a game, then it is not a game. If one player doesn't understand the rules of the game, then that person cannot really play the game. Games generally have objectives and goals for the players to achieve, and most games have rules to determine the winners and losers.

Risk and Reward

Players take a risk whenever they play a game. They risk losing, experiencing frustration, and suffering disappointment. They risk their precious time. They may even risk money or personal injury. Players expect something in return for this risk. To meet their expectations, game developers must understand what motivates players.

There are many reasons a player plays a game. This chapter describes several of these factors. To create great games, game artists should keep these factors in mind throughout the development process.

Exercise and Education

Just like the animals that play games, human beings have an instinctual need to learn, grow, and improve their skills. Games can fulfill this need in several ways, by providing physical and mental challenges; by exercising problem-solving skills; and by improving dexterity, reflexes, agility, and hand-eye coordination.

A simulation is a game designed with the principal goal of accurately modeling reality.

Games can simulate real-world problems and situations. They allow players to test their skills and strategic abilities without exposing them to what might otherwise be hazardous or perilous situations. The more believable the game, the better it simulates reality.

> My grandfather Albert Evry was a senior executive at the Department of Defense. He was responsible for the development, test, and evaluation of new systems and technologies for the United States Armed Forces. I remember traveling with him to a military base in Maryland, and being surprised to see a large room full of giant tables cluttered with tiny toy tanks, submarines, and boats.
>
> The United States' Department of Defense invests millions of dollars each year developing games and simulations. Simulations are games that are specifically designed to emulate real-life situations.
>
> The Joint Chiefs of Staff have long appreciated the educational value of games. War games and role-playing games are a time-tested staple of military training. From fighter pilots to artillery gunners, today's soldiers fight their first battles in video games.

Game artists and designers balance the artistic vision and entertainment value of a game against the accurate simulation of real-world experiences. Too much reality can be mundane, tedious, and boring. Too little reality can be confusing and disorienting.

Discovery and Exploration

You walk cautiously down a winding stairway. With every twist and turn of the path, another landing comes into view. Large iron torches, bolted to the walls, flood each landing with a pool of flickering amber light. You cross beneath an arch and emerge into a long, dark hallway. Cautiously, you move through the darkness, until your hands feel the familiar form of a …

What comes next? Would you like to know?

A close relative of education is discovery. As a player explores an environment, whether it is real, imaginary, or virtual, the player learns a little more with every step.

> **Discovery is the act of noticing or learning something for the first time in one's experience.**

> **Exploration is the act of searching or investigating for the purpose of discovery.**

> **Curiosity is a natural drive to know or learn.**

Like a movie or novel, games allow their players to discover new realms. Through games, players can discover new places, times, and characters. Each new detail a player discovers along the way feeds the player's curiosity. The more complex and mysterious the game's environment, the more opportunities for discovery the game can provide. Each twist and turn of the path provides the player with one more opportunity to discover what's around the bend. Even such a minor discovery as what lies beyond the next door can in some small way increase a player's amusement.

This is equally true for amusement park rides, zoos, exhibits, and museums. Guests riding dark rides, such as Disneyland's Mr. Toad's Wild Ride, Alice in Wonderland, The Haunted Mansion, and The Pirates of the Caribbean attractions, derive much of their enjoyment from the simple fulfillment of curiosity. They experience a small sense of discovery as they turn every corner. They may even experience a little discovery by simply turning their own heads to look around.

Whether playing in a theme park or playing a video game, players know they are not really somewhere else, but they want to believe their exploration is real. A game artist's job is to help them.

Fantasy Fulfillment

You are the captain of a star destroyer on a secret mission to save the galaxy. You could be a mighty warrior, a dragon-master, a powerful sorceress, or the Emperor of Lower Earth. Games can do more than just immerse you in another place. They can transform you into someone or something you are not.

Games allow players to experience situations and activities that would not be possible in their normal daily lifestyle. They enable players to live out fantasies.

A fantasy is an imagined situation that a person thinks about to experience pleasure or entertainment. Fantasies can be realistic, but often they involve situations and activities that are unlikely to happen in reality.

Games give players an opportunity to become someone they are not. When players have more freedom and control over their virtual alter egos, they experience a greater sense of agency.

Role-playing is the act of pretending to be someone or something you are not.

As the directness, flexibility, and intimacy of the control that players can exert on their characters in a game increases, the more the players feel that they truly are their characters. They control the characters as their agents. They experience the world through the characters' eyes.

Sense of agency refers to the player's feeling of power, control, and personal connection to a character or entity within a game.

Game artists can significantly impact the players' ability to develop a sense of agency with their characters in a game. The more responsive the characters' animation, the more the players feel in control of the character.

A very crude and unrealistic character can sometimes detract from the players' sense of agency, but many well-designed games have successfully overcome this particular weakness.

Fantasy role-playing can be extremely satisfying and entertaining. Role-playing can be much more rewarding for the player, if the player can develop a strong sense of agency with their characters in a game. Think of the difference between watching your friends play "cops and robbers" and playing "cops and robbers" yourself. Watching your friends may be amusing, but playing the game yourself is far more entertaining. When you are the cop or robber, you have a very strong sense of agency in the game. You are in fact the agent.

Dramatic Narrative

Samantha stood alone on the moonlit street. Trembling in the cold night air, she stared nervously through the fog. Running in the rain had left her soggy and exhausted. Her knees were scraped. Her feet ached and her heart pounded in her chest.

Her long blonde hair fell across her tearful blue eyes, as she looked down in exhaustion. Fighting to catch her breath, she heard the metal clack of iron boots on the cobblestones behind her. She fought to hold back a scream, as she realized there was no place left to hide, but suddenly…

For thousands of years, people have been captivated by the art of storytelling. Like games stories serve an important educational function. Stories allow one individual to pass their thoughts, lessons, and experiences to others.

Stories help prevent each successive generation from repeating the hard lessons of the many generations that have come before them. Dramatic storytelling is also an ageless form of entertainment. Games can be considered interactive stories.

Dramatic narrative is the art of telling a story in a way that captivates the audience and leaves them wanting to know more.

Screenwriter and director Alan Armer described drama as "a man walking on an empty stage holding a lit bomb." Once the fuse is lit the audience will sit captivated and attentive, curious to see what will happen when the fire burns its way up the fuse.

There are two factors at work in this example.

- The audience is curious. They want to see the results of the explosion that they expect to follow.
- The audience is worried. They care what happens to the man holding the bomb.

The curiosity factor is simply the desire for discovery. The worry is something much more powerful.

As early humans grew to depend on each other, they developed an instinctual ability to worry about each other. When a person can empathize with another person, they can share and understand their feelings. They can emotionally feel their pain.

Empathy is the ability of one person to share, feel, and understand the feelings of another person. The second person can be a friend, a stranger, or a fictional character.

Not only can people share each others feelings, psychiatrists (and many song) writers have argued that people have a basic need to relate to each other in this way.

After reading the story about Samantha, above, you have been curious to know what happens next. Hopefully you were also concerned about her. If you were even a little concerned for her safety, then you have experienced empathy. You have shared her pain and fear.

In writing Samantha's story I tried to arouse your sense of empathy for Samantha. I tried to give you enough detail to make her seem real. I wanted her to seem like a person that you might actually know, and I tried to verbally paint a picture of her feelings in a way that would help you relate to her in a very personal way.

Game artists do the same thing for the characters in games. It is far easier for players to empathize with characters that are lifelike and believable. When a character looks and acts like a real person, the players may recognize in the characters many human traits and emotions.

To maximize empathy, a dramatic writer must carefully describe the emotional state of their characters. A game artist must carefully design and animate their characters to evoke and display clear emotions that players will instantly understand.

Many great character artists began by drawing caricatures. Legendary cartoon artists like Stan Lee, Bill Justice, Marc Davis, Dave Thomas, Ollie Johnson, and Ward Kimbal were masters of caricature. They used their caricature skills to create renowned casts of characters that have earned a permanent place in the hearts of millions of children and adults.

A caricature is a representation of a person or object in which the subject's distinctive features, emotions, or peculiarities are deliberately exaggerated.

Walt Disney understood the importance of incorporating clear emotion into the design of his characters. Snow White's friends, the Seven Dwarfs, were extreme caricatures. Each dwarf was designed to express a single identifiable emotion. Happy was happy. Dopey was dopey. Grumpy was grumpy, and Bashful was bashful. Children in every part of the world immediately recognize and relate to these simple human emotions.

Thinking of a game as an interactive story is not a new concept. Some of the first text based games were adventure games, where the player was given a written description of a situation, and asked to tell the computer what they wanted to do.

Interactive storytelling is not unique to video games. During the early 1980s several series of interactive novels became extremely popular. Each interactive novel contained many different endings. At the end of each page in the book the author would invite the reader to make a decision. The reader's decision would determine the page on which the story would continue, until they reached an end.

Edward Packard wrote the first of these books, *Sugarcane Island*, which was illustrated by Barbara Carter. It was originally released by Vermont Crossroads Press and later re-released as part of the popular "Choose Your Own Adventure Books" series. The *Choose Your Own Adventure Books*, published by Random House, were so popular that more than 180 titles were released.

(continued)

(continued from previous page)

Another important step in the evolution of interactive fiction was the fantasy role-playing game called Dungeons and Dragons. Dungeons and Dragons was developed by Gary Gygax and Dave Arneson. The game is played in groups, where one player is selected as a Dungeon Master. The Dungeon Master uses a secret map and a set of dice to guide and narrate an interactive story. The other players each control their own character in that story.

New approaches and better techniques of implementing and improving the interactive storytelling process in video games is one of the most important and exciting areas of potential growth in this rapidly changing industry.

Escapism

An important aspect of role-playing is escapism. Movies, books, television, and themeparks all provide outlets for escapism. They offer audiences an opportunity to momentarily forget reality. Audiences are mentally transported to an alternative reality with its own rules, limits, and opportunities.

Escapism is the act or desire of escaping from reality.

Games are extremely powerful instruments of escapism. They offer players the chance to escape to another location, another time, another universe, and even into another body.

Game artists are responsible for designing rich and enticing alternate realities into which players wish to escape. To support escapism, a game world must seem consistent and immersive. The player should feel that they are completely surrounded by the game's virtual environment. Whatever that environment may be, it must be interesting and enticing, and it should somehow make sense to the player. Confusing inconsistencies in a game's environment can have a jarring affect on players, and completely destroy their sense of escape into another reality.

A more controversial aspect of escapism can be seen in many games. Games can allow players to escape the bounds of society's rules and morality. As a character in a fictional world, you are free to do many things you would never do in reality. Like Pinocchio entering Pleasure Island, players can be drawn in by the lure of the forbidden to escape into a world where everything is acceptable. Many popular games are based on this philosophy. Some critics feel that this is a fundamental problem with video games, but any art or technology can be exploited or misused.

Even traditional playground games like "cops and robbers" can be said to encourage some antisocial behaviors. Kids have played such games for centuries, and I have never seen any study that would indicate that playing "cops and robbers" increases the likelihood a child will choose a life of violence and crime.

Video games can offer a safe release for players' aggression and frustration, as long as the players understand that the actions they perform in a game are only appropriate within a video game.

Detractors of video games often contend that realistic video games can desensitize their players to make them more comfortable with violence, killing, death, and gore. There may be some sliver of truth to this, but the desensitizing effect of video games is probably no stronger than that of violent television shows and motion pictures.

Desensitizing is the psychological process of making a person or animal less affected by a particular stimulus by repeated or prolonged exposure to that stimulus.

In creating the look of a game, game artists have a tremendous impact on the degree to which a video game exposes its players to realistic blood, gore, and violence. It can be argued that shooting metallic robots with lasers is far less likely to desensitize a player to real-world violence than the same game played with human characters and assault rifles.

Accomplishment and Acknowledgment

When players win a game, they think, "I am that good!" When players lose a game, they think, "Well, it's just a game." In life, victories are difficult and failures are devastating. Fun games are designed to maximize the player's opportunities for accomplishment, while minimizing the consequences of failure. Victories should be celebrated and failures mitigated.

Victories can be enhanced by creating spectacular effects and long animation sequences to emphasize and extend the duration of victorious moments in a game. When the player defeats the overlord, the overlord doesn't just drop dead, but instead crawls cowering away before blowing up in a spectacle of sparks and flame.

Failures can be mitigated by quickly moving along, or by distracting the player with even cooler effects or more humorous antics. When the player is killed by the overlord, the player doesn't slowly rot on the floor, but triggers a thermal nuclear blast that melts the entire level. This may not change the fact that the player has failed, but it looks so cool that the player is glad to have seen it and will probably show it to friends.

The makers of digital slot machines have mastered the art of enhancing victories and mitigating failures. Digital slot machines erupt in a fanfare of music and animation when a player wins even the smallest victory. Losing spins are fast and quiet, yet trumpets blast and recorded coins tinkle as "winners" get rewarded with the modest return of a small part of their original bet.

Everyone likes to feel recognized and acknowledged as individuals. Acknowledging a player's accomplishments increases the player's sense of accomplishment.

How would it feel to walk through a crowded room and be noticed by no one? How much worse would it feel to achieve the greatest victory of your life and have no one take note?

When players play a game, they expect their presence and accomplishments to be acknowledged. Game artists can enhance this sense of acknowledgement by creating characters and props that respond and react to the player's actions.

Social Interaction

Games have a bad reputation for encouraging isolation and antisocial behavior. In a very few cases, this may be deserved, but historically, games are fantastic tools to foster social interaction and communication.

Games give people something to do together. They give an excuse for friends to meet and interact. Players have something to brag about, and strangers are brought together in a safe and socially acceptable forum.

Even single-player games can foster a players sense of social interaction. The introduction of rich and believable characters with intelligent interaction can open many new doors for social lubrication. Players who are too shy or lack the confidence to approach a stranger in a real-world situation might easily approach a realistic character in a game. As players find pleasure and reward in such virtual interaction, they may gain a sense of empowerment and confidence that will translate into their real-world experiences as well.

To witness a true miracle of social interaction, place two shy teenagers in a room with one video game and watch what happens. Online multiplayer games offer even more opportunities for social interaction.

Game artists can increase the sense of social fulfillment provided in a game by creating interesting, diverse, and lifelike characters who have their own individual styles, traits, postures, and gestures.

Sensory Gratification

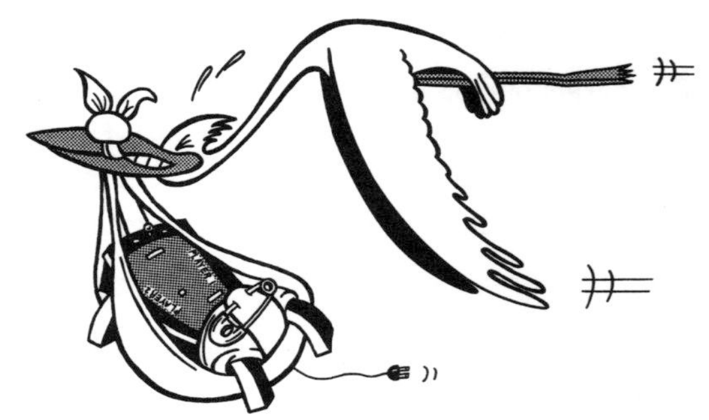

People like sparkles, gems, diamonds, and lava lamps. As a species, humans are naturally captivated by beautiful scenery, inspiring music, and dazzling effects of every kind.

Even the oldest and crudest arcade games used light and sound to attract and hold players' attention. Today's video games feature music composed by world-renowned composers and performed by entire symphony orchestras.

The earliest games filled their screens with white or green lines and dots. Today's games feature animated characters and three-dimensional worlds. As game technology has advanced, the craft of the game artist has evolved from engineering blinking technical oddities to sculpting and decorating fantastic magical landscapes. The more visually interesting and attractive a game looks, the more visually gratifying it is to its players.

Tomorrow's game artists will rely on far greater technologies to bring to life evermore immersive and captivating virtual realities. One thing you can count on in the video game industry is that tomorrow is already here.

Summary

In this chapter, you should have learned the following concepts:

- Game artists create the characters, backgrounds, objects, textures, and visual assets that create the appearance of a game.
- A game is any contest between two or more intelligent entities.
- A game is governed by a comprehensive set of rules.
- Players take a risk whenever they play a game.
- Games are a proven technique of natural education.
- A simulation is a game designed with the principal goal of accurately modeling reality.
- Discovery is the act of noticing or learning something for the first time in one's personal experience.
- Exploration is the act of searching or investigating for the purpose of discovery.
- The more complex and mysterious the game's environment, the more opportunities for discovery the game can provide.

- Role-playing is the act of pretending to be someone or something you are not.
- Sense of agency refers to the player's feeling of power, control, and personal connection to a character or entity within a game.
- The more control that players can exert on their characters in a game, the more the players will feel that they truly are those characters.
- Role-playing is more rewarding when there is a greater sense of agency between the players and their characters in the games.
- Dramatic narrative is the art of telling a story in a way that captivates the audience and leaves them wanting to know more.
- Empathy is the ability of one person to share, feel, and understand the feelings of another person. The second person can be a friend, a stranger, or a fictional character.
- A caricature is a representation of a person or object in which the subject's distinctive features, emotions, or peculiarities are deliberately exaggerated.
- Escapism is the act or desire of escaping from reality.
- Desensitizing is the psychological process of making a person or animal less affected by a particular stimulus by repeated or prolonged exposure to that stimulus.
- Game artists can increase the sense of social fulfillment provided in a game by creating interesting, diverse, and lifelike characters who have their own individual styles, traits, postures, and gestures.

Questions and Answers

Q: How does a simulation differ from a game?

A: A simulation is a game that is designed to accurately depict or replicate real-world situations and conditions.

Q: When were games invented?

A: No one knows, but games have existed long before recorded history.

Q: What is the relationship between a player's level of control of a character and his sense of agency with that character?

A: The more control the player has over a character, the more there is a sense of agency between the player and the character.

Q: What are the most important elements that define a game?

A: The rules are the most important elements that define a game.

Q: Which does more to enhance a player's sense of discovery, a very long straight hallway or a short hallway with a 50-degree turn? Why?

A: The hallway with a turn does more to enhance a sense of discovery. The entire long straight hallway is instantly in the player's view. There is no sense of discovery or exploration as they turn the corner, because there is no corner to turn.

Q: Which is more important to enhance a player's sense of fantasy fulfillment, the detail of the character or the responsiveness of the character?

A: The responsiveness of the character is far more important because it enhances the player's sense of agency with the character.

Discussion Questions

1. Compare and discuss the different sets of rules you would create for a good jet-fighter simulation and a fun jet-fighter game.
2. Why is a sense of agency important to fantasy fulfillment?
3. Describe several ways you could enhance a player's sense of accomplishment.
4. Describe several ways you could mitigate a player's failure.
5. How can a game artist increase the sense of social interaction a player receives from a game?
6. Describe a way games can be used to teach.

Exercises

1. Create your own card game using a deck of traditional playing cards. Write all the rules necessary to define your new game.
2. List three rules that would be appropriate in an automobile simulation that would probably be left out of an automobile racing game.
3. Why is it essential that a game's rules cover all possibilities?
4. List two things players risk anytime they play a game.
5. Draw a map of a level showing seven caverns. Lay out the caverns in a manner that maximizes the players' sense of discovery.
6. Describe two ways you could reduce the possible effects of desensitization in a battlefield combat game.
7. Describe several ways a video game can help people escape.
8. Describe seven reasons a player would play a game.
9. Choose any game, play it, and rate how it does or does not satisfy each of the reasons you described in Exercise 8. Explain your ratings.

Chapter 2

The World of the Game Artist

The video-game and electronic entertainment industry of today is much like the motion picture industry of 1910. At that time, movie makers knew how to use a camera and how to cut film. They were experimenting with camera angles, stunts, sets, locations, and special effects, but they were just beginning to put it all together.

The video games of today are like those first movies. Video games tend to be based around one or two key activities, locations, or effects. The stories are rather limited, designed primarily to justify the use of these activities, locations, or effects. There are certainly a few exceptions, but the video-game industry has not yet seen its D. W. Griffith or Walt Disney. Every year, a new generation of video games takes another step forward from the one-reel shorts of the early 1900s toward the two-hour artistic and technical masterpieces that eventually followed.

Introduction

The job of a game artist has changed greatly over the past 25 years. The first video-game artists were actually programmers and engineers. Traditional artists were contracted to paint artwork for marketing, advertising, and product packaging, but the images in the game were "hard coded" into the game program.

I created my first video games in the early 1980s. In those ancient days of video-game development, only one to three programmers would work on a typical professional video game. Many professional games were developed by a lone programmer.

Early game programmers might spend many months working on a game before an artist (or, often, a more artistic programmer) would join the team and create the final graphics for the game. Many of these early game artists had little experience. They were often expected to produce all the artwork for a game in a few days or a week.

My first games were programmed in assembly language, a symbolic programming language where each instruction translates directly into a single microprocessor instruction. It took pages of code just to draw a picture of a spaceship or motorcycle on the screen. It took many lines of code to divide two numbers.

There were no professional drawing programs available, so I created my own graphics software called Video Graphics. I recruited my childhood friend and neighbor Dean Parks, who used my Video Graphics program to create all of the artwork for our early games. He was the entire art department, and despite the limited technology available, his graphics frequently surpassed the state-of-the-art.

Today, most professional games are developed by a much larger team. A typical modern game studio employs 5 to 15 programmers, a team of game and level designers, a technical director, an art director, and an armada of game artists. A full-time producer and perhaps several associate producers are needed to coordinate, support, and maintain communications among the large development team.

Although professional game development teams have grown, new technology has made the game development process much easier. The combination of larger teams, better tools, and more powerful technology is opening vast new possibilities in the art of game development.

Game Graphics Technology

The very first video-game graphics were hardwired. Nolan Bushnell, who founded Atari along with Ted Dabney, created the paddles and ball in their first Pong game by using electronic timer circuits synchronized with a CRT (*Cathode Ray Tube*). See Figure 2.1.

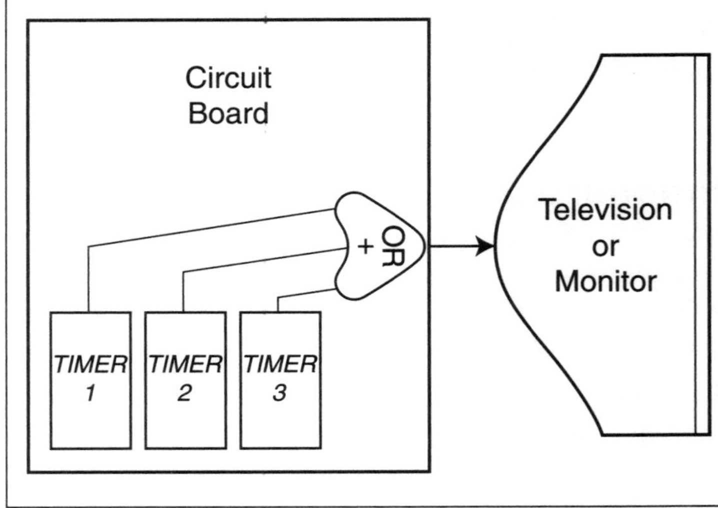

Figure 2.1
Pong used separate timer circuits to control the illumination of dots on the screen.

The CRTs used in the first Pong games were black-and-white television sets. A television uses magnets and an electron gun to sweep a beam in a zigzag pattern across and down the screen. The imaginary wall switch shown in Figure 2.2 is wired to turn the electron beam on or off as the magnets sweep it along the screen.

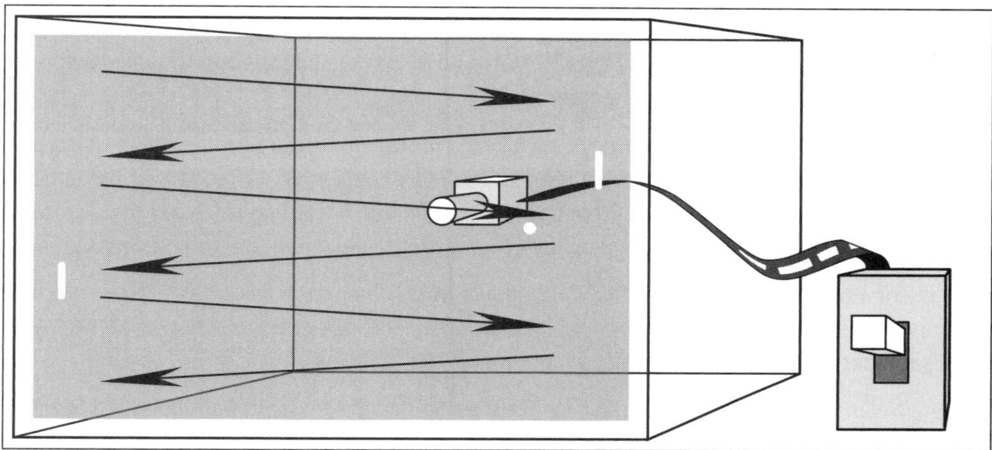

Figure 2.2
The electron beam is interrupted as it scans and sweeps across and down the screen.

If the wall switch in Figure 2.2 is turned on during the entire scan of the screen, the screen appears entirely white. If the switch is turned off during the entire scan, the screen appears solid black.

The timers shown in Figure 2.1 were engineered to turn the video signal on and off at exactly the right time to make the paddles and the ball appear in their respective places on the screen. If Timer 1 was responsible for the Pong ball, then it would transmit a signal to the CRT only when the CRT's electron gun was scanning the spot where the ball should appear.

Figure 2.3
Pong used short lines for paddles and a point of light for a ball.

The signals from the various timer circuits would be added together to turn the signal feeding the CRT on and off as the CRT scanned its moving dot across and down the light-sensitive phosphorous screen. The result looked similar to the image in Figure 2.3.

If Pong's designers wanted to change the shape of the paddle, they would have had to open up the game and rewire or replace the timer circuits that controlled the CRT. This was how the very first game artists had to work their magic.

Nolan Bushnell and Ted Dabney founded Atari with an investment of $250 each. Nolan recruited fellow engineer Al Alcorn to help design a driving game, but they decided to start with something simpler. The result of Al and Nolan's experiment was a ping-pong-like game they named Pong.

In Pong, players slide a paddle quickly across the screen in an effort to catch and return a bouncing ball. Nolan took their first Pong game to a local tavern, and the crowd's overwhelming response assured him that Pong would be a hit. Atari sold many coin-operated Pong tables before they decided to try entering the consumer marketplace.

With the help of engineer Bob Brown, they developed a prototype product for the home market. They took their prototype to New York for a large toy industry convention. Nolan carried the large box full of wires and an even larger TV from booth to booth, demonstrating it for any toy distributor that would take the time to try it. Every toy company that saw it had the same response.

The toy distributor's would first tell him, "Wow, that's neat." Then they would ask, "How much does it cost?" When he answered, he would be sent away. The conventional wisdom of the toy industry said that no one would ever spend more than $100 for a toy.

Frustrated, Nolan returned home in despair. He went to his favorite tavern, where he saw a Sears Roebuck's delivery man trying to move a large pool table into the bar. He asked the deliveryman, "How much does one of those tables cost?" Sears sold pool tables for much more than Nolan planned to sell his Pong consoles.

Nolan contacted Sears and asked if they would be interested in an "electronic pool table." Soon there were visitors from Sears' home office in Chicago knocking on Nolan's door.

Nolan and Al made several demonstrations for Sears. They nearly lost the deal completely when their only prototype failed and Al had to rebuild it in the back room, while Nolan stalled an entourage of Sears' buyers.

Sears' sporting goods manager Tom Quinn saw the potential of the product and eventually offered Atari a contract for 50,000 units. Almost immediately, Sears raised the contract to 150,000 units by Christmas. Nolan and his partners were extremely excited, until they realized they could never deliver that many units in the short time required. They had no factory, no staff, and no money to get either.

After trying to find a bank to finance their operation, Nolan was forced to call Sears and explain that they just could not meet the deadline. Mr. Quinn asked Nolan what he would need to fulfill the contract, and soon Nolan found himself talking with a vice president at the Sears Financial Group. Sears built Atari their first factory and built a Sears' warehouse right beside it. Nolan and his partners would build the new products in the factory and roll them across a line on the ground into the warehouse for Sears to ship.

Nolan soon sold Atari to Warner Communications for more than $28 million. He later found an entertainment and pizza empire operated by a singing mouse named Chuck E. Cheese.

Digital Color Schemes

By the mid-1970s, most video games were based on microprocessors.

> **Microprocessors are sophisticated large-scale integrated circuits, which can be programmed to perform a variety of functions.**

Like the original Pong games, microprocessor-based games still display their graphics by rapidly switching the signal fed to a CRT, but by the late 1970s, most game systems displayed their graphics on color monitors. Color displays operate in the same manner as monochrome displays, but instead of switching one signal that is connected to a CRT, three separate signals are used.

> **Monochrome literally means one color. Monochrome displays typically used CRTs to project and sweep a beam across a green or white phosphorescent surface, but monochrome can be used to describe any single-color image.**

In most color video systems, three separate signals control the brightness of the red, green, and blue components of each color on the screen. Red, green, and blue are called the primary colors of light. These colors can be combined in various ways to create all of the colors of the rainbow.

Most students are taught that red, yellow, and blue are primary colors. This is true of paint, where each successive particle of paint filters or subtracts some color from the solid white background of the canvas or paper.

In painting with light, colors are actually added to each other over an otherwise black background. Red, green, and blue are technically called additive primary colors. Red, yellow, and blue are technically subtractive primary colors.

In this book, and throughout most of the video-game industry, the additive primary colors red, green, and blue are the only primary colors you are likely to encounter.

Table 2.1 shows how the three primary colors can be mixed to create eight different colors.

Table 2.1 Digital Combinations of the Primary Colors of Light

Resulting Color	Red Light	Green Light	Blue Light
Black	off	off	off
White	on	on	on
Red	on	off	off
Yellow	on	on	off
Green	off	on	off
Cyan	off	on	on
Blue	off	off	on
Magenta	on	off	on

In most game systems, the job of synchronizing and switching the three color signals was delegated out of the microprocessor brain of the computer to a separate dedicated hardware component called a video display generator. See Figure 2.4.

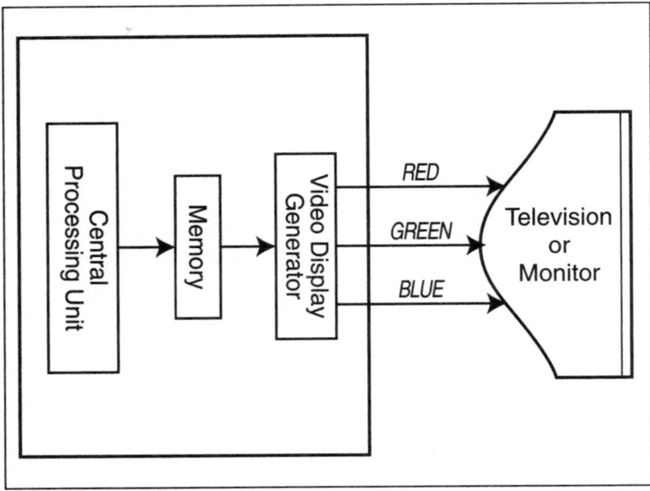

Figure 2.4
Most game systems use separate video display generator chips to generate the signals to drive the monitor.

A video display generator is a large-scale integrated circuit specifically designed to convert digital information from a computer into the video output signals necessary to drive a video display.

Video display generators typically read the contents of a section of computer memory. The individual bits of information that fill this memory can function as a map to tell the video display generator which color should be output for each point or pixel on the screen.

Pixel is short for picture element, and refers to each individual dot that makes up any image that is recorded or displayed by a computer.

All video display generators in use today rely on bitmaps throughout many stages of the display process. All computer images and the entire computer screen are typically divided into a grid of pixels, as shown in Figures 2.5 through 2.7.

A bitmap refers to a collection of data or files within a computer's memory, where each subsequent bit or combination of bits describes the color of a pixel in an image.

A bitmap is simply a file that serves as a map to show which pixels are set to which colors in an image.

Figure 2.5
This bitmap image of Dino World was modeled for International Magic Factory by my longtime friend and business partner David Sudd.

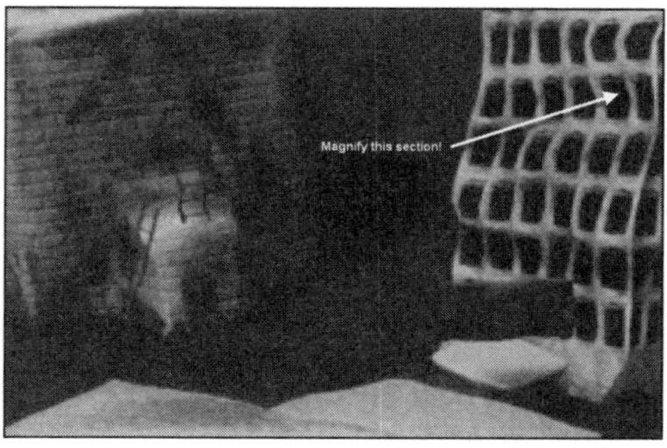

Figure 2.6
As the image is magnified, you start to see the individual pixels that make up the image.

Like the first Pong games, the earliest video display generators were entirely digital and only allowed each primary color to be turned completely off or on. Because the signals could only be switched on or off, there was no way to display twice as much red as green, which would be necessary to produce an orange color. They also could not display the color purple with twice as much red as blue.

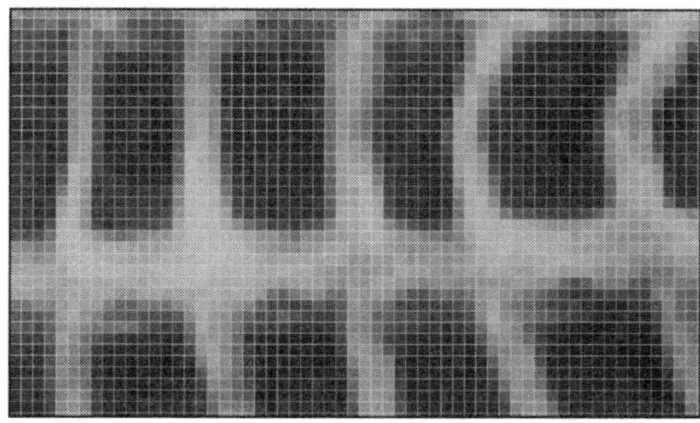

Figure 2.7
Now the pixels are clearly visible as a grid of separately colored rectangles.

Many of the earliest color video display generators limited game artists to working with only two or four colors at a time. It is pretty amazing how artfully many early game artists used patterns of only two colors.

Many early two-color video-game systems, including the Dragon and the Tandy Color Computer, had a strange timing bug that produced a very useful phenomenon. Whenever a programmer would place a white dot and black dot side by side, they would appear to artifact (shift in color) into a shade of red or blue. So many video games took advantage of this illusion that it became commonplace to see a video game described as operating in artifact mode.

Game artists could control the direction of this apparent color shift by placing the white dot or the black dot first in the pattern. However, there was a problem. Depending upon precisely when in the video synchronization process the video display generator was started, the reddish and bluish patterns could appear reversed, and all of the colors in the game would be backwards. It was almost like looking at a photograph's color negative.

(continued)

(continued from previous page)

A common solution to this problem was to begin the game on power-up by asking the players if the color of the screen looked red or blue. When they answered incorrectly, they were instructed to turn off the computer and start it again. It could take many tries before the colors looked correct.

I learned this trick originally from Steve Bjork, who programmed such early games as Zaxxon, Pole Position, and The Sands of Egypt, all of which used artifact mode.

Harnessing the Rainbow

By the time the IBM PC came along, customers were demanding a lot more colors. The long-awaited VGA (Video Graphics Array) card offered programmers and game artists the freedom of choosing from thousands of colors. This became possible through the addition of high-speed digital-to-analog conversion circuits, which allow the video display generator to ramp or dim the brightness of each color signal up and down, instead of merely turning them off and on.

An analog signal can be visualized as a chandelier being controlled with a dimmer, while a digital signal can be visualized by turning that same chandelier on or off by switching a switch at the fuse box.

Figure 2.8 illustrates a video display generator outputting analog signals through a digital-to-analog converter.

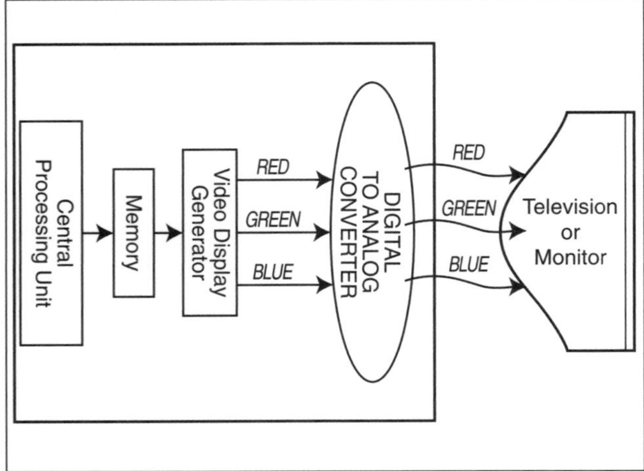

Figure 2.8
Digital-to-analog converters enable artists to combine various amounts of each primary color.

Digital-to-analog conversion refers to the process of translating digital data consisting of only 1s and 0s into analog data where each signal value can represent a broad continuous range of voltages.

With analog graphic displays, artists could have exactly the shade of purple they desired, but there was a catch. The more colors you use in a picture, the more memory it takes to store that picture.

A two-color image that is 32 by 32 pixels in size can be stored in 128 bytes of computer memory. A 32-by-32-pixel image with 256 colors requires 1,024 bytes of memory. That same 32-by-32-pixel image with 16 million colors requires 4,096 bytes of memory.

Paletting is the process where a small palette of colors is selected from a much larger set of possible colors. Instead of containing the full color information for an image, a paletted bitmap file must only hold an index number for each pixel's entry into the color palette.

Color Palettes

At a time when computer memories were typically very small, it was necessary to find a compromise that would give artists a wide selection of colors without draining the computer of all its available memory. One solution was an approach called paletting.

A palette is a small set of predetermined colors. Think of these colors as a small set of carefully selected paint colors that a painter has mixed in preparation for beginning a masterpiece.

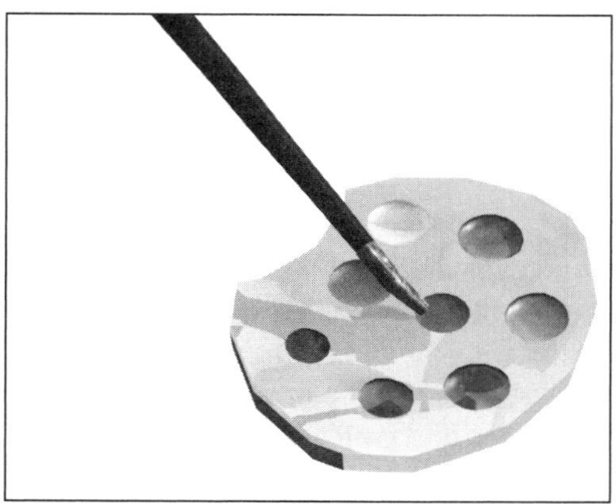

Figure 2.9
In an artist's palette, each slot can hold a different color mixture of paint.

A palette slot is an entry that defines an individual color in a palette. Think of the palette as a painter's tray, and the palette slots as the individual paint reservoirs sunk into the tray. See Figure 2.9.

By replacing the raw color data for each pixel in a bitmap with the index number of a slot in a palette, a paletted image file can hold an image with a high color depth using a small bit depth. In other words, paletted images require much less memory to store. The original VGA cards allowed game artists to select a palette of 256 colors, chosen from thousands of possible combinations of the red, green, and blue components.

A 256-color palette limits a game artist to using only 256 colors at a time, but gives the artist the freedom to select any set of 256 colors to use. Paletted color modes are seldom used in games today, but their legacy remains in many of the bitmap image formats and graphics tools with which modern games are developed.

Color depth refers to the number of colors that are available to be displayed in any pixel of an image.

Bit depth refers to the number of individual bits of memory used to hold the color information for each pixel in an image.

Compression

Color palettes were an early and effective form of image compression. In recent years, many new compression standards have become available.

The popularity of the Internet has created a hoard of new compression codecs, each with its own advantages and disadvantages.

Image compression is any process that reduces the memory required to hold the information necessary to reproduce an image.

Some codecs use lossy compression, where the original image is mutilated or changed in some manner. Figures 2.10 through 2.12 use an extreme example to illustrate the difference between lossy and lossless compression. Compressed PCX files typically implement a form of lossless compression.

Figure 2.10
The original Crystal Ball Room image, illustrated by Steve Mutz for International Magic Factory

A codec is a small utility program, function, plug-in, or service library that implements some method to compress and decompress a file. Codecs can apply one or more compression techniques and typically are designed to encode and decode their data to and from a particular file format.

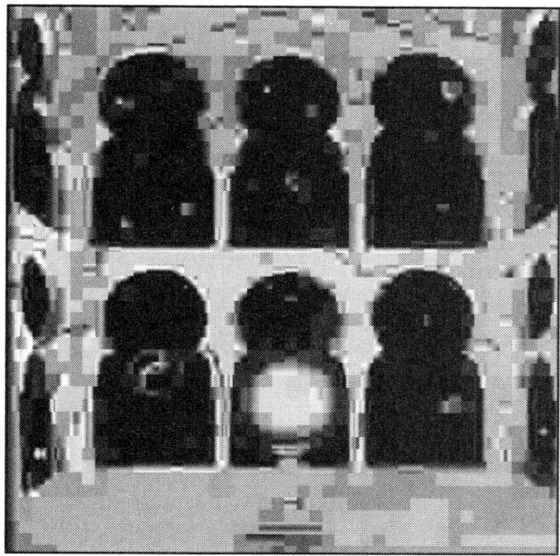

Figure 2.11
This is the same image as Figure 2.10 after a lossy compression process.

Figure 2.12
This is the image from Figure 2.10 after a lossless compression process.

Lossy compression refers to any process of compression that results in the deterioration, or any reduction in the accuracy or precision, of the original image's pixel information.

Lossless compression refers to any process of compression that does not introduce any errors or alterations in the original image's pixel information.

These are extreme examples. Most compression techniques produce acceptable results that fall someplace between those shown in Figures 2.11 and 2.12. It would be accurate to say that every image in this book has been compressed and decompressed several times before being printed on the pages you are reading.

Compressed PCX files leave an image's data unchanged, except where a single color repeats continuously. The repeating colored pixels are counted and tagged, and then the original pixels are left out of the compressed image.

If you applied such a compression technique to the song "Hi Ho, Hi Ho," you could compress it to the phrase "2Hi Ho," and save 6 bytes of memory. To decompress the compressed phrase you would strip out the number 2, and it would tell you to repeat the following letters twice. This would result in the phrase "Hi Ho, Hi Ho," which is exactly what you compressed in the first place. There is no loss of data, so this is a lossless compression technique.

Compression made it possible for early games to include more images, more colorful images, and much higher resolution images.

If a 32-by-32-pixel icon requires 4K (4,096 bytes) of memory, how much memory does it take to save an image that fills the entire screen? At a screen resolution of 800 by 600 pixels, it takes 1,920K (1,920,000 bytes). Even on today's computers, that is a big file. On the computers of the 1980s and 1990s, that was an enormous file.

Resolution is a measure of the amount of detail recorded in an image. It is typically stated as the number of columns and rows of pixels used to hold the entire screen or image file.

Figures 2.13 to 2.16 show the same image displayed at progressively lower resolutions.

Figure 2.13
This is the Crystal Ball room with 350 horizontal lines of resolution.

Figure 2.14
This is the same image with only 128 lines of resolution.

Lower resolution images require much less memory to store, but they lose clarity and detail. Too low a resolution can make an image vague and confusing. Noticeably low-resolution graphics can detract from the sense of reality and believability of a game.

Exercise caution when combining images of different resolutions in a game. Using one low-resolution image in an otherwise high-resolution game is like hanging a giant sign in the game saying, "This is just a computer game!" Placing one high-resolution image in a low-resolution game makes the rest of the game look crude and less realistic by comparison.

Figure 2.15
Here is the same image with only 64 lines of resolution.

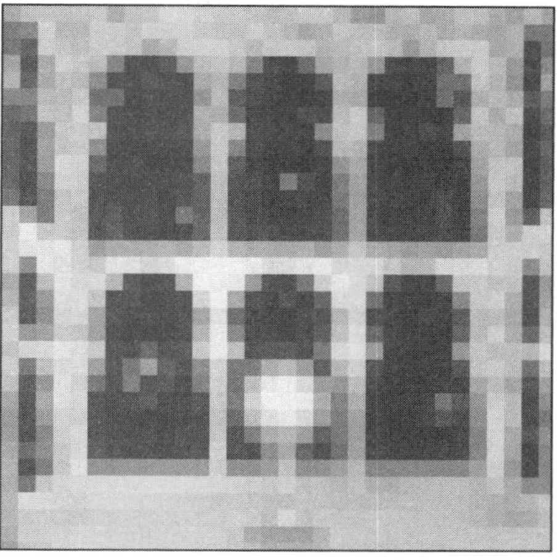

Figure 2.16
With 32 lines of resolution, the image is barely recognizable.

Sprites

Imagine a screen full of alien spaceships. The aliens descend from above, flying in a cluster, moving first left and then right. Screenshots such as the one shown in Figure 2.17 were typical of the first color video games.

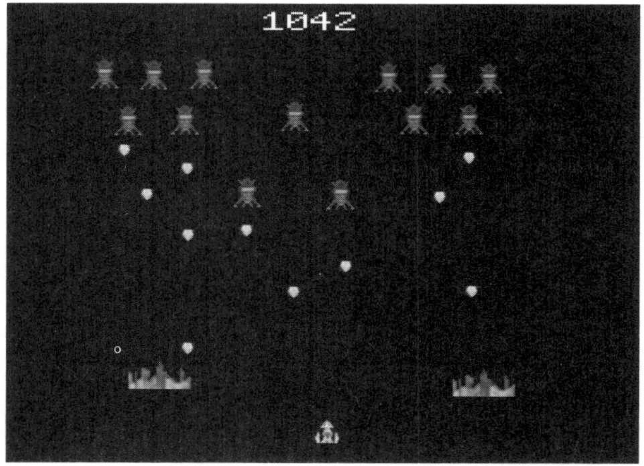

Figure 2.17
This screenshot depicts an early color video game.

The backgrounds of the earliest video games were kept simple and rarely moved. Computers had very small memories and were slow; even with compression, it was difficult to smoothly animate a complicated background image that would fill the entire screen.

The small foreground images, the ships and the gunfire, were stored as a small collection of images or sprites, which a programmer would stamp onto the screen in the appropriate locations. A sprite is a two-dimensional picture used to portray an object, character, or entity on the screen. See Figure 2.18.

Figure 2.18
Sprites are two-dimensional pictures of an object, character, or other moving entity in a game.

Figure 2.19
Sprites are like flat painted puppets that can be moved anywhere on the screen.

You can think of sprites as flat paper puppets or painted cut-out shapes that a programmer can position anywhere on the puppet stage of the screen. See Figure 2.19.

Figures 2.20 through 2.22 show the individual sprites that appear in the screenshot shown in Figure 2.17.

A sprite is a small two-dimensional picture. Sprites are usually painted as rectangular images with a black or transparent background so that they can be overlaid or stamped onto the screen in one or more locations. The characters, ghosts, spaceships, and gunfire in most 2-D games are stored as sprites.

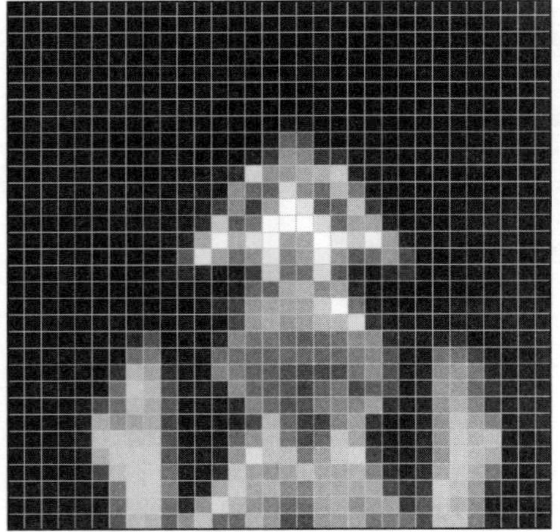

Figure 2.20
This sprite is the player's ship at the bottom of the screen.

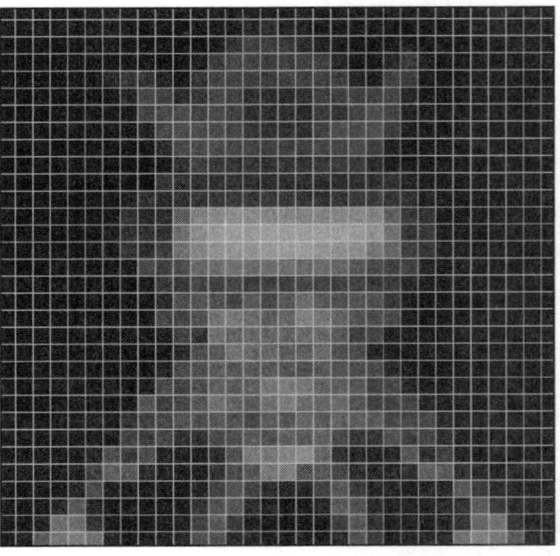

Figure 2.21
This sprite is an alien ship, which is used for all of the aliens in the level.

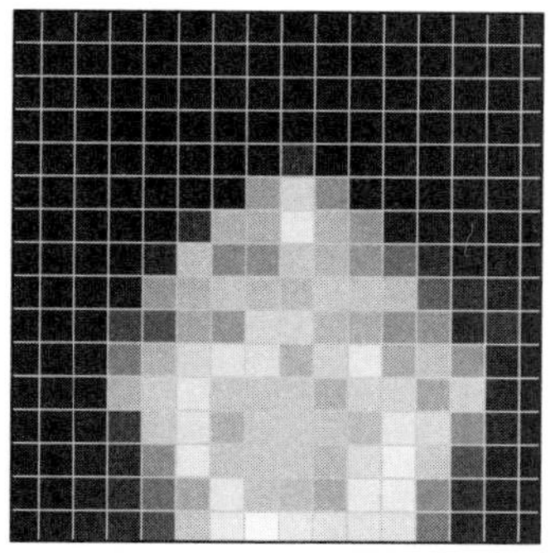

Figure 2.22
This sprite is used for the incoming bombs that are dropped by the aliens and rain down the screen.

Tiles

In the early 1980s, programmers began experimenting with the idea of using sprites to animate small pieces of a game level's background. Soon, whole backgrounds were being constructed by covering the entire screen with sprites or tiles.

Dividing a screen into small tiles began as a programming trick to substantially reduce the memory required to store a full screen of graphics. This creative strategy compresses a full-screen image by dividing the screen into a grid of many small squares or rectangles. Each rectangle is assigned a tile, which is selected from a palette of prepainted tile images. Like sprites, the tile images can contain animation or be simple static pictures.

Figure 2.23 shows a typical tiled game screen. If you look closely, you will see that the image is made up of a mosaic of tiles.

In Figure 2.24, you can clearly see the individual tiles that compose the image. Notice how the tiles are carefully designed to be generic building blocks, which the game artist pieces together and assembles in many different formations.

Figure 2.23
This screenshot is like a mosaic composed of many tiles.

This approach makes it easy for game artists and programmers to quickly build many different but similar levels. The levels have great memory efficiency be cause the high-resolution and high-color detailed images of each tile are saved only once, regardless of how many times the tile might appear in a scene.

Figure 2.24
Here you can see the individual tiles that compose the image in Figure 2.23.

The only information that is actually needed to reproduce the scene is a grid of numbers. Each number in the grid represents the index of the tile that is used to fill that position on the screen.

Figure 2.25 shows the tile index numbers used to represent every tile in the scene from Figure 2.23. The entire level uses fewer than 30 unique tiles. Several tiles, for example, Tile 1 and Tile 8, are repeated many times in a row throughout the image.

1	1	1	1	1	1	1	1	1	1	1	1	1
1	1	1	1	1	1	1	1	1	1	1	1	1
1	1	1	1	1	2	1	3	1	1	1	1	1
1	1	1	1	1	7	8	9	1	1	1	1	1
1	1	4	5	6	8	8	8	9	5	10	9	11
13	12	12	12	12	8	8	8	12	12	12	12	14
8	8	8	8	8	8	8	8	8	8	8	8	8
8	15	16	16	16	17	8	15	16	17	8	15	17
8	16	16	16	16	18	8	19	16	16	8	16	16
8	16	16	16	18	20	8	20	19	18	8	16	18
8	18	20	21	20	22	8	23	20	20	8	21	20
8	23	24	24	25	8	8	8	23	25	8	23	24

Figure 2.25
These numbers indicate the index of the specific tile image that is placed at each spot in the grid that describes the scene.

Building the levels in this manner results in tremendous savings in terms of both development time and computer memory. The savings are so significant that game developers could design games with scenes that are far wider than a single screen could display. The wide tiled image shown in Figure 2.26 can be stored in less memory than it takes to store a typical single full screen image.

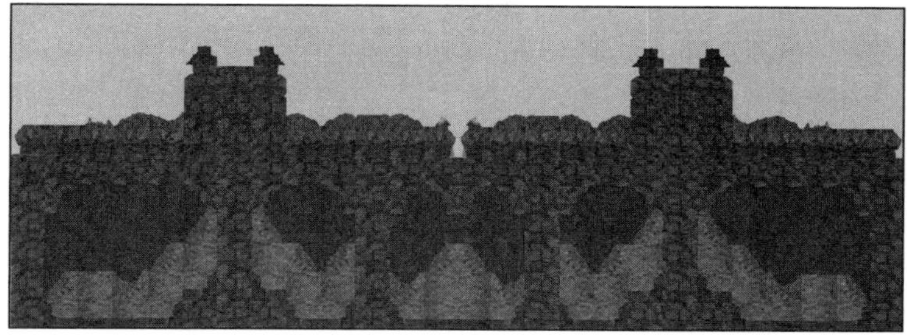

Figure 2.26
This wide tiled image requires less memory than a typical single full-screen image.

Acceleration refers to the development and use of specifically engineered electronic hardware to speed up a much repeated process of graphic display or image manipulation. Various graphic cards and video display generators offer different functions and degrees of hardware acceleration.

Game systems such as the first Nintendo, Sega Genesis, and Sony PlayStation included hardware that accelerated this process of drawing tiles on the screen. This made it pos sible for programmers to easily scroll a viewport across enormous tiled scenes.

Figure 2.27 shows how a viewport is scrolled across a tiled scene as the player progresses through a side-scrolling game.

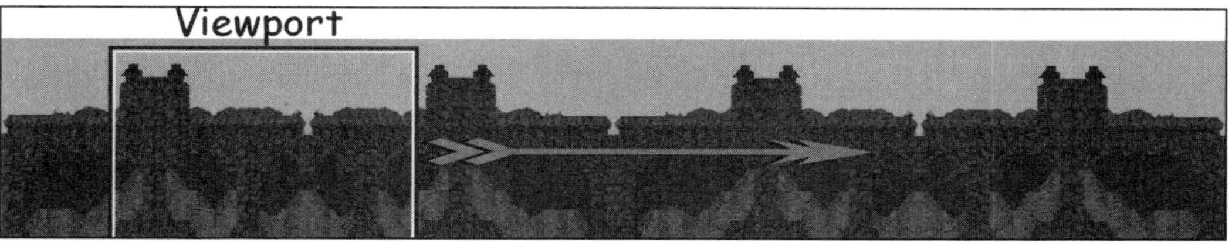

Figure 2.27
In a side-scroller, a viewport is scrolled across a large tiled scene.

A viewport is a window through which a user views a virtual world. Viewports can be thought of as cameras or eyes through which a user peers. A viewport can be stationary and immobile, or it can be programmed to slide, pan, tilt, zoom, dolly, or scroll.

Side-scrollers are a genre of video games where the player's viewport scrolls through a large scene as the player's character progresses through each level.

Side-scrollers became the favorite genre of a whole generation of video-game players. Ironically, the same drive toward software optimization and hardware acceleration that brought the side-scrollers into existence eventually led to their decline into obscurity. Tiled side-scroller games quickly disappeared from the video-game scene as new game systems offered even more powerful techniques of image compression and graphics acceleration.

Start Your Engines

When you hear two game programmers discussing the merits of their favorite engines, they are probably not talking about rebuilding their cars. See Figure 2.28.

Figure 2.28
Like the motorcar in this picture, 3-D game engines drive players through virtual worlds, labyrinths, and mazes.

In 1993, id Software released a video game called Doom. They gave a few sample levels away for free, and then asked players to license the full game if they wished to continue. This concept, called shareware, turned id Software into a leader in the video-game industry.

Shareware is the business practice of giving a limited version of a product or program away for free, and then asking customers to pay to upgrade to a better or more complete version of that product or program.

Shareware was only part of Doom's success. Doom had two other revolutionary features that have forever changed the video-game industry.

In order to create a vast 3-D maze full of places to fight and explore, the designers of Doom were not content with merely painting predrawn bitmap backgrounds or using flat tiles to build the backgrounds for their levels. The Doom engine took the concept of tiling in a whole new direction by moving the tiles away from the flat two-dimensional computer screen and painting them instead on three-dimensional surfaces, as shown in Figure 2.29.

Doom's developers broke new ground in another way. Doom's programmers completely separated the artistic design of the game's levels from the actual coding of the game program itself. They created a generic game engine that could be used independently of its artwork to create any number of levels or games. The artistic details of the specific game levels could be changed by an artist without altering or rebuilding the game program itself.

Figure 2.29
The Doom engine pulled its background tiles away from the screen and projected them instead onto 3-D surfaces in a virtual game world.

Eventually, id Software released Doom's game engine and a complete set of design tools to the world, which ushered in the next generation of video games. Today, most new video games are developed using some form of tool-based game design.

Tool-based game design refers to the process of using either a generic game engine or a highly customized one, with a suite of design tools to create the artwork, geometry, and layouts for each level.

Doom changed the face of the video-game industry. It heralded a new wave of 3-D games, and it motivated a vast expansion in research and development that led to a new generation of inexpensive hardware for 3-D video graphics acceleration.

In the professional world of video-game development, tool-based game design helped define and popularize two new career tracks, level designers and game artists.

Level designers direct, plan, and implement the placement, blocking, actions, and behavior of every object, character, and location in a game. Level designers are frequently responsible for developing and implementing the puzzles, challenges, and layouts of every level of a game.

Game artists are responsible for the visual appearance of every object, surface, and entity in a game. Game artists design, implement, and build the props, characters, surface textures, and assets that level designers use to construct the virtual world or worlds of the game.

With the evolution of 3-D game engines, game programmers now focus almost exclusively on the technical aspects of game development. Game artists produce every object in a game as a 3-D model, and level designers place and arrange these models into massive mazes or virtual worlds.

Art in Three Dimensions

A typical photograph, and most movies and television shows, are based upon images in two dimensions. Like a piece of paper, a two-dimensional image has height and width, but it is flat and can only hint at depth through careful use of color, form, and perspective.

Architects and sculptors work in true three-dimensional space. Real buildings and statues have not only height and width, but depth as well. Parts of a 3-D object are actually in front of or behind other parts. See Figure 2.30.

Figure 2.30
Places and objects in 3-D games must be created in three dimensions.

Although most computer screens can still only display flat two-dimensional images today, most game artists and level designers use design tools to create three-dimensional virtual worlds through which their characters and players can live and explore.

Orthographic Viewports

It is necessary for level designers and game artists to look at a two-dimensional screen and somehow see and understand the three-dimensional spaces and objects they are creating. A simple system called orthographic projection has emerged as the unrivalled standard for modern three-dimensional visualization.

Despite the long and fancy-sounding name, the concept is really quite simple. Orthographic projection simply means that we look at the same object from three specific angles at one time. The best way to understand this is to imagine that you are trying to model a car. You want to see it in its entirety, so you place a camera above it looking down. This is a good start, but you can't see the handles on the doors or the details of the hubcaps, so you add another camera off to one side. Now you are set, except you can't see the license plate or the engine grill, so you add one more camera in front of the car. Now you

Figure 2.31
Three cameras are placed orthogonally to show three orthographic views.

can see the car in all of its dimensions. Figure 2.31 shows the three cameras placed at right angles to each other to show three orthographic views.

Figure 2.32
This is the front view.

Figures 2.32 through 2.34 show three orthographic views of the same object.

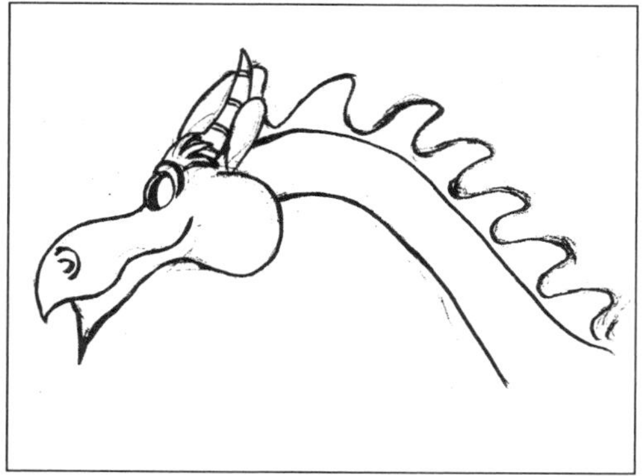

Figure 2.33
This is the side view.

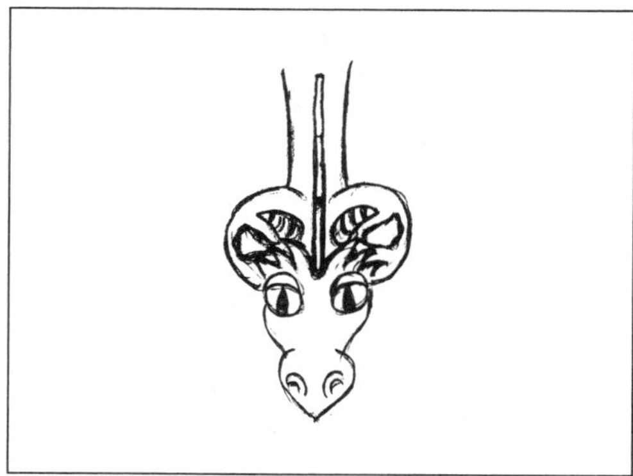

Figure 2.34
This is the top view.

Game artists use these three simple views to model almost anything in a game. Obviously, there will eventually come a time when you want to spin the car around and see it from a variety of angles. For this, you commonly add a fourth view, which can be moved anywhere around the scene. This is commonly called a perspective view or 3-D view, because it allows you to view your objects from any number of perspectives.

Orthographic projections are multiple flattened views of a single object or scene, where each view is taken at right angles from the others.

Perspective views show an object or a scene as it would appear from a specific point in or around the object or the scene. In a perspective view, the objects in the distance appear smaller and closer together than the objects near the viewer.

The Building Blocks of 3-D Games

The characters, objects, walls, and floors in a modern video-game level are not made of wood, bricks, flesh, mud, or dirt. Game levels are constructed from pure geometry. See Figure 2.35.

Figure 2.35
Game artists build fantasy worlds from simple geometry.

Today's video graphics controllers excel at drawing three-dimensional geometry. Most video graphics controllers are optimized to draw three-dimensional triangles with almost inconceivable speed.

Game objects are defined by individual points called vertices. These points are then connected with lines to form the edges of polygons. See Figure 2.36.

Figure 2.36
Vertices are connected with lines to form the faces of polygons.

A vertex is a single point in space. Vertices are used to define the corner points of faces or polygons in 3-D games.

A face is a solid surface in 3-D space. Faces are defined by their corners and edges.

A polygon is a flat shape made up of multiple sides. The simplest polygons used in 3-D games are triangles. Most 3-D video accelerators break higher order polygons (polygons with more edges) into triangles before drawing them.

Groups of polygons are joined together to form meshes, which appear as solid objects in a game. See Figure 2.37.

A mesh is a collection of connected faces. Meshes define the shapes of the objects in a 3-D game.

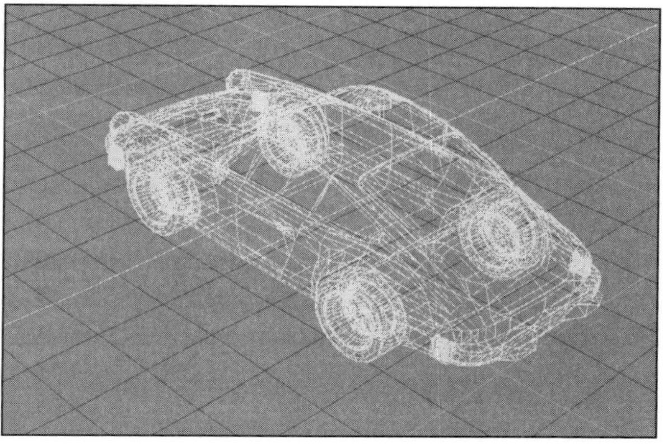

Figure 2.37
A mesh of polygons defines the shape of this car.

In a video game, every object is defined by some number of triangles. A pyramid might have just one triangle for each side. A square is just two triangles stuck together, so practically any geometric shape can be represented.

Polygon count refers to the number of separate faces that make up an object.

What happens when the objects need to be rounded or curved? Most game engines cannot deal with actual curved geometry. Instead, they approximate the curved surfaces by dividing them into many smaller flat surfaces.

A hi-poly model is a 3-D model where many faces are used to create very precise detail and curvature.

A smooth billiard ball can be modeled with a large number of tiny triangles. The more triangles used to define the billiard ball, the smoother it appears. There is a trade-off however: the fewer triangles in the billiard ball, the faster it can be drawn.

A low-poly model is a 3-D model where very few faces are used, resulting in far less precise detail and very chunky curvature.

Game engines frequently require that their objects have low polygon counts, though improvements in hardware and game engine efficiency have helped to lessen this restriction over the past few years.

Bringing Reality to Geometry

In a video game, a simple six-sided box could be a room, a closet, a subway car, or a locked steel vault.

Figure 2.38 shows the inside of a simple cube.

3-D game engines bring a sense of solidity and reality to the geometry in a game by painting images of textures onto the faces that make up each object, as shown in Figure 2.39.

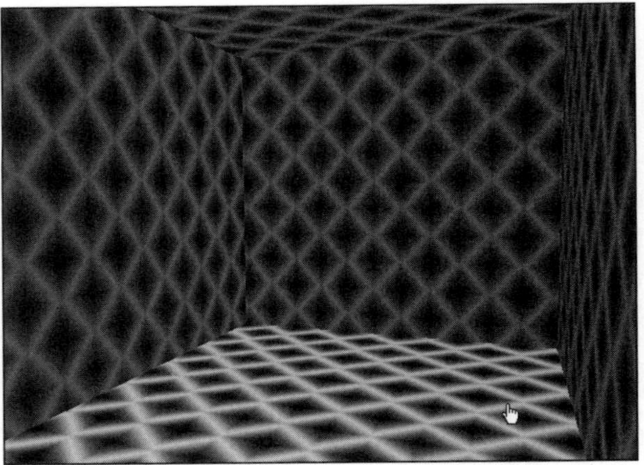

Figure 2.38
This is the inside of a simple hollow cube.

> **Texturing is the process of painting an image onto the faces of a 3-D object in order to give that object the illusion of solidity and reality.**

Figure 2.39
Game artists paint textures onto every object and surface in a scene.

Figure 2.40 shows the same hollow cube from Figure 2.38 after all the cube's surfaces have been painted with a texture image.

The cube walls seem much more solid and realistic, but the room still appears flat and artificial. In the real world, you seldom see such evenly lit textures. A large part of the human brain's natural mechanism of depth perception is based on the analysis of the subtle changes in brightness that you see in the textures all around you.

No matter where you are reading this book, if you look around at the walls and other surfaces, you are bound to see subtle, if not dramatic, changes in the surfaces' brightness. These are caused by the light sources in the environment.

Game engines add reality and depth to a game level by simulating the effects of lighting on the surfaces within the level.

Figure 2.40
An image of bricks has been painted onto the faces of the cube.

Figure 2.41
Lights placed within the room add a sense of depth and realism.

Figure 2.41 shows the room from Figure 2.40 with the addition of simulated lighting.

Modern video cards accelerate both the lighting and texturing of the triangles they draw.

Lighting is the process of simulating the effect of lights and light sources in an environment to give the illusion of depth and reality.

The Anatomy of a Texture

Texture images are generally just simple bitmaps, like the tiles used in two-dimensional side-scroller games.

Figure 2.42 shows a photographic image captured for a texture in a game.

Mapping this bitmap onto the walls of the cube results in the image shown in Figure 2.43.

Figure 2.42
This photo was taken with a digital camera.

Figure 2.43
The room has been textured with the bitmap shown in Figure 2.42.

There is a problem with the texture. If you look at the walls of the cave, you can't help but notice the straight lines going across and down the walls. On either side of these lines, the rocks on the wall seem disjointed and out of alignment.

Looking at the image in Figure 2.42, the problem is not obvious, but if you roll the image to the left and down, you can clearly see the cause of the seams. See Figure 2.44.

Figure 2.44
The original texture image has been rolled downward and to the side so that the original edges are now in the center of the image.

Figure 2.45
The reddish rock in the center has been cloned and merged with the rock underneath.

Seams refer to the subtle lines that appear where a texture image fails to tile properly.

An inspection of Figure 2.44 reveals that the seams occur wherever the rocks that were on one edge of the picture are out of line with the rocks on the other. This can be corrected by using a paint program to clone and merge the opposite sides of the image. Figures 2.45 through 2.47 show how the seams are removed.

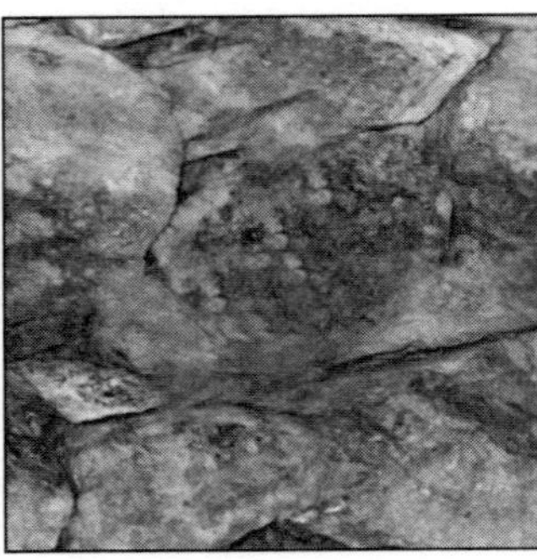

Figure 2.46
The seam lines have all been removed.

Figure 2.47
With the seams removed, the image is rolled again to be sure no new seams have developed.

The seamless texture image can now be painted onto the surfaces in the scene.

Figure 2.48 shows the cube with the new seamless texture on all of its faces.

Figure 2.48
The cube is now textured with the seamless image.

The Tools of the Trade

There are many game engines available, and even more design tools with which you can create the levels and objects to use in the various engines. It is hard to find two programmers who can agree on the best, fastest, or easiest of the game engines, and few artists can agree on the best tool or tools to create the visual assets for games.

When you build a house, there is no one best tool, but there are many useful tools that are occasionally perfect for the job at hand. Game development tools are just the same. Regardless of the tools you choose, they all employ very similar concepts and processes. They all allow you to model objects in a variety of ways, and they offer a multitude of methods to create, build, sculpt, texture, and animate your 3-D objects. See Figure 2.49.

Figure 2.49
Like contractors building a house, game artists use many different tools to model, texture, and bring to life the objects in a game.

This book demonstrates a variety of these methods using a powerful and flexible design tool called gameSpace. Whether or not you choose gameSpace as your primary modeling tool, you should be able to apply many of its concepts to almost any 3-D game tool you are likely to encounter.

Keep in mind that the video-game industry is constantly changing, and the tools and techniques you learn today are only stepping stones to the tools and techniques that are likely to be available to you in the near future. Video-game technology is still rapidly evolving, but the fundamental methods and tools that you encounter in this book are likely to remain dominant forces in the game industry for many years to come.

Summary

In this chapter, you should have learned the following concepts:

- The earliest video game graphics were produced using hardwired circuits.
- Computers display images on CRTs by precisely timing the signal being sent to the CRTs electron gun as is scans across the screen.
- Monochrome displays can display only two colors.
- Color displays use three signals to control the amount of red, green, and blue in each point on the screen.
- Red, green, and blue are the primary colors of light.
- Digital signals can only be on or off.
- Digital color displays can only display a small number of colors.
- Video display generators are integrated circuits that handle the regulation and timing of the signals that a computer outputs to a monitor.
- Pixels are individual dots that make an image.
- Bitmaps are collections or files of sequential pixel data that record and describe an image.
- Analog signals can vary across a range of values.
- Analog color displays can mix colors in a wide variety of ways.
- Palettes can be used to give an artist a vast selection of colors, while still limiting the number of colors that can be simultaneously displayed in an image.
- Resolution is an indication of the amount of detail or number of pixels contained in an image.
- Color depth is the measure of how many colors can be used in an image.
- Bit depth refers to the number of bits or memory allotted to store the colors assigned to each pixel.
- Sprites are bitmap images that can be quickly displayed and moved around the screen.
- Tiled backgrounds are produced by building a mosaic or grid from a small set of tile images.

- Compression is the process of reducing the amount of memory required to store a bitmap file.
- Lossy compression occurs when the original image is changed or mutilated in the course of the compression and decompression process.
- A codec is a program, library, or plug-in that implements a specific compression and decompression process.
- Tiled backgrounds are highly compressed and require far less memory than ordinary bitmaps.
- Side-scrollers are games where a large, usually tiled, background scrolls past the players as they travel through each level.
- Tool-based game design refers to the process of building a game using dedicated design tools and a pre-existing game engine.
- Orthogonal viewports allow you to see all of the dimensions of an object simultaneously.
- Vertices are individual points in space used to define the corners of objects in a 3-D game.
- Faces are polygonal surfaces formed by connecting the vertices with edges.
- Meshes are collections of connected faces that define the shapes of object in a 3-D game.
- Texturing is the process of painting an image onto the faces of a 3-D object in order to give that object the illusion of solidity and reality.
- Lighting is the process of simulating the effect of light and a light source in an environment to give the illusion of depth and reality.
- Seamless textures are texture images that can be tiled without noticeable incongruities and irregularities.

Questions and Answers

Q: What would happen if the luminance signal to a black-and-white CRT display was switched on for the entire duration of a screen sweep?

A: The entire screen would be solid white.

Q: How were the first video-game graphics created?

A: Electronic timers were wired to turn on or off a video signal whenever a CRT was scanning across the appropriate points on the screen.

Q: What are the three primary colors of light?

A: Red, green, and blue.

Q: What is hardware acceleration?

A: Hardware acceleration refers to the use of specially engineered circuitry that is designed to speed up frequently repeated graphics operations.

Q: Why do tiled backgrounds take less memory than ordinary bitmaps?

A: The detail pixel information that defines each tile must only be stored once, although the tile may be repeated many times in the scene.

Q: Why is lighting important to a game environment?

A: The human brain uses changes in brightness and shadows as an indicator of depth. Textures in reality are seldom seen with perfectly flat lighting.

Discussion Questions

1. Why do analog video displays offer more artistic freedom than digital video displays?
2. Why was the technique of using tiled backgrounds so important to the development of side-scrollers?
3. Describe some texture images that are naturally seamless.
4. Why would it be a bad idea to add a very high resolution character to a medium-resolution game?
5. Would a 3-D game or a side-scroller be more likely to enhance a player's sense of agency? Why?
6. How could you use triangles to model a round object such as a ball?

Exercises

1. Explain why it would have been very difficult to change the ball in the original Pong games into a bird with flapping wings.
2. If the red signal coming out of a video display generator was disconnected, what colors would you still be able to display?
3. You are asked to paint a beach scene using a paletted display mode. Describe four colors you would definitely select for your palette.
4. Design a set of tiles that you could use to create a side-scroller set in a jungle.
5. Create a level for the jungle game, using the tiles you designed for Exercise 4. Create a grid showing the appropriate tile number for each location on the screen.
6. Play an old arcade-style game and list any sprites that you see.
7. Examine the view displayed in Figure 2.50. Is this an orthographic view or a perspective view?

Figure 2.50
Is this a perspective view or an orthographic view?

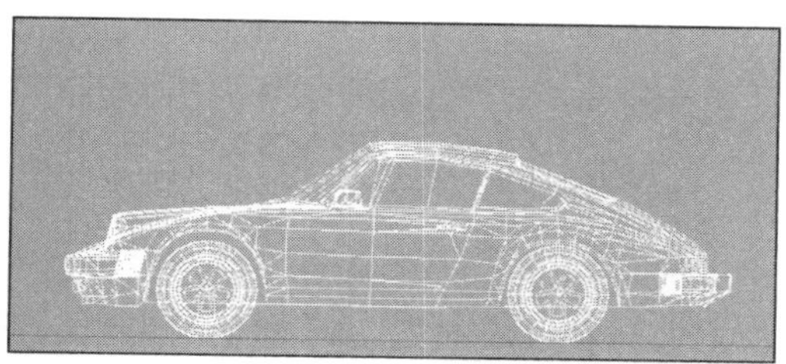

Figure 2.51
Is this a perspective view or an orthographic view?

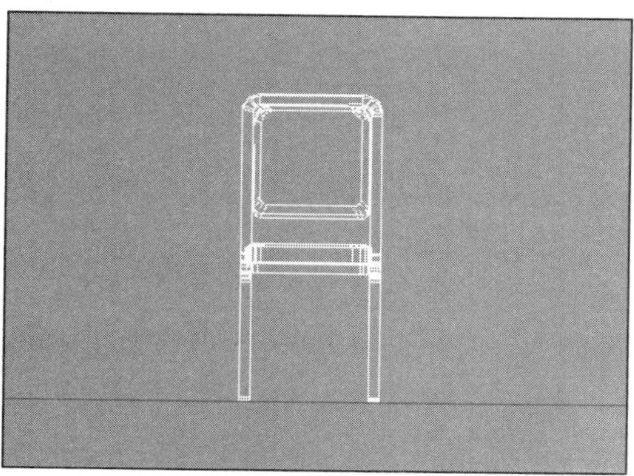

Figure 2.52
This is a front view.

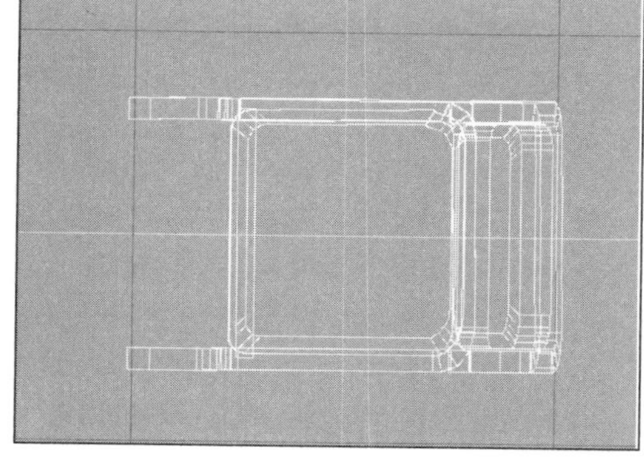

Figure 2.53
This is a top view.

8. Examine the view displayed in Figure 2.51. Is this an orthographic view or a perspective view?
9. Study the projections shown in Figures 2.52 through 2.54. They are all different views of the same object. What is that object?

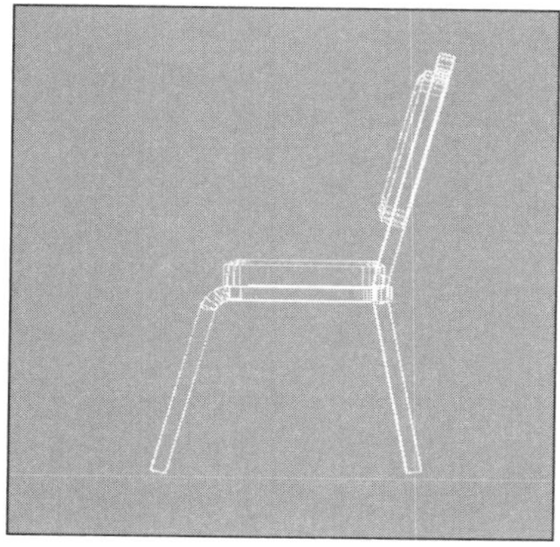

Figure 2.54
This is a side view.

10. Study the projections shown in Figures 2.55 through 2.57. They are all different views of the same object. What is that object?

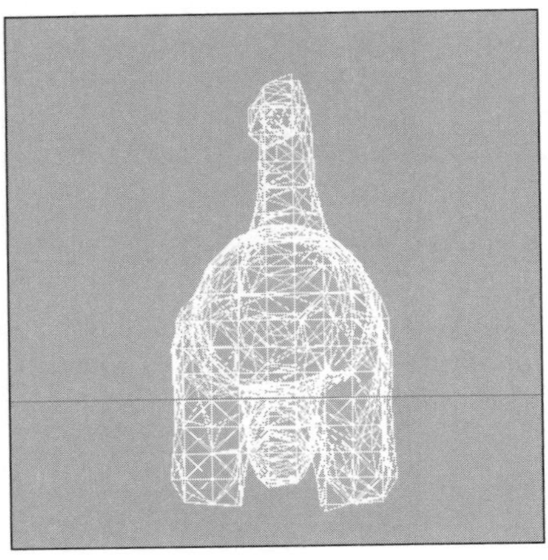

Figure 2.55
This is a front view.

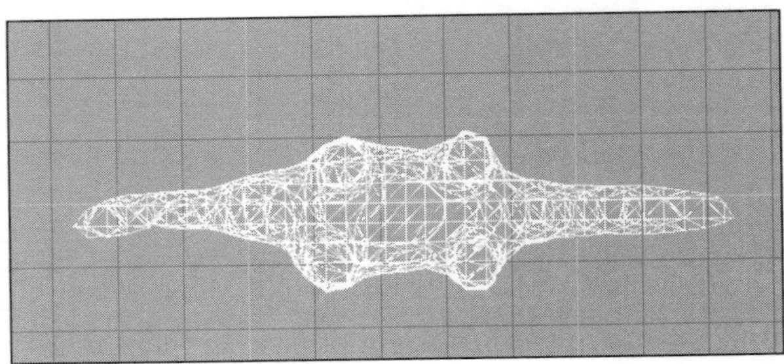

Figure 2.56
This is a top view.

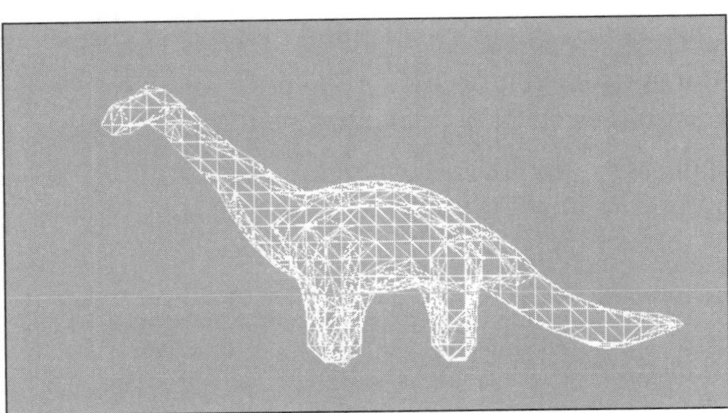

Figure 2.57
This is a side view.

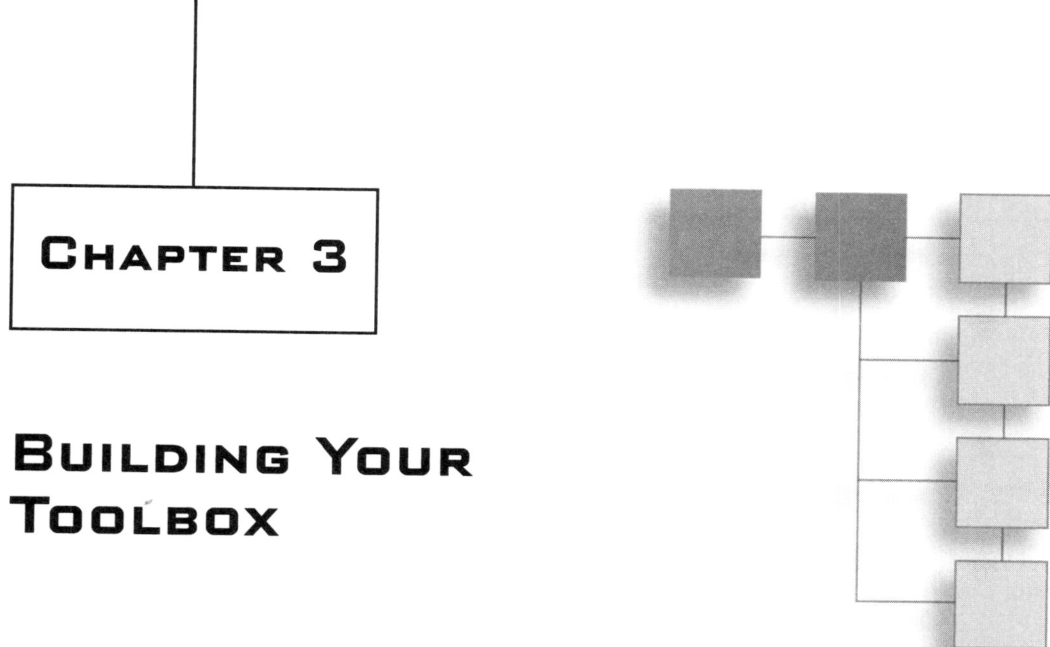

Chapter 3

Building Your Toolbox

You walk through your favorite bookstore. An artfully crafted cover catches your attention, and you pick up a fantastic graphics book. The book seems to teach exactly what you want to know. The book is well written, beautifully illustrated, and has hundreds of screenshots to guide you through one wonderful project after another.

You buy the book and take it home. You are excited to try the first project, when those three horrifying words hit you: "software not included." There are dozens of wonderful graphics books on the market. Most of them focus on a single software package, and most of these software packages are extremely expensive.

Most computer graphics books assume that their readers have already purchased whatever software they require. On the rare occasion when graphics books do include the necessary applications, they usually only offer a time-limited demo that might last long enough to complete the first project in the book. This book is different.

Introduction

When I began developing my game graphics course for Gamescapers, I had several goals in mind. I wanted to provide my students with a set of tools that would allow them to experience a wide range of artistic styles and 3-D modeling techniques. I felt the students needed a powerful graphics toolbox that they could take home and easily install on their own computers. It had to be powerful and inexpensive, and it had to allow them to experience the thrill of actually exporting their own models into a real working video game. I found a perfect solution in a program called gameSpace.

gameSpace Light

The CD that accompanies this book contains a fully functional version of gameSpace Light. gameSpace Light is a sophisticated 3-D modeling and animation package.

gameSpace was developed by Caligari Corporation, known for its award-winning trueSpace Reality Designer. gameSpace enables game artists to easily export models to a wide variety of game engines. gameSpace Light offers all of the modeling tools of gameSpace, without imposing any expiration dates or usage limits.

The only limit to the models you can build with gameSpace Light is the number of polygons the model can contain. Because all game artists strive to build objects with the lowest possible polygon counts, this limit can actually be seen as a useful set of training wheels that can help to instill and reinforce efficient modeling practices in novice game artists.

Depending upon your computer's settings, when you insert the Beginning Game Graphics CD in your computer's CD-ROM drive, the CD's user interface should launch automatically. If the user interface does not launch automatically, right-click on the Windows Start button. Use Windows Explorer to browse to the root directory of the CD. From the CD's root directory, double-click on the application named Start. Read and accept the software license for the CD and click on the button labeled gameSpace Light, as shown in Figure 3.1.

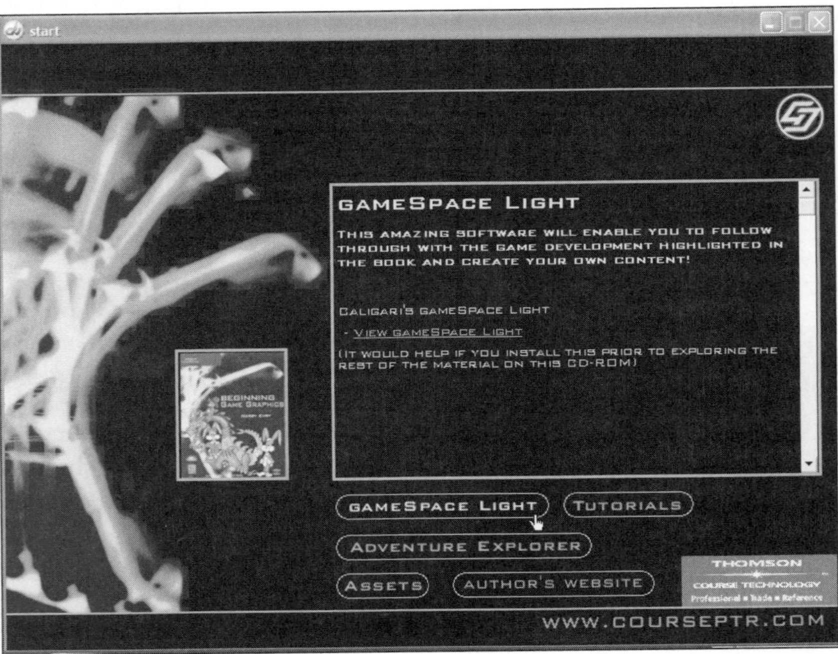

Figure 3.1
Click the gameSpace Light button.

Click the link labeled View gameSpace Light to open the gameSpace Light setup directory. The programs you need to install gameSpace Light are found in this directory.

Run the gameSpace Light setup program and follow its prompts to install gameSpace. You might need to register and acquire a serial number from Caligari. This is a fast and easy process. It is completely free and requires only an e-mail address and access to the Internet.

Once installation is complete, you should have a new icon on your desktop, as shown in Figure 3.2.

Figure 3.2
Click this icon to launch gameSpace Light.

Adventure Explorer

Once you have installed gameSpace, use the CD's user interface to install Adventure Explorer. Adventure Explorer is a simple 3-D video game, which you will be using throughout the projects in this book.

To install Adventure Explorer, click the button labeled Adventure Explorer on the CD's user interface. See Figure 3.3.

> I developed Adventure Explorer using DarkBasic Professional and DarkMatter. Both products are distributed by an innovative software company called The Game Creators.
>
> DarkBasic Professional is a powerful game programming language. DarkBasic Professional uses simple commands but offers a wealth of powerful graphics and animation features that make video-game programming fast and easy. DarkMatter is a collection of textures, models, characters, props, and other assets developed for use with DarkBasic Professional. Portions of the game physics exhibited in Adventure Explorer were implemented using the NGC Collision System, developed by a company called Nuclear Glory Enterprises.
>
> I programmed the ObjectImporter application using Microsoft's Visual C++, which is sold as part of its Visual Studio products.
>
> Links to these and other useful development tools can be found on this book's companion Web site at **www.gamescapers.com/GameGraphics**.

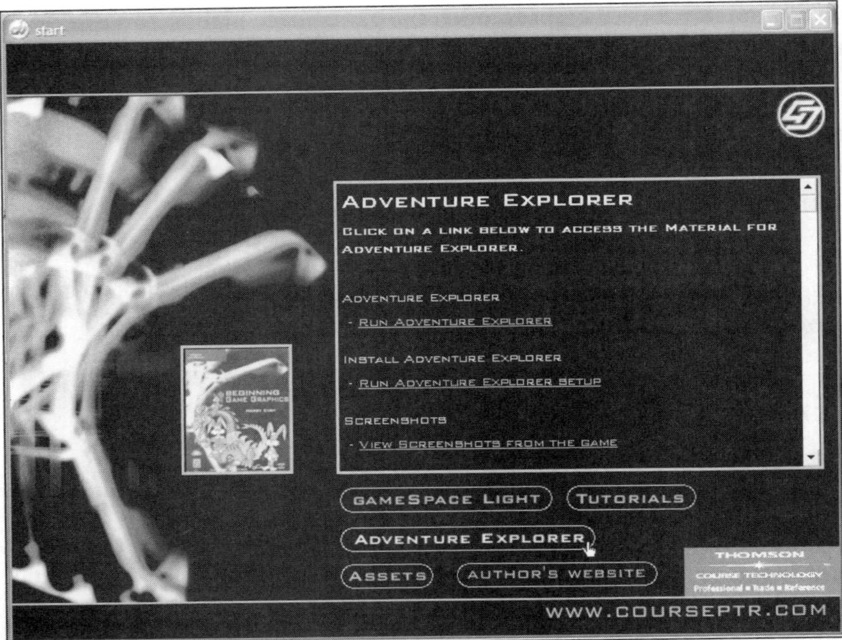

Figure 3.3
Click the Adventure Explorer button.

Click the link labeled Run Adventure Explorer Setup to install Adventure Explorer on your computer. Follow the prompts to complete the installation. I recommend that you accept the installer's recommended defaults wherever possible.

You can play Adventure Explorer from the CD with a preset collection of game objects, but you must install it onto your computer's hard disk before you can use it to complete the projects in this book.

Figure 3.4
Double-click the icon labeled Adventure Explorer to launch the game.

Throughout the remainder of this book, you will be recreating and replacing the objects in Adventure Explorer. The Adventure Explorer Setup program adds two icons to your desktop, as shown in Figure 3.4.

Figure 3.5 shows a screenshot from Adventure Explorer.

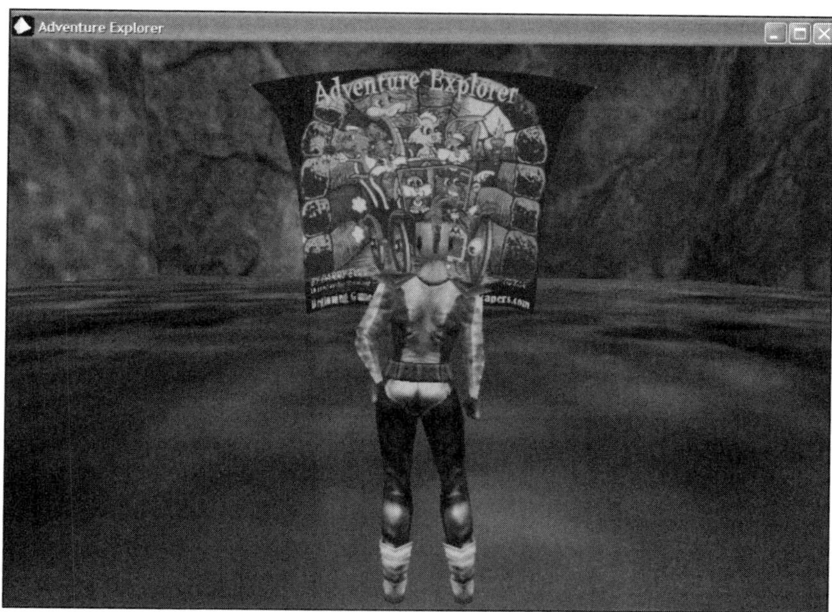

Figure 3.5
This is a screenshot from Adventure Explorer.

The second icon in Figure 3.4 is used to launch ObjectImporter. ObjectImporter makes it easy for you to replace the objects in Adventure Explorer. See Figure 3.6.

You can also launch ObjectImporter and Adventure Explorer using the All Programs list on the Windows Start menu.

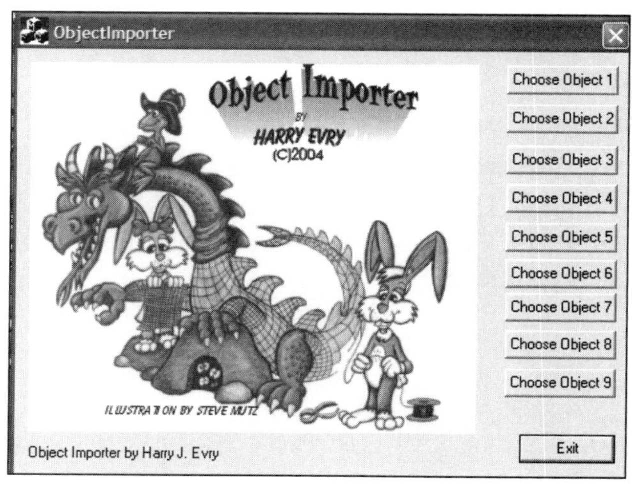

Figure 3.6
ObjectImporter replaces the game objects in Adventure Explorer.

Textures

Several of the projects in this book require image files that are contained in the Textures menu on the book's CD. gameSpace can read these files directly from the CD, but you might wish to copy the Textures folder to a more convenient location on your computer's hard disk.

Summary

In this chapter, you should have learned the following concepts:

- gameSpace Light is a powerful and flexible 3-D modeling package.
- gameSpace Light makes it easy to export object models into a wide range of game engines.
- gameSpace Light has no expiration date or usage limit.
- gameSpace Light has all of the modeling tools of gameSpace, but sets a limit on the complexity of the models it can save.
- Adventure Explorer is a simple 3-D game.
- ObjectImporter is a utility program that enables you to replace the game objects in Adventure Explorer.
- The Textures folder contains textures and image files you will need to complete many projects in this book.

Exercises

1. Install gameSpace Light.
2. Install Adventure Explorer.
3. The Tutorials section of the companion CD's user interface contains a great tutorial called Spirit of the Interface. Watch this tutorial for a brief introduction to the gameSpace interface.

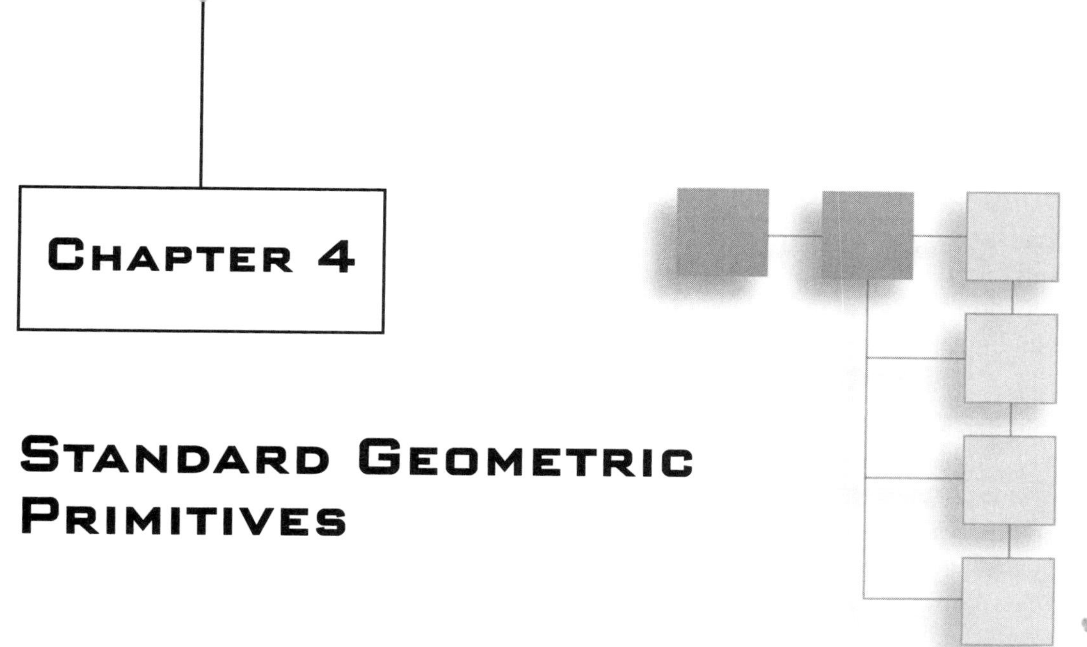

Chapter 4

Standard Geometric Primitives

The chapter titles are starting to sound more impressive, but don't worry. Like most computer terms, "geometric primitive" is just a big name for something so simple that it can be identified by almost any child.

Introduction

If you are like me, you may have, at some point in your past, pleasantly wasted hundreds of hours building with wooden blocks or plastic molded Legos (see Sidebar).

I remember building fantastic castles, pirate ships, space stations, dragons, rockets, and UFOs sitting on the floor of my den with my childhood friends and my extremely cool uncle Bruce. We thought we were just playing and having fun, but my mother somehow knew we were really mastering the fine art of modeling with geometric primitives. Of course, she would never have used those words for it.

So what exactly is a geometric primitive? Geometric primitives are the basic shapes we all know and recognize. They are simple three-dimensional shapes such as cubes, spheres, cylinders, and cones, and they work just like the blocks in a typical preschool building set.

> Many years ago my good friend Dean Parks, who has helped to contribute some of the designs and models for this book, and I appeared briefly in an episode of the *P.M. Magazine* television program. We were building a space station in a Lego exhibit at the Los Angeles Children's Museum. Twenty years later, we are still building imaginary space stations.

In this section, you will learn how to model with these basic shapes, and you will discover once more how to turn primitive building blocks into the fantastic figments of your imagination. You will learn to use the gameSpace user interface to create and manipulate primitives, and then you will bring them into an actual game.

Bring Out the Blocks

Everybody grab your preschool building set and dump all the blocks on the floor. In case you don't happen to have your preschool building set handy, take a look at Figure 4.1.

Figure 4.1
The basic primitive building blocks

Here you see a plane, a cube, a sphere, a cylinder, and a cone. In Figures 4.2 through 4.6, you can see these same five geometric primitives as they appear in typical orthographic views, which were discussed earlier in the book. Remember that orthographic views allow you to see the same object simultaneously from multiple directions.

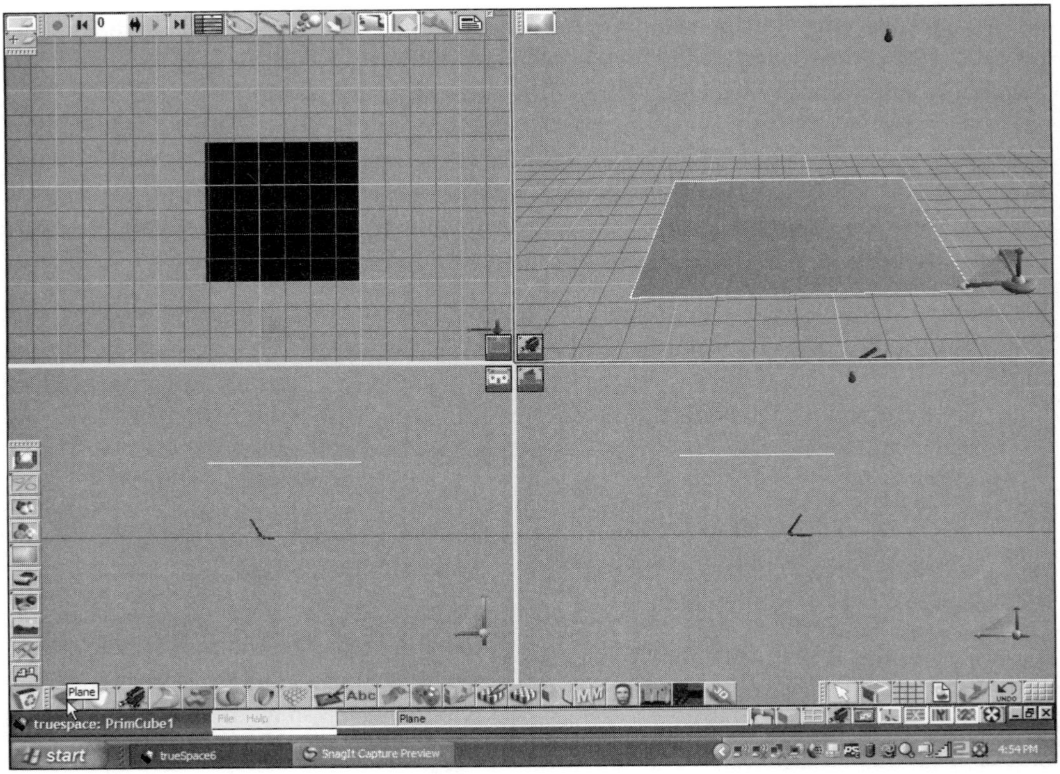

Figure 4.2
A plane is an extremely thin square. Picture a sheet of thin paper.

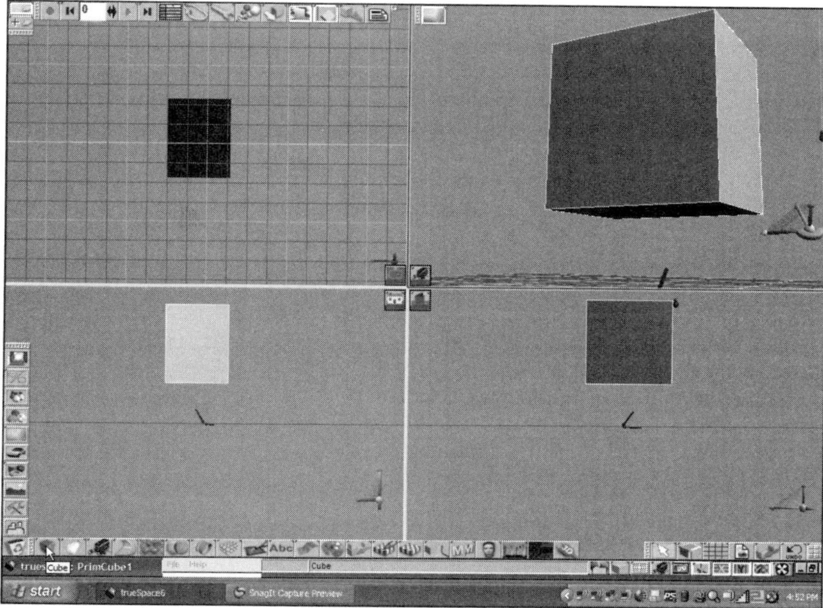

Figure 4.3
A cube is a six-sided square shape. Picture a square shipping carton.

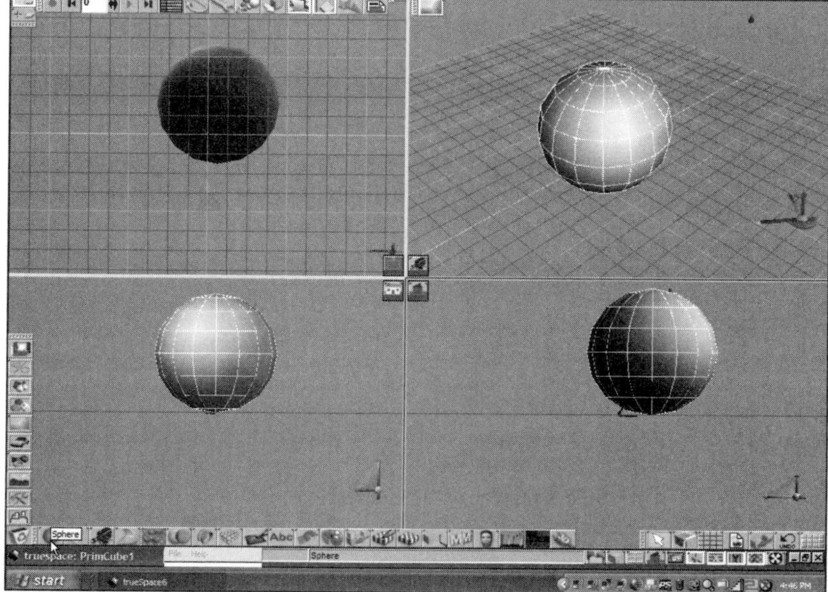

Figure 4.4
A sphere is a round ball. Picture a smooth beach ball.

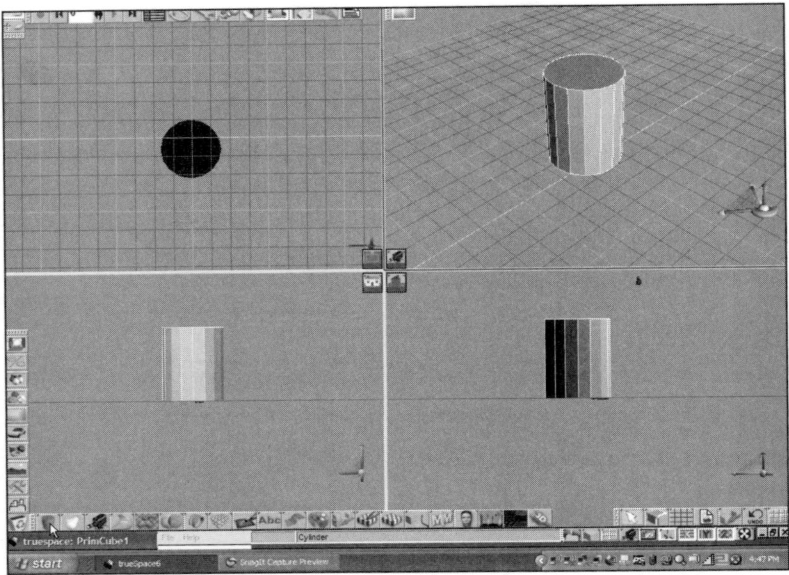

Figure 4.5
A cylinder appears round from one side and rectangular from the others. Picture a can of soda.

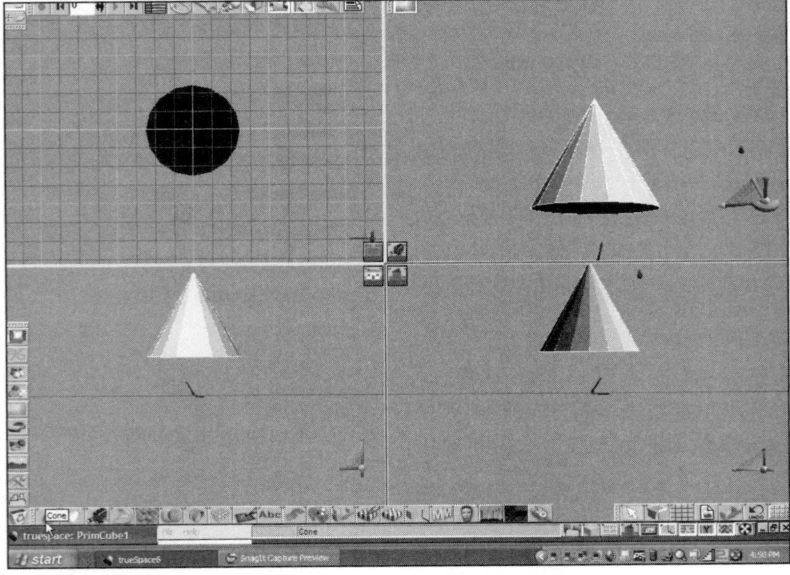

Figure 4.6
A cone appears round from one side and triangular from the others. Picture a funnel or a road safety cone.

Geometric primitives are the most basic three-dimensional shapes, such as planes, cubes, spheres, cylinders, and cones.

Primitives All Around Us

Children find it easy to look at a shoebox and see a house. They find it natural to pick up a basketball and pretend it is a planet. Yet often as children grow up, they find it harder to see the simple shapes in things that once seemed so obvious.

Geometric primitives are everywhere around us. The glass in your window is a plane. The wheels of your car are cylinders, and so is the shiny muffler pipe that sticks out the back. Perhaps the handle of your gear shift is a cylinder or a sphere, and I would bet the shaft of the gear shift is some kind of cylinder.

Look around the room that you are in right now. How many basic primitive shapes do you see around you? If you are one of those serious people who expect their cubes to be perfectly square or their spheres to be perfectly round, then you may not count too many. Artists, of course, tend to like their lines curved, their cubes squashed, and their spheres compressed. If you can accept that primitives can be stretched in one direction or another, then you are certain to find them everywhere you look.

I remember a delightful conversation I once had with Kathy Kirk, the chief show designer at Walt Disney Imagineering. I suggested that computers and computer-aided design software could help expedite the accurate drawing of straight lines and geometric shapes. She swept her hand grandly about and pointed to the fanciful storyboard drawings all around her office. "This is Disney," she said. "We don't use straight lines or geometric shapes here." She was right; Disney artists certainly use a lot of beautiful curves. But most Disney animators happily admit that they still depend on geometry. As Disney legend John Hench explained, they just like to squash and stretch their geometry as if it's somehow alive and moving.

Two Primitives Are Better Than One

Although there are many game objects that can be built from simple primitives, think of the objects that you could build if you were to stick your primitives together. Wasn't this the idea behind the popular Legos building blocks? See Figure 4.7.

Figure 4.7
Combining geometric primitives

Two cylinders make a top hat. Three cylinders can make a weight lifter's barbell, and three simple spheres might appear to millions of children around the world like a very famous cartoon mouse.

With a little imagination, you can probably think of hundreds of everyday objects that you could easily make from a few combined primitives. With a modeling tool that can create, combine, and distort geometric primitives, you can easily produce an endless array of game objects and models.

The Power of Primitives

The real power of primitives is not in the software. It's the portable supercomputer you call your brain that really fills in the gaps between geometry and illusion. The human brain has a unique ability to extract real everyday objects from even the simplest lines and shapes. Take a look at the rough collection of lines in Figure 4.8. What do you see?

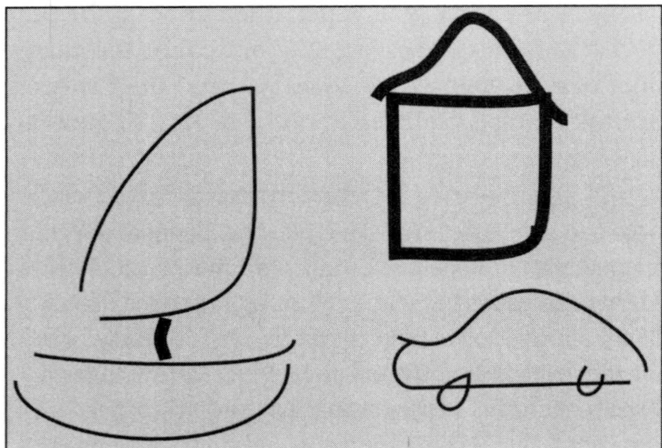

Figure 4.8
What do you see?

> Have you ever gazed at a cloud in the sky and saw a dolphin, a shark, a fish, a whale, or a really large frosted jelly donut?
>
> Even thousands of years ago, our ancestors saw such things in the clouds and in the tiny little dots that fill our nighttime skies. All right, I'll admit they probably never saw a large frosted jelly donut, but you get the idea.

A fundamental skill of good game artists is the ability to communicate and bring to their viewers' minds the most complicated of objects, using only the simplest forms, shapes, and patterns. Primitives are typically the simplest forms around.

It should be pretty easy to see why simple geometric primitives have become some of the most popular tools of modeling for 3-D games. Nearly every 3-D modeling package on the market supports some form of 3-D primitive modeling.

What makes modeling with primitives so popular?

- Geometric primitives are easy enough for any child to understand.
- Most artists can easily visualize geometric primitives.
- Programmers can implement and manipulate geometric primitives easily.
- Computer graphics hardware can draw geometric primitives extremely quickly.
- Geometric primitives can be combined and manipulated in a huge number of ways.

Game artists use geometric primitives to create a vast number of the common and not-so-common objects you may need in your games.

An important side benefit of modeling with primitives is that 3-D models created from primitives tend to be built efficiently. A game programmer would say "They have a very low polygon count." Although there are certainly exceptions to this rule, breaking your objects into large simple blocks tends to result in game models with less wasted detail and fewer complex parts.

gameSpace offers a powerful selection of tools to create, modify, combine, and manipulate geometric primitives.

Building with Blocks

In this section, you will learn to create and manipulate geometric primitives within gameSpace. You will build some simple game objects, and you will use these objects to enhance and improve a real computer game.

3, 2, 1, Launch

It's time to launch gameSpace. If you haven't installed gameSpace on your computer, go back to Chapter 3 and install it now. Also be sure to install the Gamescapers' Adventure Explorer software which was discussed in Chapter 3. See Figure 4.9.

Figure 4.9
Click this icon to launch gameSpace from your desktop.

Once you have installed gameSpace, you can launch the program in a couple of ways:

- Click on the gameSpace icon, which the installer program usually places on your desktop. See Figure 4.9.
- Click on the Windows Start button, then choose All Programs, and finally click on Caligari gameSpace or Caligari gameSpace Light.

Everything in Its Place

When you launch gameSpace, it usually remembers the last scene that you edited, so you may see some leftover objects from a previous tutorial or from your own projects and experimentation. You can save these items, if you wish, by choosing File > Save > Scene from the File Menu at the bottom of the gameSpace screen. See Figure 4.10.

tip

By default, gameSpace's menu item File/Preferences has an option/setting called "Auto Load." If this option is checked on the Preferences panel, gameSpace will reload the last scene you were working on. If you prefer to have a fresh, blank scene every time you start gameSpace, simply uncheck the option.

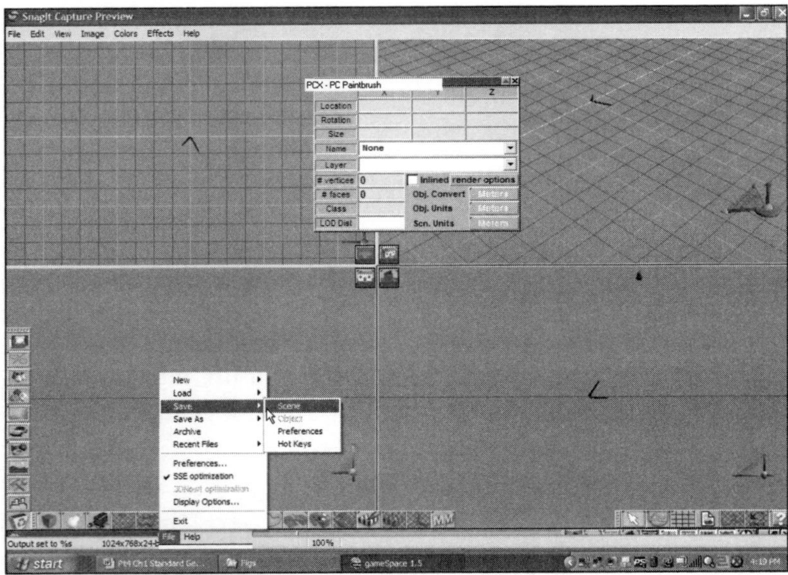

Figure 4.10
Saving a gameSpace scene

Now choose File > New > Scene from the File Menu to clear out the workspace, and you are ready to begin a new scene. See Figure 4.11.

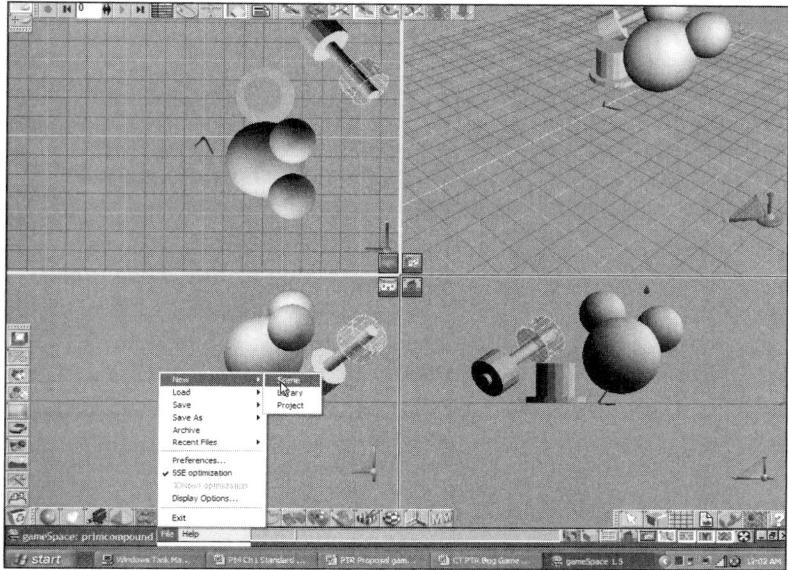

Figure 4.11
A brand new scene: imagine the possibilities!

Surprisingly, gameSpace has perhaps the smallest and simplest menu bar in the business. The menus, which are found at the bottom of the screen, are used only for file handling, user preferences, and easy access to the useful help files. If you are using the free version of gameSpace, you will unfortunately be missing the bulk of these help files.

If this is your first time working with gameSpace, you might, at first glance, feel a bit overwhelmed. Don't worry. It's actually much simpler than it appears.

Many Windows programs hide their commands in sprawling menus that you pull down from the top of the screen. Most typical graphics programs complement busy menus with a maze of elaborate panels, floating windows, and adjustable sidebars.

The creators of gameSpace have taken floating graphic toolbars to a whole new level. They obviously don't care much for menus. They created a visual interface where any possible command or feature is only one or two mouse clicks away.

They accomplish this by organizing hundreds of picture buttons into neat stacks. Imagine that the screen is a giant board game, and that each little picture box on the bottom of the board is actually a pile of game cards. To play a card, you choose the card you wish to play from the appropriate stack and place it on the top of that stack. That is exactly how the picture buttons, also known as icons, in gameSpace are arranged.

Icons are small buttons containing pictures that visually depict the actions they are meant to perform.

You might think that all of these stacks of little buttons would get in the way, but the buttons are organized in a simple and logical way. Once you understand the purpose of each set of icons on the gameSpace toolbars, you can easily find any tool you may need.

As you start your first model, you will quickly see how this works.

Toolbars are clusters of icons or groups of icons arranged in a row. gameSpace has a default set of toolbars that appear on the bottom, top, and sides of the screen, but you can easily modify these toolbars or even create new toolbars of your own.

Your First Model

For your first primitive model, you will create a simple box. A box may not sound so exciting, but in the magical world of video games (and the not-so-magical world of moving and shipping), they can be very useful. I can assure you that the models you make will get more interesting as we go.

This may be your first opportunity to experience the unique gameSpace interface. Remember the stacks of picture buttons (or icons) discussed above. The first slot on the toolbar, right next to the recycle bin at the bottom left of the screen, is what gameSpace calls the primitive library. I would describe it as a pile of icons for creating primitives. See Figure 4.12.

Few nongamers recognize the incredible power and versatility of boxes. Boxes can block your escape. They can shield you from gunfire. They can contain deadly, precious, or life-changing cargo. You can slide them across the floor. You can climb them, break them, shoot them, blast them to pieces, and if you are really careful, you can randomly jump from one box to another. A few very fortunate boxes have even made it to stardom as the lead characters in successful, if somewhat primitive, video games. Someone has to build them. So why not you?

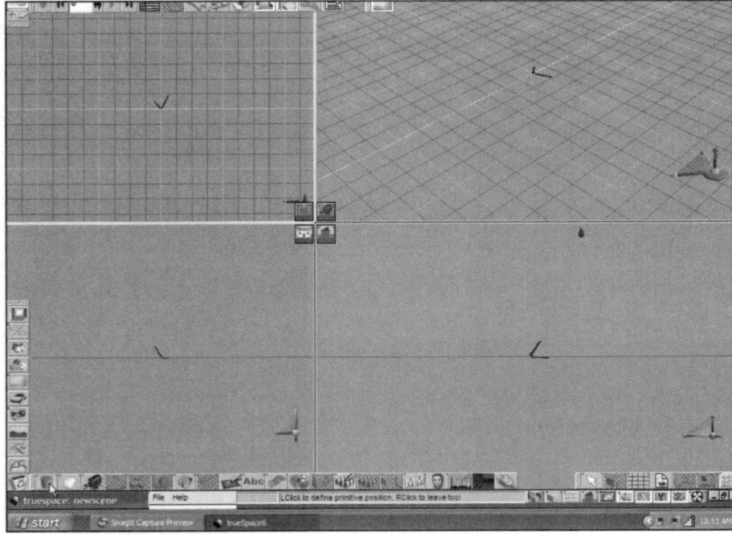

Figure 4.12
The primitive library or the pile of primitives

You might see an icon with a picture of a cube here. If you do, the proverbial "cube card" is at the top of the stack, and you can simply click on it. See Figure 4.13.

Figure 4.13
The cube icon

If, as in Figure 4.12, you see a picture of a cylinder, cone, plane, sphere, or anything other than a cube, then you must pull the "cube card" from the proverbial pile and bring it to the top of the deck.

To do this, simply click on and drag whatever icon is currently visible in the first slot beside the recycle bin. If your screen looked like Figure 4.12, you would click on and drag the picture of the cylinder. This reveals the full set of icons that can appear in this slot. See Figure 4.14.

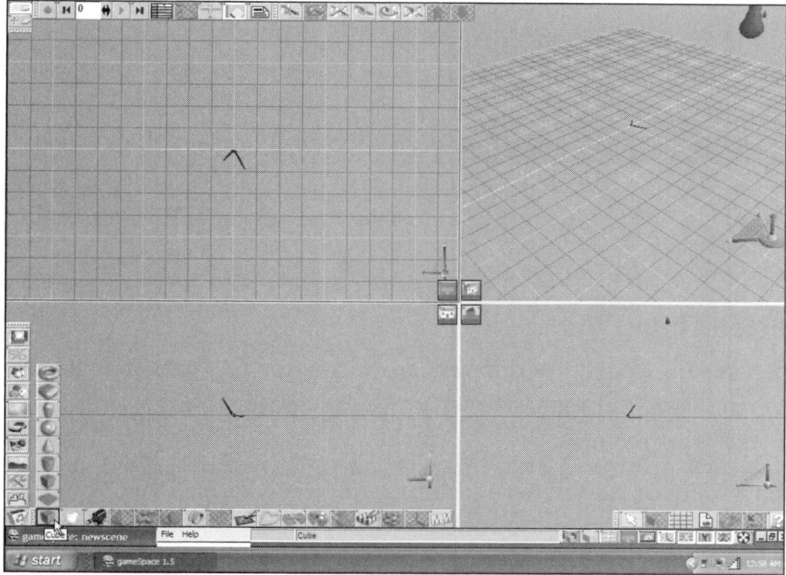

Figure 4.14
Click and drag to see every available card in the "pile of primitives."

Drag toward the top of the screen until the moving border appears around the cube icon shown in Figure 4.13, and release the mouse button.

The screen should now appear as in Figure 4.15, with the cube icon sitting next to the recycle bin. Notice the amber glow that appears around the cube icon. This tells you that gameSpace is now in Primitive Creation Mode. You may also notice that the mouse pointer on the screen will now appear with a little picture of a cube beside it.

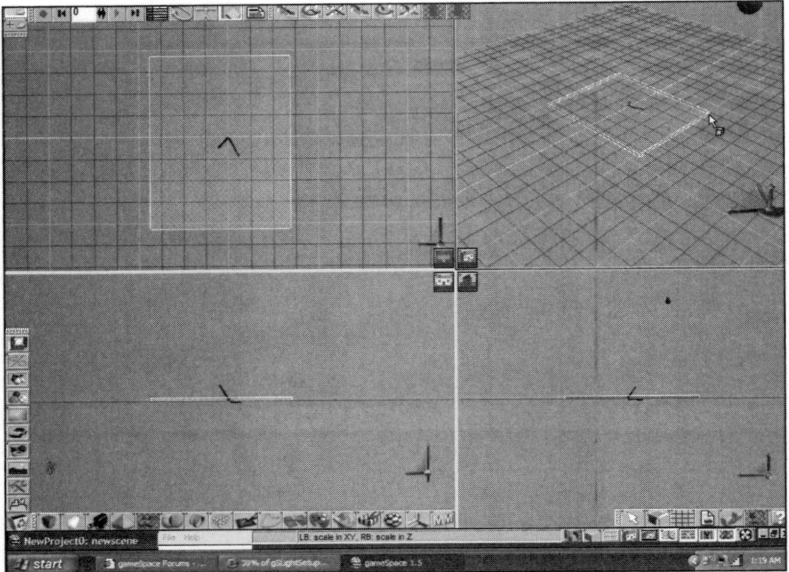

Figure 4.15
Ready to draw a cube.

Four Views Are Better Than One

Your gameSpace screen may still look quite different from the one in these screenshots, however. The screenshots indicate four separate viewports or windows on the screen, but you may only have one viewport on yours.

gameSpace can work in a variety of ways. There are times when it is easier to work in one single viewport, such as when you need to examine extremely small and intricate details. You should remember from Chapter 2, however, that four views allow you to see an object's details in all three dimensions.

Viewports are the windows through which you view the three-dimensional virtual world within gameSpace. gameSpace lets you change the number of visible viewports and the specific viewing angle from which each viewport is drawn.

To change the layout of your gameSpace screen, work the toolbars exactly as you did when selecting the Cube tool. This time, however, you will choose from the viewport configuration library, which appears on the lower toolbar at the far right-hand side of the screen. See Figure 4.16.

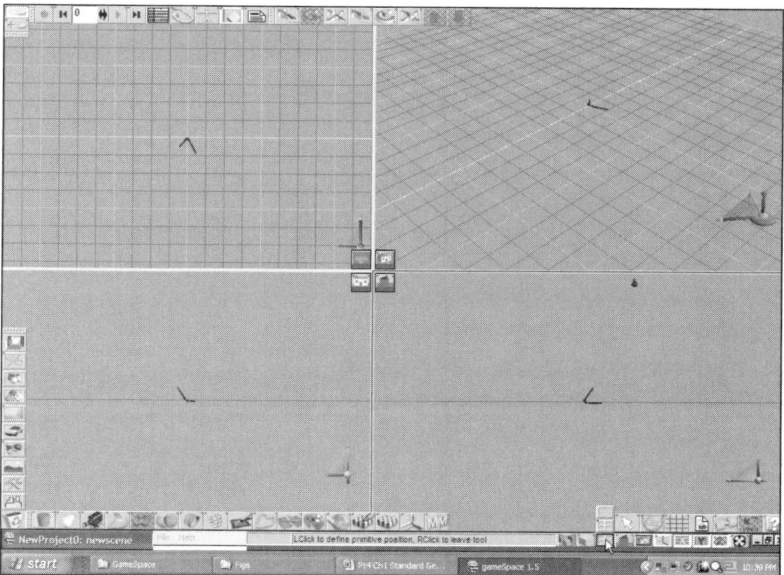

Figure 4.16
Choose a screen layout.

The screen layout icons, shown in more detail in Figure 4.17, allow you to select either one viewport, which fills the whole screen, or four smaller viewports, as seen in Figure 4.15.

Figure 4.17
Use these icons to choose between single viewport and multiple viewport modes.

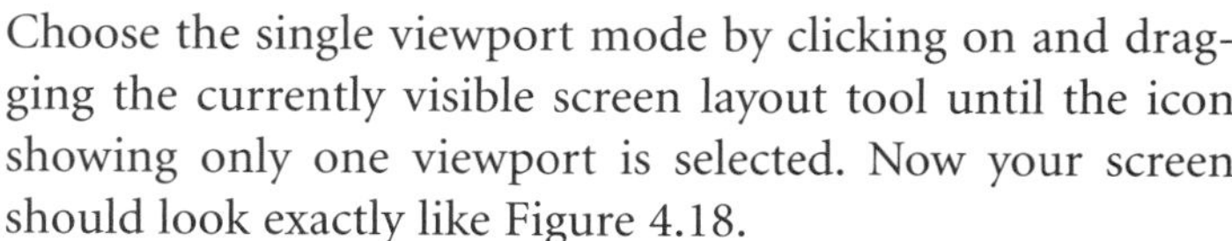

Choose the single viewport mode by clicking on and dragging the currently visible screen layout tool until the icon showing only one viewport is selected. Now your screen should look exactly like Figure 4.18.

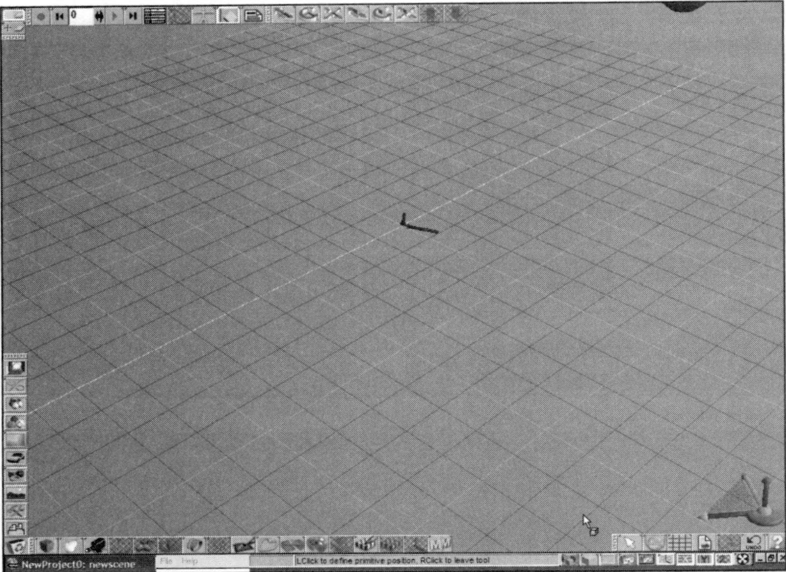

Figure 4.18
Single viewport mode

You are almost ready to make your first model.

Navigating in Three Dimensions

Before you can create a cube, you must understand how to move around and draw in three-dimensional space. It is one thing to view objects in three dimensions, but it is quite another to actually use a mouse to move them in three dimensions.

It is easy enough to use the computer's mouse to draw on a flat, two-dimensional surface. You simply move the mouse up, down, left, and right, and the mouse pointer moves exactly where you want it. When you are working in top, front, and side orthographic viewports the mouse can function in the usual way. These are two-dimensional windows into a three-dimensional scene. But what about a perspective viewport? At some point, you still need to draw in three dimensions.

tip

It is often convenient to use the two-dimensional orthogonal views to manipulate and position objects precisely. In these views, your mouse is restricted to two-dimensional movement up, down, left, and right within the active viewport.

It is obviously a little harder when you have to move the mouse in six possible directions, but the ability to do so can significantly enhance your modeling capabilities. Ideally, you should be able to draw three-dimensional forms that flow up and down, left and right, and forward and back all at the same time.

This problem has been solved in many different ways by almost every 3-D program on the market, but here is where gameSpace really shines. The geniuses at Caligari did a fantastic job of inventing one of the most simple, intuitive, and elegant 3-D navigation interfaces in the industry.

> There have also been some very creative and innovative hardware solutions to this problem. From swinging armatures and floating position trackers to control gloves and three-dimensional mouse-like devices, hardware manufacturers are racing to find a good three-dimensional control device that will achieve mass market acceptance.
>
> I have recently been playing with a new product from 3D connexion called the SpaceBall 5000. It is like a trackball with 12 buttons, but it can sense very fine hand movements in more than six directions, including up and down, left and right, forward and back, and several directions of rotation. Unfortunately the manufacturer does not yet provide direct support for the gameSpace interface, but this may change in the very near future.

The basic concept is quite simple. First, drag the mouse to move left and right or forward and back, then right-click-drag the mouse to move up and down. Mathematicians would say left-click-drag to move on the X and Y axes, then right-click to move on the Z axis, but if you are not a mathematician, an example may be in order.

A Cube Is Born

It is much easier to show this visually than to adequately describe it in words, so check out Figures 4.19 to 4.23 and then try it for yourself.

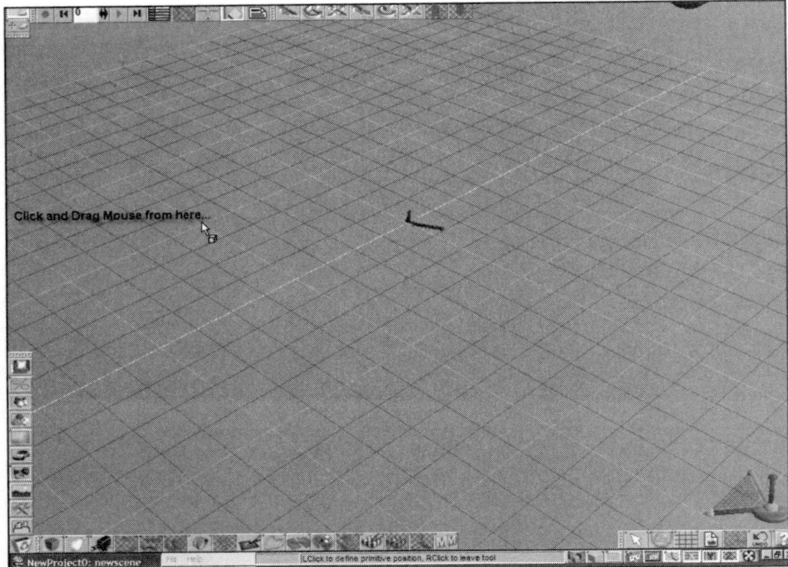

Figure 4.19
Making a cube, step 1

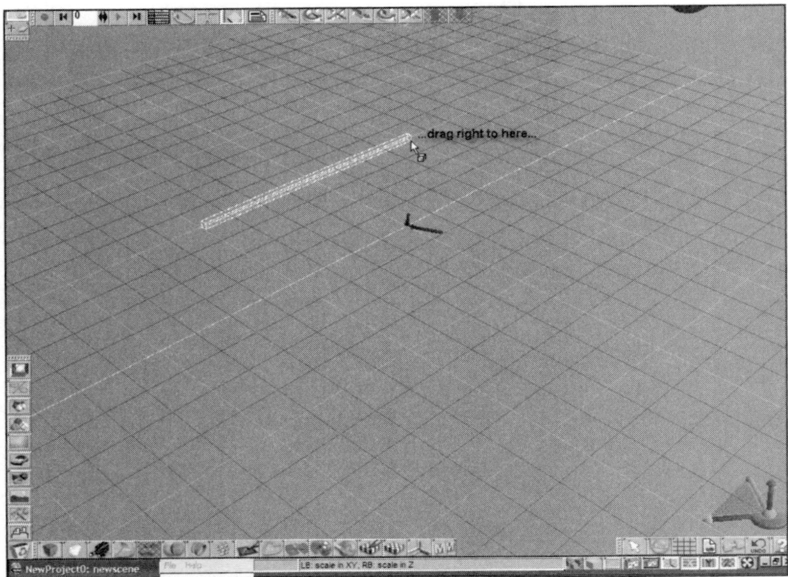

Figure 4.20
Making a cube, step 2

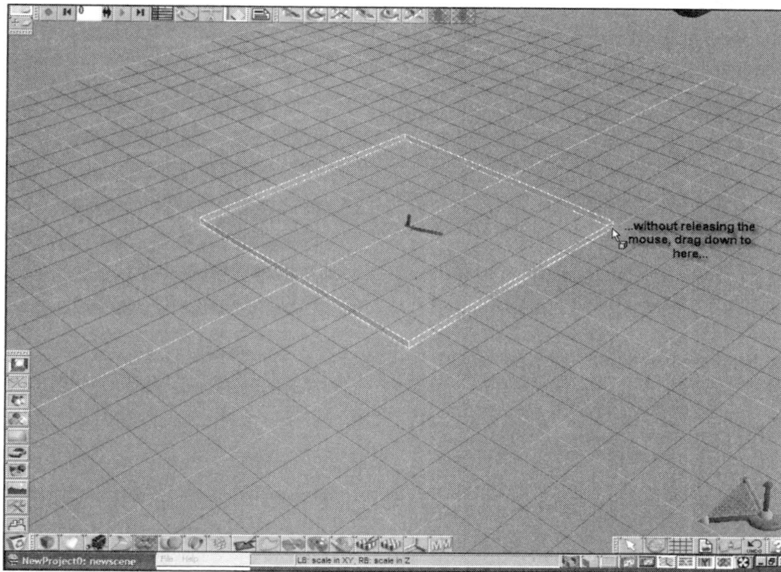

Figure 4.21
Making a cube, step 3

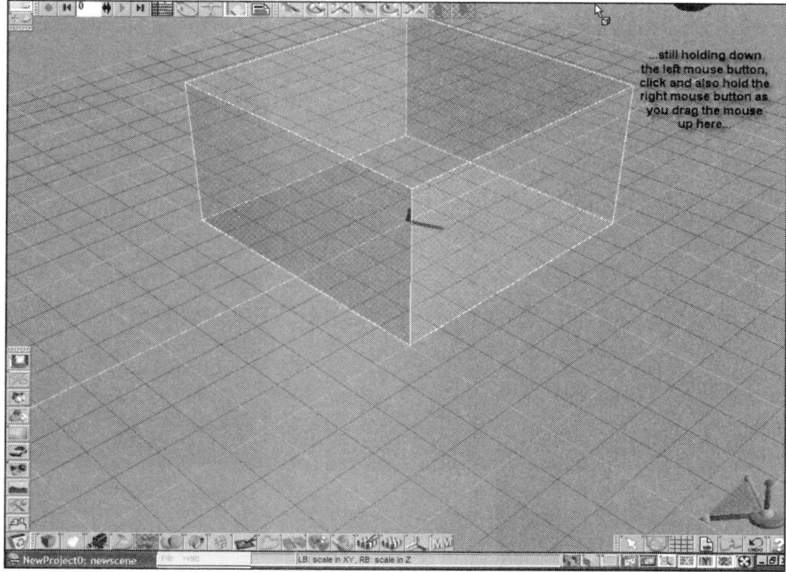

Figure 4.22
Making a cube, step 4

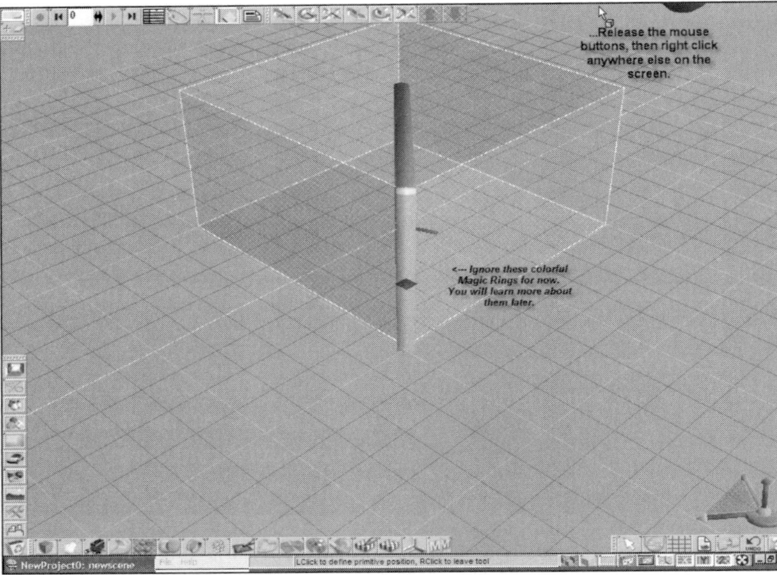

Figure 4.23
Making a cube, step 5

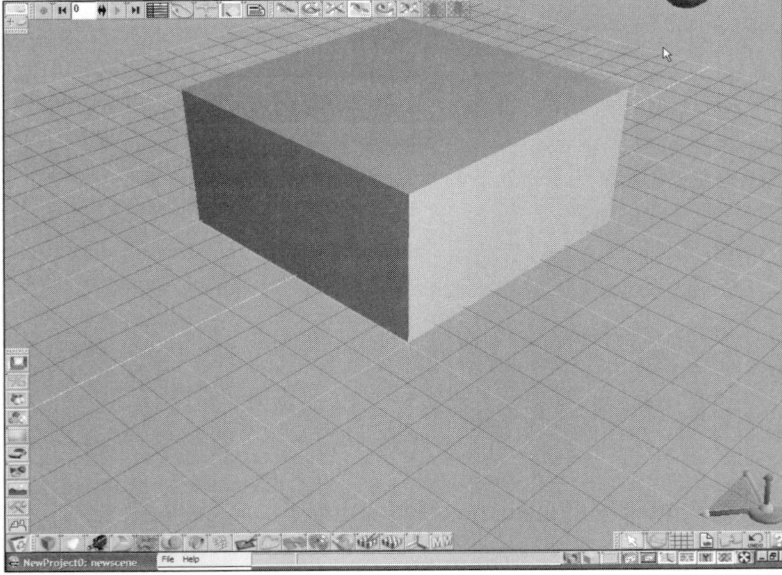

Figure 4.24
The completed cube

Hit the Delete key to erase the cube, and repeat the above process until you feel comfortable working in three dimensions. Try building a variety of cubes, from thin tall cubes to wide short cubes.

Adjusting Your Cube

Creating your cube is just the beginning. Sometimes it is just not possible to get exactly the shape you need. Most of your time in modeling is spent tweaking and finely adjusting the objects once they are created, and gameSpace makes this pretty easy.

Your cube is a pretty simple shape, but you may still want to adjust it a little. Select the object scale tool from the toolbar at the top of the gameSpace screen. You can also activate this tool by pressing the C key. See Figure 4.25.

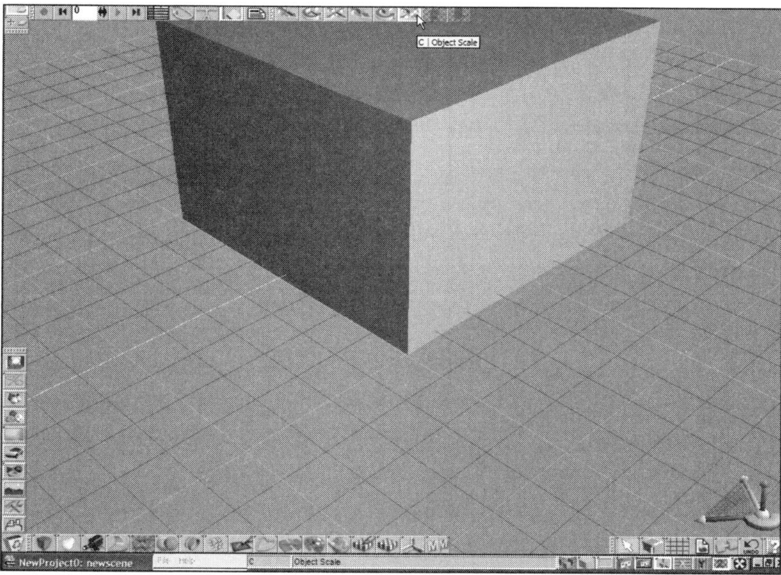

Figure 4.25
Select the object scale tool.

Now you can drag your mouse to scale, shrink, or stretch the cube in any direction. If you want to make the cube taller or shorter, remember to hold down the right mouse button as you drag. The right mouse button will scale the cube in the up and down direction.

With only one viewport, it may be difficult to determine when the cube is precisely square. So choose the multiple viewport icon from the screen layout tools at the bottom of the screen. See Figure 4.26.

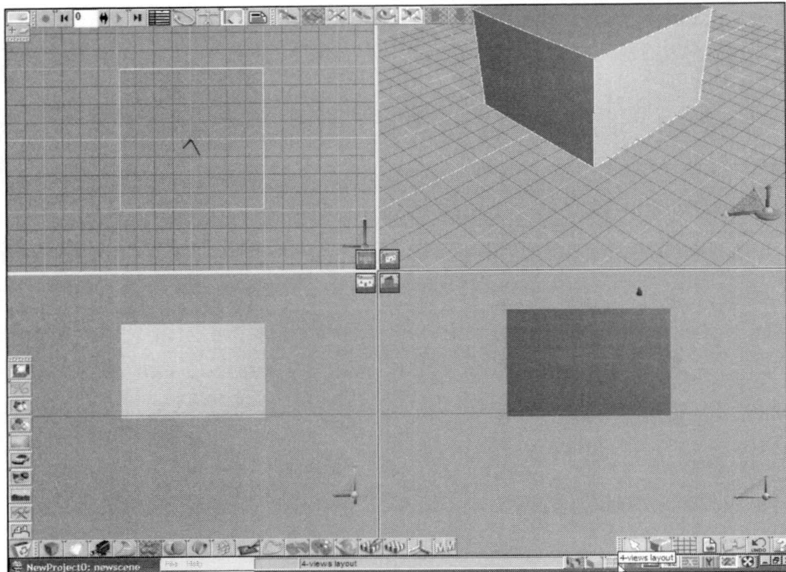

Figure 4.26
Change to a multiple viewport configuration.

Now you can use the three orthogonal viewports (top, front, and side) to see exactly how long or short the cube appears from each direction.

The buttons in the slots just to the left of the object scale tool allow you to move or rotate the selected object. Try using these tools to reposition the object and turn it around. Note how the use of left-click-drag and right-click-drag affects each of these tools.

If you need to zoom in or out for a better look in any viewport, click in that viewport, and then use your mouse scroll wheel or center button to move the viewport's viewing position toward or away from your object.

tip

Use the Z, X, and C keys to quickly activate the object move, object rotate, and object scale tools, respectively.

You might think these are odd letter choices for these functions, but notice that they are the first three keys on the bottom row of letters in any standard QWERTY keyboard. This makes it quite easy for you to quickly move between them, as long as you can remember their order. Object move is the first key, object rotate is the second, and object scale is the third, just as they appear on the toolbar.

Taking More Control

Modeling things visually using gameSpace's simple graphical interface can be easy, but often you need a little more control. Maybe it is enough that your cube model is almost a perfect cube, but sometimes the game requires a cube that is perfectly square. What you need is a little more precision.

Perhaps the level designer has planned for the cube to slip precisely into a specific hole in the level, or perhaps the programmers have programmed the game physics and collision code to some exact specification. It could just be that your producer has had too little sleep lately and thinks numerical precision can make up for an inadequate budget and a overzealous schedule. It really can't, you know.

Whatever the reason, the visual interface is just not enough. It is time for you to take control. Find the icon of the white arrow on the higher of the two toolbars on the bottom right of the screen. This is the object selection icon. See Figure 4.27.

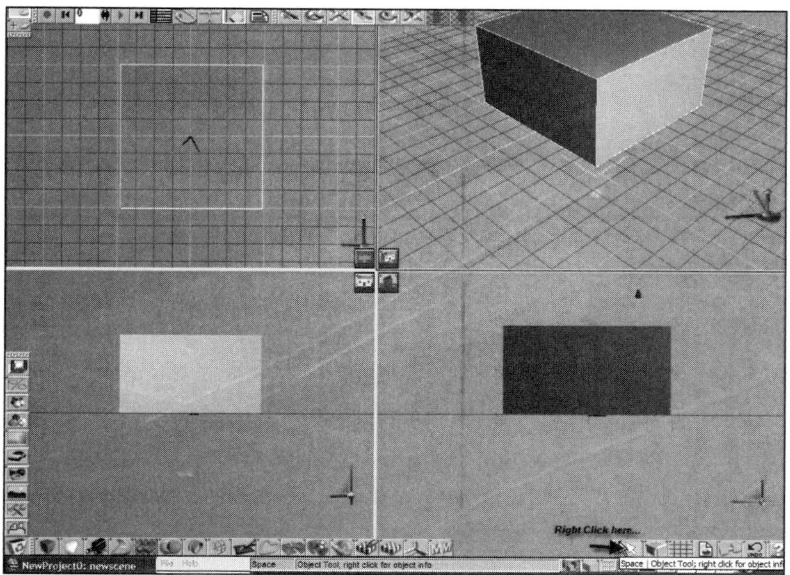

Figure 4.27
Right-click on the object selection tool.

Right-click the arrow icon to open the Object Info Pane. See Figure 4.28.

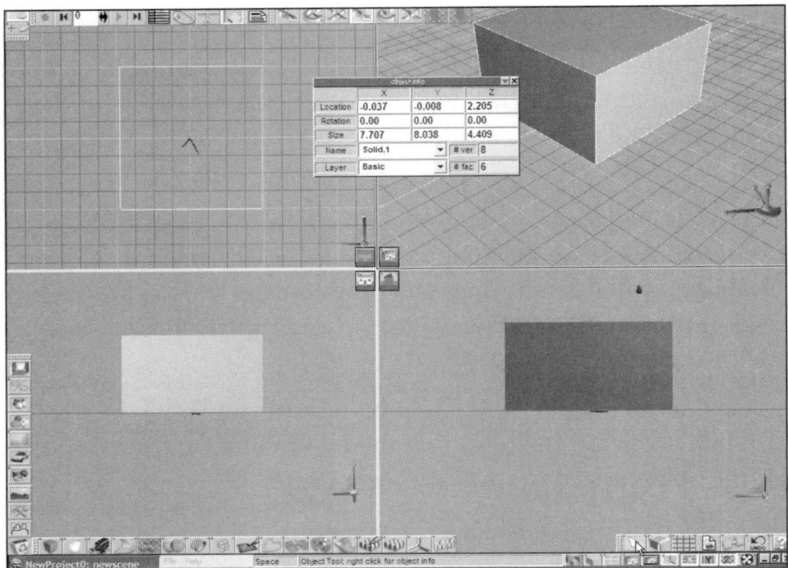

Figure 4.28
The Object Info Pane

The Object Info Pane tells you the precise location, rotation, and size of the selected object. In this case, the only object in the scene is the cube. The location, rotation, and size are each specified with three numbers, which describe the object in units along the X, Y, and Z axes.

In gameSpace, the X axis runs left and right. The Y axis runs in and out of the screen, and the Z axis is up and down. The grid that you see in the perspective viewport typically shows lines running in the X and Y directions.

Looking at the Object Info Pane in Figure 4.28, you can see that the cube in the screenshot is located near the center of the world, offset from the center by exactly 2.205 units in the up and down (Z) direction. If you wanted to precisely center this cube, you could replace all three location numbers with the number 0.0.

To do this, click on the first location number, beneath the X column title, and type in the new number. Use 0.0 if you wish to center the object. Repeat this process for the location numbers beneath the Y and Z column title. See Figure 4.29.

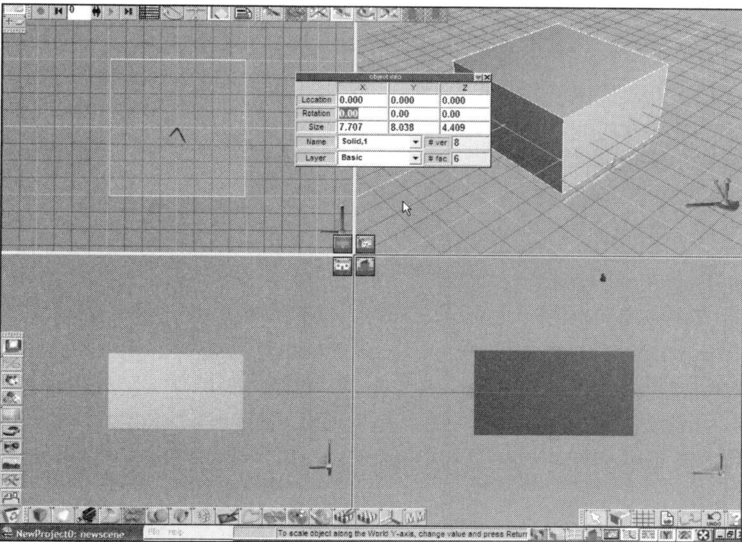

Figure 4.29
Here the cube is perfectly centered, but not perfectly square.

You can also see that the cube is far from perfectly square. Its size in the X and Y directions is nearly twice its size in the Z direction. To make it perfectly square in all directions, make sure the three size numbers are set to the same value. In Figure 4.30, they have been each set to exactly 7.0.

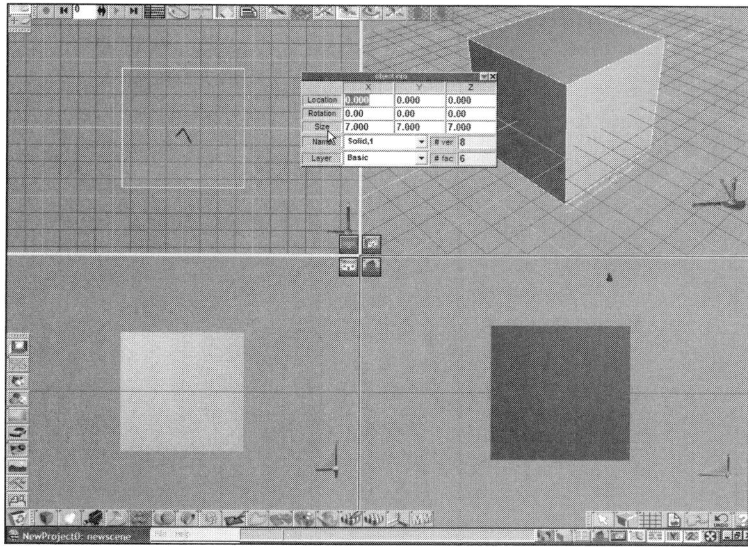

Figure 4.30
The cube is now perfectly squared.

If you are not happy with the location of the Object Info Pane, you can drag it anywhere around the screen by clicking and dragging on the blue title bar, where it says the words "object info." This can be very useful because it allows you to see objects that might otherwise be hidden by the Object Info Pane. gameSpace remembers where you last placed the Object Info Pane and tries to reposition it there the next time you open it.

Calibrate Your Rulers

You have seen how to change the numbers in the Object Info Pane, but do you really know what they mean? When I say the cube is 7 units wide, does that mean it is 7 inches or 7 miles? This is particularly important when you are making objects to import into a video game. Imagine the confusion if one game artist creates a cool player character for a game, while another makes the nifty supercharged atomic minivan that the player will ride in. If the player is modeled at 7 meters and the vehicle is modeled at 7 feet, the players are going to have a little problem.

To prevent this situation from arising, and ironically, to enable it as well, gameSpace lets you choose what the coordinates should mean for any given object. To see this information, you must open up more of the Object Info Pane. Notice the little red triangle (technically, it's an arrow tip) at the top right corner of the Object Info Pane. This downward-pointing triangle tells you that there is more of this Object Info Pane that is not currently visible. See Figure 4.31.

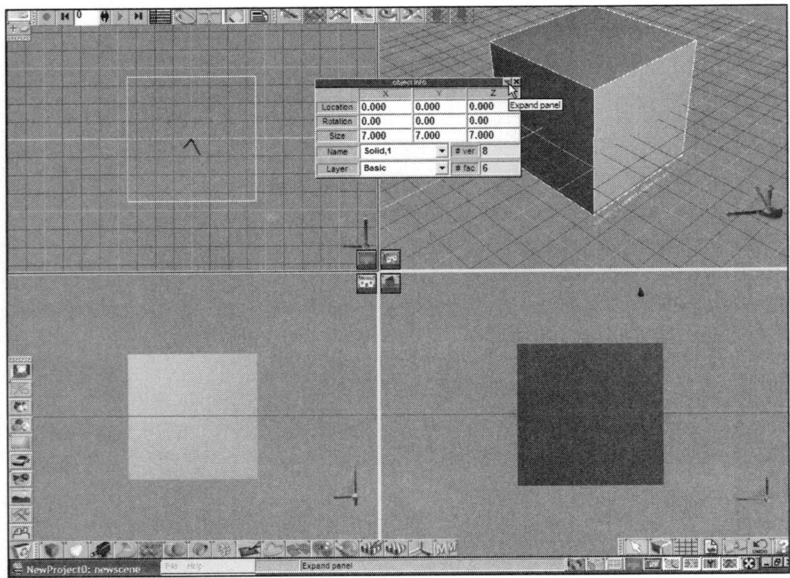

Figure 4.31
The downward-pointing triangle tells you there is more to view.

Click on the red triangle to expand the Object Info Pane. You will see a lot more details and options.

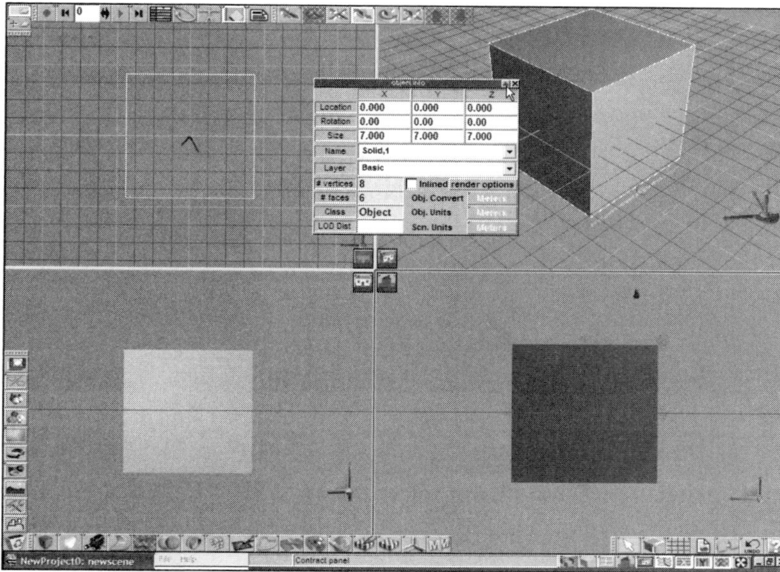

Figure 4.32
This is the full Object Info Pane.

Notice that the red triangle now points upward. Clicking on the arrow once again would collapse the Object Info Pane to once more hide the extra information.

The expanded Object Info Pane answers the questions about the meaning of units. Figure 4.32 tells us that the units are being measured in meters. Meters are good for engineers and surveyors, but most video-game programmers think in points and pixels. I recommend that you set all of your unit measurements to points. I will be using points throughout the examples in this book. Figure 4.33 shows the same object with its units set to points.

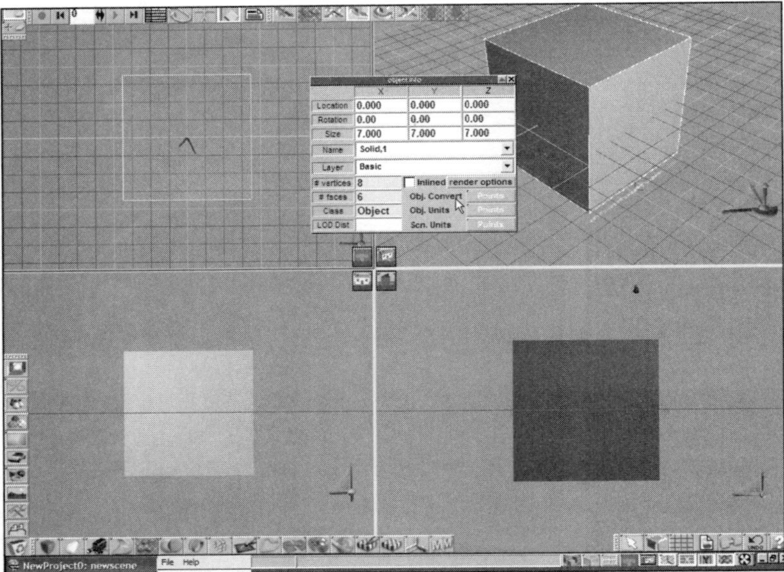

Figure 4.33
Now the units and screen units are both set to points.

The Price of Detail

Another important detail disclosed in the Object Info Pane is the number of vertices and faces used in the selected object. Remember that all objects in a 3-D game are made up of vertices (points), edges (run between vertices), and faces (polygons). In the case of this cube, there are eight vertices. These vertices are the corners of the cube. There are also exactly six faces, which are the cube's six sides.

Game artists must think about face counts far more critically than film artists, animators, architects, or illustrators. The more detail you add to your game objects, the more faces and vertices they require. As a general rule, the more faces you use in your game objects, the slower your game executes. This can and will impact game play significantly. In extreme cases, it can even force a video game to misbehave and crash in a variety of ways.

In less extreme cases, high "poly count" almost always increases the hardware requirements for the consumers who want to play your game. This translates into fewer players, fewer purchasers, fewer fans, less job security, and much less money in your yearly bonus.

As a game artist, your duty is to carefully balance the look of your objects against the efficient and economical use of faces. Game objects are typically low-poly objects. They must have a very low face count.

If you are using gameSpace Light, which comes with this book, then don't worry. gameSpace Light has a strict limit to the number of faces you can use in your objects, which can be a bit constraining, but may make you a better game modeler. It certainly forces you to model more economically.

Saving the Scene

When you have a good square cube, save it by choosing File > Save As > Scene, from the File menu. See Figure 4.34.

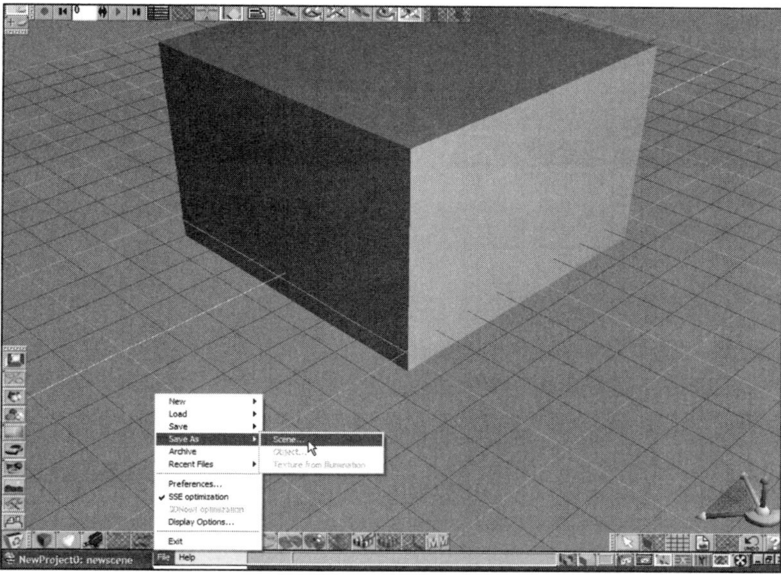

Figure 4.34
Saving your first model

gameSpace opens a window asking you to choose a name and a location to save your scene. It also gives you a choice of file types in which to save it. For now, choose the default Caligari .scn file type, and let gameSpace save the file in the suggested directory. See Figure 4.35. Once we start working with other file formats, you will want to save each object's files in its own separate directory.

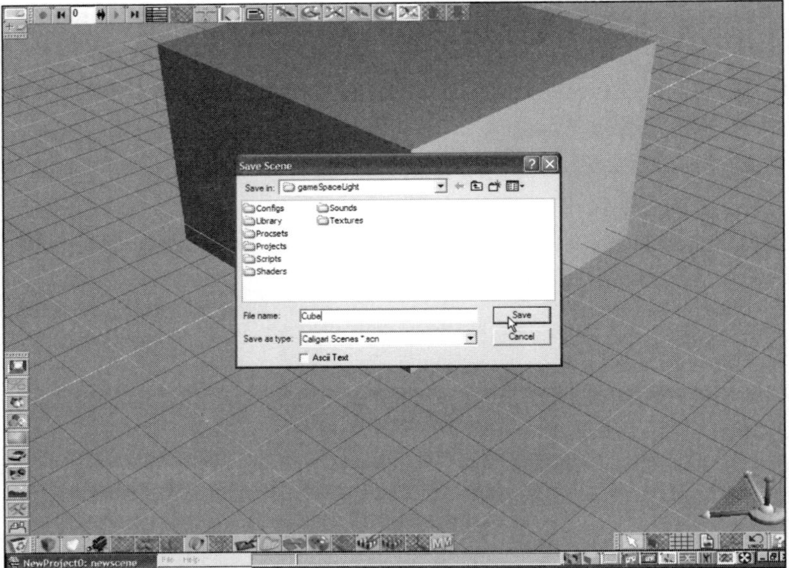

Figure 4.35
Saving Cube .scn

Kicking Around a Ball

The very first electronic video game, Pong, contained the very first video graphic ball. It is only fitting that your first video game should contain a ball or two as well. Pong's ball was only a dot that bounced between two little lines (paddles), but your first ball will be a real regulation soccer ball, or at least a close virtual simulation. You can probably guess what's coming next.

1. Choose File > New > Scene from the File menu.
2. Drag on the cube icon until you see the whole primitive library.
3. From the primitive library, select the sphere icon, which shows a picture of a smooth round ball, and release the mouse button.

Notice that the sphere icon has a close twin, the geosphereicon. This sort of subtoolbar works just like the regular toolbars you have seen before, only in this case, it is hidden deep inside another toolbar. See Figure 4.36.

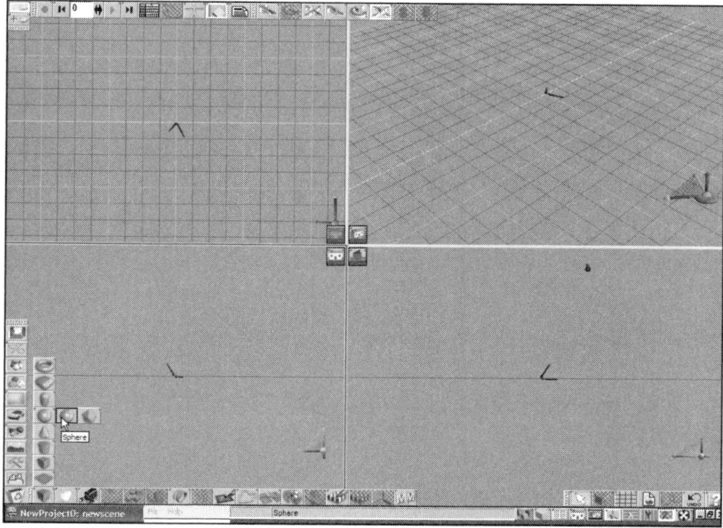

Figure 4.36
Choose the smooth sphere primitive icon.

Click in the center of either the top or the perspective viewport on the screen and drag the mouse to create a round ball. See Figure 4.37. It doesn't really matter how large you make the ball, as long as you can see it on the screen. You will use the Object Info Pane to scale and position it appropriately.

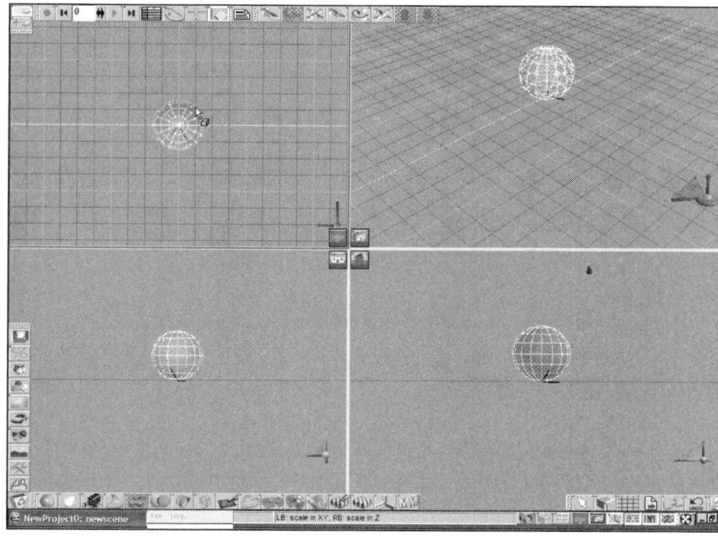

Figure 4.37
Click and drag to create a sphere.

Right-click anywhere else on the screen to get rid of the colorful Magic Rings.

You are going to use this object in a game, so it is important that you position and scale it precisely. That means that it is time to open the Object Info Pane. If necessary, open the Object Info Pane by right-clicking on the arrow icon, as shown earlier in Figure 4.27.

Set the object parameters exactly as shown in Table 4.1 and in Figure 4.38.

Table 4.1 Ball Object Parameters

	X	Y	Z
Location	0.146	0.2	0.926
Rotation	0	0	0
Scale	1.764	1.764	1.764

All units and screen units are set in Points.

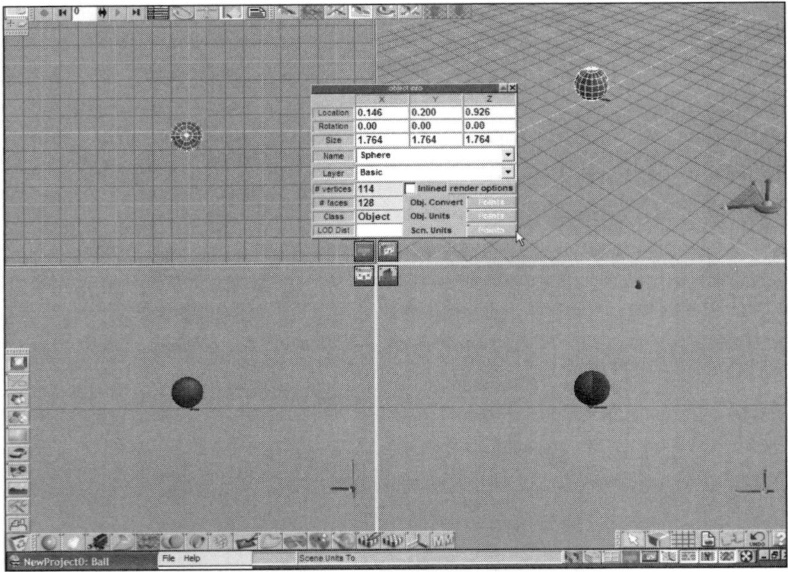

Figure 4.38
Set the ball location, rotation, scale, and units as seen here.

You have a ball, but it is not clearly a soccer ball. It could be a pretty round rock. To make it a soccer ball, you need to see the little black and white facets that are known and loved throughout the world, at least, that is, throughout Europe, Australia, and South America.

Painting on the Detail

You could create a true faceted sphere, which in this case might even reduce the face count of your object. But often, adding such details increases the face count and certainly increases the complexity and difficulty of building the model. You can accomplish the goal easily without spending hours meticulously modeling a soccer ball and then hand painting its various sides.

Textures are the minute details, colors, and visual artifacts that help the brain to sense and recognize the surface structure and internal content of any object.

Great textures are the secret ingredient of great game models, and gameSpace has a powerful and versatile Material Editor that makes texturing fun. gameSpace also comes with a Material Library full of useful textures and a sophisticated Library Manager to help you find, modify, and build your own libraries of models, textures, shaders, and bitmaps.

Materials are gameSpace elements that represent combinations of procedural (computer-generated) images and user-created images that combine and layer together to create the illusion of real-world textures.

The Material Library is a storehouse for prepackaged or user-customized gameSpace materials.

Shaders are programs and numeric procedures that instruct gameSpace how to generate various textures and individual components of textures based upon specific user-controlled parameters. Think of a shader as an automated texture factory, where you can control the texture's appearance by setting and adjusting its dials and controls.

The Material Editor is a pop-up panel where you can layer, edit, and modify any number of shaders and bitmaps to build highly complex and realistic textures for your objects.

Bitmaps are computer files that contain numeric representations of visual images. These can be digital photographs, retouched photos, scanned drawings, animated videos, or visual content from any other source. In other words, a bitmap is a picture.

Open the Material Library by clicking on its icon on the vertical toolbar to the left of the gameSpace screen. Its picture looks like a bowl full of painted balls. See Figure 4.39.

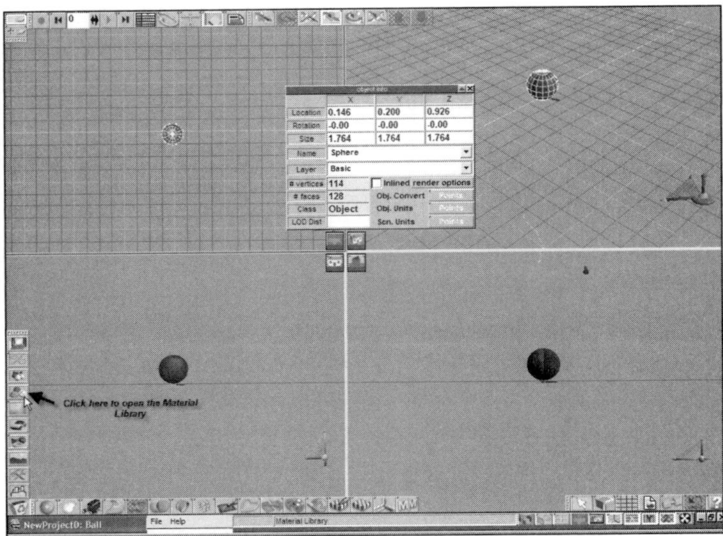

Figure 4.39
Click here to open the Material Library.

In the Material Library, you will see a wide variety of materials. These are only a small sample of the many thousands of rich textures that gameSpace can generate. Click on any material in the Material Library to open it for inspection in the Material Editor. See Figure 4.40.

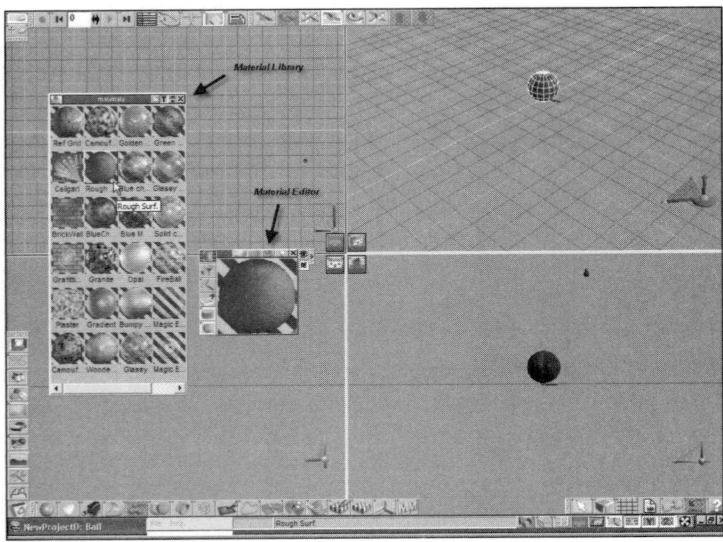

Figure 4.40
The Material Library and the Material Editor

To apply a material to your object, simply drag the material from the preview window in the Material Editor to the object in gameSpace. This is demonstrated in Figure 4.41.

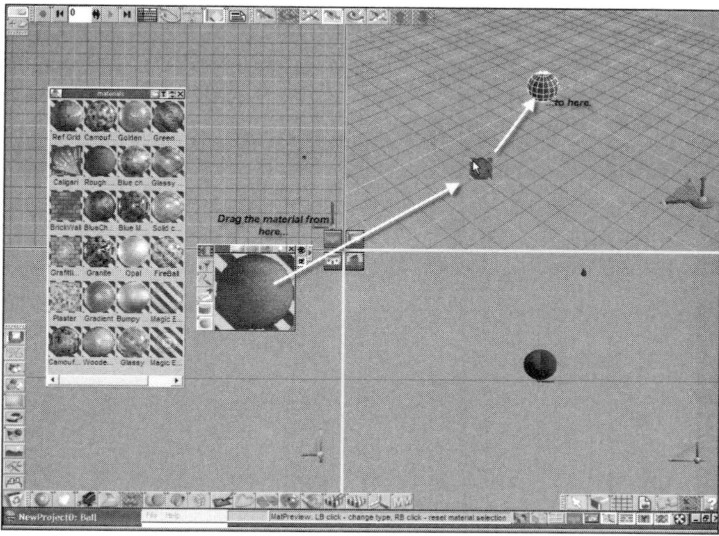

Figure 4.41
Dragging a material onto an object

The Material Editor offers lots of great materials, but none of them are right for your soccer ball. So you need to create your own.

To start with, you should choose a material that is somewhat like the material you need. None seem too close, so choose a simple one like the Ref Grid at the top of the Material Library. See Figure 4.42.

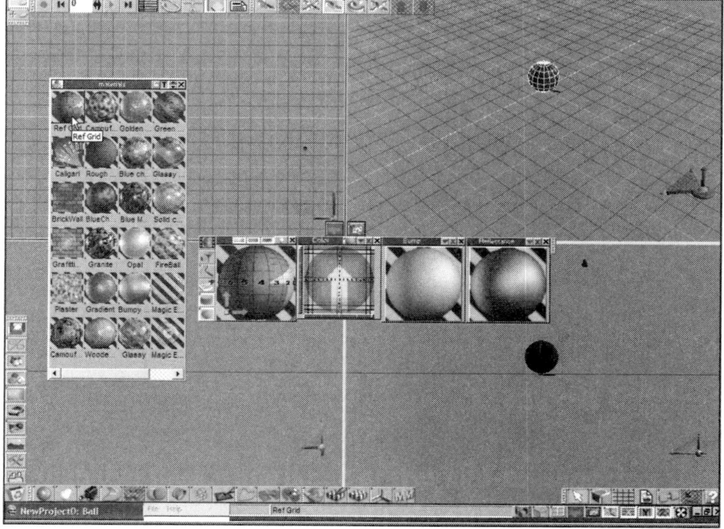

Figure 4.42
Click on Ref Grid to bring it into the Material Editor.

The Ref Grid uses a very simple shader that copies a bitmap image, a picture of a grid, directly onto the object. To see the details of this shader, click on the arrow pointing toward the right on the far right side of the Material Editor. This exposes the various shaders that make up the selected material.

You want to replace this shader with another more appropriate for a soccer ball, so open the Color Shader Library, which is the rainbowlike gradient just beneath the Material Library icon.

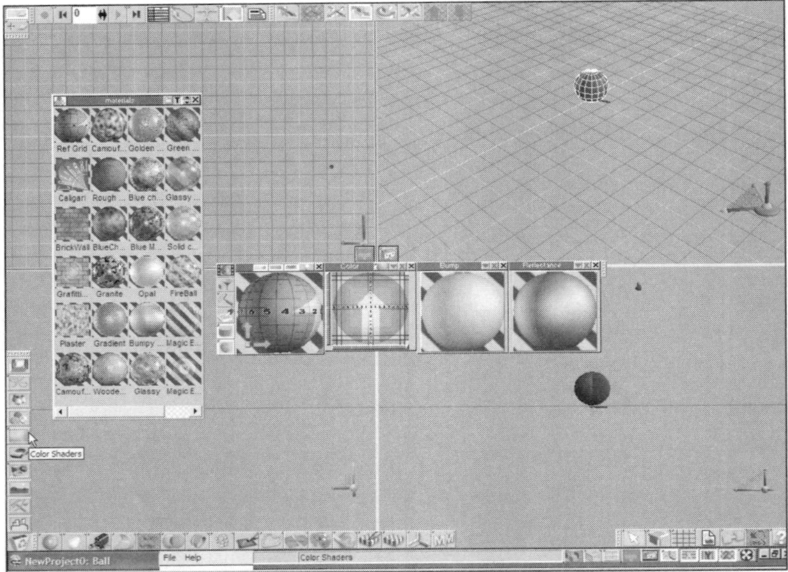

Figure 4.43
Opening the Color Shader Library

When you click the Color Shader icon, as shown in Figure 4.43, the Color Shader Library opens, and the Material Library vanishes. The Material Editor stays open, however.

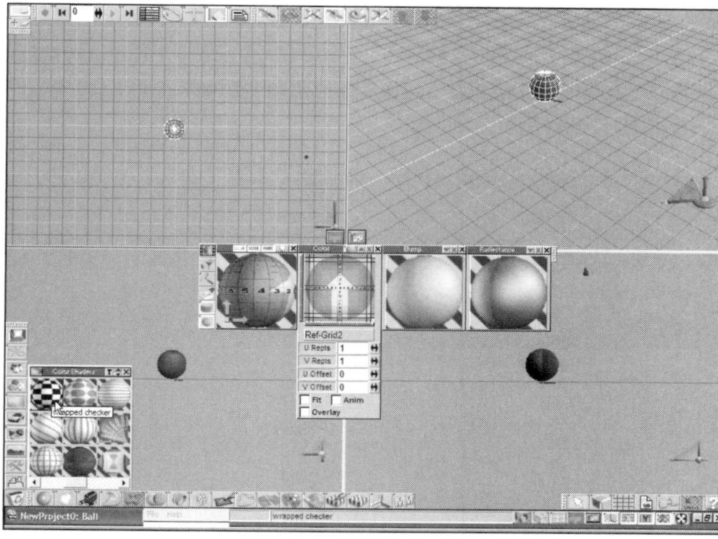

Figure 4.44
Choose the Wrapped Checker shader.

Drag the scroll bar at the bottom of the Color Shader Library until you see the Wrapped Checker shader. See Figure 4.44. Don't confuse this with the Cube shader, which looks quite similar. Click on the Wrapped Checker shader and see how it changes the material in the Material Editor. See Figure 4.45.

Figure 4.45
The Wrapped Checker shader at work

The Wrapped Checker shader is a procedural program that automatically generates its texture from a set of inputs that you can control. To see these inputs, click on the red triangle in the top right corner of the Color panel in the Material Editor. It works exactly like the red triangle in the Object Info Pane. See Figure 4.46.

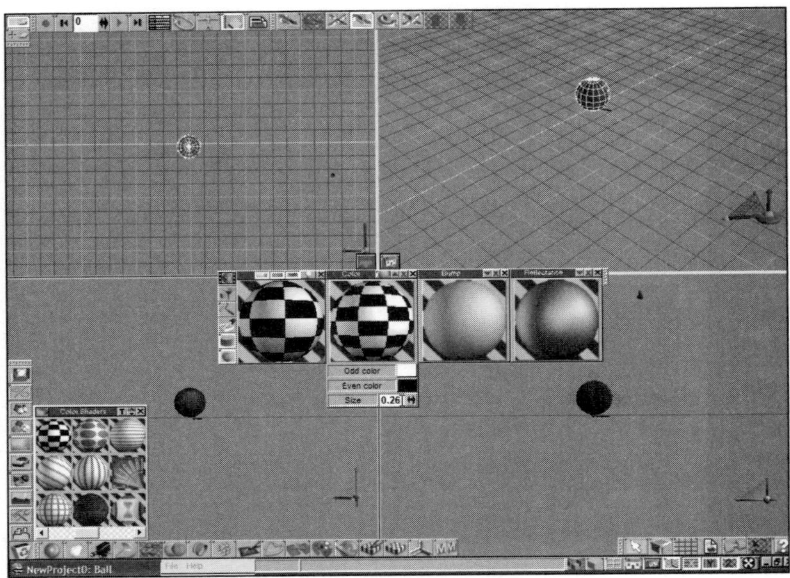

Figure 4.46
Adjust the parameters of the Wrapped Checker shader.

You can see that the Wrapped Checker shader allows you to choose the color for each set of checkers, as well as the size and density of the checker pattern. Try changing the number in the Size parameter in various steps between 0.0 and 1.0. You can also drag on the little spinner (looks like a bidirectional arrow) to raise or lower this value. Watch the Material Editor's main preview window to see the impact of the changes.

I found that a size setting of around 0.19 makes a pretty good soccer ball, but feel free to use any setting that you please here.

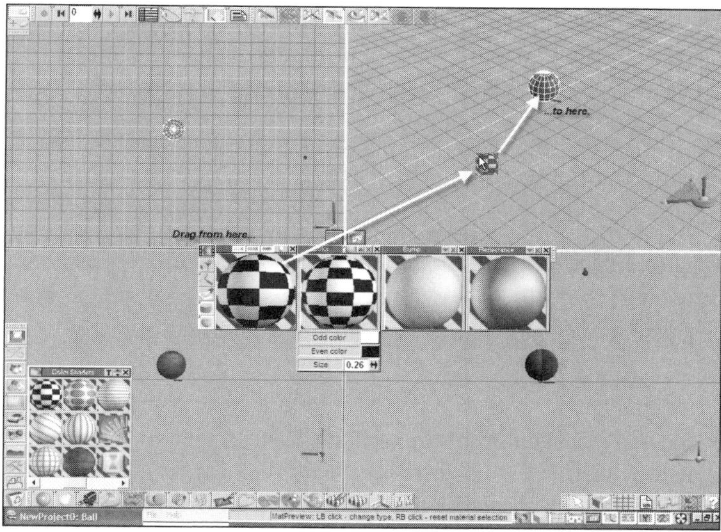

Figure 4.47
Drag the material onto the ball.

Finish the soccer ball by dragging the new material onto the ball. See Figure 4.47.

Saving a Game Object

It's time to save the ball. First, you should save the scene exactly as you did before. This is the file you will reopen if you ever want to change the ball in the future. I have a pretty strong feeling you will want to change it, so definitely save the file. If you have forgotten how to save the scene, see Figure 4.48.

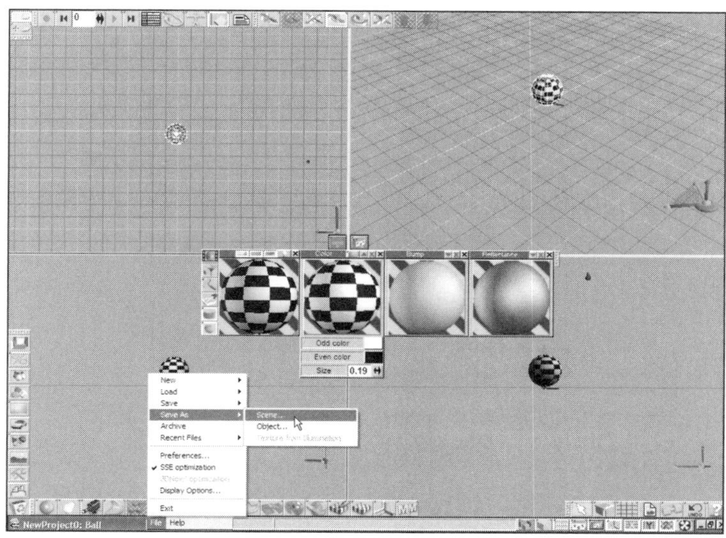

Figure 4.48
Save the scene for the ball.

Unlike your last model, you are actually going to bring this one into a game. That means you need to save it in a format that a game can understand. The Caligari .scn file format is a great way to save your work, but it is not recognized by any game engine I have used. Depending upon your specific target game, you may need to save your object files in a variety of formats.

For the sample games I have included with this book, the format to use is a DirectX .x file. I made this choice in programming the demo game, but it won't always be the same for any other game you produce.

Another significant design decision I made in programming the sample games was that every object's files should be housed in that object's own private directory. This also is not always the case for every other game, but it has definite advantages when working with a lot of .x files.

> DirectX .x files store the model and the model's textures in separate files. Sometimes they are stored in a great many separate files. By placing each object's files in its own directory, it is easy to keep all of these files together, and it is much harder for them to become lost or separated.

For the remainder of this book, you should always save your object files as DirectX .x files and place them in their own directories. It's easy, it's a good way to keep things organized, but most importantly to remember for the projects in this book, it's not optional. Here's how it's done.

1. Select File > Save As > Object from the File menu. See Figure 4.49.

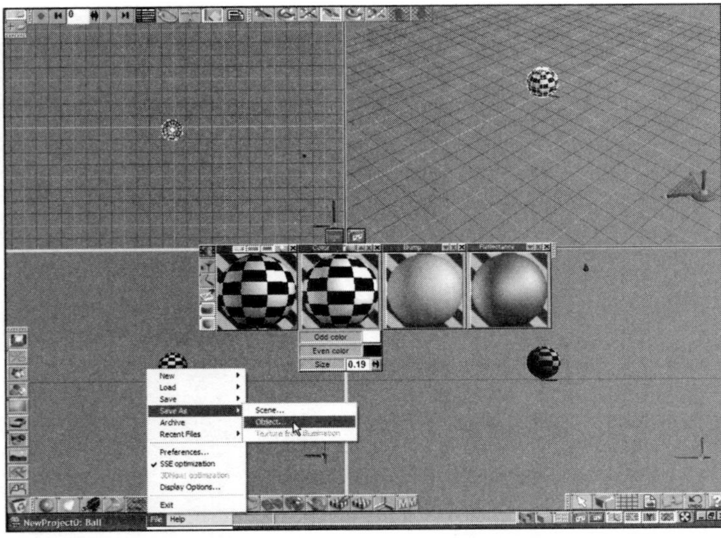

Figure 4.49
Choose File > Save As > Object.

2. Create a new directory to store your ball object. See Figure 4.50.

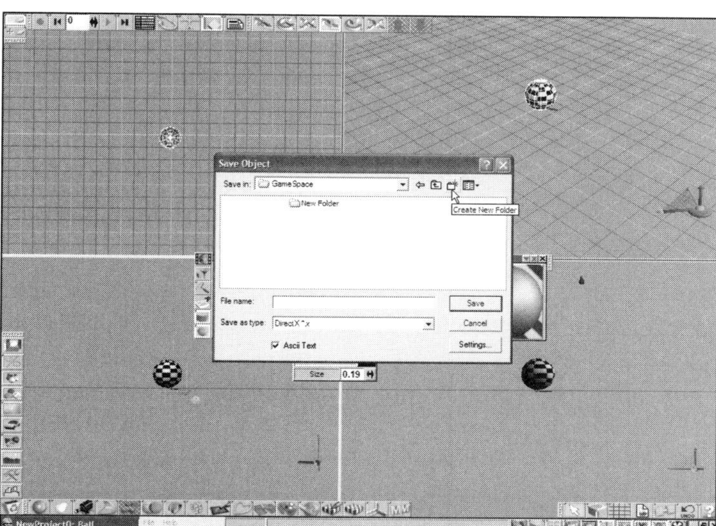

Figure 4.50
Create a new directory by clicking on the Create New Folder button above the directory view.

3. Click on the name of the new folder, and change the name to Ball. See Figure 4.51.
4. Be sure to choose DirectX .x file format from the file type list.
5. Double-click on the new Ball folder to choose it as the destination for your file.
6. Type the name Ball.x into the file name field at the bottom of the Save As window.
7. Click Save.

Your object files should now be saved appropriately.

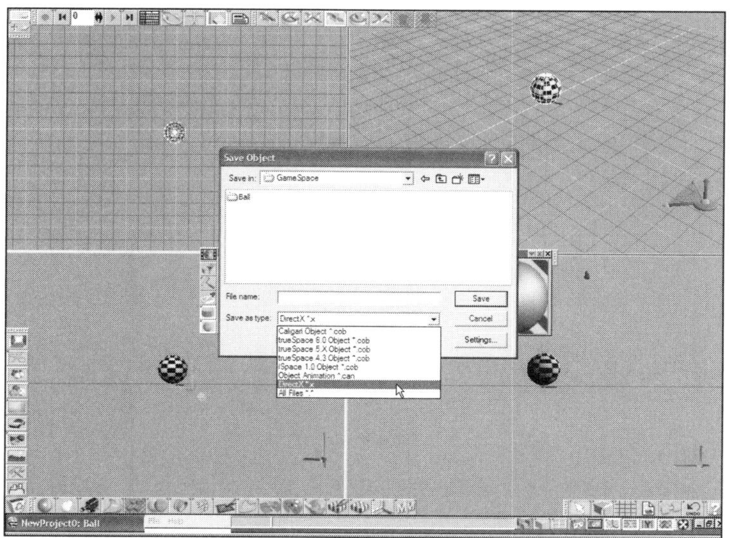

Figure 4.51
Rename the new folder and select the DirectX .x file format.

Close gameSpace by clicking on the little X at the bottom right-hand corner of the screen. Get out some quarters. It's time to play a video game!

Gaming with Objects

Congratulations. You have created your first game model. You have given it a texture. You have even saved it as a real game object file. Now all you need to do is to make a game. Fortunately, I just happen to have a game that's seriously in need of new game objects. If you combine your objects and my game, just think of the fun we can have.

Adventure Explorer is technically a third-person adventure game. Unfortunately, in its current state, it is not very exciting. Actually, without your new game models, it is nearly impossible to play, but it still looks kind of neat. If you haven't taken a look at it yet, this is a good time to give it a try.

Launch Adventure Explorer and take a moment to explore.

Playing in the Water

Adventure Explorer drops you into an underground cavern. See Figure 4.52.

Like most adventure games, your goal is to collect treasure and to find your way out. You will have to create many of the objects necessary to complete the game.

Figure 4.52
Explore the banks of a shimmering river.

Use the Left and Right Arrow keys to turn around. Use the Up and Down Arrows to move forward and back, and hit the spacebar to jump. See Figure 4.53.

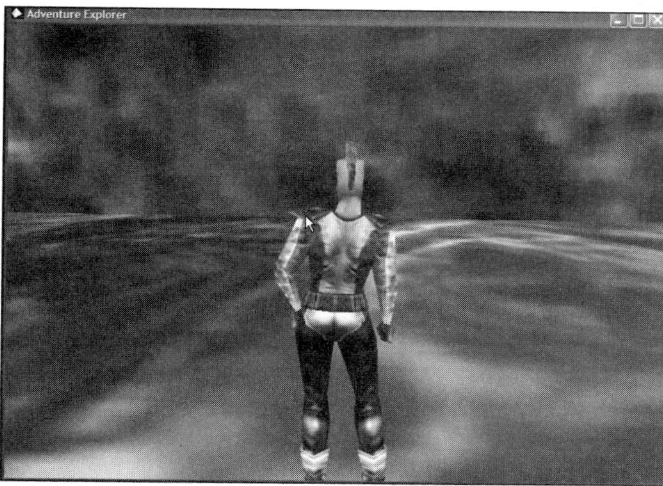

Figure 4.53
Try to jump the stream, but be careful. Don't fall in!

If you happen to get too close to the water, you may find yourself stuck beneath the river. You can always press the R key to restart the game.

It shouldn't take you long to realize that the stream is a bit too wide to cross. I'll admit this is not a whole lot of fun yet, but you can see there is a lot of room to grow. What this game really needs is something to do with the water. Perhaps a half dozen soccer balls will do the trick.

When you get tired of watching the water or diving into it, you can press Esc to quit. If more than thirty minutes have passed and you are still trying to cross the water, congratulations, you obviously have the heart of a master gamer. Now stop playing in the water and get back to work.

Adding Models to a Game

The process of bringing a new model file into a game is traditionally called importing. The game engine with which I programmed Adventure Explorer understands the very same .x files that gameSpace saved.

The only trick to using your own models in Adventure Explorer is in the process of moving, copying, and renaming the appropriate files so that they can be easily located by Adventure Explorer.

To make this process as easy as possible, I created another program called ObjectImporter. See Figure 4.54. It has a simple dialog box with a bunch of clearly marked buttons. It is not very pretty, and it's far from impressive, but it couldn't get much easier to use.

You will find ObjectImporter in the same directory as Adventure Explorer. It only functions in this directory, so please don't try to move it.

Launch ObjectImporter and click on the button labeled Choose Object 1. Do not try any of the other buttons yet. You will get to them soon enough.

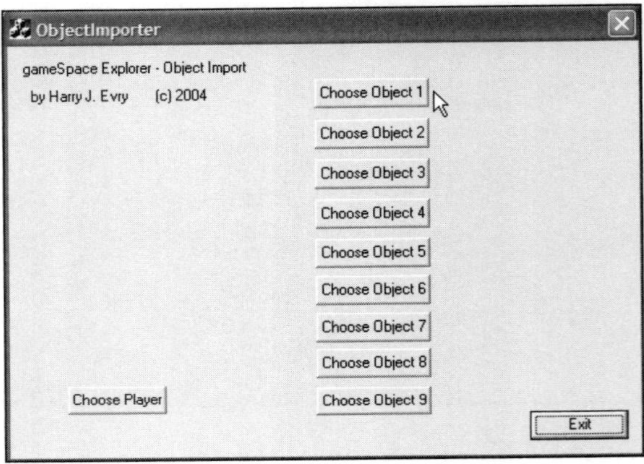

Figure 4.54
ObjectImporter takes the pain out of importing your models.

Another window opens, asking you to "Select a Model File to replace Game Object 1." Navigate to the new directory where you saved the object files for your ball. When the name of your .x file appears in the file selection window, click it. Then click on the button labeled Open. See Figure 4.55.

Finally, ObjectImporter asks you to confirm your decision. See Figure 4.56. This is your last chance to keep your old model files as they were.

ObjectImporter does not delete any of the original files that you place into your own new object directories; it simply copies these files to its own internal directories. That means you can safely go back and forth between different object models for the same game objects, as long as you originally saved them each in their own separate directories.

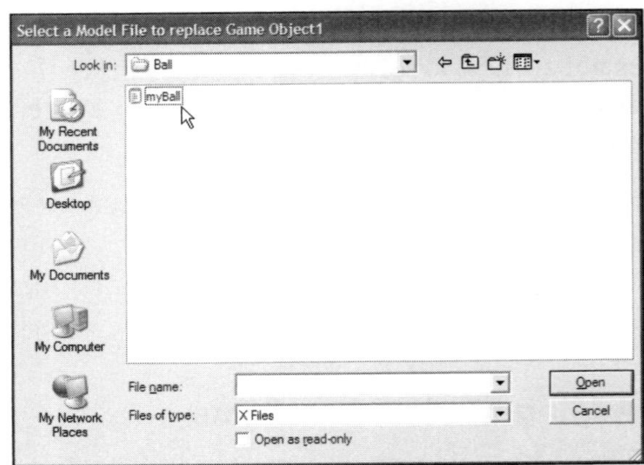

Figure 4.55
Find your object's .x file in the new directory you created for it.

On the other hand, if you later change your object's .x files and want to see the changes in the game, you must run ObjectImporter again to reselect the updated model file. ObjectImporter takes a virtual snapshot of the current state of your selected object file, but never updates that snapshot unless you tell ObjectImporter to select the object file again.

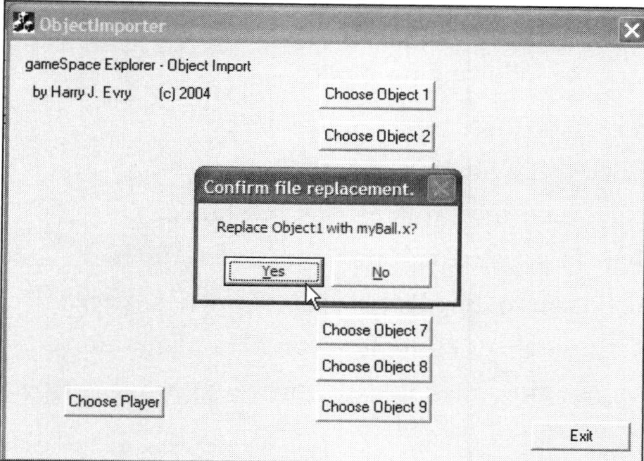

Figure 4.56
Click the button labeled Yes to import your new object files.

Once you have clicked on Yes, close ObjectImporter and launch Adventure Explorer. You should immediately notice a change above the water. I am not sure that floating soccer balls are the answer to all the game's problems, but if your screen looks anything like Figure 4.57, you are well on your way to becoming a game artist.

Figure 4.57
Your new objects have been added to the game.

Summary

In this chapter, you should have learned the following concepts:

- Geometric primitives are the most basic three-dimensional objects.
- Many game objects can be modeled using simple geometric primitives.
- Geometric primitives can be scaled, deformed, rotated, and combined.
- gameSpace uses icons and toolbars to organize its commands and features.
- gameSpace uses the right mouse button to drag things up and down in space.
- gameSpace lets you choose between single or multiple viewport configurations.
- Orthogonal viewports restrict mouse movement to two dimensions, while perspective viewports allow mouse movement in three dimensions.
- The Object Info Pane gives you precise numeric control of your objects' parameters.
- The Object Info Pane reports the number of faces and vertices contained in any object.
- Game artists must carefully balance the detail of their models against the number of faces and vertices they require.
- Placing an object at location 0,0,0 centers the object in the gameSpace world.
- Always use consistent units to describe your object models.
- Textures can be used to enhance the illusion of reality and detail in game models.
- gameSpace materials are used to assign visual textures to an object.
- gameSpace materials are made from combinations of shaders and bitmaps.
- Shaders are like automated numeric texture factories that can be modified and controlled by user-supplied parameters.
- Game object files should always be saved in their own separate directories.
- gameSpace .x files can be directly imported and used in Adventure Explorer.
- ObjectImporter copies new object models into Adventure Explorer.

Questions and Answers

Q: What are common geometric primitives?

A: Geometric primitives are the most basic three-dimensional objects, such as cubes, cones, and spheres.

Q: What numeric location is considered the center of the gameSpace world?

A: The X,Y,Z coordinates 0,0,0 represent the center of the gameSpace virtual environment.

Q: In terms of the X, Y, and Z axes, what directions do the lines on the visible grid in the gameSpace perspective view typically point?

A: In the gameSpace perspective viewport, the grid lines run in the same direction as the X and Y axes.

Q: What mouse maneuver would you use to move an object up in the air when working in the gameSpace perspective viewport?

A: Right-click and drag upward to move a gameSpace object up in the air when working in the perspective viewport.

Q: What mouse maneuver would you use to move an object up in the air when working in a side viewport?

A: Side viewports, like any orthogonal viewport, are two-dimensional projections of a scene. Therefore, you merely left-click and drag to move an object up and down in a side viewport.

Q: If the cone icon was visible in the first slot to the right of the recycle bin, how would you set up gameSpace to build a cylinder?

A: To select the Cylinder tool, click and drag upward or downward on the visible cone icon until the cylinder icon is visible and highlighted. Then you can release the mouse button and click and drag to draw a cylinder.

Q: What key would you press to quickly select the Object Move tool?

A: The Z key is the keyboard shortcut for the Object Move tool.

Q: How can you find the number of vertices and faces in an object?

A: The Object Info Pane contains data fields that display the vertex count and face count for any selected object.

Q: How do you expand the Object Info Pane or the Color Shader Panel?

A: Click on the red triangle or red downward-pointing arrow tip in the upper right corner of either panel.

Q: Where can you find gameSpace's predefined materials? How do you get there?

A: The Material Library contains a variety of predefined sample materials. Click the icon showing a bowl of painted balls to open the Material Editor.

Q: Why is it a good idea to save different .x files in their own separate directories?

A: DirectX .x files can save their meshes and textures in separate files. It is not uncommon for a single object model to require a number of supporting files. Placing these files in their own directories makes it easy to track which of these files must work together.

Discussion Questions

1. Pick any object in the room and discuss how you would model it using geometric primitives.
2. What are the key differences in concerns and approaches between a 3-D artist building models for video games and the same artist building models for movies, architecture, or illustration?
3. What are some advantages of building models from geometric primitives?
4. What geometric primitive typically requires the most faces? Why?
5. What are the principal goals of texturing in a game model?
6. What are the advantages and disadvantages of working in a multiple viewport configuration?
7. What are some important differences between .x files and .scn files, and when would you use each?
8. In what situations would you need to use the Object Info Pane?
9. If you were going to replace your soccer ball model with something more appropriate or useful to players in the Adventure Explorer, what might it be?

Exercises

1. Design a game vehicle using only standard primitives.
2. Use gameSpace to model a cylinder that is perfectly circular at its base and is exactly twice as high as it is wide.
3. Use gameSpace's primitive tools to create a witch's hat and save it as a .x file.
4. Change the texture of your soccer ball to make it look like a beach ball.
5. Use ObjectImporter to replace your soccer ball in Adventure Explorer with the new beach ball from exercise 4 as Object 1.
6. Use ObjectImporter to load the witch's hat from exercise 3 into Adventure Explorer as Object 1. You should first scale the hat model so that it is similar in size to your ball model.

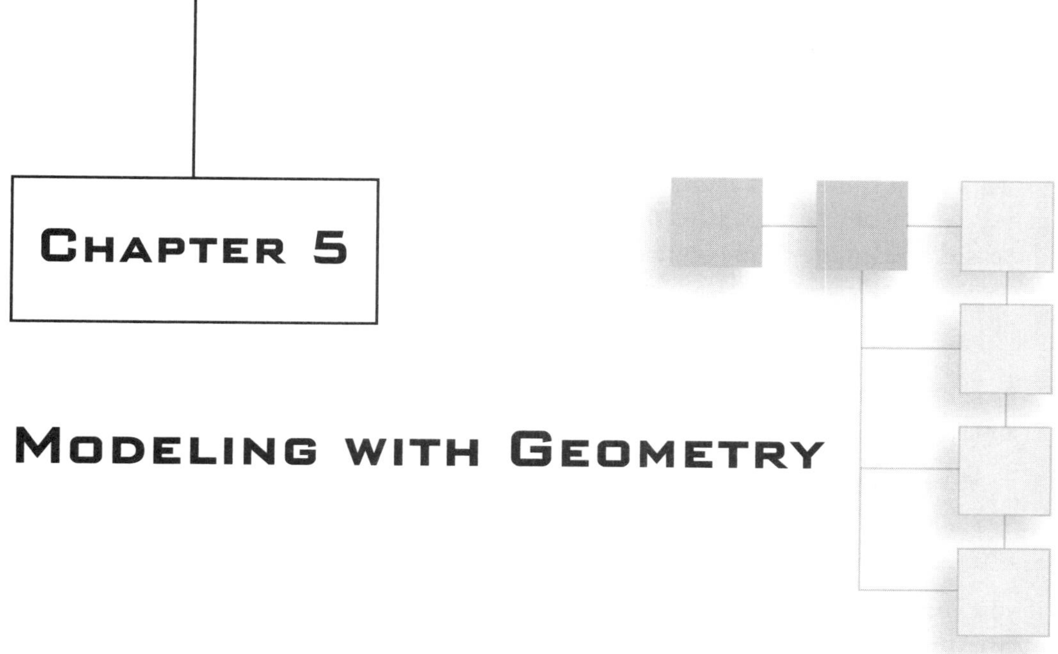

Chapter 5

Modeling with Geometry

In the last chapter, you used gameSpace primitives to model simple geometric shapes. In Chapter 5, you will continue to work with geometric primitives and learn to manipulate them in a variety of ways. The model you build in this chapter will be much more detailed, and will be made up of many parts.

Introduction

You're standing at the edge of a river. There is no bridge. There's no boat, and you're longing to reach the other side. After several failed attempts to jump across the river, you stand, dripping, staring into the sky. Surely, the all-powerful, all-knowing game designers will send you aid in your time of need.

A startling transformation begins. Millions of tiny bits and sparks fly through the air. Your heart jumps for joy and then falls as you see a bunch of useless soccer balls materialize upon the river. How odd is that?

OK, I'll admit the soccer balls add very little to the game. They don't exactly fit the environment, and they certainly won't help you cross the river and advance in your quest.

The Meaning of Existence

Throughout history, the world's greatest scholars have asked the questions, "Why are we here? What is the meaning of existence?" Usually these questions are met with confused stares and polite silence. If you happen to be an object in a video game, you should have a good answer to these questions.

Like the actors in a movie and the players in a baseball game, video-game objects usually serve a purpose in a game. Also like actors in a movie and players on any professional athletic team, video-game objects are not free. Even relatively simple models require hours of work from game artists, level designers, and programmers. As you have already seen, game objects can be expensive in terms of their faces, textures, and vertices and the increased burden they place on the game engine.

How do you determine when an object should be added to your game? Typically, you might ask yourself the following questions:

- Does the object fit the setting, the period, and the theme of the game?
- Does the object add to the realism or authenticity of the game?
- Does the object serve a purpose in the gameplay?
- Does the object help or hinder the players in accomplishing their goals?
- Does the object add to the general entertainment value of the game?

If you answer no to any of these questions, you may need to redesign the object. If you answer no to all of these questions, the object clearly does not belong in your game.

The soccer balls from the last chapter fail to meet any of these tests. If you completed the exercises from Chapter 4, where you replaced the soccer ball with a beach ball, the object could pass a couple of these tests. Either way, the ball has done its job, and it is time for something better.

Keeping with the Theme

A soccer ball doesn't belong in a deep underground chamber. A half dozen of them certainly don't belong floating in your underground river. They don't fit the theme.

The word *theme* refers to an overall design concept. It sets the overriding look, feel, and period of a game or level.

My good friend and former boss, Rolly Crump, explains it this way: "When someone creates a theme, you stick to it. You set a theme, an overall style or design idea, and you reflect it in everything else you do, from the ticket booths to the trash cans." Rolly is a legendary artistic director and Disney Imagineer who helped create much of Disneyland's Haunted Mansion, Enchanted Tiki Room, Mr. Toad's Wild Ride, and It's a Small World attractions.

Another friend and former boss, Michael Okuda, the graphic designer responsible for much of the look of *Star Trek*, had slightly different but complementary advice. Michael would frequently tell me, "You set a pattern, stick to the pattern, and then once it is established, you break it." If something in the scene doesn't appear a little different or out of place, then the scene looks too obviously perfect, fake, and unnatural. Taken together, these two simple design philosophies can produce powerful results.

Violating the theme in a game can seem to the players as if they are watching a movie in a theatre when suddenly the director yells "Cut!" and the actors walk off the set. One bad object in the wrong place is like a neon sign flashing the message, "This is just pretend." One little thing that clearly doesn't belong can shatter the illusion of reality for the player.

Multiplying Primitives

You will begin this section by modeling a simple log. Of course, a log by itself is not all that useful. Any good scout knows, however, that a log is the primary building block of a much more useful object, a log raft.

In building a log raft, you will learn to duplicate and combine your primitives (the logs) and to assemble them into a raft that could carry you across the river.

Modeling a Log

Begin building a log by selecting File > New > Scene from the gameSpace File menu. For the screenshots in this section, I worked in the single viewport configuration. I chose this configuration because it makes things easier for you to see.

Bring the Cylinder tool to the top of the Geometric Primitive Tools slot by clicking on and dragging whichever primitive tool is currently visible and selecting the primitive icon with the picture of a cylinder. Remember that a cylinder is round on the sides but flat on the top and bottom.

Once you have activated the Cylinder tool, click in the center of the viewport and drag to create the cylinder. See Figure 5.1.

tip

Remember, left-click and drag the mouse to begin building a primitive. When you add a right-click-hold and drag you can adjust the height of the new primitive. As an alternative you could simply click in the viewport to create a default primitive.

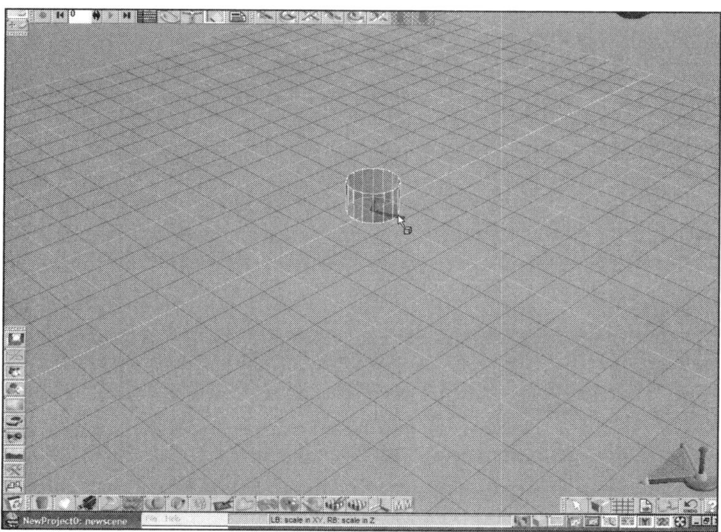

Figure 5.1
Use the Cylinder tool to create a cylinder.

Right-click on the Object tool to open the Object Info Pane. Recall from the last chapter that the Object tool's icon looks like an arrow. Expand the Object Info Pane by clicking on the small red triangle, and set all the units to Points. Set your cylinder's scale, location, and rotation parameters to match Table 5.1 and Figure 5.2.

Table 5.1 Cylinder Object Parameters

	X	Y	Z
Location	0.0	0.0	0.5
Rotation	90	0	0
Scale	2	2	15

All units and screen units are set in Points.

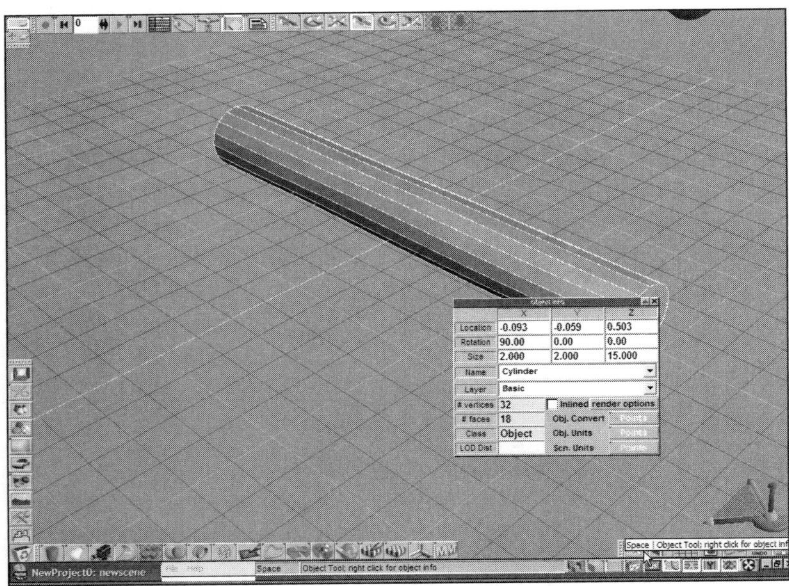

Figure 5.2
Use the Object Info Pane to set the precise location, rotation, and scale.

Naming Your Blocks

This is a good time to establish a very important professional habit. The Name field of the Object Info Pane allows you to assign a meaningful name to the currently selected object.

Left-click and hold the left mouse button and then drag across the name "Cylinder" in the Object Info Pane. When the name "Cylinder" is highlighted, release the mouse button, and type the word "Log." This will rename the object. See Figure 5.3.

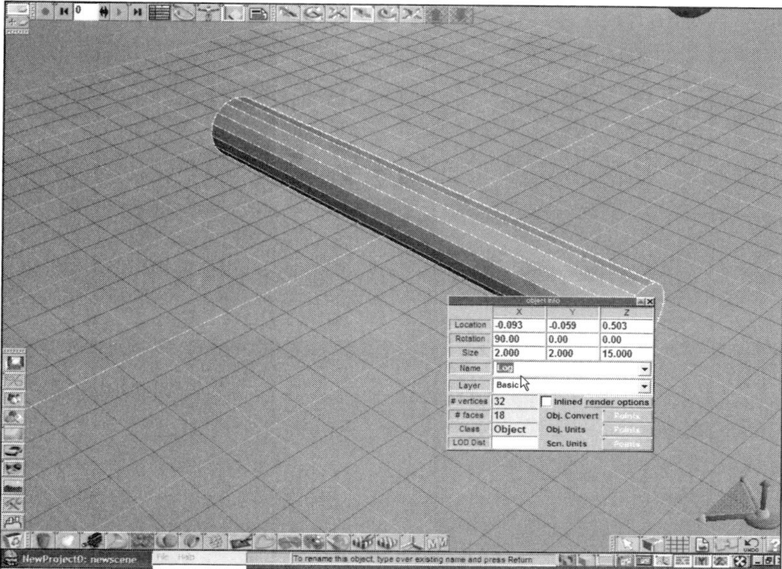

Figure 5.3
Change the name of your cylinder to "Log."

Naming your objects may not seem that important when there are only a few simple primitives in your scene, but just wait until you build your first scene with more than a hundred assorted pieces. Names such as Object 1 or Cylinder 20 are hardly informative when you have many objects and two dozen of them are cylinders.

One sign of professionalism and experience in a 3-D artist, is the manner, consistency, and clarity with which they name their objects. This is especially important when you are working in a professional team situation. Another artist may be required to inspect, manipulate, or edit your models, and she will certainly appreciate a good naming scheme.

As a rule, you should name your objects immediately after you create them. Don't wait until you have too many objects to easily recognize and then try to go back and name them all later. This just leads to confusion and an increased likelihood of error.

tip

The small downward pointing triangle immediately to the right of the Object Info Pane's Name field can be used to quickly select any object in the scene by name. This can be very useful when working with a cluttered and complicated scene.

Painting the Grain

The most important step in transforming your cylinder into a log is applying an appropriate texture. In Chapter 4, you saw how to use the Material Library to apply a texture. See Figure 5.4.

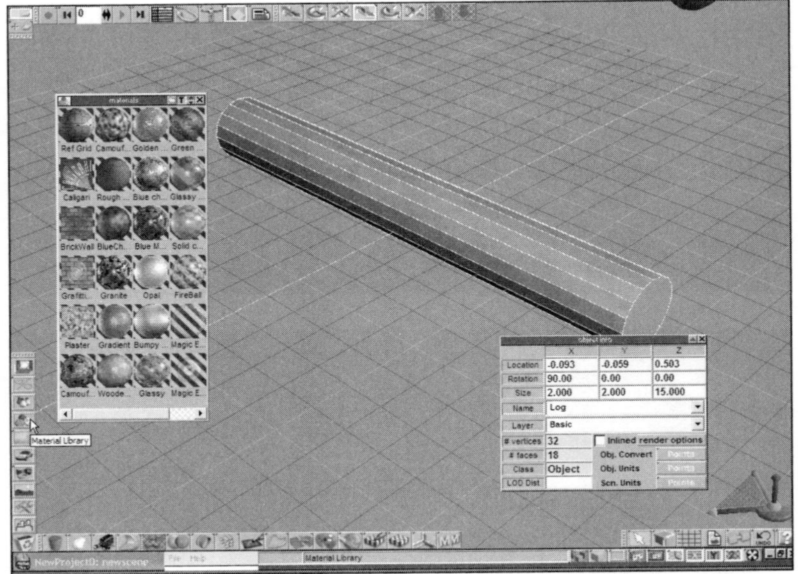

Figure 5.4
Open the Material Library.

Open the Material Library by clicking on the Material Library icon on the left-hand side of the screen. Scroll down and double-click on the Wooden Doll material to open the Material Editor. See Figure 5.5.

Use the little black arrow to expand the Material Editor to show the Color panel. See Figure 5.6.

Figure 5.5
Double-click the material to launch the Material Editor.

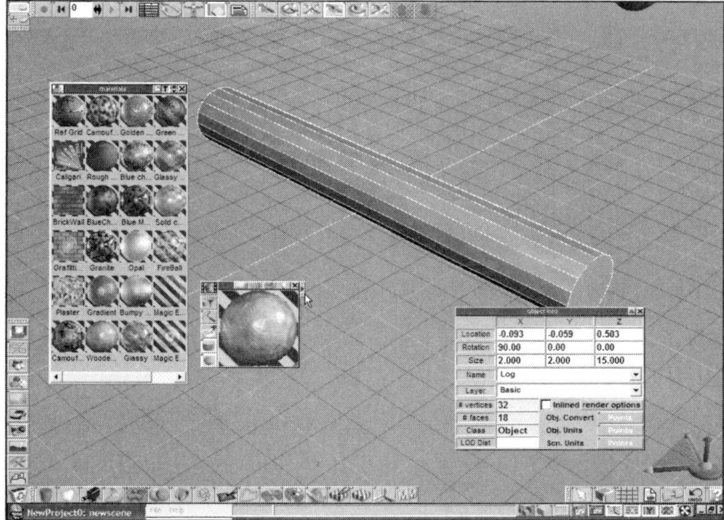

Figure 5.6
Click on the small black arrow on the far right border of the Material Editor.

Click on the red triangle on the top of the Color panel to further expand the Color panel. See Figures 5.7 and 5.8.

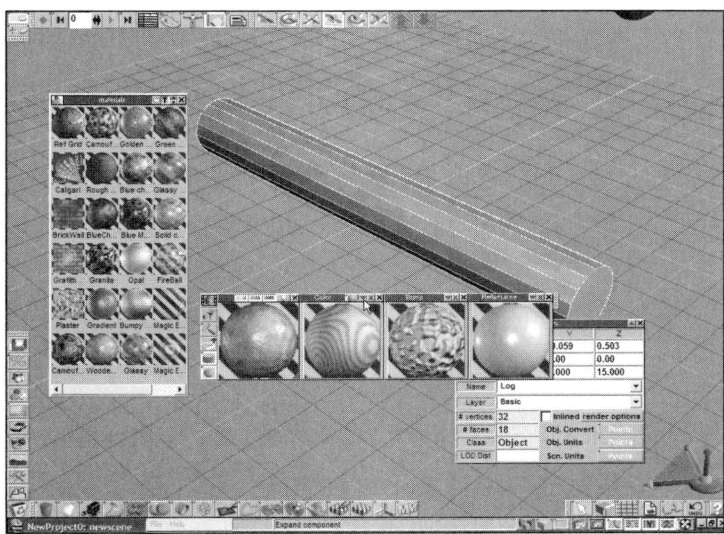

Figure 5.7
Click the small red triangle to expand the Color panel.

Figure 5.8
The wood shader parameters allow you to choose between many types, colors, and details of wood grain.

Try experimenting with the various options and parameters displayed in the expanded Color panel. Notice that you can select the type of wood and adjust many of the details that define the look of the wood grain. You can also change the specific colors that make up the wood.

For the log model, I chose the Pine texture. You may do the same, or feel free to use any style of wood you choose.

Once you have found the perfect texture, click on the icon in the Material Editor showing a picture of a funnel and a block. This is the Paint Object button. It applies the current texture to whichever object is currently selected. See Figure 5.9.

Figure 5.9
Click the Paint Object tool near the top-left corner of the Material Editor.

Close the Material Editor by clicking on the small X in the upper-right corner of the Material Editor's preview window. See Figure 5.10.

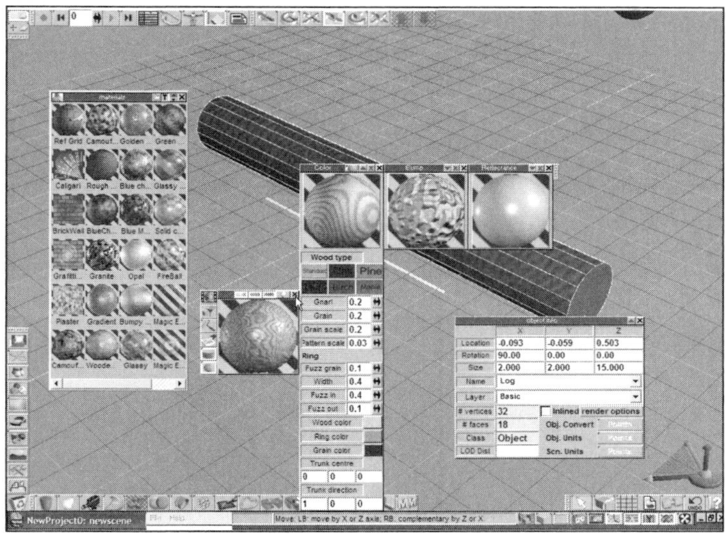

Figure 5.10
Close the Material Editor.

Now that you've applied the wooden texture to your log, take a good look at it. Note the direction of the wood grain. There is something wrong with the new log's texture. Look at the image in Figure 5.11. It looks a lot like wood, but can you tell what's wrong with it?

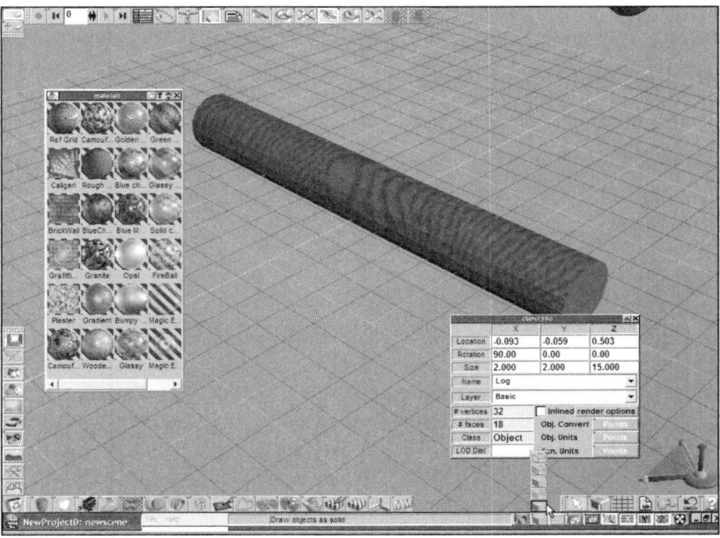

Figure 5.11
What's wrong with this log?

tip

gameSpace viewports can be set to display objects in a variety of ways. When working with materials it is sometimes preferable to work with some or all of the viewports set to Solid Render Mode where objects are displayed as solids with detailed texture

Anyone who has spent more than a few days in woodshop class will probably see the problem immediately. If this log was only a few inches long, it is possible, although unlikely, that the grain might really stretch in this direction. If, on the other hand, this is supposed to be a large log from a real tree, the grain would normally run along the length of the log.

Materials and Projections

When you are working with a simple colored material or a perfectly square checkerboard pattern, the orientation of the texture may not be significant. With an irregular texture such as wood, however, you need to understand and control exactly how the material is applied to your object.

The technical term for what you are trying to accomplish is "projection." You project the texture image onto the object, much as a slide projector projects a picture onto a wall. In the example of a slide on a wall, you have what is called "planar UV projection." This means that the image is spread evenly across a simple flat surface (a plane). If you were to imagine a large round room, like a planetarium, where special projector lenses spread the slide's image evenly in all directions, you would instead be describing "spherical UV projection."

Planar UV projection refers to the process of mapping an image onto an imaginary two-dimensional surface.

Cubic UV projection refers to the process of mapping an image onto all sides of an imaginary cube. This is similar to using three separate plane projections, one each for the front, the side, and the top of the object.

Spherical projection refers to the process of mapping an image onto an imaginary round globe.

Cylindrical projection refers to the process of mapping an image onto the curved sides of an imaginary cylinder. This is like spherical projection, but it curves in only one direction.

> The letters U and V are traditionally used to describe the horizontal (left to right) and vertical (up and down) positioning of a texture image. The same way that typical 3-D graphics artists and programmers use the letters X, Y, and Z to describe the three orthogonal directions of movement in a virtual world, the letters U and V are reserved for descriptions of any entity's internal texture-mapping coordinates.

gameSpace makes it very easy to choose the UV projection system that works best for your object. The UV projection tool icons are located on the main gameSpace toolbar toward the bottom center of your screen.

The default projection mode is planar UV projection and is represented by a picture of a very thin, short, rectangular box with a checkerboard on top and matching stripes down the sides. This mode is best when you have an object surface that is only visible from one direction or from two opposite directions. For example, a wall that is seen from its front or back side would be a perfect candidate for planar UV projection.

In the case of your log, you want the stripes of the grain to run the length of log, which is a cylinder. Cylindrical UV projection seems an appropriate choice. Right-click on the UV projection tools icon and drag the mouse up until you have selected the UV projection icon featuring a picture of a little can with a checkerboard pattern wrapped around its sides. See Figure 5.12.

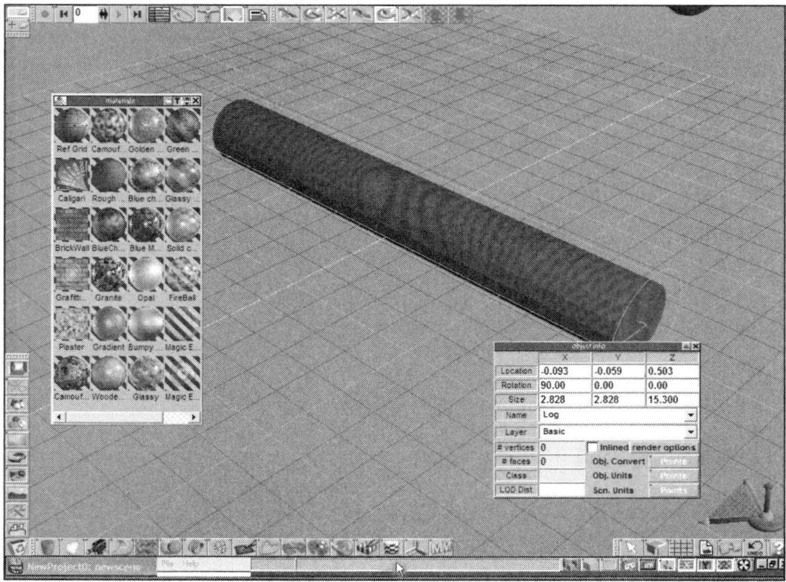

Figure 5.12
Map the textures onto the log with cylindrical UV projections.

Notice the thin blue lines that appear around the log. These represent the imaginary projection object, in this case, a cylinder, around which the log's material is stretched before it is applied. You can see that the projection may have changed, but the grain lines are still running in the wrong direction.

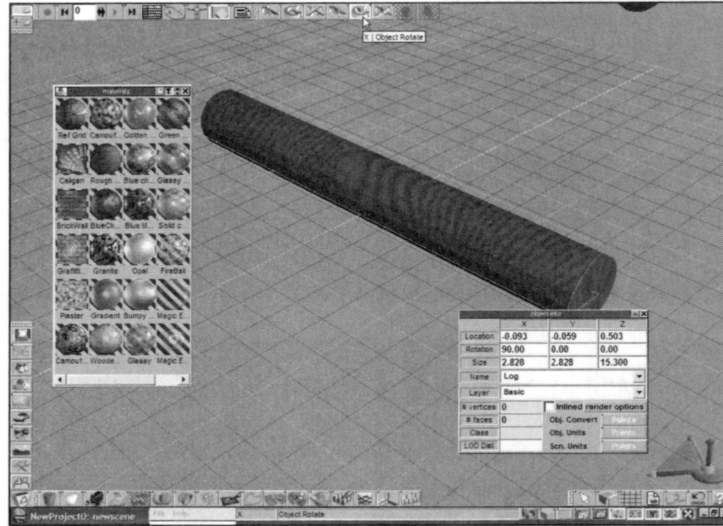

Figure 5.13
With the projection cylinder visible, select the Object Rotate tool.

With the blue projection cylinder visible, choose the Object Rotate tool, or simply hit the X key. Notice that the cylindrical UV projection tool remains active and the blue projection cylinder remains visible, even though the object rotate tool is now active as well. See Figure 5.13.

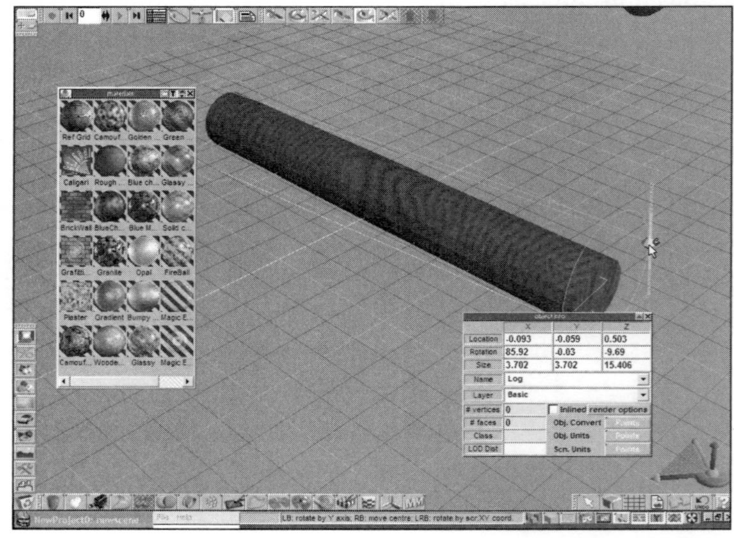

Figure 5.14
Rotate the blue UV projection cylinder using this rotation handle.

You can now use the mouse to rotate the blue projection cylinder by clicking and dragging in various directions. Without pressing the mouse button, move the mouse around the blue projection cylinder and notice the various "rotation handles" that appear as you do. Click and drag on the large diamond-shaped rotation handle that is shown in Figure 5.14.

As you move the blue projection cylinder, notice that the log model does not move, but the texture patterns that appear on it do. As long as the UV projection tool remains active, you can use the Object Rotate, Object Scale, and Object Move tools to easily manipulate the object's UV projection coordinates. Using the projector analogy, described above, this is like moving, rotating, or zooming the projector.

In many other modeling programs, these types of adjustments to an object's UV projection coordinates must be calculated by hand and typed in numerically. gameSpace makes it easy to visually determine the most appropriate UV offsets.

Play around with the UV projection cylinder, and try some of the other UV projection shapes to see how they affect the texture of the log. When you are done experimenting, select the cylindrical UV projection tool again, and rotate the cylinder until the grain lines run the length of the log. Figure 5.15 shows the UV projection cylinder rotated to produce a more realistic projection for the log's texture.

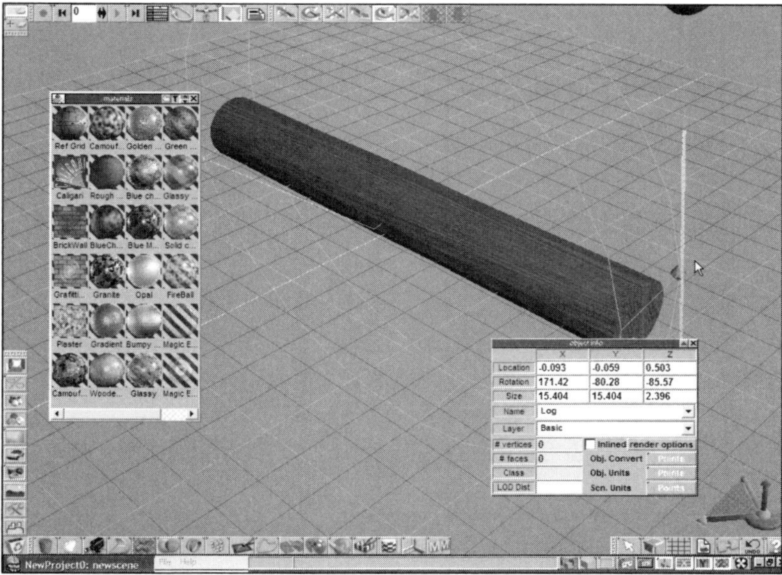

Figure 5.15
Rotate the UV projection cylinder until the wood grain flows in the proper direction.

When the log looks correct, save the scene, and then save the object as a DirectX .x file. See Figure 5.16. Remember to save the DirectX file in its own directory, as shown in Figure 5.17.

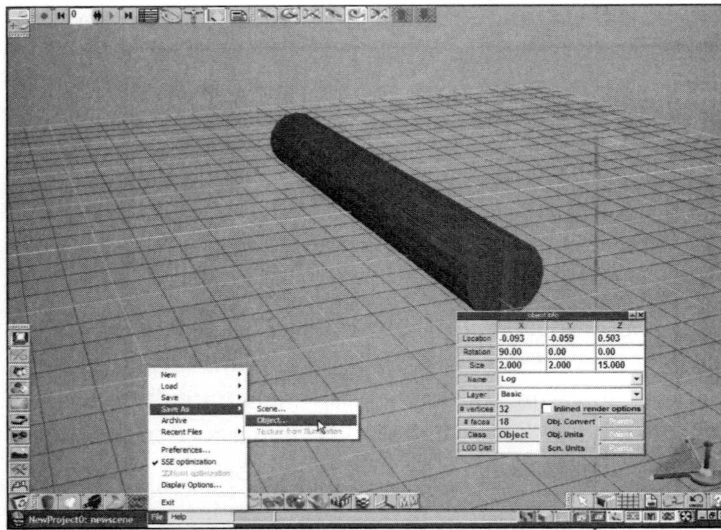

Figure 5.16
Use File > Save As > Object to save the log model.

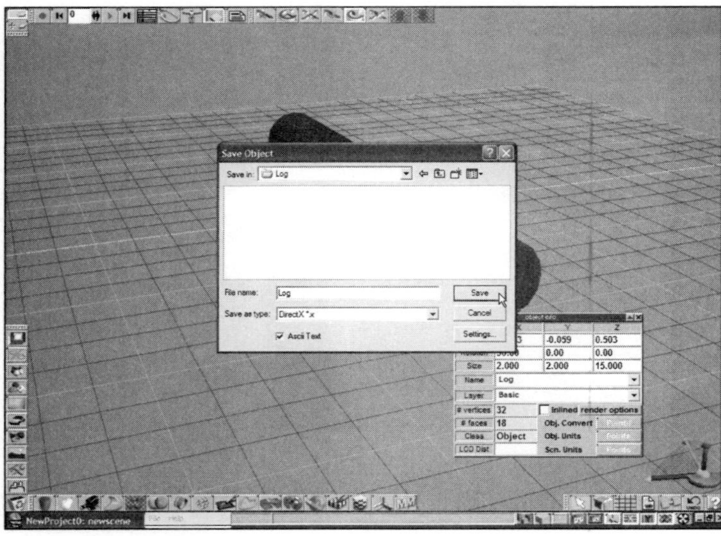

Figure 5.17
Save the log model into its own directory.

Use the ObjectImporter to import your new log object as Object 1, and then play the Adventure Explorer game to see your new logs in action. See Figure 5.18.

Figure 5.18
Import your new log as game Object 1.

The logs are quite an improvement, but it is still extremely unlikely you will get across the river. In the next section, you will use your logs to create a raft that will make it much easier.

Assembling a Raft

If it is not already open, load the scene you saved when you built your log model.

To build a raft, you will need a few more logs and a little glue. Fortunately, your gameSpace building set has an endless supply of both. You already have one log in your scene. Rather than create several more logs from scratch, you can simply duplicate the log you have.

Toward the bottom right of the screen, find the Copy tool. Use the Object tool to select the log, and then activate the Copy tool, as seen Figure 5.19.

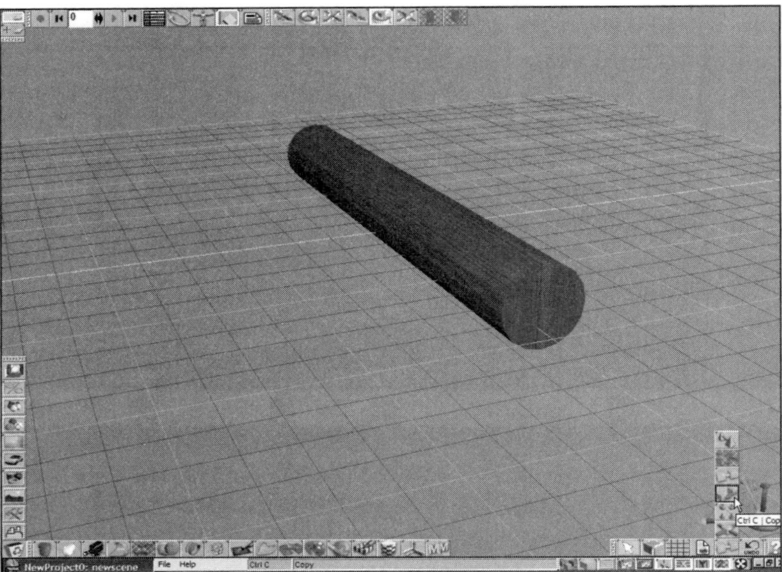

Figure 5.19
Use the Copy tool to make an exact duplicate of an object.

You may not actually see the new copy of the log yet. It has probably been created directly on top of the original log. When you later try to move the log, however, you will see that another identical log is left in its place.

The next step in building your raft is to slide the new log into position beside the first log, and then to repeat the process. Ideally, you would slide the new log only in the X direction, leaving it precisely aligned with the original log in the Y and Z directions. Unless you cheat a bit, this can be harder than it sounds. Fortunately, this isn't a test, and when it comes to building 3-D models, game artists cheat all the time.

Locking the Wheels

Imagine that the Object Move tool is actually a moving dolly. It's like a mouse-controlled cart with really smooth wheels. Picture your objects sliding around on this invisible dolly as you drag your mouse around the screen. The dolly's flexible wheels spin in any direction, so you can roll the dolly anywhere you move your mouse.

At times, this freedom is great; it gives you unlimited freedom to move your objects in any direction. What if you are building a raft and want to move the object in exactly one direction at a time? Wouldn't it be nice if you could just flip a switch and lock the wheels so that your dolly moves precisely and only in the direction you require? That is exactly what the three axis enable buttons do.

Three buttons at the very bottom of the gameSpace screen display the letters X, Y, and Z. Think of these as wheel-locks or brakes on the dolly. When the X button is selected, you are free to move, scale, or rotate objects in the direction of the X axis. Likewise, the Y and Z buttons enable or disable movement in the Y and Z axes' directions, respectively.

tip

Press the A, S, and D keys to quickly enable or disable movement along the X, Y, and Z axes, respectively. Note that these three keys are directly above the Z, X, and C keys, which are the keyboard shortcuts for Object Move, Object Rotate, and Object Scale.

The actual directions that are controlled by the X, Y, and Z enable buttons depend upon the type of viewport in which you are moving. When working in a viewport that is set up to display a front, back, top, bottom, or side view, the X enable button allows or prevents movement that is right or left in relation to the screen display of that viewport. Likewise, the Y enable button allows or prevents movement up or down in that same viewport. In a 3-D perspective or camera viewport, the X, Y, and Z enable buttons directly correspond to the directions of the global X, Y, and Z axes.

An Assembly Line for Logs

Disable movement in the Y and Z directions by setting the three axis enable buttons as shown in Figure 5.20.

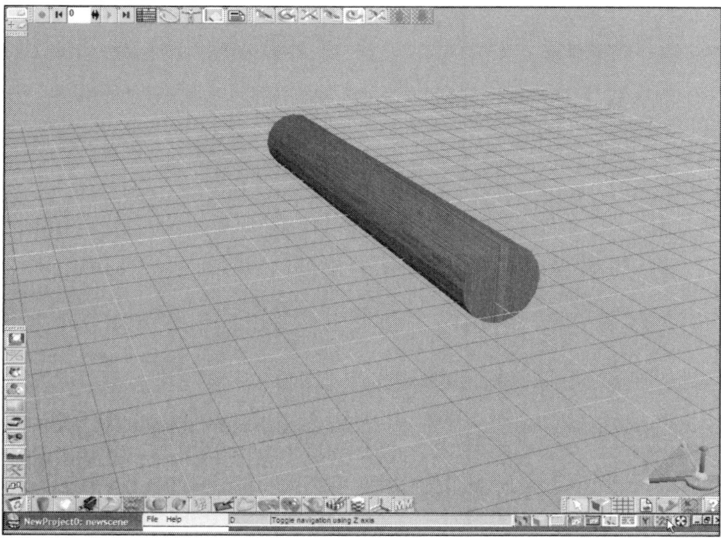

Figure 5.20
Movement is enabled on the X axis and disabled on the Y axis and Z axis.

Now when you move the log using the Object Move tool, it only moves along the X axis.

Use the Object Move tool to slide the copy of your log so that it sits side by side with the original log. See Figure 5.21.

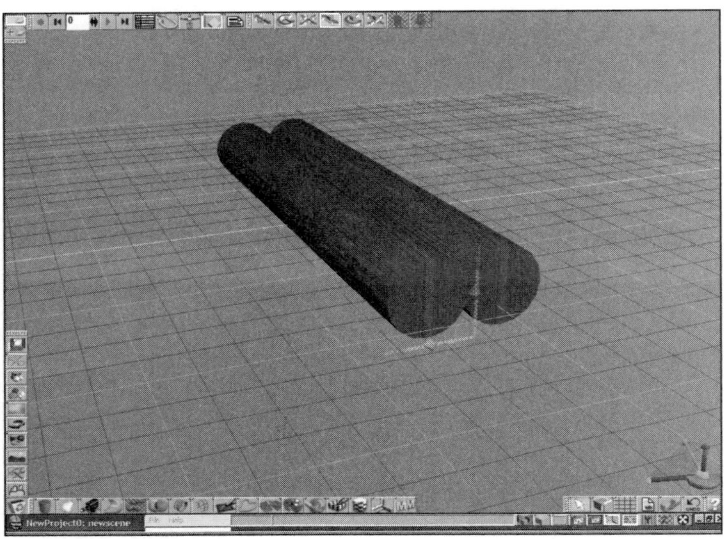

Figure 5.21
Slide a copy of your log into position.

Click the Copy icon once again. This will create another new copy of your log. See Figure 5.22.

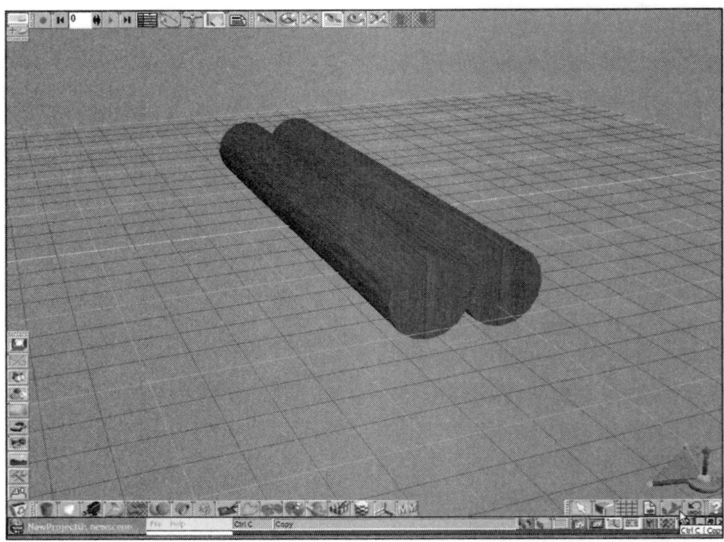

Figure 5.22
Use the Copy tool to make a third log.

Drag the new log into its proper place, immediately beside the first two. See Figure 5.23.

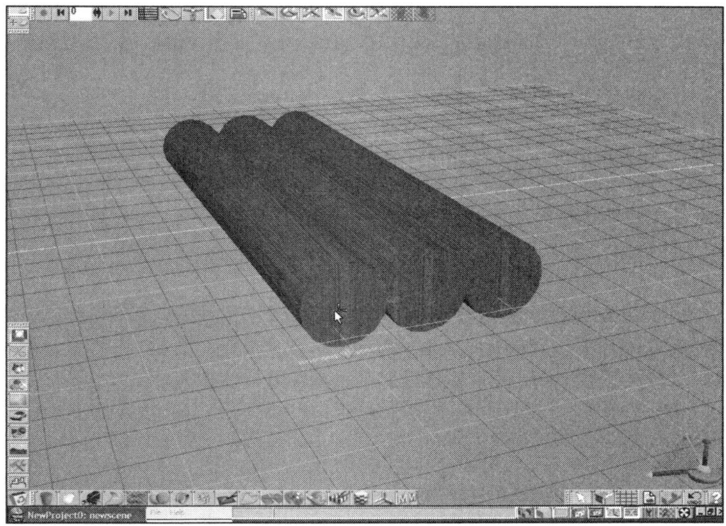

Figure 5.23
Use the Object Move tool to slide the new log into position.

Click the Copy icon yet again. This will give you a fourth log. Slide the new log into position, exactly as before. Your scene should now look like the scene shown in Figure 5.24.

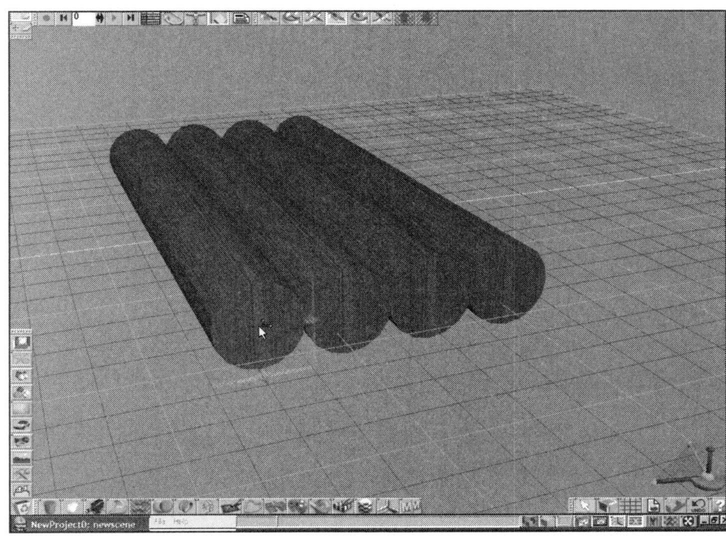

Figure 5.24
Copy and reposition your fourth log.

You now have a basic raft, but it doesn't look very believable. You can apply a number of simple tricks to make your raft seem more realistic. Can you think of a few?

The Balance of Believability

Almost all inexperienced game artists make two fundamental mistakes. The first mistake most novice game artists make is stopping too soon. They make overly simple models that are too perfect, too regular, too geometric, and too crude to be believable. This is a serious problem, because video games, like movies, books, and many other art forms, are based on the viewer's willing suspension of disbelief. The players of your game are trying to make themselves forget that the game isn't real. Any obvious weakness or inconsistency in the quality of a game model disrupts this effort and reminds the player that the game is clearly fake.

The second common mistake is just the opposite of the first. Overly ambitious game artists work endlessly to sculpt and polish the tiniest details of their models. This tireless dedication and perfectionism is often encouraged by many well-meaning 3-D modeling teachers and art schools. Although quality of work and artistic pride are very important, they are rarely the most important aspects of video game art.

It is difficult to say which of the two common mistakes is worse. Ironically, the latter of the two is probably more dangerous to your career as a game artist. Game companies often value a game artist who can quickly crank out a whole level full of simple but recognizable models, but very few game producers are likely to keep a game artist who could produce the most stunning and detailed game models but never completes them.

A game artist must constantly balance the believability of the models against artistic vision and the economies of time and schedule. Part of defining the artistic style of a game should be establishing and agreeing upon an acceptable balance of visual quality, artistic style, work efficiency, polygon efficiency, and believability. This ability to balance believability with economy may be the most important skill a game artist can master.

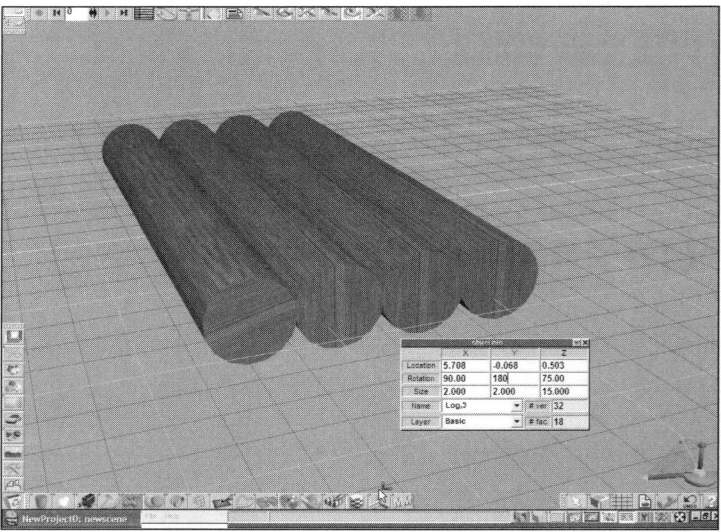

Figure 5.25
One log is rotated differently than the others.

In the case of your raft, the balance of believability translates into questions such as, "How do I keep all of the logs from looking exactly the same, when they are all based on the same original model?" There are many solutions to this problem, and one may be just as good as any other. One simple solution is to rotate each log into a different orientation. Compare the screenshots depicted in Figures 5.25, 5.26, and 5.27.

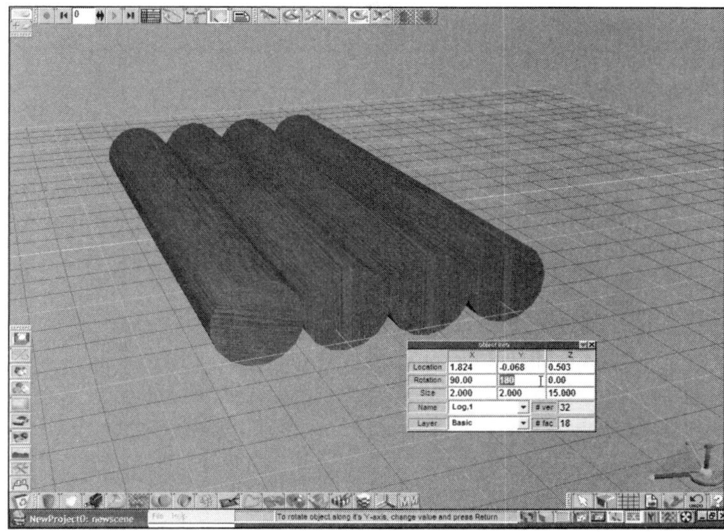

Figure 5.26
Use the Object Info Pane to flip another log.

Another way to enhance believability might involve adjusting the scale of each log to make some slightly longer, shorter, wider, or narrower than the others. Try experimenting with either of these approaches, or a combination of the two. You can also try any similar approach of your own design. Just be sure that the overall shape and size of the raft remains pretty much unchanged.

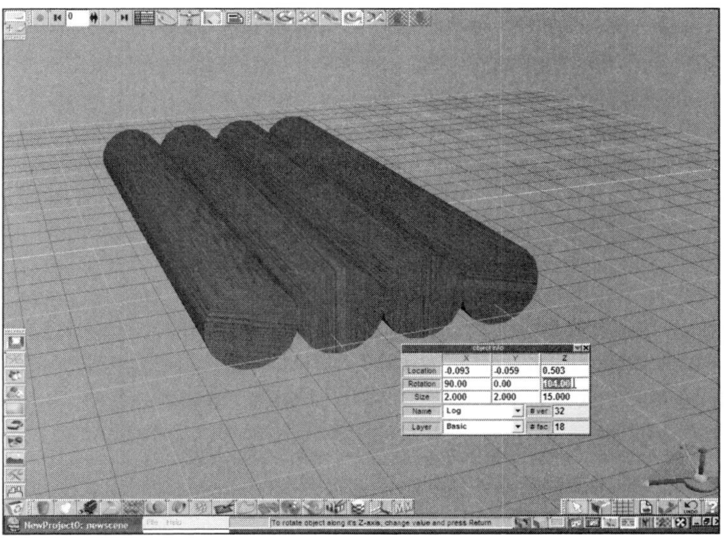

Figure 5.27
All of the logs have slightly different orientation.

Another apparent defect in your raft model arises from its simple construction. A child can build a miniature raft by gluing together a bunch of sticks, but rarely would you expect to see a real water-worthy raft with no obvious signs of fastening, binding, or cross-bracing.

Here you see a real test of the delicate balancing act I described before. You can spend hours or even days making a raft model with so much detail that you could actually build it. This would be too much work, and even if done with the greatest accuracy, might still completely fail to satisfy the needs of your game.

What's really needed is just enough obvious detail, however false it may be, to send the message to the viewer that upon closer inspection, more details would be visible. Such closer inspection will never happen, so it is merely the illusion of this detail that you need to convey.

> Douglas Adams, in his extremely popular, funny, and insightful novel *The Hitchhikers Guide to the Galaxy*, makes the brilliant, if offbeat, suggestion that travelers would be wise to carry a towel with them wherever they may go. Adams humorously makes the point that once people see that you have a towel, they will assume you are the type of prepared and thoughtful individual who would also own a toothbrush, soap, food, water, and other such necessities, and as such, they are far more likely to trust you with their own.
>
> This philosophy can be applied equally to video-game models. When a player sees some evidence of a rivet, a bolt, a belt, a wire, or a cross-beam in an object, they somehow assume that if any such detail is visible, then far more must be hidden just beneath the surface.
>
> This is also the strategy behind the business executive, professor, or author who attends a dressy meeting wearing only a dress shirt and a pair of nice slacks, knowing that people will automatically assume that there is a matching well-tailored jacket hanging nearby in an office or car. The professional gets all the benefits of appearing well-dressed for the occasion, without the effort or discomfort of completely dressing up. My uncle, Michael Schoenbrun, was the Vice President of Production at Paramount Studios and Gracie Films, he called this his "I left my tie in the car look." It really works.

To create the illusion of detail in your raft model, add a couple of cross-beam elements placed near either end of the raft. These add to the raft's believability, while requiring very little effort from you. They also add very few new faces and vertices for the game engine to render.

Detailing the Raft

Change the screen layout so that you can view the model from multiple viewports. This will make it easier to position things properly in all three dimensions. See Figure 5.28.

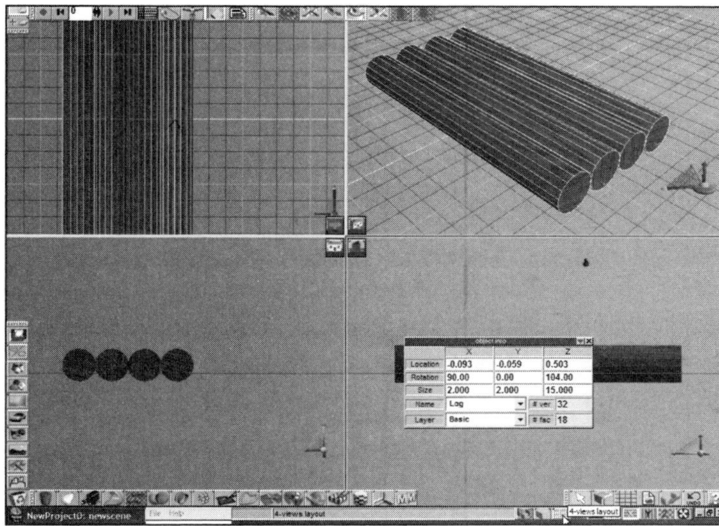

Figure 5.28
Select the multiple viewport layout.

Your cross-beams, like the logs, are cylinders. You just position and stretch them so that they appear to hold together the rafts of your log.

Use the Cylinder icon to create a new cylinder. See Figure 5.29.

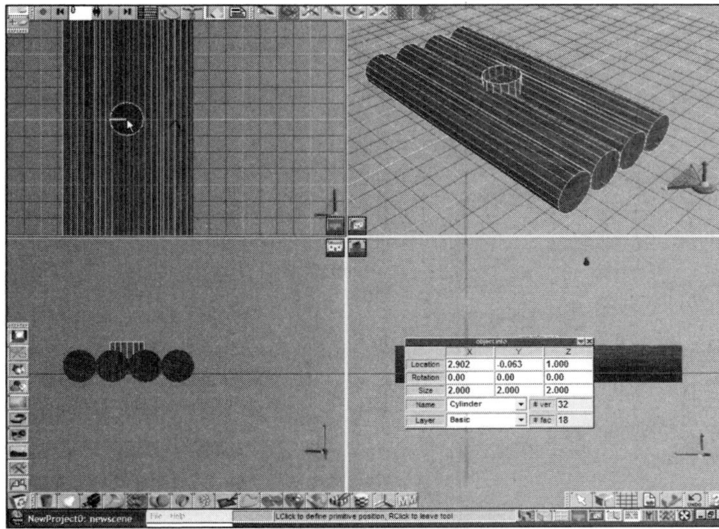

Figure 5.29
Create another cylinder.

Use the Object Info Pane or the Object Scale and Object Rotate tools to adjust the new cylinder, as shown in Figures 5.30 through 5.32.

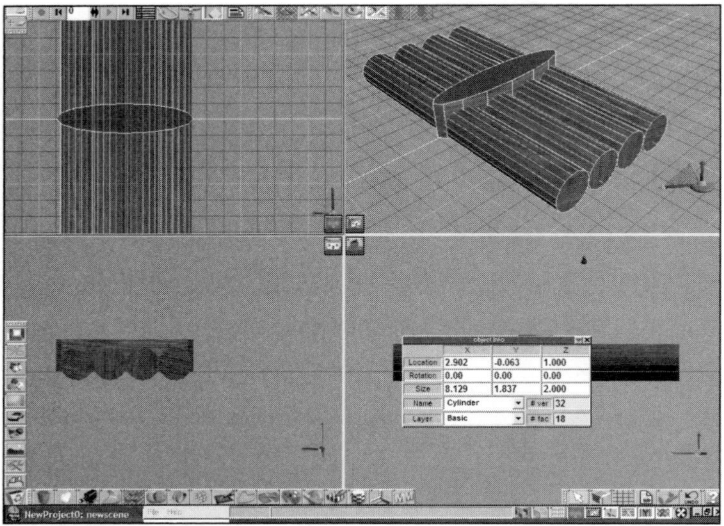

Figure 5.30
Adjust the scale and rotation of the new cylinder.

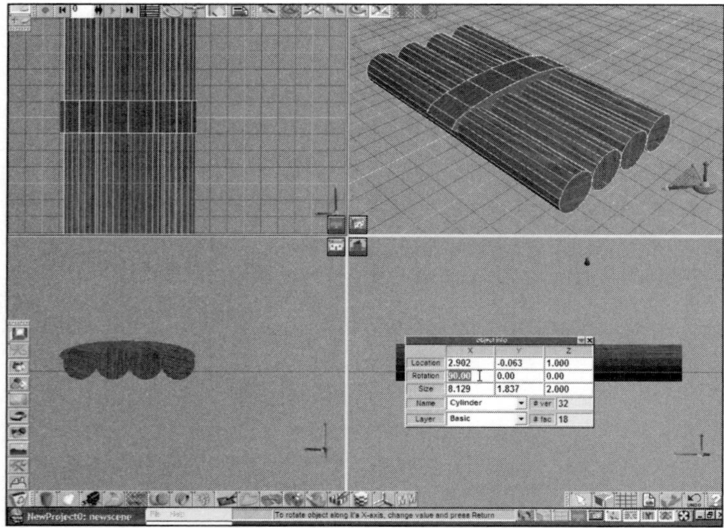

Figure 5.31
Rotate the new cylinder.

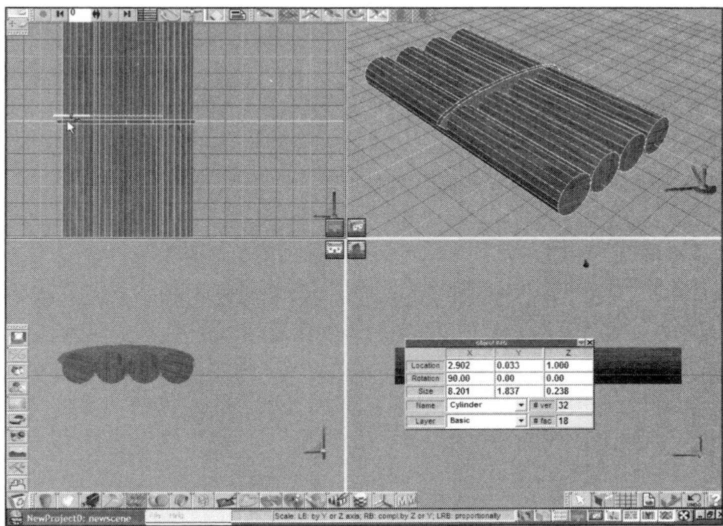

Figure 5.32
Scale the cylinder.

Before you duplicate this cylinder, take a moment to adjust its texture. Open the Material Library. See Figure 5.33.

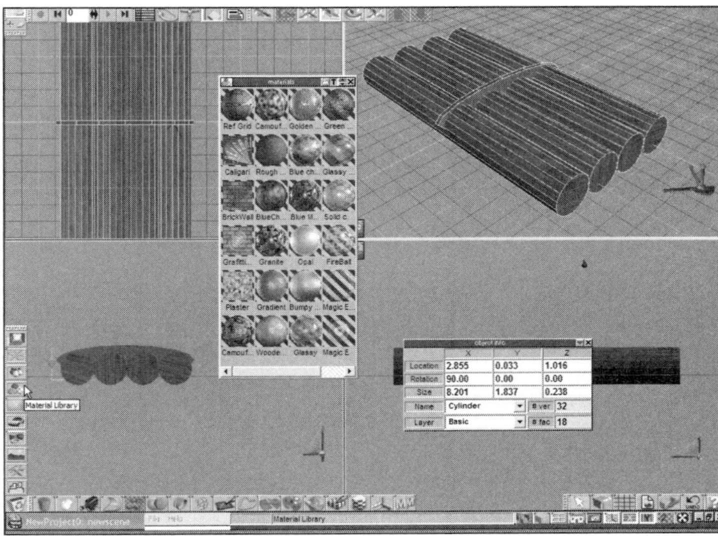

Figure 5.33
Open the Material Library.

Choose a different material from the Material Library by dragging the material named Rough Surf to a spot near the center of the new piece. See Figure 5.34. The new texture helps to make the detail stand out from the rest of the model. It also helps to give the impression that the raft was constructed out of a variety of materials.

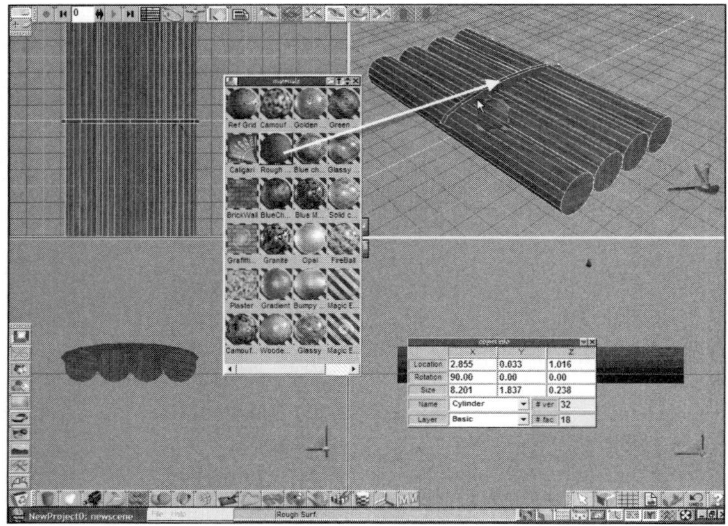

Figure 5.34
Drag the Rough Surf material and drop it onto the new piece.

Set the three axis enable buttons, as shown in Figure 5.35. This enables movement along the Y axis, while disabling movement along the X and Z axes.

Select the Object Move tool. Drag the new piece downward in the top view, which is displayed in the viewport at the top left-hand side of the screen. The final position should look similar to that shown in Figure 5.35.

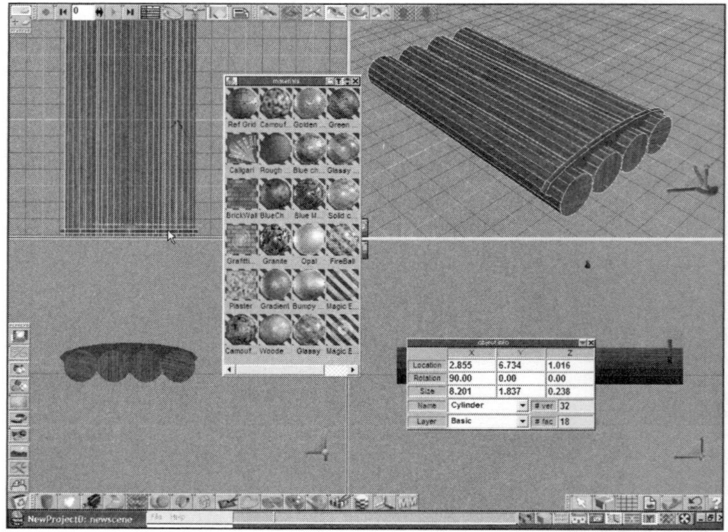

Figure 5.35
Use the Object Move tool to slide the new piece toward the front of the raft.

Press the A and D keys once each to re-enable movement in the X and Z directions.

Select the Object Scale tool, and drag the new piece to stretch it using the front view, which is located in the bottom left viewport. See Figure 5.36.

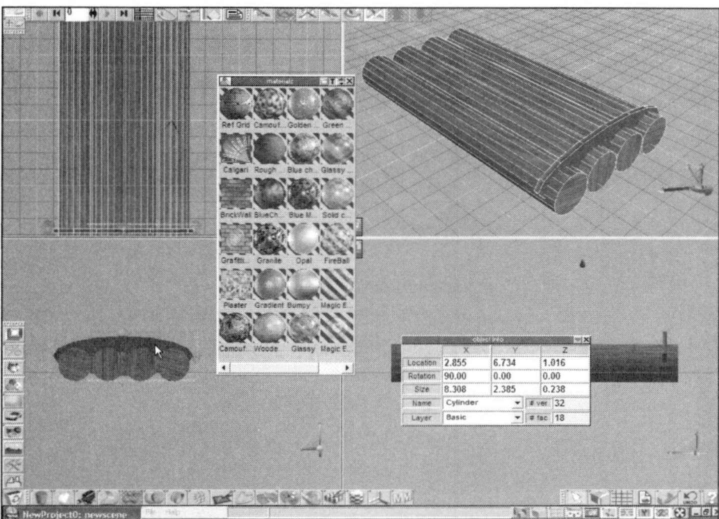

Figure 5.36
Use the Object Scale tool to stretch the new piece in the front view.

Select the Move Object tool, then drag the new piece in the front view until it appears similar to Figure 5.37.

Press Ctrl+C or click the Copy icon to duplicate the new piece. Remember that you may not see the newly created duplicate until you try to move it. See Figure 5.38.

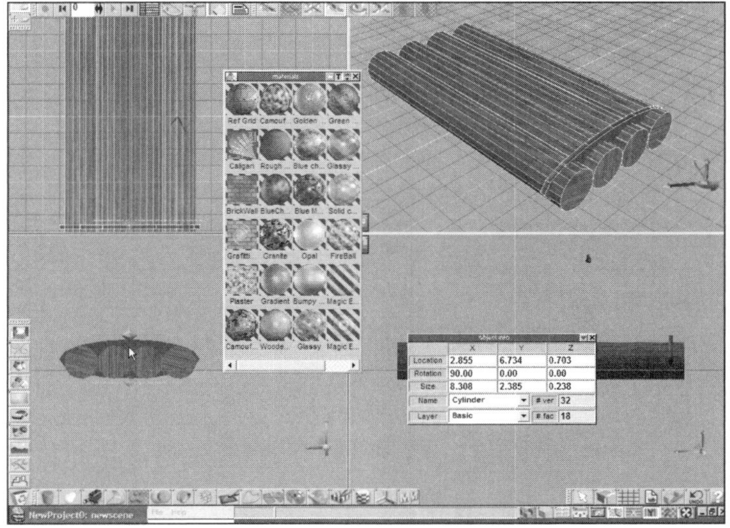

Figure 5.37
Use the Object Move tool to reposition the new piece in the front

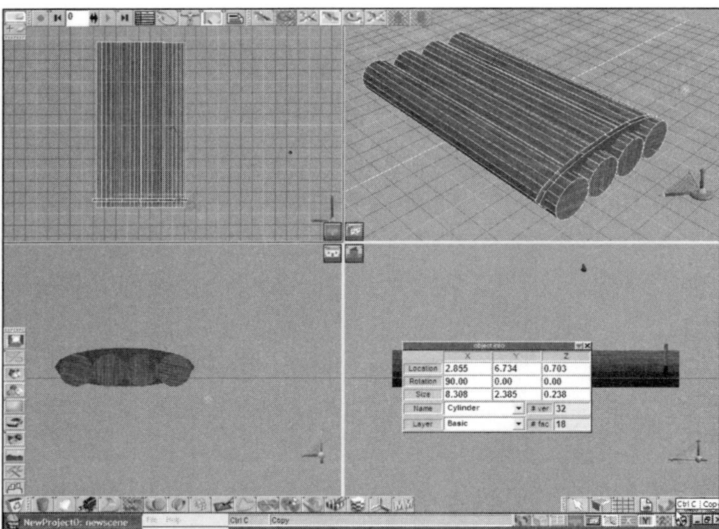

Figure 5.38
Click the Copy icon.

Press the A and D keys once each again to disable movement in the X and Z directions.

Working once again in the top view, use the Object Move tool to slide the new piece up toward the other end of the raft. It should now look like Figure 5.39.

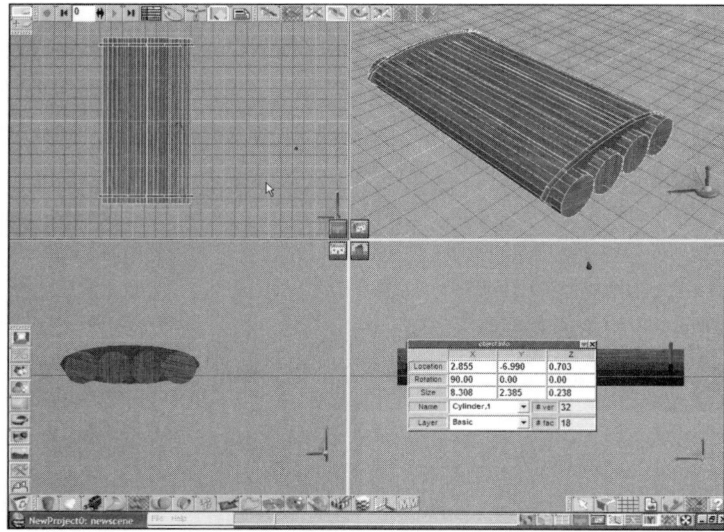

Figure 5.39
Working in the top view, slide the new object up.

Select File > Save As > Scene to save your raft model as a Caligari Scenes .scn model. When prompted for a name, simply name it "Raft."

In the next chapter, you will complete the raft. You will learn how to connect the various pieces together and combine them into a single object, which you can use in the game.

Summary

In this chapter, you should have learned the following concepts:

- All game objects should have a purpose and serve some need in the game.
- A good game object fits the theme, style, period, and setting of a game.
- Once you set a theme, stick to it and apply it throughout the objects in your level.
- Set patterns, but break them occasionally to make things more realistic.
- Every object in a game should help the player to suspend disbelief.
- Materials can be dragged directly from the Material Library onto an object.
- The Copy tool allows you to make an exact duplicate of any object.
- Movement in various directions can be enabled or disabled with the axis enable buttons.
- The axis enable buttons work differently in the 3-D perspective and camera views than they do in the front, back, top, bottom, or side views.
- The axis enable buttons can limit the effective directions of the Object Move, Object Rotate, and Object Scale tools.
- The Object Info Pane can be used to assign a new name to any object.
- Objects can be selected by name by choosing them from the object list that is attached to the Name field in the Object Info Pane.
- The Paint Object button in the Material Editor applies the current material to the currently selected object.
- Texture images can be mapped onto an object in a variety of ways.
- The letters U and V are typically used to represent the horizontal and vertical mapping of a texture image onto a 3-D surface.
- gameSpace allows you to choose between various shapes of UV projection.
- You can use the Object Move, Object Rotate, and Object Scale tools to move, rotate, or scale an object's assigned UV projection shape.
- UV projection shapes can be manipulated separately from the object to which they are attached.

- Game artists must carefully maintain the balance of believability in their objects.
- Sometimes just the obvious hint of detail can make an object model seem far more complicated and detailed than it is.

Questions and Answers

Q: What are five questions a game object should be able to positively answer?

A:

1. Does the object fit the setting, the period, and the theme of the game?
2. Does the object add to the realism or authenticity of the game?
3. Does the object serve a purpose in the gameplay?
4. Does the object help or hinder the player in accomplishing the goals?
5. Does the object add to the general entertainment value of the game?

Q: What are the keyboard shortcuts to enable or disable movement along the X, Y, and Z axes?

A: The A, S, and D keys toggle the state of the X, Y, and Z axis enable buttons, respectively.

Q: If you are working in a viewport displaying a front view and movement along the Y axis is disabled, in which directions are you still able to move an object?

A: You are only able to move the object left and right, which is along the X axis of this viewport and, coincidentally, the global X axis as well.

Q: If you are working in a perspective viewport and movement along the Z axis is disabled, in which direction are you not able to move your object?

A: You are not able to move your object up or down in the air.

Q: What is the keyboard shortcut for the Copy tool?

A: The keyboard shortcut for the Copy tool is Ctrl+C.

Q: If you were trying to apply a material to a golf ball, which UV projection mode would be most appropriate?

A: Spherical UV projection would be the best fit for a golf ball or other completely round object.

Q: What gameSpace icon displays a picture of two small boxes side by side with a blue arrow passing in front of them?

A: The icon represents the Copy tool.

Q: How can you select an object by its name in gameSpace?

A: Click the small downward pointing triangle to the right of the Name field on the Object Info Pane, and then select the name from the list of objects.

Q: You use the gameSpace Copy tool, but you do not see any change in the scene. Why is this?

A: There are two possible answers to this question.

1. No object was selected when you chose the Copy tool.
2. A new object was created, but it is hidden by the original object, which still sits at exactly the same location.

Discussion Questions

1. Select a real object or a picture to use as the artistic basis for a design theme for a level. How might that theme affect the way you would model other important objects in the level?
2. Describe a situation where cubic UV projection would clearly be the best choice for projecting a texture onto an object.
3. How does spherical UV projection differ from cylindrical UV projection?
4. You are asked to build an object by duplicating four identical primitives. How might you quickly adjust these primitives to conceal the fact that they are all nearly identical?
5. Why is the hint of detail often more effective than actually modeling accurate details for an object?
6. What are some of the considerations a game artist should consider when balancing the believability of models?
7. Why is it important to assign meaningful names to your objects?

Exercises

1. Add another piece of detail to your raft. It should add to the sense of believability of the model, without adding many new faces or vertices. It is also important that it does not change the overall size or shape of the raft.
2. Use the Cube tool and the Copy tool to create five identical cubes, then use the Material Editor to give each of them a similar but slightly different texture.
3. Use gameSpace to create four identical cubes and four identical spheres. Apply the same texture to each of these objects, and then change the UV projection modes of the objects so that no two cubes and no two spheres are assigned the same UV projection mode.

4. Use the Cube tool and the Object Info Pane to create a long narrow cube. Apply a woodlike texture to the cube, and then change its UV projection mode to cubic UV projection. Move, rotate, and scale the UV projection cube to change the look of the wood grain.
5. Create one cube, then use the Copy tool and the three axis enable buttons to create a grid of evenly spaced cubes, as shown in Figure 5.40.

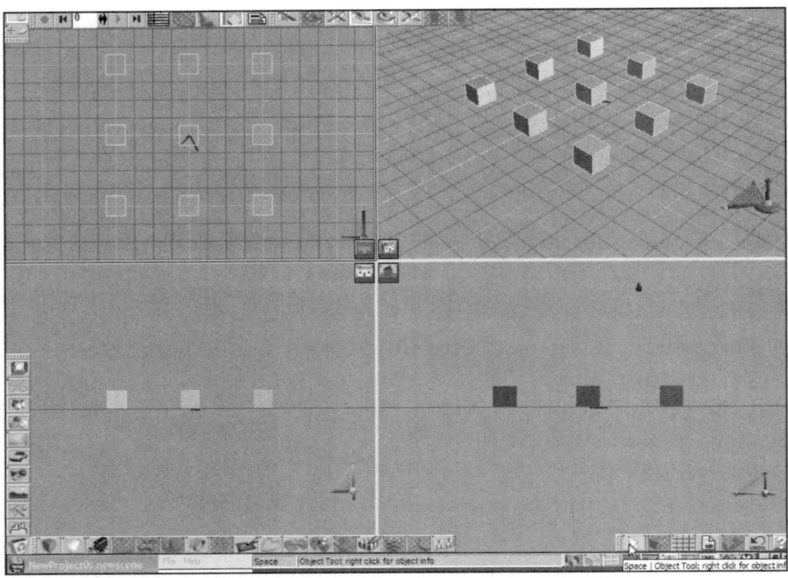

Figure 5.40
How precisely can you build this grid of cubes?

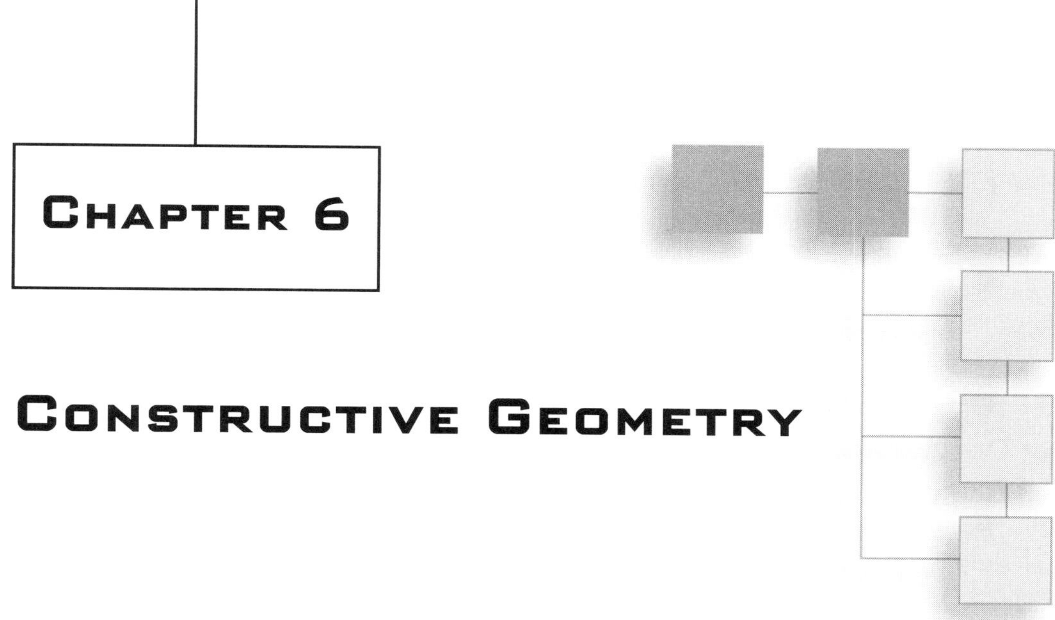

Chapter 6

Constructive Geometry

Introduction

In the last chapter, you built a log raft by duplicating and manipulating a number of individual cylinders. In this chapter, you will see how these cylinders can be combined and connected in a variety of ways.

Keeping It Together

You have nearly completed the raft, but at this point, your raft is just a loose collection of isolated logs and crosspieces. If you were to use the Object Move tool to drag around one log, it would leave the rest of the raft behind with a big gaping hole.

If there is one memorable lesson that I learned early in my 3-D modeling career, it is that when you build a water-going vessel, such as a raft, you must be sure the various pieces will always stick together.

> I remember a time when I was very young, and my extremely cool Uncle Bruce had spent the better part of a week building a giant sailing ship. His ship took almost every Lego I owned, and he even went so far as to take apart a few of my own Lego masterpieces to get a few extra pieces for this gigantic sailing vessel. The morning that his ship was complete, I awoke very early to admire Uncle Bruce's late-night work.
>
> What makes this incident so memorable was not merely the size of this Lego ship, though it was extremely big. The thing that engraved this experience so clearly in my memory was the manner in which I decided to test the sea-worthiness of Uncle Bruce's masterpiece.
>
> With great ceremony and a child's sense of scientific wonder, I launched the giant Lego ship by tossing it lovingly into the deepest part of my backyard swimming pool.
>
> *(continued)*

(continued from previous page)

I learned a very important lesson that day, and so did my uncle. I learned never to sail a Lego boat without first sealing its many hundreds of pieces together with some very strong and waterproof glue. Uncle Bruce learned never to leave his Lego masterpieces where his young nephew Harry could find them in the morning, and my whole family learned how long it can take to skim hundreds of tiny Lego blocks from a very large pool.

Get Out the Glue

To complete your raft, you'll need some glue to hold the pieces together. gameSpace has a name for this glue, and it is simply "glue." In an industry that prizes itself on patented buzzwords and elaborate techno-babble, it is refreshing to find a program that uses simple words like "glue" to mean glue.

A compound object is an object made up of a combination of other simpler objects.

gameSpace allows you to construct elaborate and complicated models by gluing together any number of simple objects.

A group is a compound object, which can be built in gameSpace by using the glue tools to add a new level to the object hierarchy.

You will find the glue tools in the same toolbar slot where you found the Copy tool. Remember you can click and hold the toolbar slot with the Copy tool to expand the toolbar vertically. Drag up to select and expand the sub-toolbar of glue tools. If necessary continue to hold the mouse button, as you drag horizontally to select the appropriate glue tool, as shown in Figure 6.1.

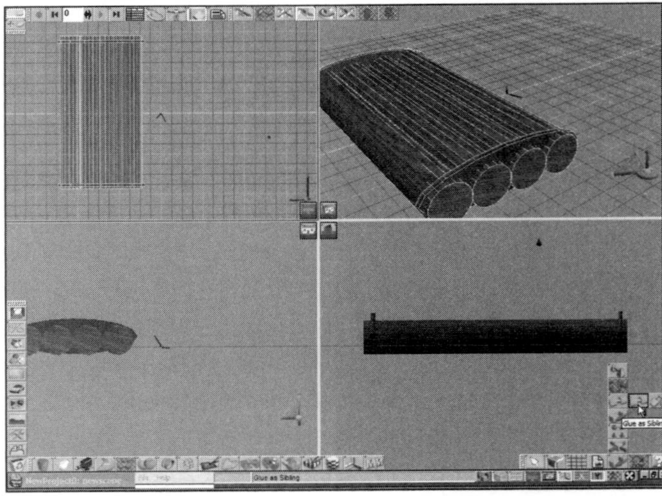

Figure 6.1
There are two glue tools.

gameSpace's glue is a lot better than that thick white liquid or that foul-smelling clear stuff that you might have played with in your past. gameSpace glue is safe. It is waterproof. It is nontoxic. It comes in an unlimited supply. It can never stick to your fingers, but it will hold together any number of objects within gameSpace.

Unlike most glue, if you happen to glue the wrong things in gameSpace, you don't have to worry. Removal and clean-up is clean and easy. There is another very important difference between gameSpace's glue and its real world counterpart. When you glue objects together with gameSpace, you can still access and manipulate the original objects individually.

The gameSpace glue tools have another important function. You can use the two different glue tools to intelligently organize your objects in a powerful and flexible way. The glue tools help you organize and group your objects together, using the same simple language with which people identify the members of their families.

The Glue as Sibling tool is used to join two or more objects at the same level of hierarchy, whereas the Glue as Child tool places the new objects at a lower level in the object hierarchy. This sounds reasonable, but what exactly is an object hierarchy?

Hierarchies and Family Trees

Have you ever drawn a family tree? Figure 6.2 shows a typical generic family tree. On the top of the family tree are your grandparents or great grandparents. In the lower levels of the family tree, you see your parents and possibly some aunts and uncles. On the next level down, you find yourself and perhaps your brothers or sisters.

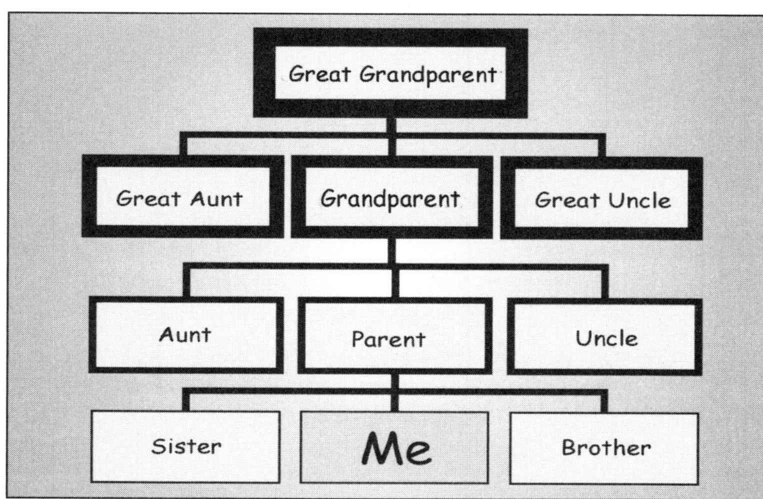

Figure 6.2
Typical family tree

Objects in gameSpace can be organized in exactly this manner. Of course, objects in gameSpace don't normally have names like Grandpa, Mom, or Dad.

The two gameSpace glue tools make organization easy, once you understand how they work. When you glue together two objects in gameSpace, you are telling gameSpace not only what you want to connect, but also how the two objects will relate to each other in their internal family tree.

To make things a little clearer, here are a couple of examples using the family tree shown in Figure 6.2. For these examples, assume that you are the "Me" listed in the lowest level of the family tree.

Imagine that your parents announce over dinner that they are about to bring a new baby into the family. You would then have a new brother or sister. The specific details of this process are far beyond the scope of this book, so let's just say you run from the table in an excited rush to update your digital family tree.

To add your new brother or sister to your family tree, you would grab the Glue as Sibling tool and use it to glue the new baby into your own level of the family tree. Remember, you use the Glue as Sibling tool to add a new object to an existing level. Your new family tree would now look like Figure 6.3.

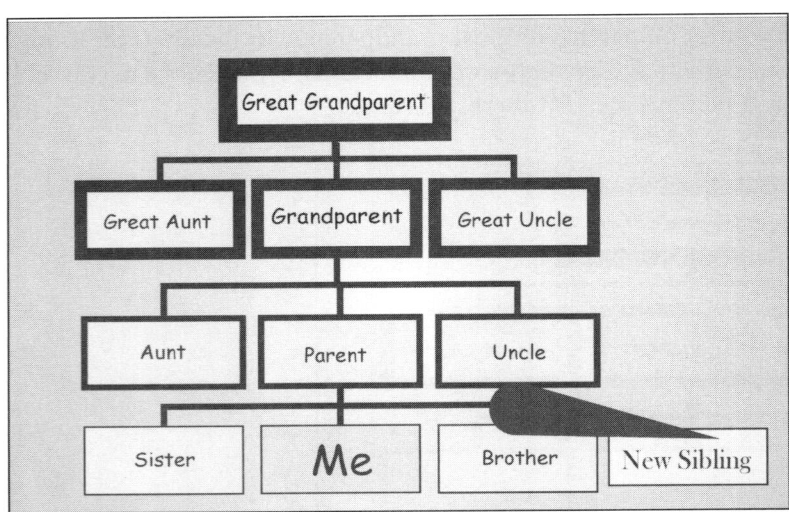

Figure 6.3
A new sibling joins the family.

Now, imagine instead that the new child was not your parents' baby, but your very own. You would probably be in even more of a rush to update the family tree, but this time you would not be adding a sibling. You would instead add a child. When you glue an object as a child, you are creating a whole new level beneath an already existing object in the family tree. See Figure 6.4.

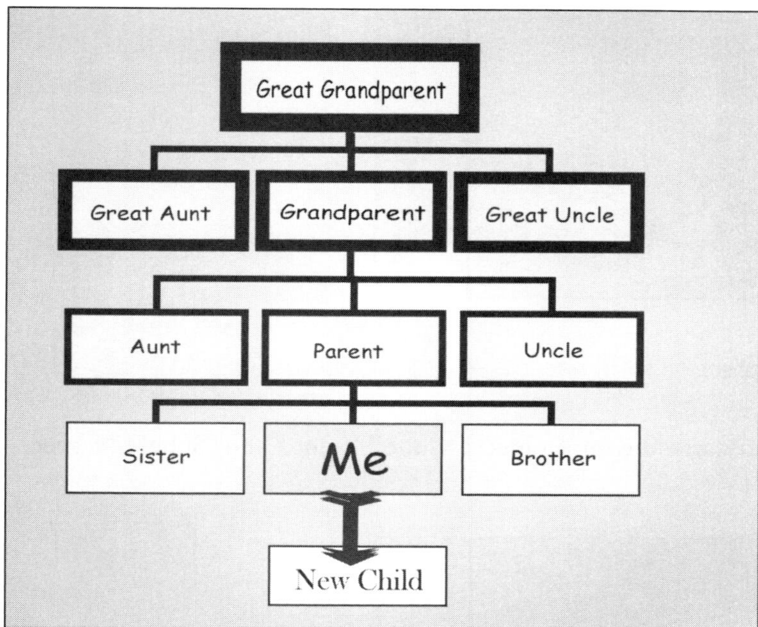

Figure 6.4
Congratulations, it's a child!

Now that you understand family genealogy, you may be wondering, "How does any of this apply to gameSpace?" To see how this applies to objects in gameSpace, try the following demonstration.

Choose File > New > Scene to start a new gameSpace scene. You could also use the Create New Scene tool, which is found on the same toolbar as the Object tool.

Use the primitive tools to create one cube, one cone, and one sphere, as shown in Figure 6.5.

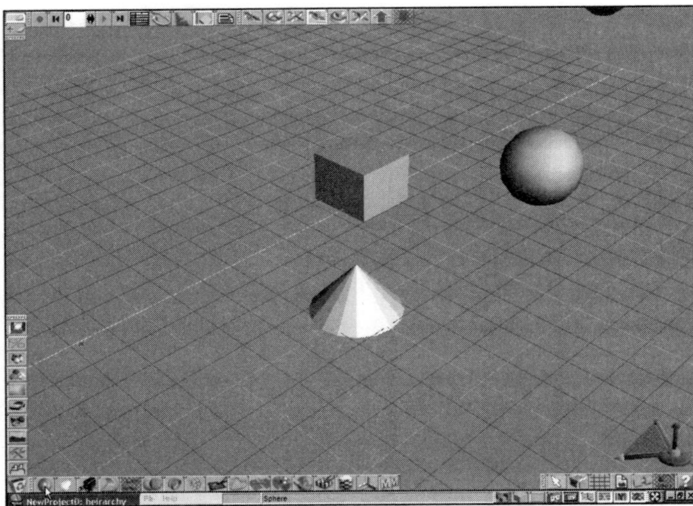

Figure 6.5
Create a cube, a cone, and a sphere.

Use the Object Info Pane to name the three objects "Cube," "Cone," and "Sphere," respectively. See Figure 6.6.

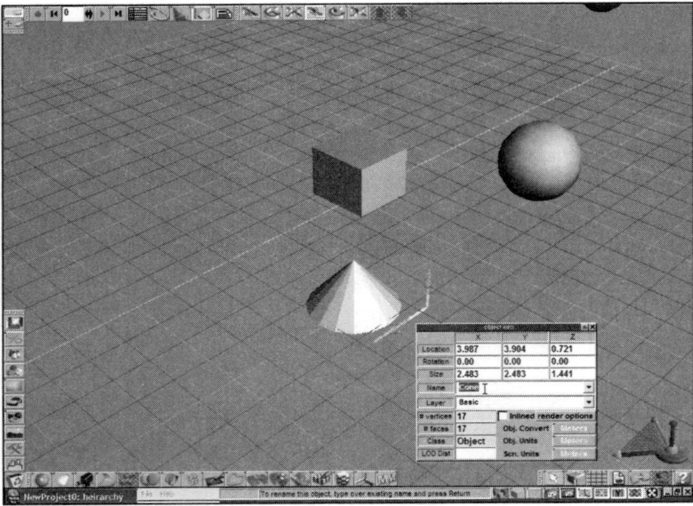

Figure 6.6
Use the Object Info Pane to name the three objects appropriately.

Use the Object tool to select the sphere. After the sphere is selected, activate the Glue as Sibling tool. The Glue as Sibling icon looks like two small brown boxes connected by a short green line. Notice that the mouse cursor changes into a small glue bottle.

With your Sphere object already selected, just click on the Cone object. See Figure 6.7.

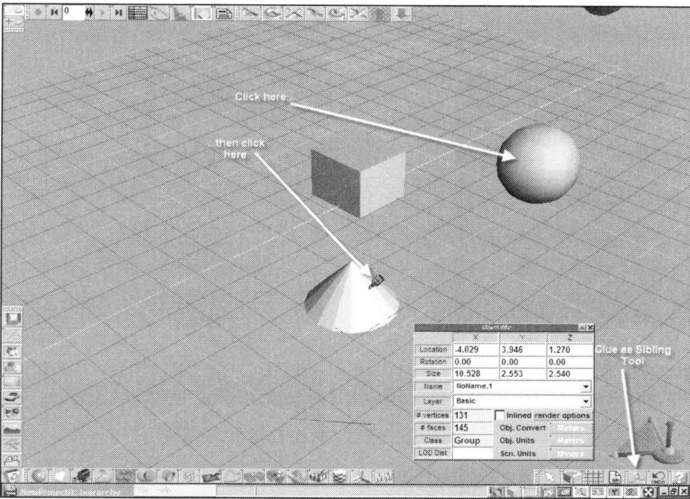

Figure 6.7
Glue the cone and the sphere together as siblings.

Select the Object Move tool and use it to drag the sphere or cone around the screen. You will see that they now move together as a single object. Also notice from the Object Info Pane that the combined object has a new name, NoName,1. No one said it would be a useful or creative name. You will change it soon.

The Scene Editor

In order to better understand what the glue tool has actually done, you can use the gameSpace Scene Editor. The Scene Editor allows you to see every object that exists in your scene in a whole new way. See Figure 6.8.

Click on the Scene Editor icon, which is located in the toolbar at the very top of the gameSpace screen.

Notice the small plus sign (+) beside the new object's name, NoName,1. This indicates that NoName,1 is a group that includes other objects. Click this small plus sign to see the sub-objects that make up this compound object. See Figure 6.9.

tip

You can move the Scene Editor window anywhere around the gameSpace screen by clicking and dragging the blue title bar that contains the words "Scene Editor."

You can shrink or stretch the Scene Editor window by moving the mouse over any edge of the window until the mouse pointer becomes a two-headed arrow. You can then use the two-headed arrow to click and drag that edge of the window in either direction. This can be very helpful if you have a lot of objects to view at once, or when you wish to see more objects in the viewport that would otherwise be hidden behind the Scene Editor.

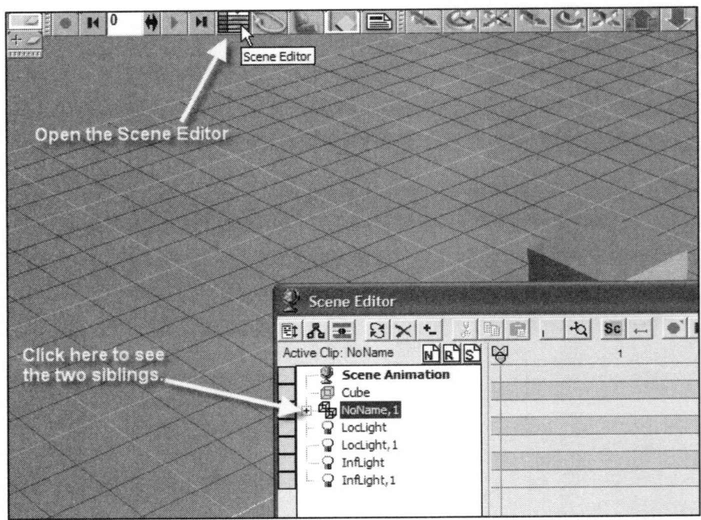

Figure 6.8
Use the Scene Editor to examine the object hierarchy.

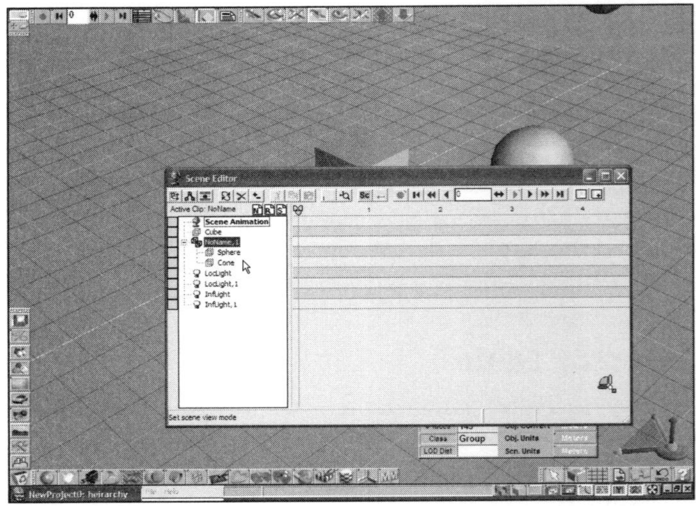

Figure 6.9
The Cone and Sphere objects constitute the NoName,1 object.

tip

The Scene Editor can be configured to show or hide certain types of objects. The leftmost icon on the Scene Editors' toolbar opens the Scene Editor Preferences panel. Use this panel to choose which types of objects should be displayed in the Scene Editor.

Click once on the name NoName,1 in the Scene Editor to select it, then click it once again to edit the text of the name. Change the name from NoName,1 to SphereAndCone, as shown in Figure 6.10.

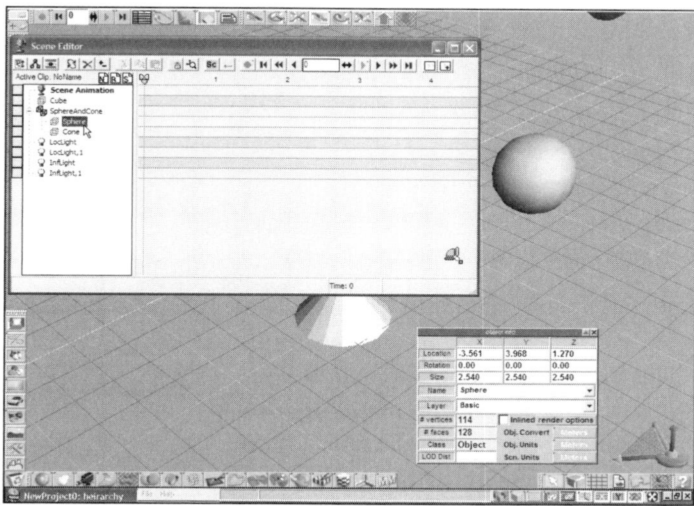

Figure 6.10
You can rename any object in the Scene Editor.

While you are looking at the Scene Editor, try clicking on the names of the Cone and Sphere objects. Notice that you can select each object individually with the Scene Editor, even though they are still part of the SphereAndCone compound object. Also note that the thick bar to the right of the object name turns yellow to indicate which object is selected. See Figure 6.11.

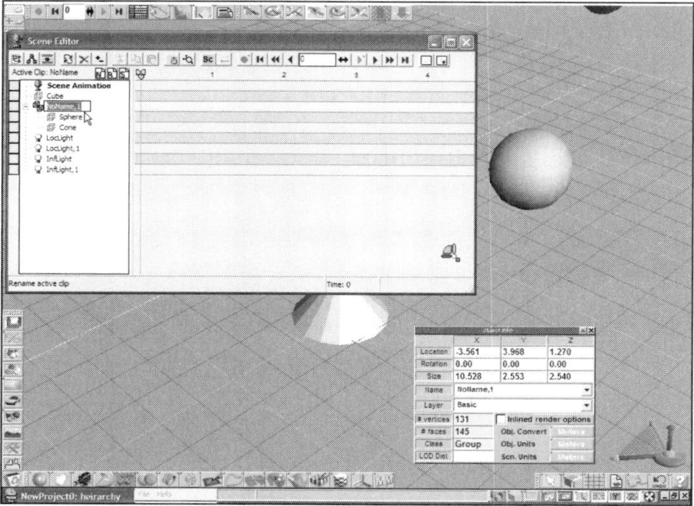

Figure 6.11
Use the Scene Editor to select objects, even when they are contained as part of another object.

Select the whole SphereAndCone compound object again, and then close the Scene Editor by clicking the small X in the upper right-hand corner of the Scene Editor window.

gameSpace gives you another way to navigate your way down a compound object's internal hierarchy. Notice that the Move down in Hierarchy icon at the top of the screen is available whenever you have selected the SphereAndCone tool, but neither of the Hierarchy icons (Up Arrow or Down Arrow) are available when you select the Cube object. The Move down in Hierarchy icon indicates that there is a lower level of objects contained within the currently selected object. See Figures 6.12 and 6.13.

Click the Move down in Hierarchy icon to move to a lower level of the selected object's object hierarchy. Notice that when you click this icon, the Move up in Hierarchy icon becomes available, and now only one part of the compound object (either the Sphere or the Cone) is selected at a time.

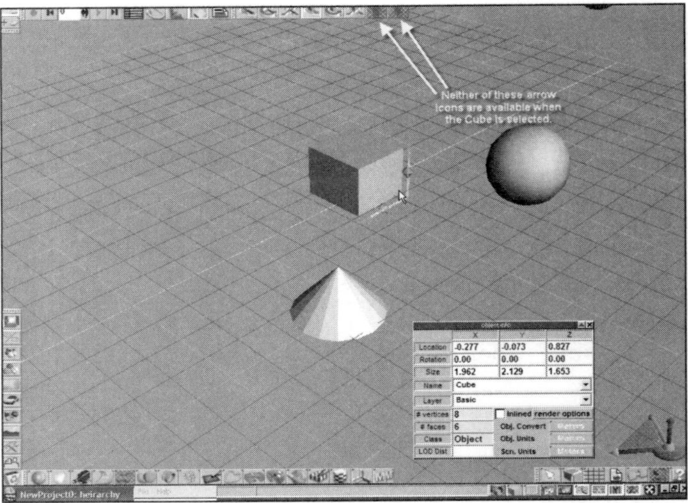

Figure 6.12
These arrow icons are used for navigating the hierarchy of compound objects.

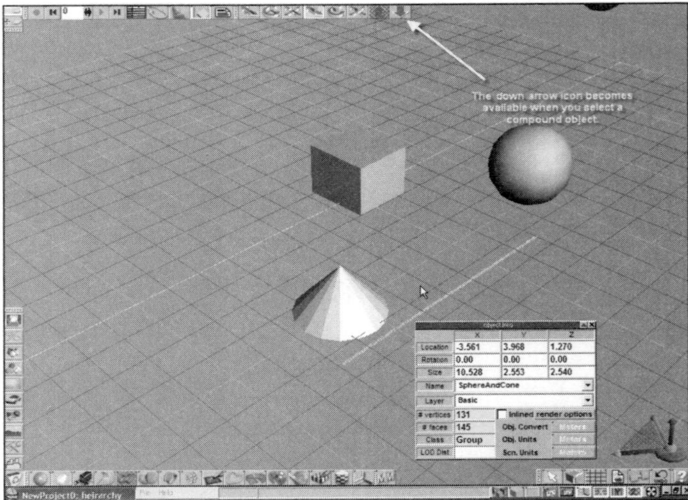

Figure 6.13
The Up Arrow and Down Arrow icons allow you to navigate up and down the hierarchy.

Use the Object Move tool, while working in this lower level of the hierarchy, to adjust the relative positions of the Cone and the Sphere. See Figure 6.14. When you are done adjusting the pieces individually, click the Move up in Hierarchy icon to return to the higher object hierarchy level.

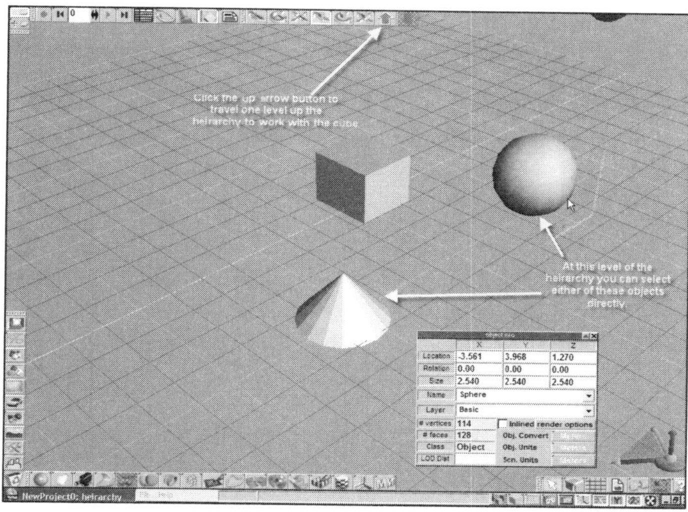

Figure 6.14
gameSpace is working at a lower level of the object hierarchy.

tip

You can use the Up Arrow and Down Arrow keys on the keyboard as shortcuts to move up or down the object hierarchy.

Use the Up Arrow to move back to the highest level of the object hierarchy. The SphereAndCone compound object should be selected. Activate the Glue as Sibling tool again and use the mouse cursor, which now looks like a glue bottle, to click on your Cube object. See Figure 6.15.

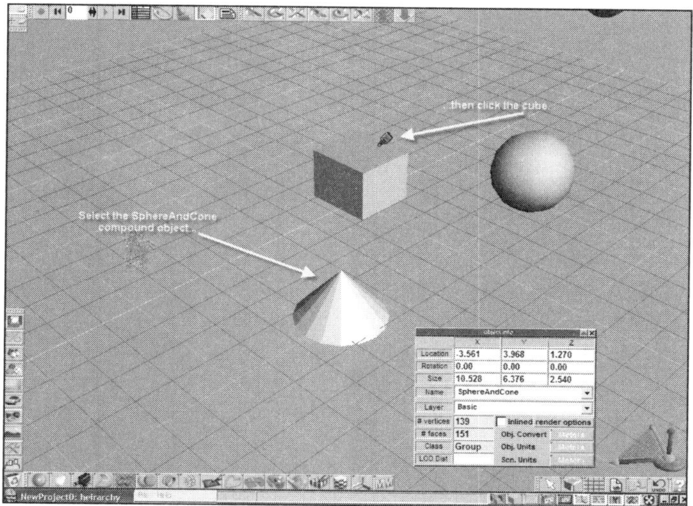

Figure 6.15
Gluing the Cube object into the SphereAndCone compound object.

You have just told gameSpace to add the cube to the existing compound object as an equal sibling of the Sphere object and the Cone object.

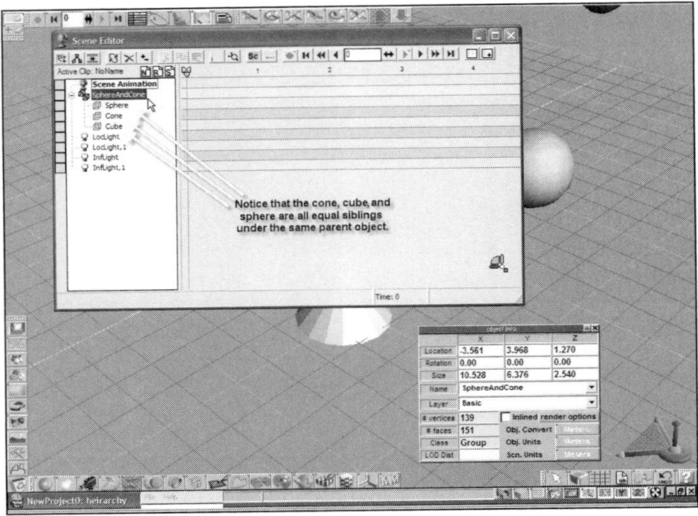

Figure 6.16
SphereAndCone now contains all three objects.

Open the Scene Editor to see how the Glue as Sibling tool connected the three objects. See Figure 6.16.

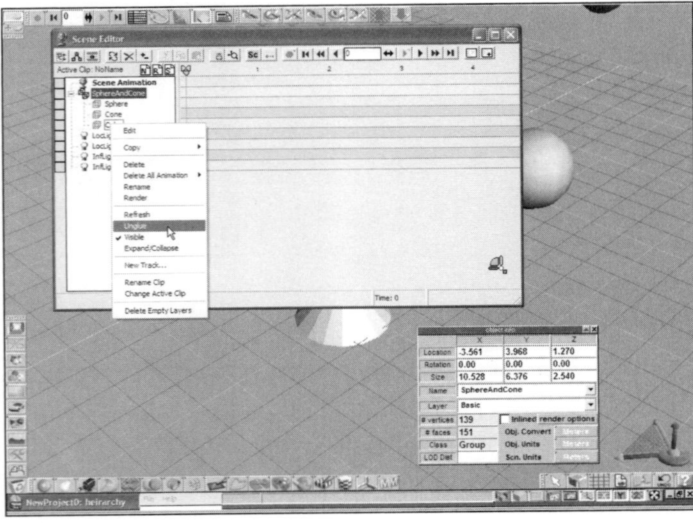

Figure 6.17
Unglue the Cube object by right-clicking on its name in the Scene Editor.

To continue the demonstration, you will need to remove the Cube object from the compound object. Do this by right-clicking on the name "Cube" in the Scene Editor and selecting Unglue from the pop-up menu that appears. See Figures 6.17 and 6.18.

Close the Scene Editor once more by clicking the X button in the corner of the Scene Editor window.

You will now glue the Cube object to the other two objects again, but this time you will reverse the order of the attachment. Start by selecting the Cube object, then activate the Glue as Sibling tool and click on the SphereAndCone compound object. See Figure 6.19.

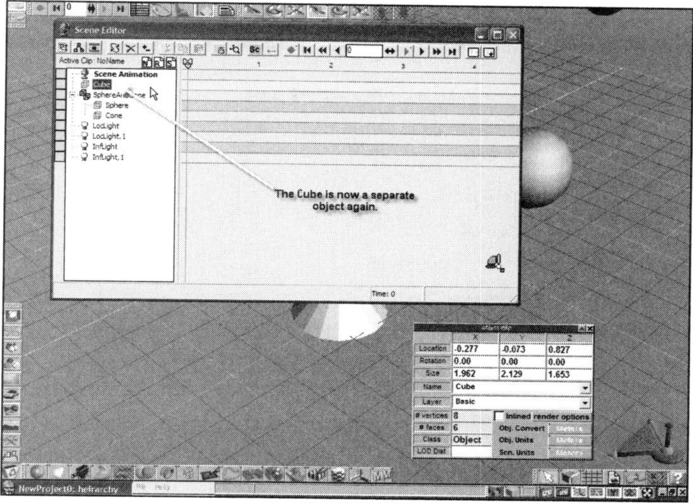

Figure 6.18
After the Unglue command, the cube is no longer part of the compound object.

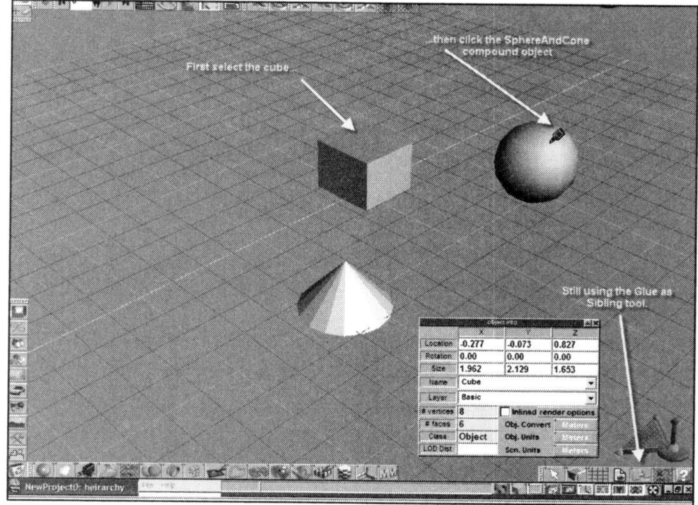

Figure 6.19
Glue the SphereAndCone compound object to the Cube object.

Open the Scene Editor to see the result of this glue operation. You will quickly see that that the order of selection makes a big difference. See Figure 6.20. This can be a source of confusion until you become comfortable with the process.

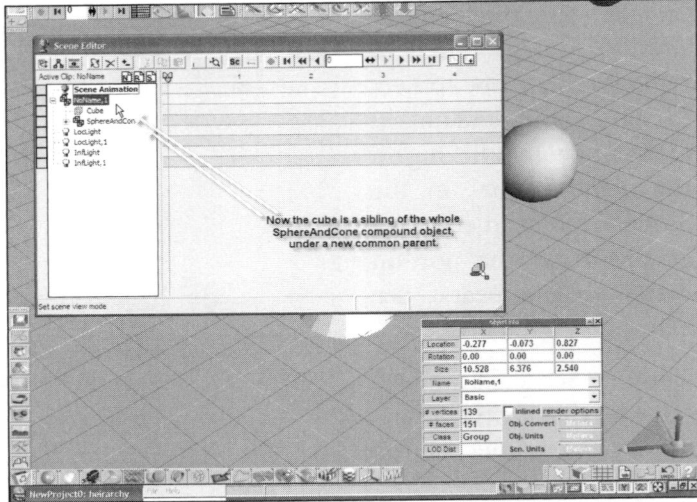

Figure 6.20
The SphereAndCone compound object has been glued to the Cube object.

In a sense, you have just created a new parent with two children. One child is the Cube object, and the other is the SphereAndCone compound object. This is the same result you would get from the Glue as Child tool, regardless of which object you chose first.

When you begin by selecting a simple noncompound object before using the Glue as Sibling tool, it behaves exactly as if you chose the Glue as Child tool. The Glue as Child tool, however, never combines the new objects into a single existing level of the hierarchy, regardless of the order in which you select the objects. See Figure 6.21.

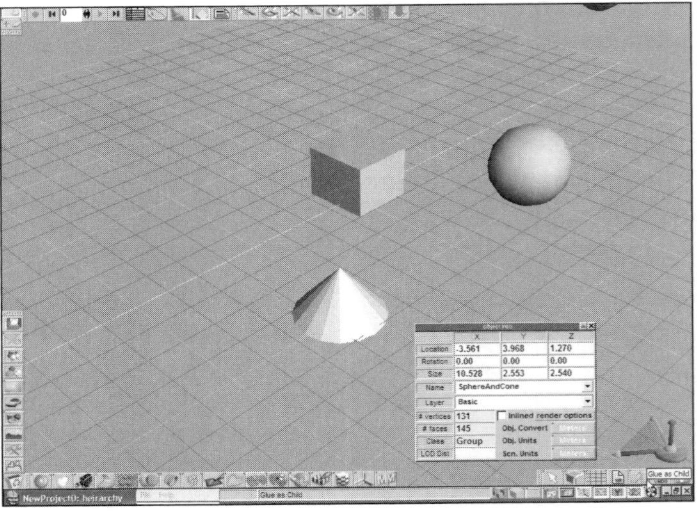

Figure 6.21
The Glue as Child tool always places the attached object into a lower level in the hierarchy.

Once again, unglue the Cube by right-clicking on its name in the Scene Editor and choosing the Unglue command. Notice that the new compound object NoName,1 disappears because there are no longer two or more sub-objects within it. Close the Scene Editor once again.

Try using the Glue as Child tool to join the Cube to the SphereAndCone object again. See Figure 6.22.

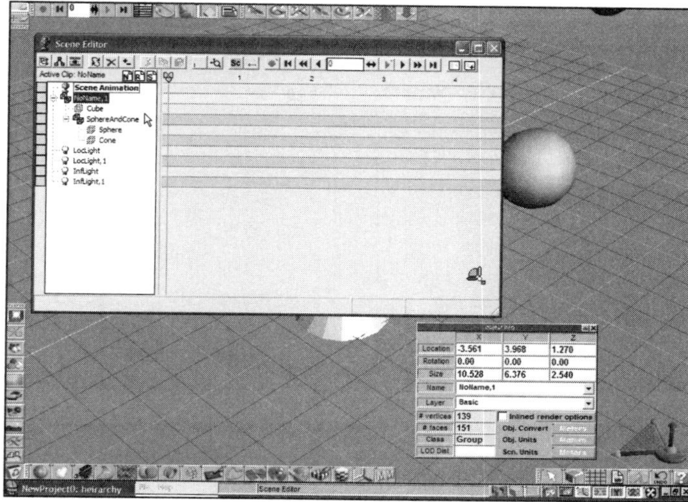

Figure 6.22
The results of the Glue as Child tool.

Moving the Camera

Before you close the scene with the cone, cube, and sphere, I will use them to demonstrate another important aspect of working with gameSpace. Be sure to unglue all three objects before continuing.

So far, the models you have built have been relatively simple. It has been pretty easy to select any of the pieces using the standard viewports. As your models get more complicated, it becomes more difficult to clearly see all the pieces.

gameSpace allows you to alter the viewing angle of any viewport. In the case of a Perspective or Camera viewport, you can reposition the camera or virtual eye anywhere around the scene.

Remember from Chapter 2, "The World of the Game Artist," that a Perspective viewport shows a view of the world as if it were viewed through the lens of an invisible camera or floating eye that is located somewhere within the scene.

> A Camera viewport is just like a Perspective viewport, but with a Camera viewport, the camera is not invisible. In other words, with a Camera viewport, you can actually see the viewport's camera represented as an object in all the other viewports. You can adjust the view displayed in a Camera viewport by moving and rotating its camera entity as it appears in the other viewports.

tip

In gameSpace any object can be used as a camera. To use an object as a camera, select the object and then choose the View from Object icon. If you have used the Camera icon to insert an actual camera, and you wish to see through that camera, you must select that camera object before choosing the View from Object icon.

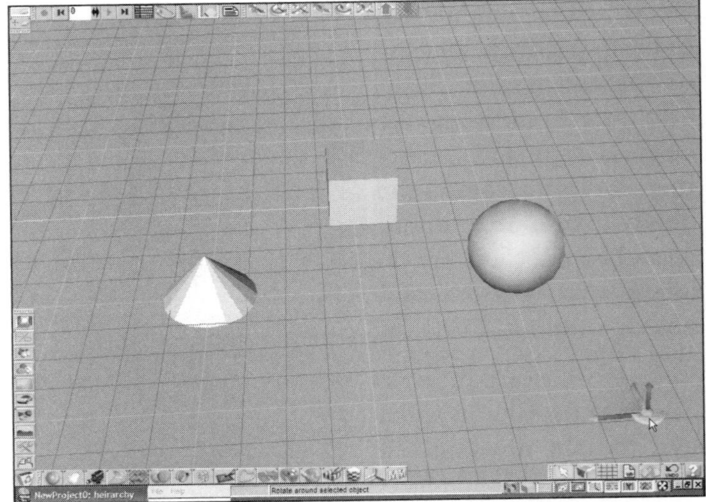

Figure 6.23
Use the 3-D navigation tool to rotate the viewport's eye around the selected object.

Even though a Perspective viewport's floating eye is not itself visible, you can still maneuver it around to find the best angle for the objects with which you are working. To adjust the eye of a Perspective viewport, use the 3-D navigation control near the corner of the viewport. See Figures 6.23 and 6.24.

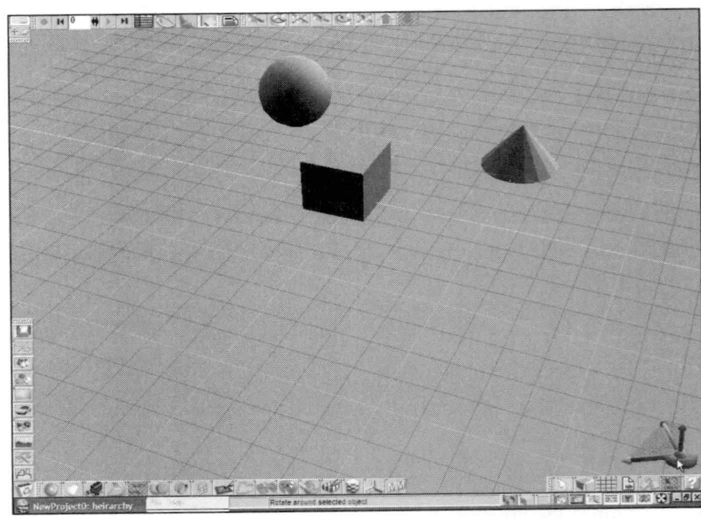

Figure 6.24
The eye of the viewport has rotated around the cube.

To rotate a Perspective viewport's eye around any object in your scene, select the object you wish to rotate around, and drag on the green washerlike ring at the base of the 3-D navigation control.

Try selecting the Cube then dragging the mouse up, down, left, and right over the large green ring in the 3-D navigation control. Every object in the scene should appear to revolve around your cube. Select the Cone object and try dragging the viewport around it in the same manner.

The 3-D navigation control offers several other ways to adjust the view. You can use the three rods that radiate from the hub of the 3-D navigation control to rotate the viewport around the global X, Y, and Z axes. See Figure 6.25.

Two semitransparent planes extend between these rotation rods. Drag the mouse across either of these planes to slide or dolly the viewport along the direction of that plane. See Figures 6.26 and 6.27.

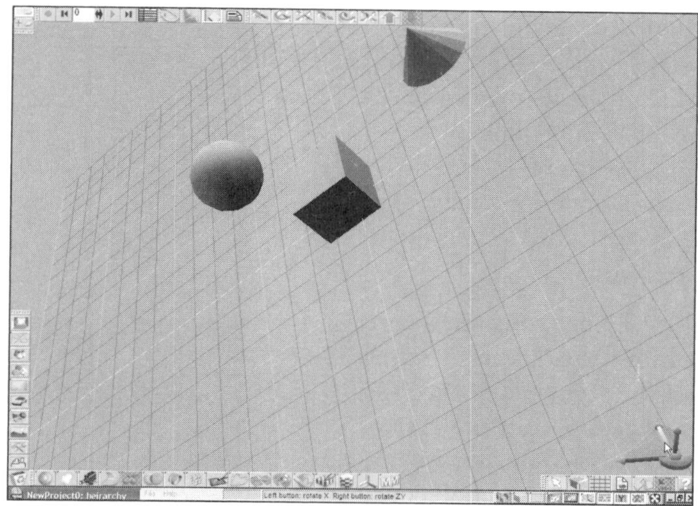

Figure 6.25
Drag the mouse over any of the three rods that extend from the hub of the 3-D navigation control to rotate the viewport along the world's X, Y, and Z axes.

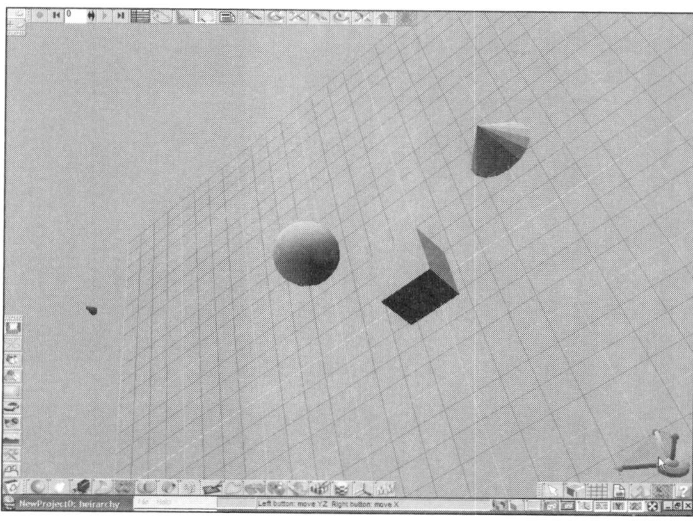

Figure 6.26
Drag the viewport up and down using this semitransparent plane.

You can also move the viewport's eye or camera directly in its own local X, Y, or Z directions by dragging over one of the three cones or arrowheads that point outward at the end of each rod.

Try flying your viewport around the objects using all of the segments of the 3-D navigation control. Try to imitate each of the viewing angles depicted in Figures 6.23 through 6.28.

tip

Orthographic viewports, such as the top, bottom, left, right, front, and back viewports, also have their own navigation controls, but in these 2-D viewports, the navigation control only pans the viewport horizontally and vertically, as in Figure 6.29.

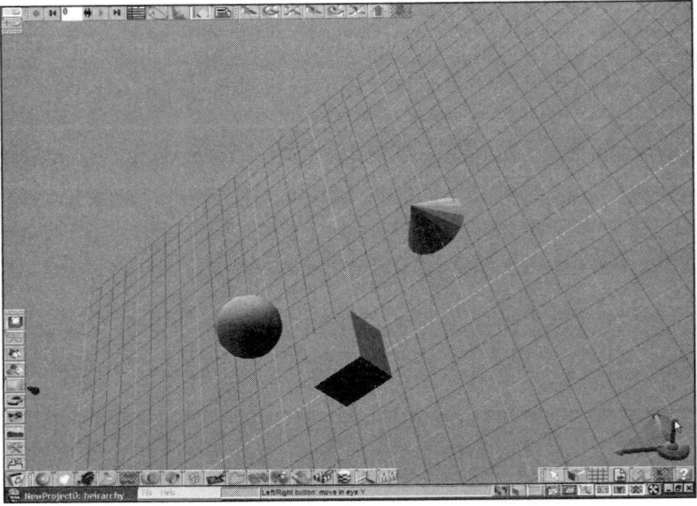

Figure 6.27
Drag these arrowheads to move the viewport's eye along its local X, Y, or Z axes.

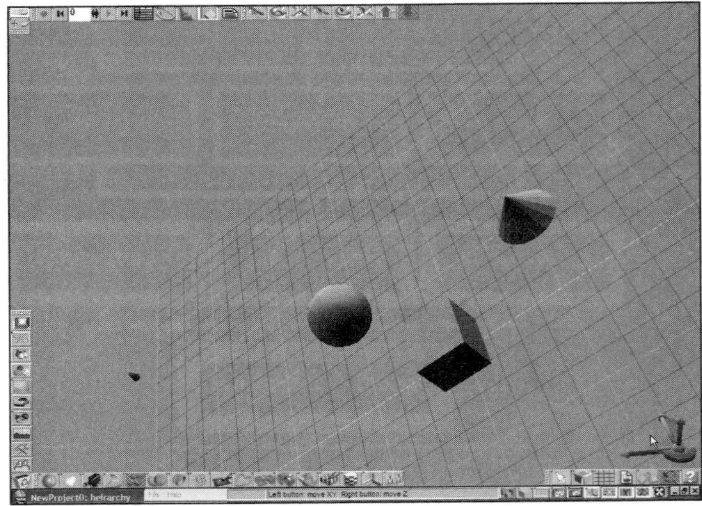

Figure 6.28
Drag the viewport in and out using this semitransparent plane.

Gluing All the Pieces

Now that you understand how to use the gameSpace glue tools, you are ready to glue together your raft. Use File > Load > Scene to reload the objects you built for your raft in Chapter 5, "Modeling with Geometry."

Use the Object tool to select your first log, then activate the Glue as Child tool, as shown in Figure 6.30.

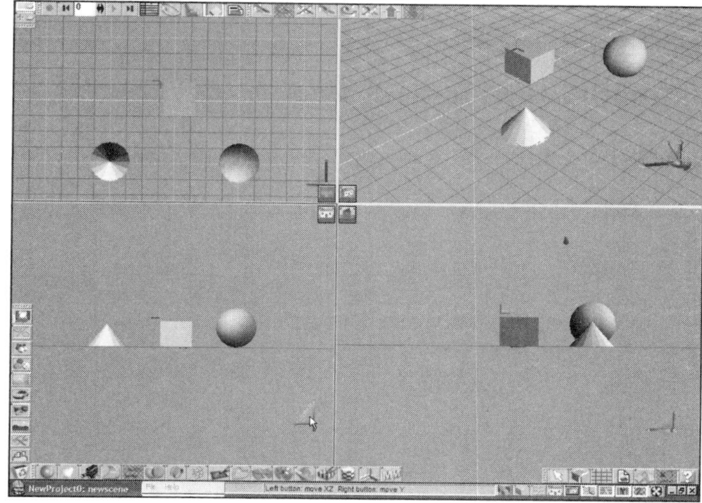

Figure 6.29
The two-dimensional orthogonal views have their own 2-D navigation tools.

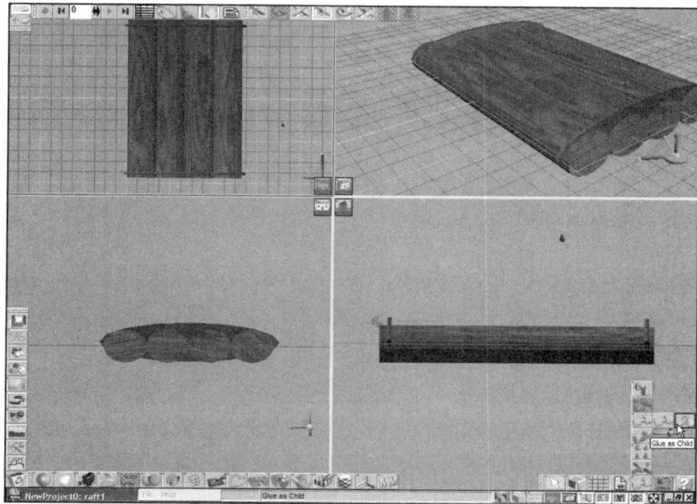

Figure 6.30
Use the Glue as Child tool to create a new group to hold the pieces of your raft.

Using the mouse cursor, which now looks like a small glue bottle, click on your second log, as shown in Figure 6.31.

You have now added a new level to your object hierarchy. You can see this using the Scene Editor. Click the Scene Editor icon near the top of your gameSpace screen to open the Scene Editor. See Figure 6.32.

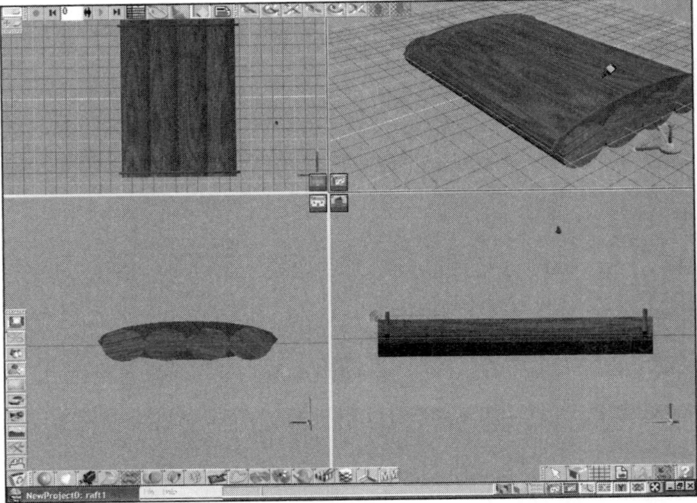

Figure 6.31
Use the small glue bottle to click on the second log.

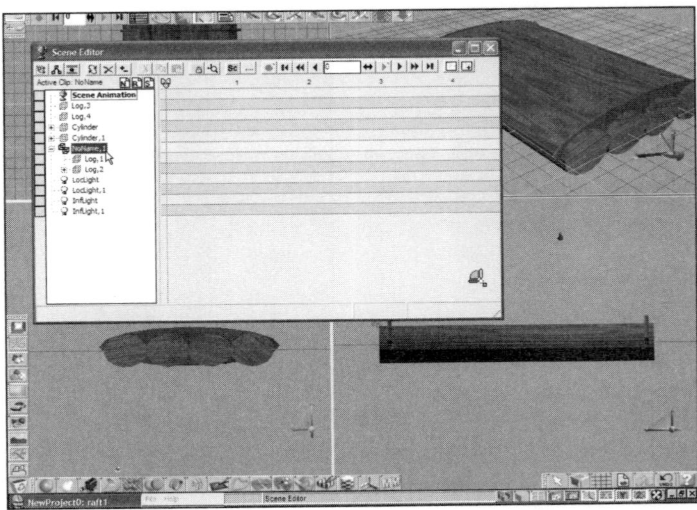

Figure 6.32
The Scene Editor now shows the new group in the object hierarchy.

Click on the new group name, NoName,1, once to see the two logs that make up the group. Click the group name again, and type in a new name. Name it something more meaningful, such as "Raft." See Figure 6.33.

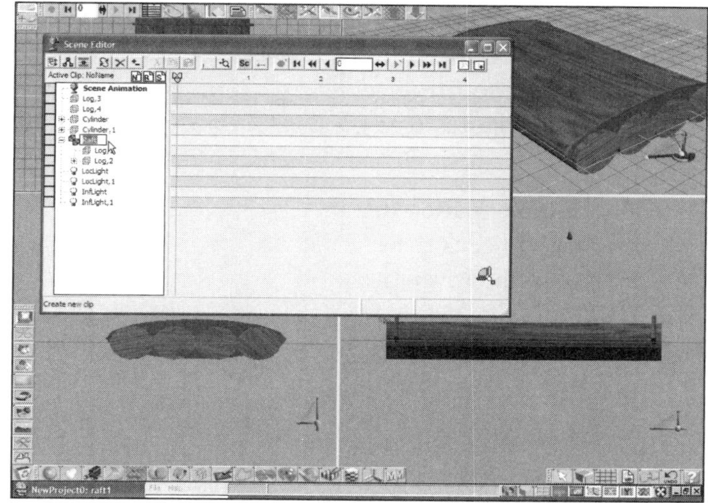

Figure 6.33
Rename the new group Raft.

Close the Scene Editor for the moment. Select either the first or second log. These both should already be part of the new raft object. With the Raft group selected, activate the Glue as Sibling tool, as shown in Figure 6.34.

This time, use the Glue as Sibling tool, because you want to add the rest of the logs to your existing Raft group. You do not want to create a new subgroup for the third and fourth logs, so you must be sure that you have selected the existing group first before activating the Glue as Sibling tool.

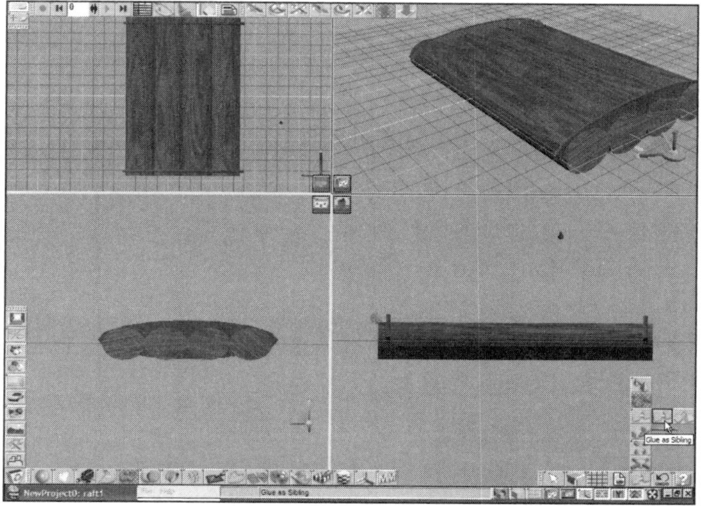

Figure 6.34
Change to the Glue as Sibling tool.

Use the little glue bottle to click on the third log. You can click on the fourth log now, too. See Figures 6.35 and 6.36.

It really doesn't matter in which order you click these last two logs, however, it will determine the order in which you can navigate between them once they are glued.

tip

The left-arrow and right-arrow keys on the keyboard can be used to navigate between two or more objects that are glued as siblings at the current level of the hierarchy.

Once you activate the Glue as Sibling tool, any logs you click on are added to the existing Raft group.

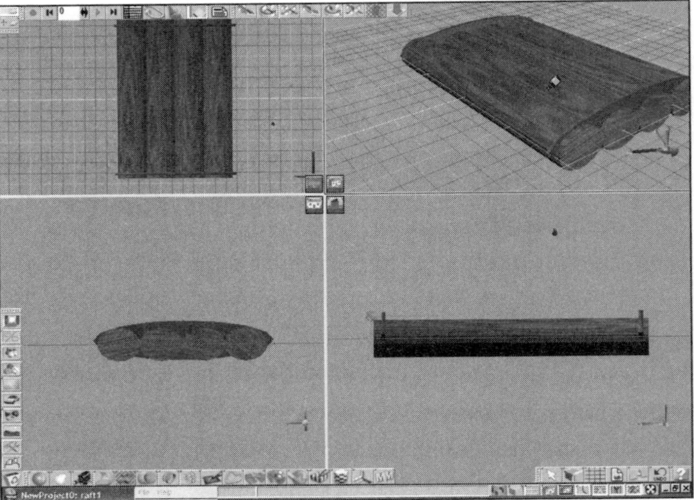

Figure 6.35
Using the Glue as Sibling tool, click on the third log to add it to the Raft group.

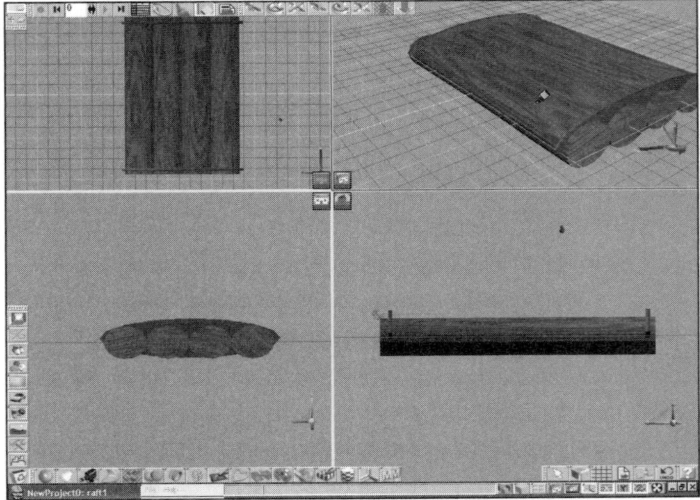

Figure 6.36
Click on the fourth log to add it to the Raft group, as well.

Click on the Scene Editor icon to see the new additions to the Raft group. See Figure 6.37.

Notice that the two remaining cylinders, your crosspieces, are still listed separately in the Scene Editor. They are not yet part of the Raft group. You could use the Glue as Sibling tool to add these, just as you added the logs, but don't.

There is another way to move objects in and out of any group using the Scene Editor. Simply click on and drag any object's name in the Scene Editor and slide it anywhere in the object hierarchy. You can even drag one object or group in or out of any other group.

Use this method to drag the cylinder objects into the Raft group. Click on the name of the first crosspiece and drag it until the mouse is directly over the name of the Raft group in the Scene Editor. Release the mouse button to drop the crosspiece into the Raft group. See Figure 6.38.

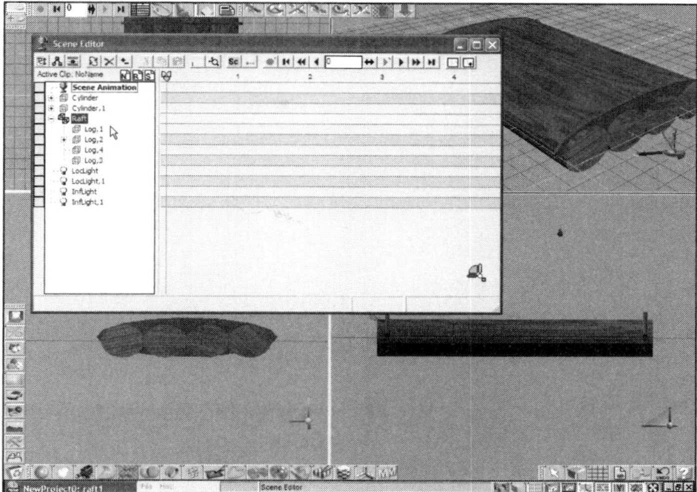

Figure 6.37
The Scene Editor shows all of the logs together in the Raft group.

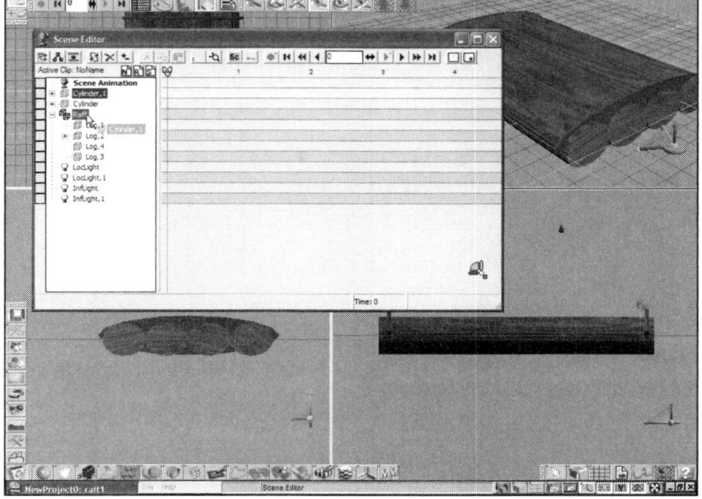

Figure 6.38
Drag one of the cylinder objects into the Raft group.

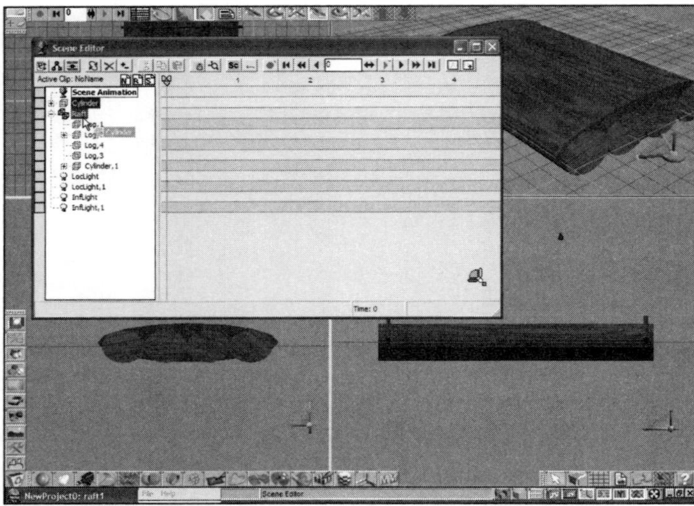

Figure 6.39
Drag the other cylinder into the Raft group in the same manner.

Add the second crosspiece in the same way. Click on its name, and drag it into the Raft object, as shown in Figure 6.39.

Use the Scene Editor to select the whole Raft group, and then close the Scene Editor. See Figure 6.40.

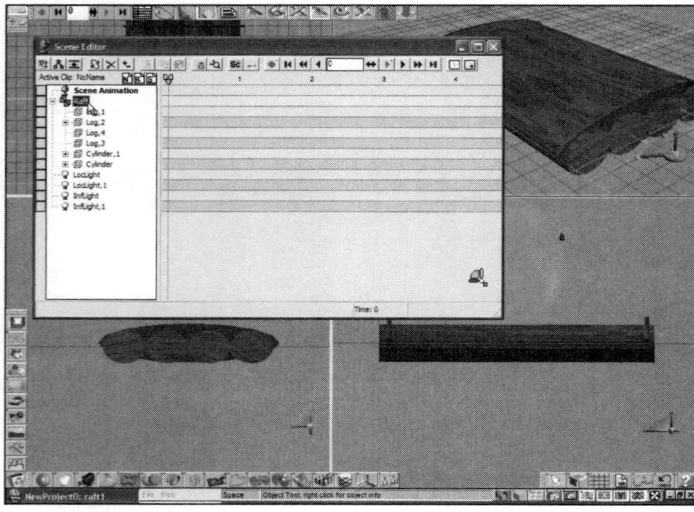

Figure 6.40
Select the whole Raft group by clicking its name in the Scene Editor.

Open the Object Info Pane, and adjust the location, rotation, and scale of the entire raft so that it appears as described in Table 6.1 and in Figure 6.41.

Table 6.1 Raft Object Parameters

	X	Y	Z
Location	0.0	0.0	0.5
Rotation	−90	0	52
Scale	7.37	8.87	15

All units and screen units are set in Points.

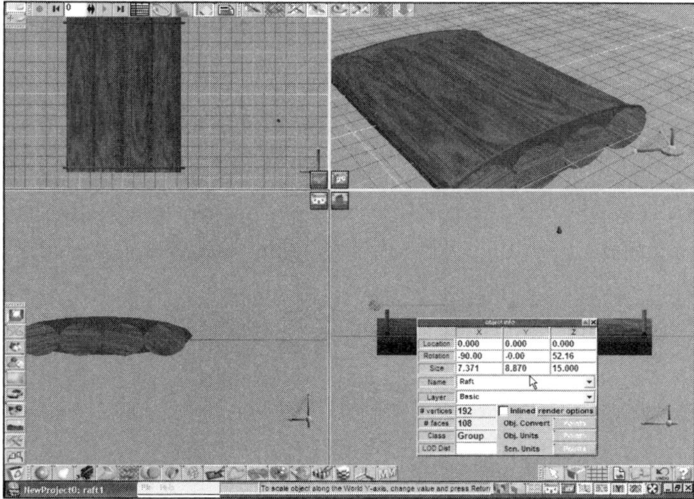

Figure 6.41
Your raft should look like this.

Crossing the River

Your raft is ready to float down the river, but you still need to save it and import it into the game. Use the File > Save > Scene menu command to save the entire finished scene.

Select the whole Raft object and use the File > Save As > Object menu command to save the object as a file named Raft.x. See Figure 6.42.

It is important that you are at the top of the object hierarchy before you save the object. It is very easy to forget where you are in the hierarchy, and save only a small section of your object. Remember to save the new object file into a separate Windows folder called Raft, as shown in Figure 6.43.

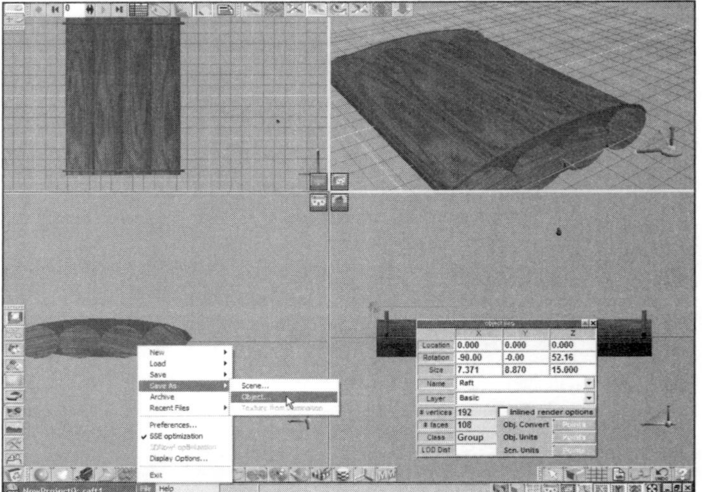

Figure 6.42
Save the whole raft as an object file.

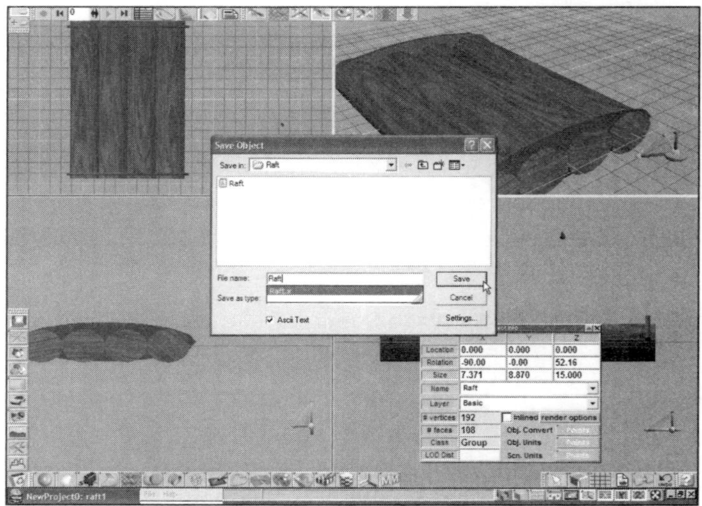

Figure 6.43
Save the raft as a DirectX .x file in its own folder.

Close or minimize gameSpace and launch the ObjectImporter. Use the ObjectImporter to replace the game's Object 1 with your new raft model. See Figure 6.44.

Close ObjectImporter and launch Adventure Explorer. Several clones of your new raft should appear floating up and down the river. If you scaled the raft correctly, there should be just enough rafts to serve as a series of moving steppingstones on which you can easily cross the river. See Figure 6.45.

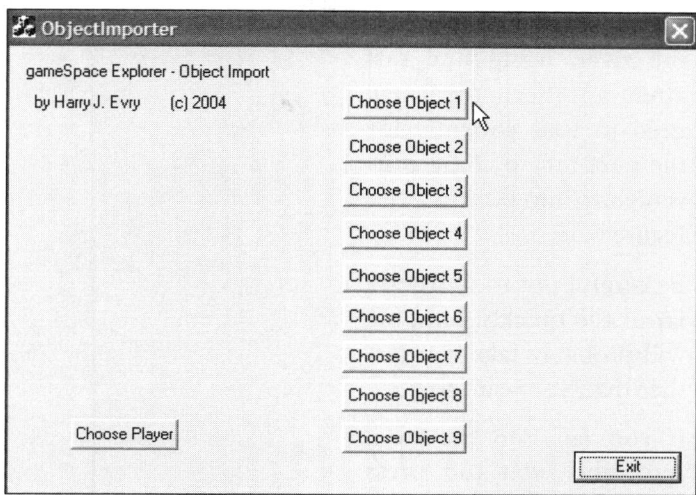

Figure 6.44
Use ObjectImporter to import your raft model as Object 1.

Figure 6.45
Several instances of your new raft float upstream and downstream in Adventure Explorer.

Try walking slowly across the river, using one raft after another. You may need to wait patiently for the next raft to come conveniently into position. See Figure 6.46.

Be careful not to move too far or too quickly. Jumping will probably take you farther than you want to go.

If you fall into the river, remember you can press the R key to restart the game.

Figure 6.46
Cross the river, raft by raft, one little step at a time.

Summary

In this chapter, you should have learned the following concepts:

- Compound objects are built by gluing together simpler objects.
- gameSpace's glue tools are used to join individual objects into groups.
- gameSpace organizes all of the objects in a scene into a hierarchy that is arranged like a family tree.
- gameSpace offers two different glue tools, the use of which allows you to specify how the newly connected objects should be arranged in the object hierarchy.
- The Scene Editor allows you to inspect and manipulate the entire object hierarchy.
- The name of every object in the scene appears somewhere within the Scene Editor.
- Conjoined objects appear embedded together beneath the same group.
- The Glue as Sibling tool joins an object into an existing group or level of the object hierarchy.
- The Glue as Child tool forces gameSpace to create a new level or subgroup.
- The Move up in Hierarchy and Move down in Hierarchy icons allow you to navigate up and down the object hierarchy.

- Objects and groups can be dragged around in the Scene Editor to alter their place in the object hierarchy.
- Objects and groups can be renamed in the Scene Editor.
- Objects can be unglued by right-clicking their names in the Scene Editor and selecting Unglue from the pop-up menu.
- The 3-D navigation controls allow you to adjust the position and angle of the eye in any Perspective viewport or Camera viewport.
- 2-D navigation controls allow you to pan around horizontally and vertically in any two-dimensional viewport.
- Any group that can be selected in the Scene Editor can be saved as a single object using the File > Save As > Object menu command.
- When using the Glue as Sibling tool, the order of object selection is significant.
- When adding an object to an existing group, select the existing group before activating the Glue as Sibling tool.

Questions and Answers

Q: What are the two gameSpace glue tools?

A: The two gameSpace glue tools are Glue as Sibling and Glue as Child.

Q: What is the keyboard shortcut to move down one level in the object hierarchy?

A: Use the Down Arrow key to move down one level in the object hierarchy.

Q: What does the green washerlike ring at the bottom of the 3-D navigation control do?

A: The green ring at the base of the 3-D navigation control is used to revolve the viewport's eye around the currently selected object.

Q: What should you select before you activate the Glue as Sibling tool?

A: Always select the group into which you wish to add the other object before activating the Glue as Sibling tool.

Q: What do the arrowlike cones at the ends of the rods in the 3-D navigation control do?

A: The cones on the rods in the 3-D navigation control move the viewport's eye in the direction of its own local X, Y, and Z axes.

Discussion Questions

1. Describe two different ways in which you can add an object into an existing level of the object hierarchy.

2. If you plan to glue together two primitive (noncompound) objects, does it matter which of the two objects you select first? Explain why or why not.
3. You wish to add a new finger into an existing hand group. What glue tool would you use? What would you select first, and why?
4. Describe two different ways to separate an object from an existing group.
5. How can you select one piece of a compound object without ungluing it from the compound object?
6. Describe the differences between the viewport navigation controls in the Perspective viewport and the viewport navigation controls in the Top viewport. Why are they different?

Exercises

1. Use gameSpace to create three spheres, and then use the Glue as Sibling tool to join them all together into a single level of the object hierarchy. The result should look like Figure 6.47.

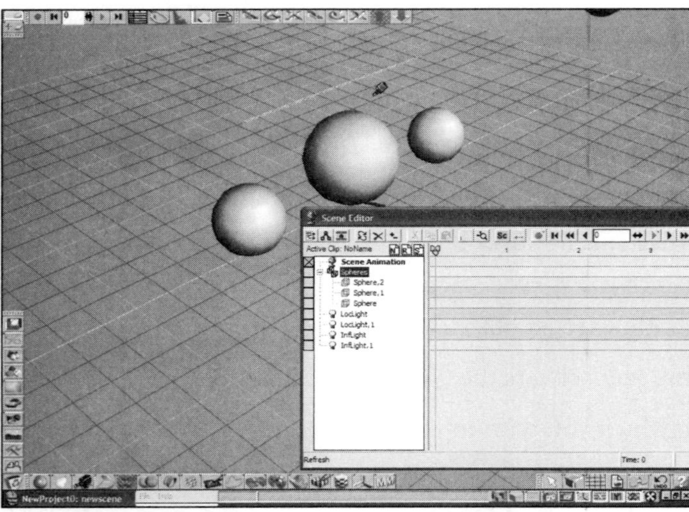

Figure 6.47
Join three spheres together in a single group.

2. Start a new scene, then use the Rounded Cylinder primitive tool to create two rounded cylinders. Position them as the two segments of a thumb. Use the glue tools to combine them into a new group, and name the group Thumb. See Figure 6.48.

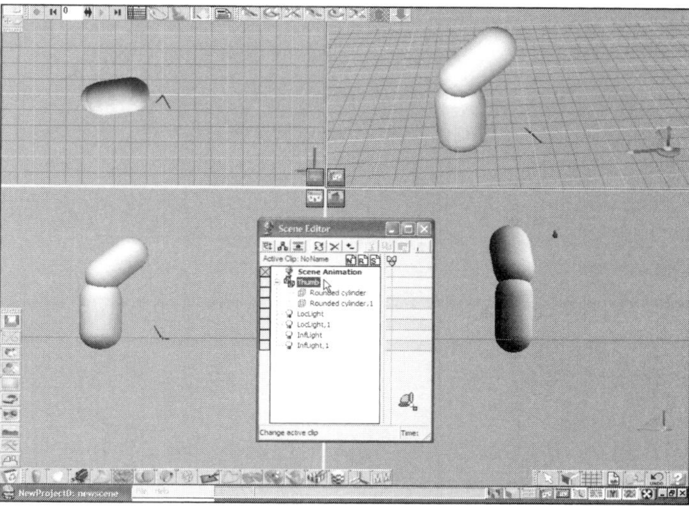

Figure 6.48
Glue two rounded cylinders together to form a thumb.

3. Create another rounded cylinder, and duplicate it twice. Position the three new primitives as if they were three segments of a finger. Glue the three pieces together as shown in Figure 6.49.

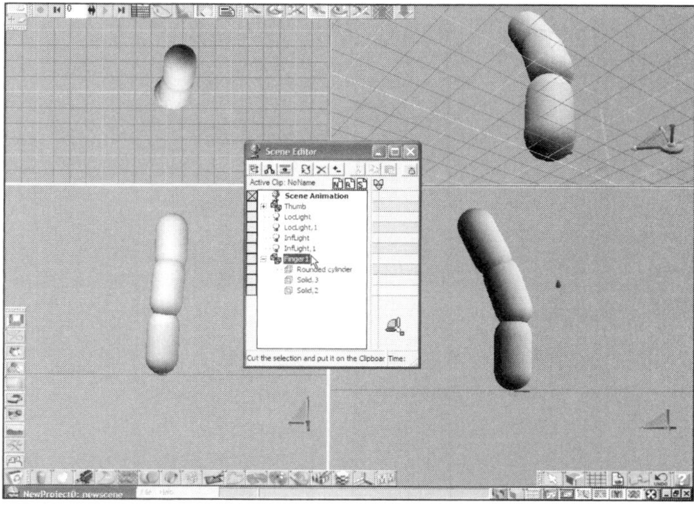

Figure 6.49
Glue three rounded cylinders together to make a finger.

4. Duplicate the finger group four times. Position, rotate, and scale all four fingers and the thumb so they appear as if they were part of a hand. See Figure 6.50.

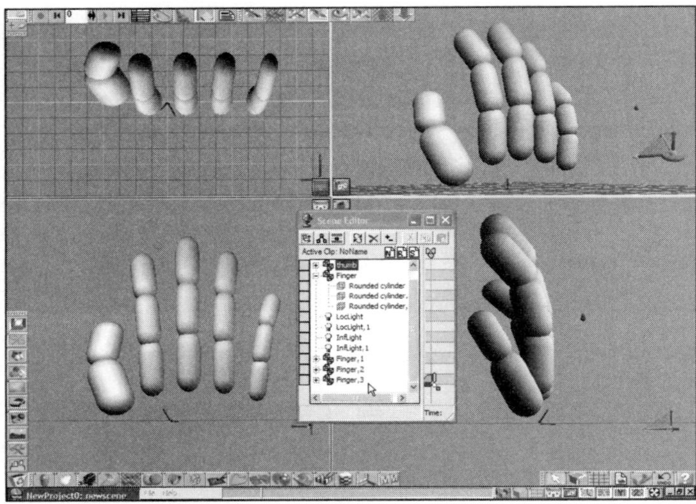

Figure 6.50
Arrange the five groups of rounded cylinders as if they were four fingers and a thumb.

5. Create a large rounded cube to form the palm of the hand, and then use the glue tools to attach the fingers and the thumb to the palm, as shown in Figure 6.51.

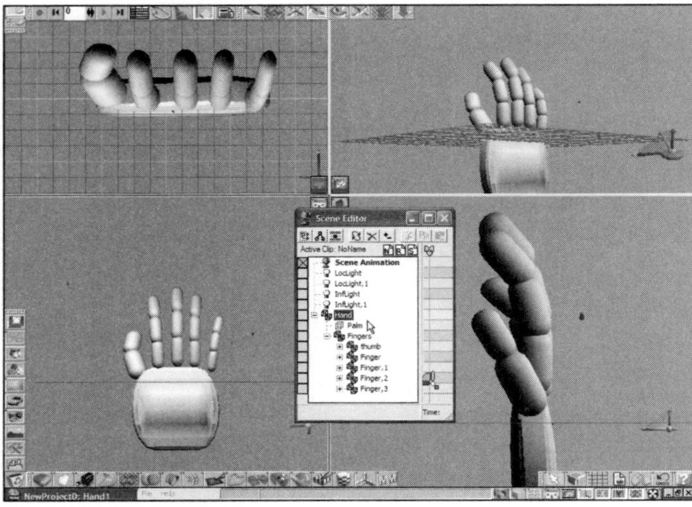

Figure 6.51
The final hand should be arranged like this.

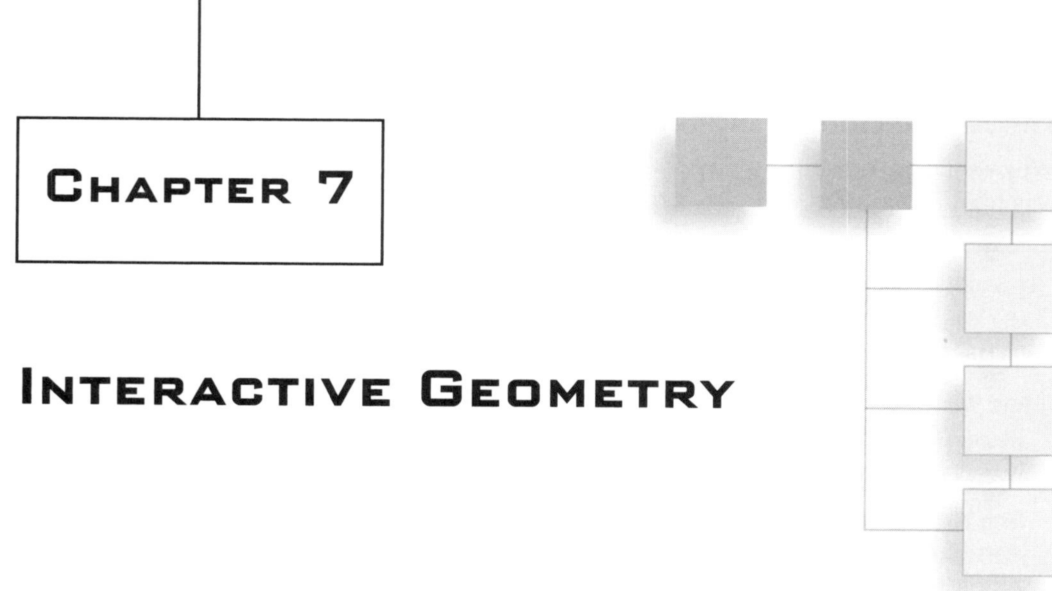

Chapter 7

Interactive Geometry

In the last chapter, you learned to build compound objects by gluing together simple primitives in a number of ways. You learned several ways to adjust the gameSpace viewports. You also learned how gameSpace organizes objects internally inside a scene, and how to inspect, manipulate, and reorganize any object, group, or subgroup within your scenes. This chapter will teach you to carve more intricate and geometrically complex models. It also showcases a number of useful tricks and techniques to help you create more realistic objects and environments for your games.

Introduction

With the help of your rafts, you can finally cross the river, but the far shore of the river offers little in the way of entertainment. As you gaze up in dismay, your eye catches the glint of some light escaping from a doorway to another chamber high above.

Priceless treasures might await you in that bright distant chamber. Unfortunately, the only visible route is a stairway overhead, which seems to stop much too short of reaching the ground. See Figure 7.1.

Figure 7.1
This staircase is a bit out of reach.

The Architecture of Interaction

Why would anyone build a staircase that doesn't reach the floor? Who would place a doorway high in the air?

> The Winchester Mystery House in San Jose, California, is a marvel of architecture and level design. Mrs. Winchester was the widow of an infamous gun maker and inventor and the heiress to the Winchester Rifle Company.
>
> Mrs. Winchester visited a psychic and was instructed to begin a project that would never be completed. Guided by the psychic, she began construction on an enormous mansion. She feared that immediately upon completion of her house, she was destined to die.
>
> With the help of her psychic, a small army of builders, and a very innovative architect, she spent years constructing one of the oddest homes in the world.
>
> The Winchester Mystery House has stairways that lead nowhere and columns that don't quite reach the floor. It has secret passages, trapdoors, and gaping holes in the floors. There is even a bedroom door that drops unsuspecting trespassers three floors down into an outside garden.
>
> The house was designed as an elaborate maze, built to ward off the spirits who Mrs. Winchester knew were eventually coming to take her away.

Several years ago, I was asked to teach a class in architectural design for videogame level designers. The class was originally proposed as a general survey of the history and principals of architecture. I spent a week considering how I might teach such a class, and finally reached the following conclusion: Level designers and architects have radically different needs and need radically different philosophies in designing their works.

Architects think about utility, organization, circulation, and statement. They design buildings to be sensible, efficient, attractive, safe, and impressive. Architects place doors where they are obvious and arrange rooms so that they are easily accessible and generally make sense.

Level designers think differently. Level designers think about challenge, confusion, defense, motivation, emotion, and containment. They design rooms with hidden uses, halls and tunnels that ramble, and vast chambers that serve no purpose but to get the player hopelessly confused and disoriented. Architects might design a building to make a statement, but level designers design their levels to tell a story.

Architectural storytelling is an art that is unique unto itself. This is the domain of art directors, show designers, level designers, and theme park Imagineers. Architectural storytelling involves architectural simulation but emphasizes emotion, illusion, and psychological manipulation.

A good level designer creates levels that support and enhance the overall illusion and function of the video game. A great level designer creates levels that motivate, inform, and propel the players along their paths. An epic level should draw the players deeper into the story, spirit, and false reality of the game world.

Rather than teach level designers to think like architects, the name of my architecture class became Architectural Storytelling and Environmental Simulation. I dispensed with the typical slides and blueprints and taught the class at Disneyland instead. Nowhere else on earth can you find better examples of architectural storytelling and environmental simulation.

Environmental Simulation

Game artists are not archeologists or architects. Building a precise and accurate model of an Egyptian pyramid or a Greek temple is great, but unless you are building a virtual tour or an exhibit for a museum, it probably does not belong in your game.

> My fiancée's brother, Geoff Prince, built a model of the Parthenon for a sixth-grade class project. The assignment was to build a model of a famous building. He had only one night to complete it, so he very creatively selected a building that he could model quickly. Searching through an encyclopedia, he found an old photograph of the Parthenon, which he used as a reference.
>
> Using dowels, salt, and flour, he meticulously recreated the historic Greek ruin. He proudly turned in the model, but his teacher took one look and said, "That doesn't look right. That is not a building." His teacher obviously knew the Parthenon from movies, paintings, and historical illustrations. The teacher expected the Parthenon to look like the grand monument that it was, and not the exploded ruin that it had become. The next day, Geoff's parents had him take in the picture from the encyclopedia to prove to his teacher that he really had faithfully recreated the legendary building.
>
> Like Geoff, a game artist can create the most accurate reproduction of a place, time, and setting only to find they have disappointed their players. Accurate depictions of reality often fail to meet the players' own unrealistic expectations.

Game artists strive to create a mental picture of a real civilization, place, or time, but only as long as that picture doesn't compromise or interfere with the visual story of the level or the creative vision of the game.

> ***Lifting* is my word for the process of capturing and replicating the most critical aspects of a real world object or setting and infusing them into a game level in a manner that efficiently sells the illusion of the original object, place, or time.**

Video games are works of interactive fiction. As works of fiction, games are not constrained to reality. Players rightfully expect their games to be more interesting, creative, and entertaining than any true reality. The game artist's challenge is to sell the illusion of a real and consistent place or time, while inflating and mutating that reality into something more inspiring, dramatic, interactive, and entertaining.

I created an acronym to describe the key ingredients to consider when lifting an environment:

L Layout
I Important features
F Forms
T Textures
E Environment
D Dressings

Layout refers to the overall arrangement of the most significant objects and paths through an environment. Important features are those things that are immediately obvious when first viewing the environment. Forms refer to the general shapes of these important features. Textures are the apparent materials that make up the prominent structures and features. Environment refers to the setting's overall lighting, conditions, and predominant background sounds. Dressings are the most obvious furnishings, fixtures, wall and floor coverings, items, decorations, relics, and artifacts.

By carefully incorporating these six critical aspects of a real-world setting into your game level, you can create a believable simulation of that culture, period, and location. By staying true to these most critical aspects of the original setting, you are free to distort and manipulate the rest of the level to best serve the functional needs and creative vision of your game.

Putting the Level to Work

The stairway in Figure 7.1 is an example of how a game level can motivate game play. The bizarre placement of the staircase requires the player to find a way up the wall. An architect would build a longer staircase or perhaps a wheelchair ramp.

A level designer would see this as a challenge for the player and an opportunity for game play. The goal of a level designer is not to find the most elegant solution to a problem, but to find the solution that is the most fun for the player.

> Rolly Crump, the world-renowned art director and Disney Imagineer, presents a wonderful seminar entitled "Follow the Fun." Rolly uses countless personal stories to demonstrate that some of his and Disney's most creative, popular, and memorable ideas came from a very simple strategy: Find something that seems fun, invest a bit of time in it, and follow where it may lead you.
>
> In this spirit, Walt Disney ordered Rolly and Yale Gracey, a fellow Imagineer, to spend many months playing in a large dark room. They spent days experimenting with projectors, mirrors, illusions, lights, mechanical rigs, air compressors, and various ghostly effects. Years later, their work would be the basis for most of the effects in Disneyland's popular Haunted Mansion attraction.

Rolly tells a hilarious story of a poor superstitious janitor who found their haunted playroom very unsettling. The maintenance department finally had to demand that Rolly and Yale leave the room lights on and the effects off each night, if they wanted the janitor to clean their lab. Dutifully they complied and left on all the lights. Unfortunately for the janitor Yale had been experimenting with position sensors and triggering devices. That night as the janitor swept the center of the room, the room lights went out, the effects turned on, ghosts filled the room, and a giant inflatable sea captain began dancing off the ground.

The next morning Rolly came into the lab to find the lights off, the ghosts floating, and a hastily discarded broom lying in the center of a half swept floor. Dick Irvine the vice president of Imagineering informed Rolly that "the janitor had left the building and was never coming back."

You will add a fun challenge to Adventure Explorer by assembling a not-so-obvious staircase out of a series of crates. You will climb up to the ledge by jumping from crate to crate, with each new crate larger than the last.

Building a Crate

Create a new scene by selecting File > New > Scene. Use the primitive tools to create a cube. Open the Object Info Pane by right-clicking on the Object tool, and set the cube's parameters as shown in Table 7.1 and in Figure 7.2.

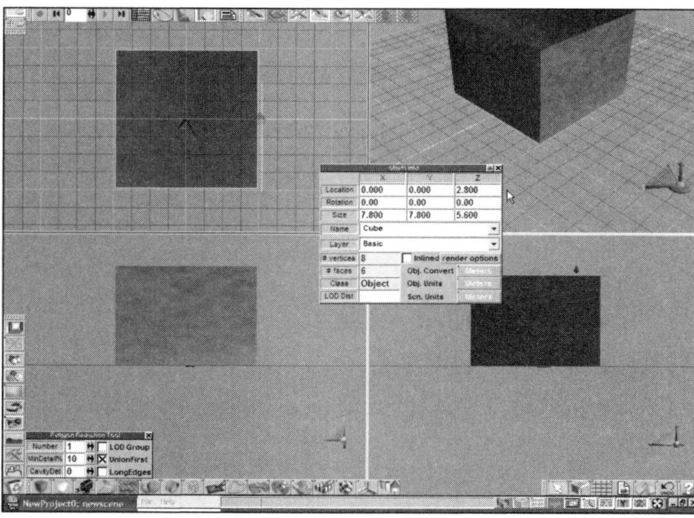

Figure 7.2
A crate begins with a simple cube.

Table 7.1 Crate Object Parameters

	X	Y	Z
Location	0.0	0.0	2.8
Rotation	0	0	0
Scale	7.8	7.8	5.6

All units and screen units are set in Points.

A crate in its simplest form is just a cube, but it would seem odd that such a simple crate could be strong enough to hold much weight. To give the crate a sense of strength, you need to add some construction detail. This can be done in many ways.

You can create a set of cross-beams and use the glue tools to build a compound object, just as you built the raft. The results of this approach are shown in Figure 7.3. However, you will build your crate another way.

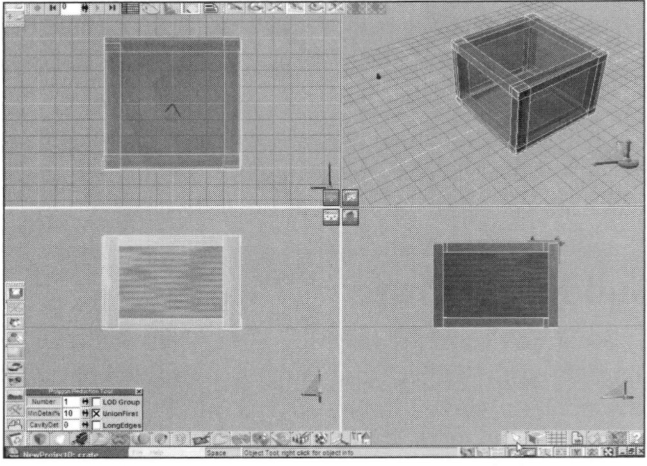

Figure 7.3
One approach involves gluing four wooden beams to each side of the crate.

Wallpapering the Crate

Open the Material Library by clicking on the icon that looks like a bowl of painted balls. Select the Caligari material that shows a picture of Caligari's logo. See Figure 7.4.

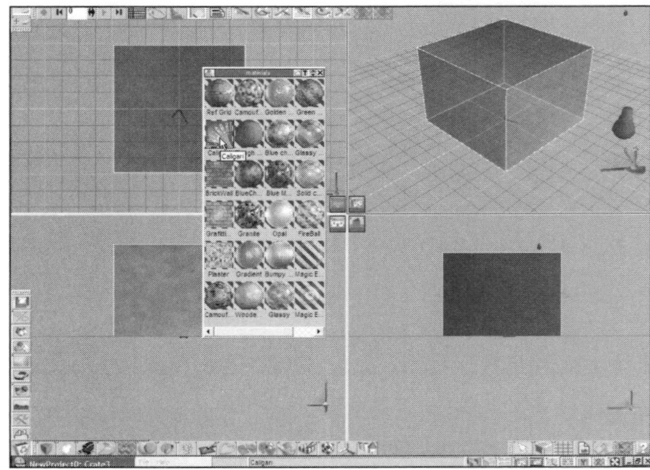

Figure 7.4
Choose the Caligari material from the Material Editor.

Double-click the Caligari material to open the Material Editor, then click the Color: texture map button near the top of the Material Editor. See Figure 7.5. This button displays the Material Editor's Color panel without expanding the entire Material Editor.

In the Color panel, click the large button labeled with the name CALIGARI. See Figure 7.6.

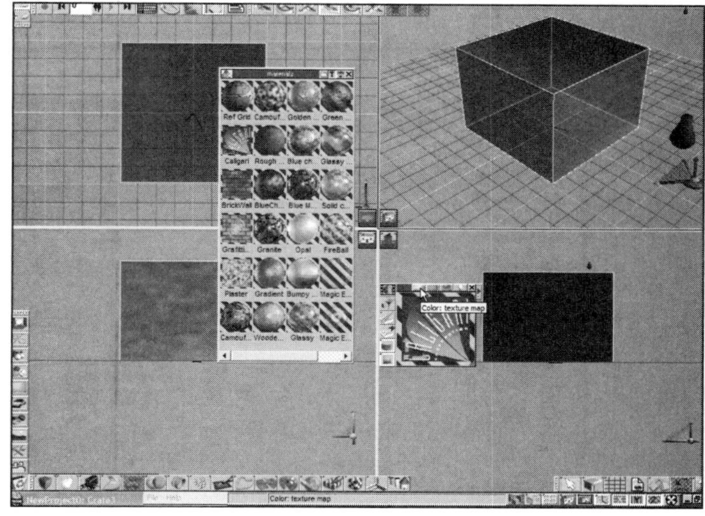

Figure 7.5
Click here to display the Color panel.

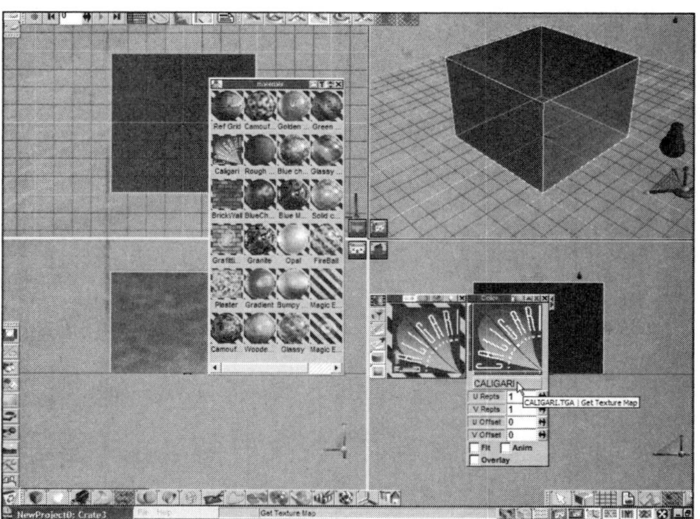

Figure 7.6
Click this button to select a new texture image.

This button allows you to replace Caligari's logo with an image from any other bitmap file. The Texture Browser, shown in Figure 7.7, allows you to navigate to any image file on your system.

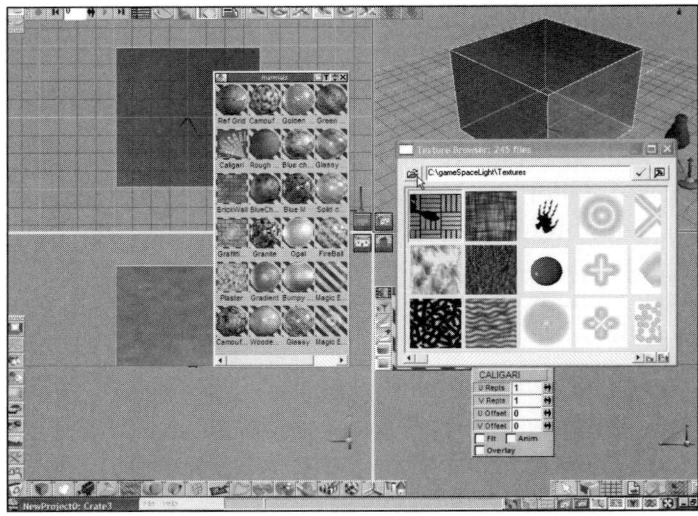

Figure 7.7
Use the Texture Browser to explore the image files on your system.

Bitmap texture files can come from any source. You can find many great texture images on the Web. You can also photograph your own textures using a digital camera or make texture images using any image-editing software. Adobe Photoshop is probably the most popular image-editing tool in use today. Corel Photo-Paint, Discreet Combustion, Macromedia Fireworks, and Adobe After Effects all offer fantastic tools that can help you create a huge variety of texture images.

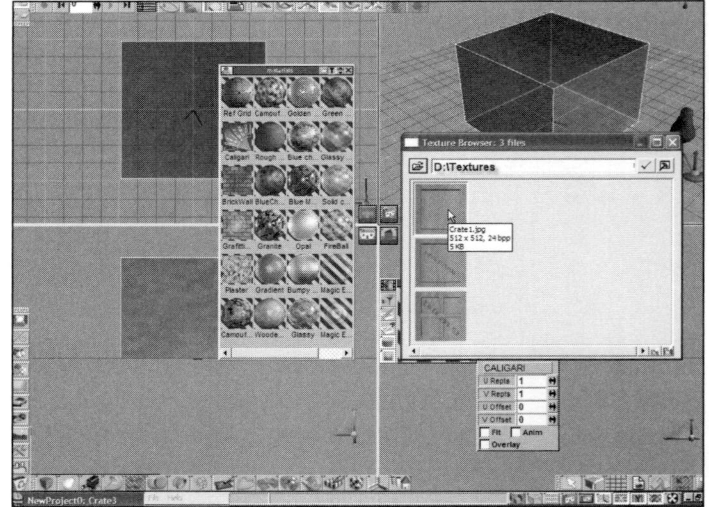

Figure 7.8
Choose the Crate1.jpg file from the Textures folder of the companion CD.

Other powerful, but often overlooked, tools for texture creation are 3-D programs such as gameSpace, Caligari trueSpace, or Discreet 3D Studio Max. Any program that can render its output to a bitmap file can be used to create a texture.

Use the Texture Browser to select the Crate1.jpg file, which can be found in the Textures folder on this book's companion CD. See Figure 7.8.

> **Base textures are the primary prototypical textures that make up a level. In order to maintain consistency in their levels, many game artists create a small set of base textures and then modify them to make a much larger set of variations of each base texture.**

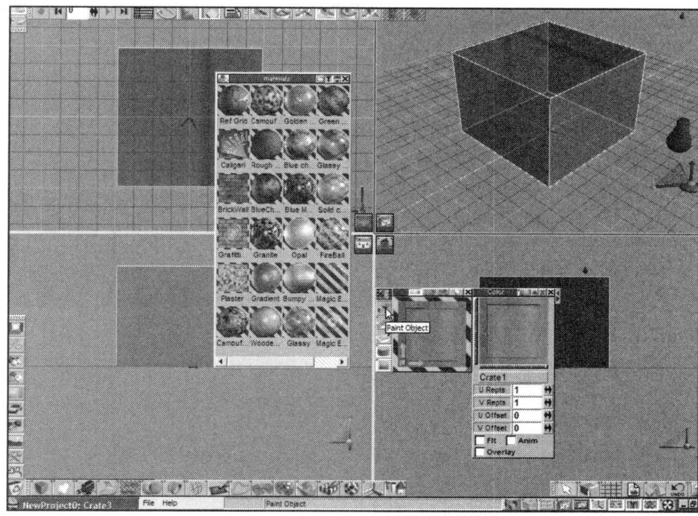

Figure 7.9
Use the Paint Object tool to apply the material to the cube.

I created the various Crate texture files using CorelDraw and Corel PhotoPaint. Crate1.jpg is the base texture. The other Crate .jpg files are variations on this base texture.

Click the Paint Object icon on the left side of the Material Editor to apply the crate texture to the cube, as shown in Figure 7.9.

Activate the Cubic UV Projection tool to apply the texture evenly on every side of the cube. See Figure 7.10.

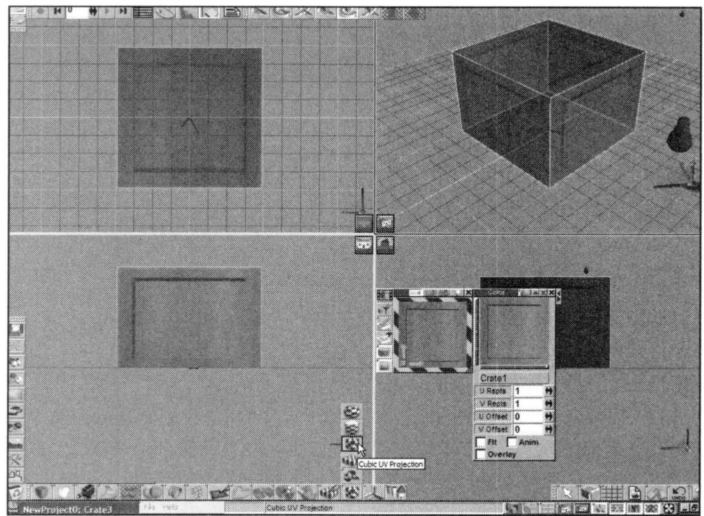

Figure 7.10
Activate the Cubic UV Projection tool.

Testing the Crate

Save the scene by selecting File > Save As > Scene, and then save the crate as a DirectX object file. See Figure 7.11.

Remember to save the crate in its own folder. See Figure 7.12.

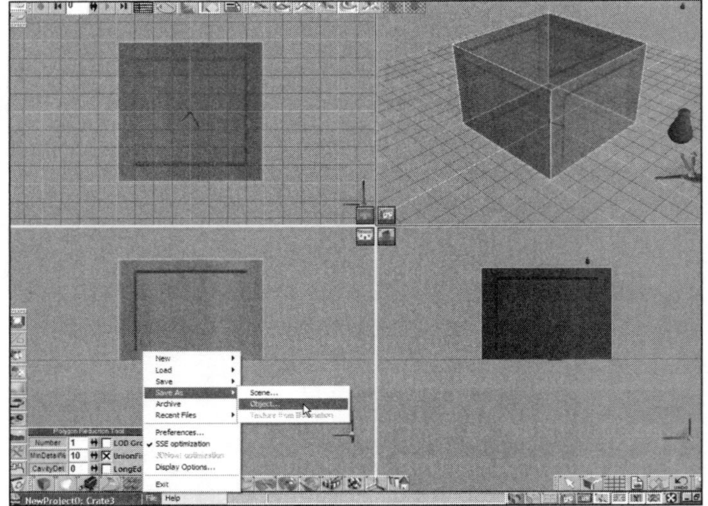

Figure 7.11
Save the object as a DirectX .x file.

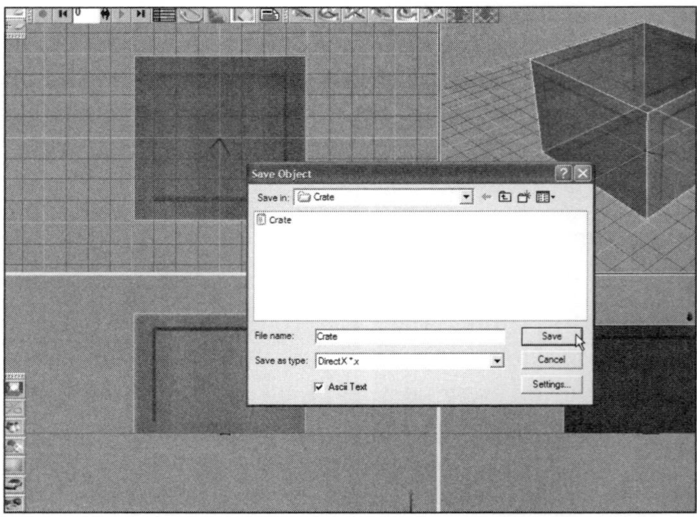

Figure 7.12
Save the Crate file in its own folder.

Close gameSpace, and launch ObjectImporter. Click the Choose Object 2 button, as shown in Figure 7.13.

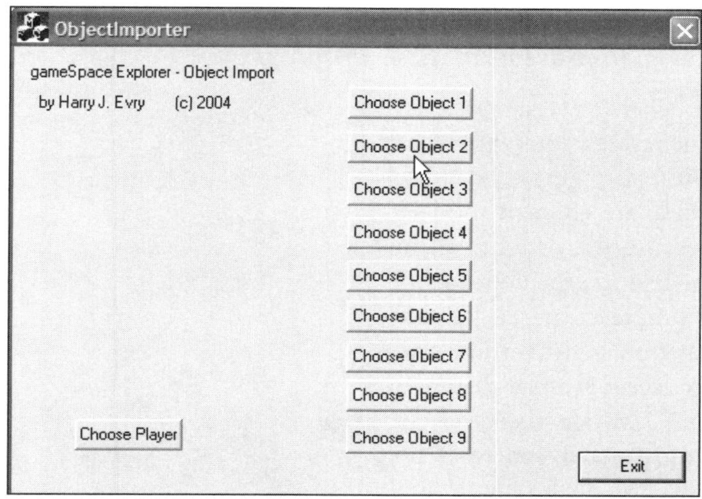

Figure 7.13
Use ObjectImporter to replace Object 2.

Find your Crate model, select it, and confirm the selection. See Figure 7.14.

Figure 7.14
Browse to your Crate model.

Close the ObjectImporter and launch Adventure Explorer.

Cross the river and try to push around some crates. If you find it too difficult to cross the river, try pressing the left bracket ([ ) key. Programmers often build secret shortcuts into their games to save themselves time while they are developing new games. Sometimes these backdoor shortcuts remain enabled even after the game is released.

Figure 7.15
Try shoving the painted crates around the level.

Figure 7.15 shows the crates in Adventure Explorer.

The crates look all right until you get very close. These are efficient models. Because the detail is all in the texture, the crate is still a simple cube. Each crate has only eight vertices and six faces. From a distance, this works very well. Unfortunately, there is no way to push the crates without getting very close. As you push against the crates, their lack of physical detail becomes obvious.

The programming team loves you because your crates are so efficient, but your art director and producer decide the crates deserve some more polygons. Stop playing games and get back to work.

Exit Adventure Explorer and return to gameSpace. If necessary, reload the scene for the crate.

Carve Out Some Faces

Have you ever carved a pumpkin? Every Halloween, millions of boys and girls draw silly faces on a big orange fruit. Some kids use a knife or chisel to carve out the pumpkin guided by these bold painted lines. gameSpace objects can be sculpted in much the same way.

You will use the crate's texture as the guidelines on the pumpkin. Unlike pumpkins, gameSpace objects can be carved with incredible precision and accuracy.

Boolean Subtraction

Figure 7.16 shows a cube and a sphere.

In Figure 7.17, the sphere has been repositioned so that it intersects and protrudes from the side of the cube.

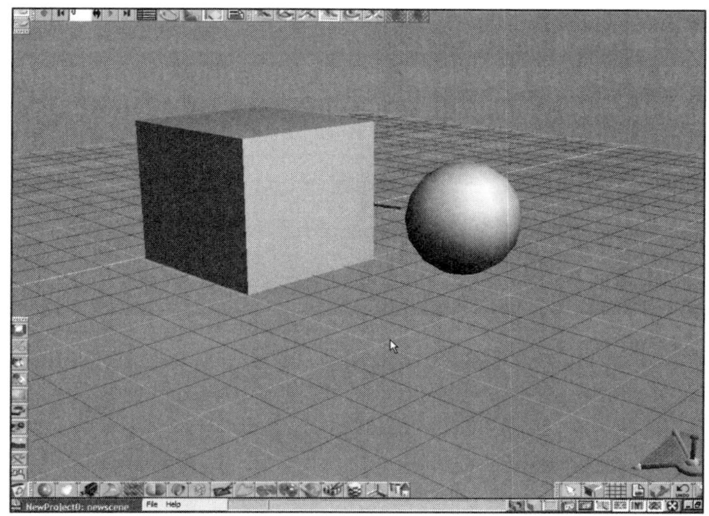

Figure 7.16
A cube and a sphere.

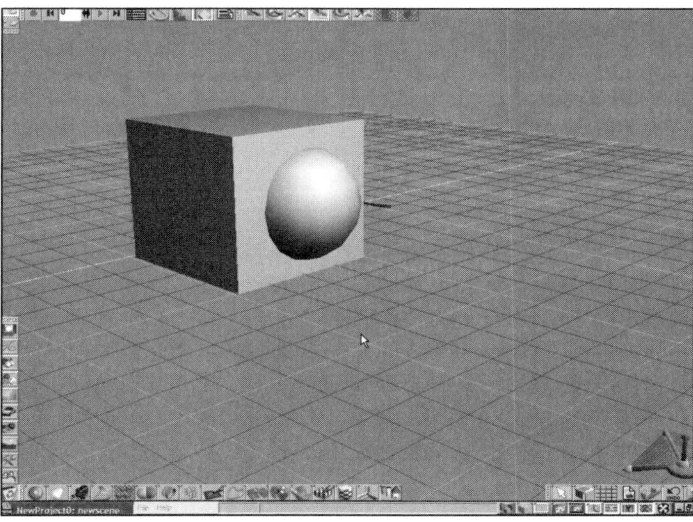

Figure 7.17
The sphere intersects the cube.

If the sphere is Boolean subtracted from the cube, the cube will have a hole in it wherever the sphere once appeared, as in Figure 7.18.

Boolean subtraction is a mathematical operation in which the entirety of one solid object is removed or drilled away from another solid object.

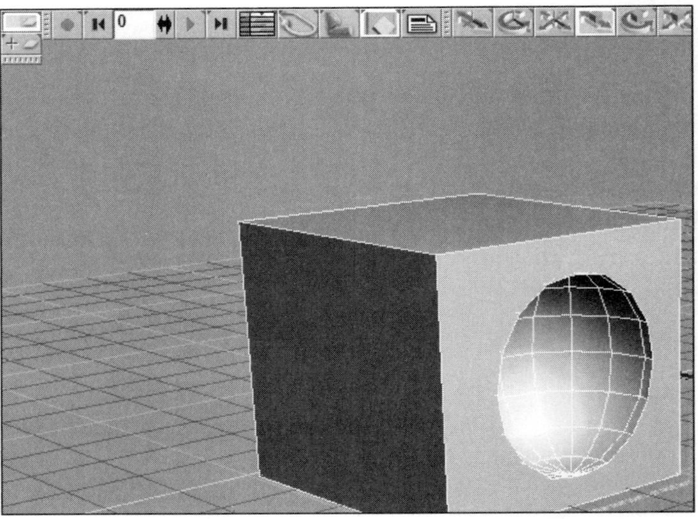

Figure 7.18
The sphere has been Boolean subtracted from the cube.

Mathematically, you would write: Cube – Sphere = CubeWithHole. Like any subtraction operation, the result is different if you reverse the order of the operands. In arithmetic, the formula 2 – 1 is not the same as 1 – 2. Subtraction of geometry works the same way. In Figure 7.19, you see another cube and another sphere.

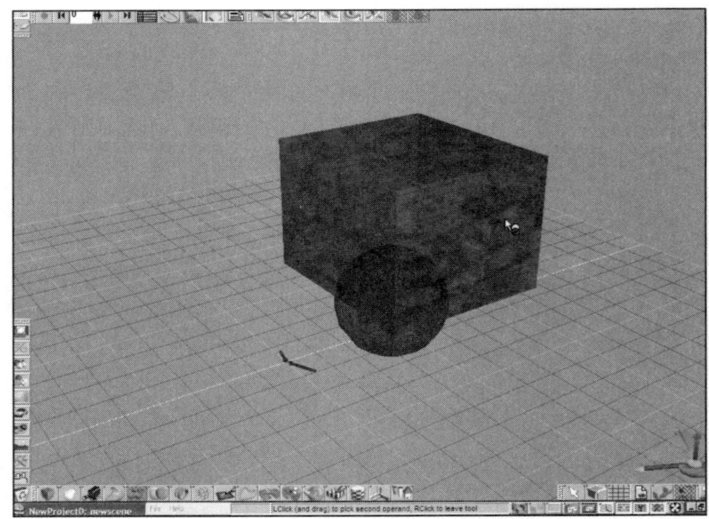

Figure 7.19
A sphere protrudes from the bottom of a cube.

The sphere is placed partially beneath the cube so that it sticks out from the bottom. This is similar to the arrangement used in the previous example. This time, however, the cube is subtracted from the sphere, instead of subtracting the sphere from the cube. The result is shown in Figure 7.20.

Mathematically, you would write: Sphere – Cube = PartialSphere

You can use Boolean subtraction to carve the inset regions out of the crate object.

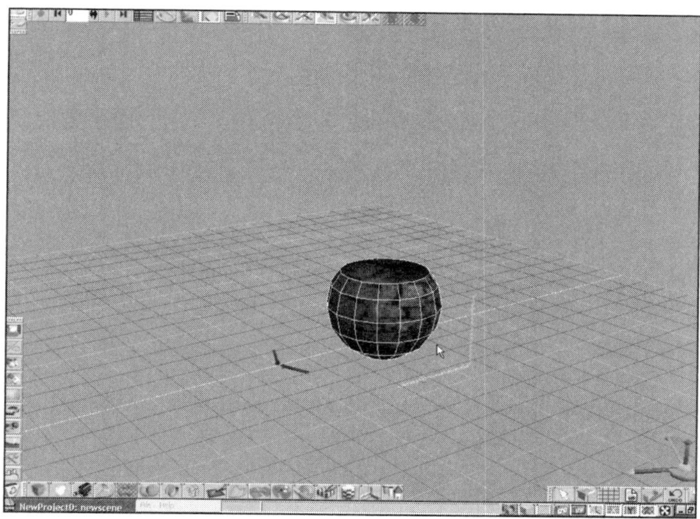

Figure 7.20
The cube has been Boolean subtracted from the sphere.

X-Ray Vision

Performing the next steps is much easier if you can look through the objects you are carving. gameSpace allows you to set the transparency of the objects in every viewport.

Figure 7.21 demonstrates how you can make all the objects in the active viewport transparent with a wire-frame outline.

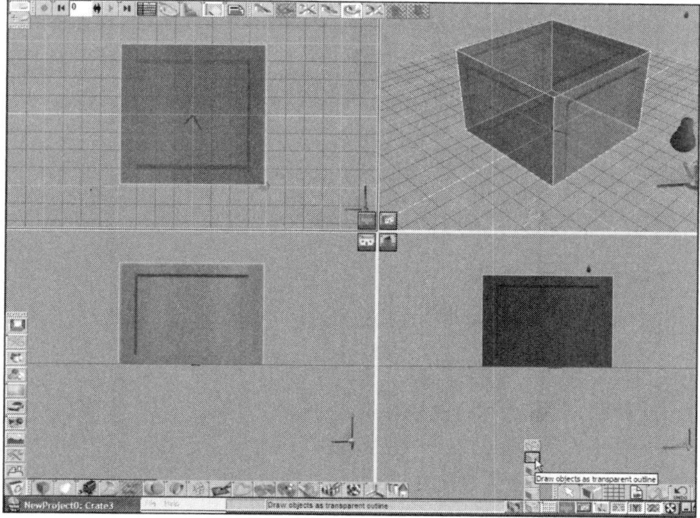

Figure 7.21
Click in each of the viewports and use this icon to make the objects in that viewport transparent.

The icons in this toolbar slot allow you to choose between the following configurations:

- Draw Object as Wire Outline
- Draw Object as Transparent with Outline
- Draw Object as Solid with Outline
- Draw Object as Transparent
- Draw Object as Solid

Remember that you can set the transparency or opacity of each viewport individually.

tip

It is often helpful to keep one of the viewports solid while the others are transparent. This gives you all of the advantages of working with transparent viewports, but helps eliminate confusion about whether one object is behind, inside, or in front of another.

Get Out the Drill

There is no standard chisel or drill shape in gameSpace. In gameSpace, you can use any solid object as a drill to carve a hole in another object.

In order to precisely carve out the inset that is outlined in the crate texture, you will create a new rectangle that precisely matches the inset lines in the texture image.

Activate the cube primitive tool to create a new cube. Working in the top viewport, place the mouse pointer on the upper-left corner of the dark painted inset lines in the crate texture. Click and drag the mouse down and to the right, until it is over the lower-right corner of the inset lines. See Figure 7.22. Do not release the mouse yet.

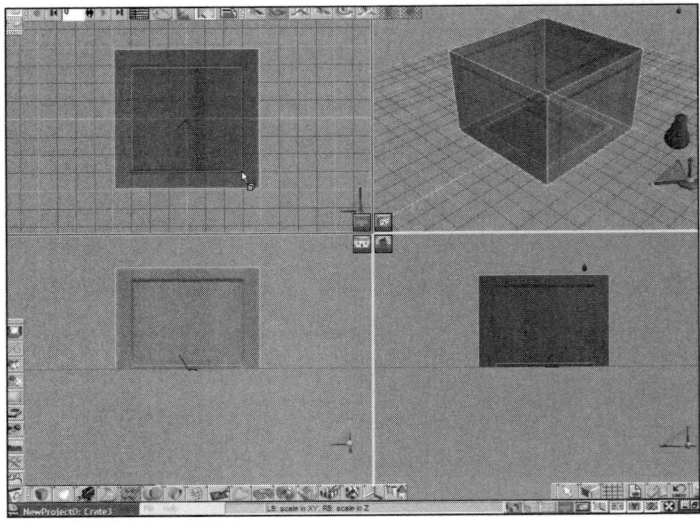

Figure 7.22
Create a rectangle that is aligned with the texture's painted inset rectangle.

Without releasing the left mouse button, press down on the right mouse button and drag the mouse upward to stretch the cube in the vertical direction. Release both mouse buttons when the new cube is similar in shape to the one shown in Figure 7.23.

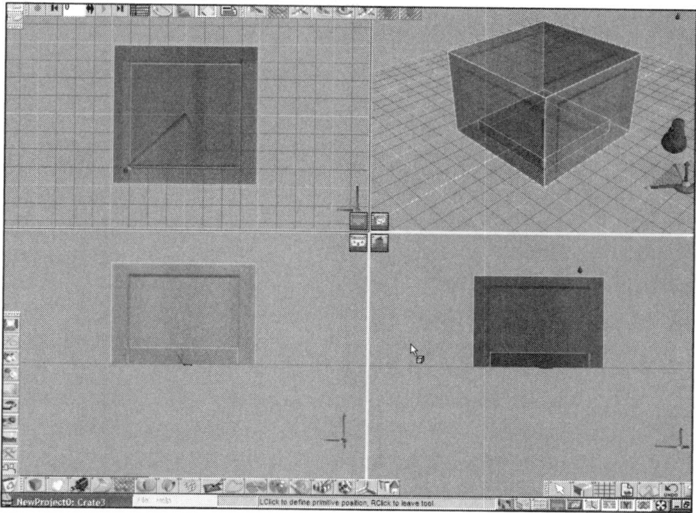

Figure 7.23
Right-click and hold to inflate the cube in the Z direction.

Bring On the Magic Ring

You have already seen the colorful rings that appear whenever you create a new primitive object. gameSpace calls these the Magic Ring controls.

tip

The Magic Rings disappear the moment you select any other object or tool. Once the Magic Rings go away, you can only bring them back by deleting the new primitive and creating it again.

The Magic Ring controls are the colorful rings that appear around a new primitive the moment it is created. The rings allow you to adjust various parameters of the new primitives by clicking and dragging over each individually colored segment of the rings.

The various segments of the Magic Rings are color-coded by function. Find the green segment of the new cube's Magic Ring controls. The green segment adjusts the height of the new primitive. Don't be confused when the green segment turns yellow once it becomes active.

Note the pop-up hints that appear when your mouse hovers over any segment of the Magic Ring controls. These tips tell you the two possible functions of that segment.

tip

Each of the various colored segments of the Magic Rings has two different functions. Depending upon which mouse button you click, you can select either the first or the second function of that segment.

Click and drag upward on the green segment of the Magic Ring, as shown in Figure 7.24.

The new cube should line up with the crate object, as seen in Figure 7.25.

Preparing the Cut

If you were to subtract the new cube from the crate now, you would have a hollow crate. Of course, there is no advantage to having hollow crates in Adventure Explorer, and this would needlessly create a lot of extra vertices and faces.

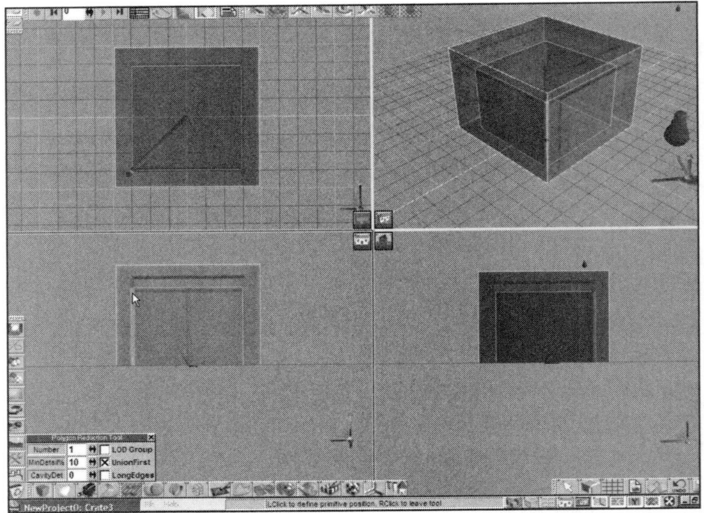

Figure 7.24
Drag on the green segment of the Magic Ring.

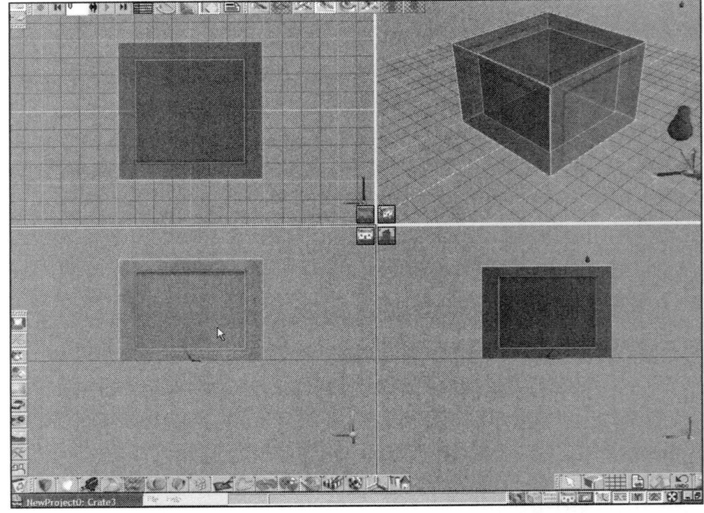

Figure 7.25
These cubes are properly aligned.

Select the Move Object tool. Press the A key to disable movement along the X axis, and use the top viewport to drag the new cube downward into the position shown in Figure 7.26. Be sure that it overlaps slightly into the side of the crate object.

Choose the Object Subtraction tool from its slot in the toolbar at the bottom of the screen. The Object Subtraction tool can be found in the slot directly above the File menu. See Figure 7.27.

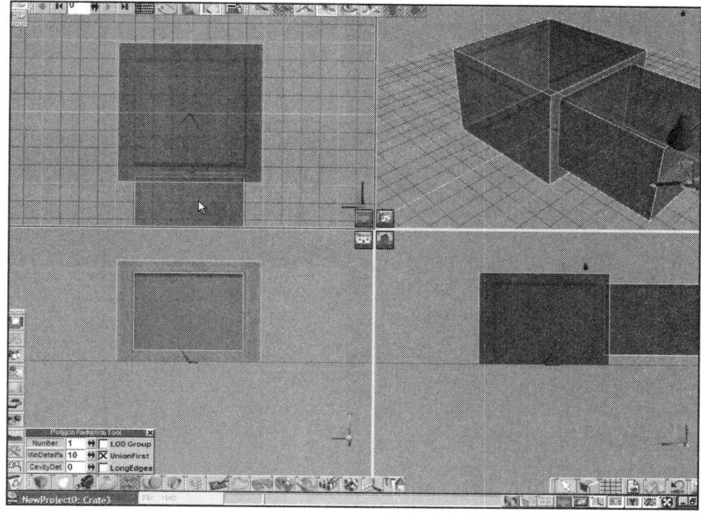

Figure 7.26
Drag the drill cube downward in the top view.

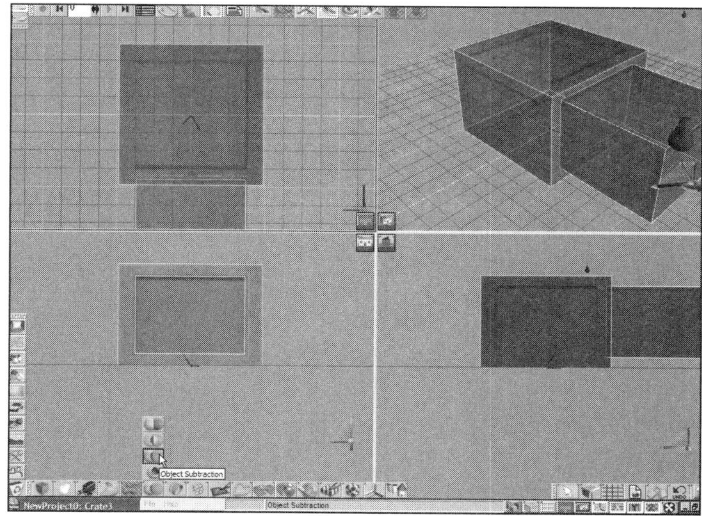

Figure 7.27
Activate the Object Subtraction tool.

A number of options are available when using the Object Subtraction tool. Right-click the Object Subtraction icon, to open the Boolean panel. Be sure the four check boxes are set as indicated in Figure 7.28.

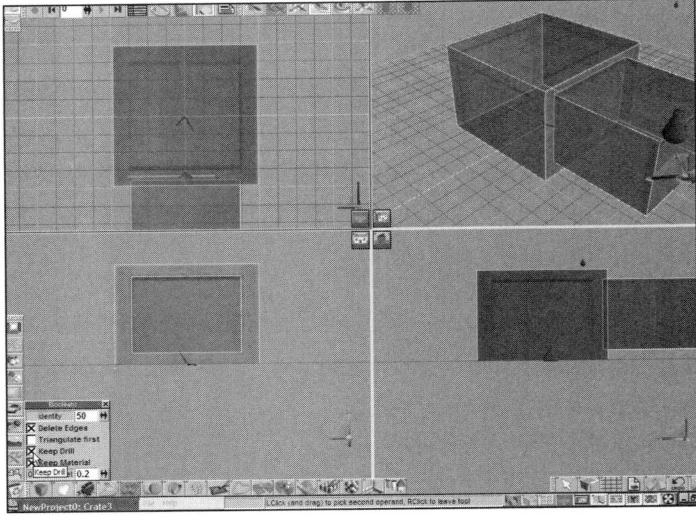

Figure 7.28
Set the options of the Boolean panel as shown here.

The Keep Drill option instructs gameSpace to preserve the new cube after the Boolean Subtraction operation. Choosing this option allows you to reuse the same drill object as you make multiple identical cuts.

You are almost ready to make your first cut, but the wrong object is selected. Because this is a subtraction operation, the order of object selection makes a difference. The new cube is probably still selected, so you will need to use the Object tool to reselect the crate object.

Activate the Object tool, and click on the crate object in any viewport. See Figure 7.29.

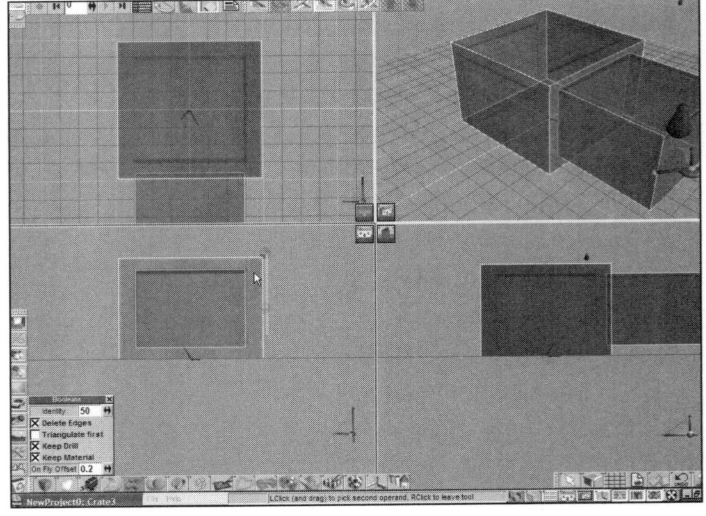

Figure 7.29
First select the crate object.

With the crate object selected, click on the Object Subtraction icon. The mouse cursor should indicate the Object Subtraction tool is active. Move the mouse until it is positioned over the drill cube. Click on the drill cube, as shown in Figure 7.30.

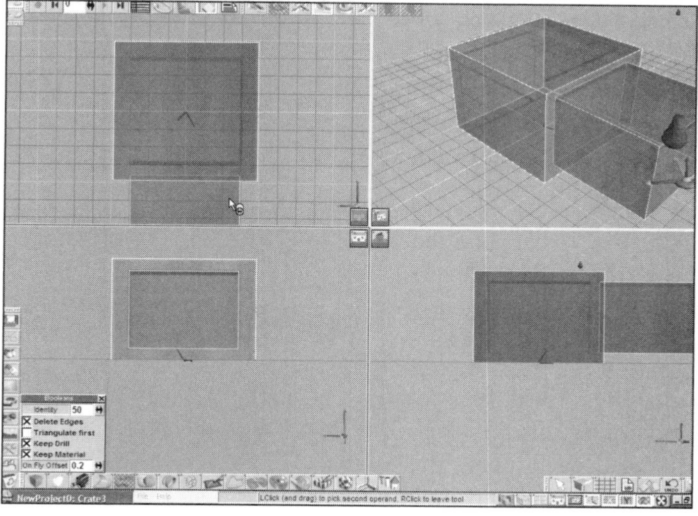

Figure 7.30
Use the Object Subtraction tool to cut away the drill cube.

Use the Object tool to select the drill cube, and drag it upward in the top viewport.

Figure 7.31 shows the drill cube in its new position. It should now slightly overlap the opposite side of the crate.

Once you have moved the drill cube out of the way, you can see the new edges where the first inset region was carved away.

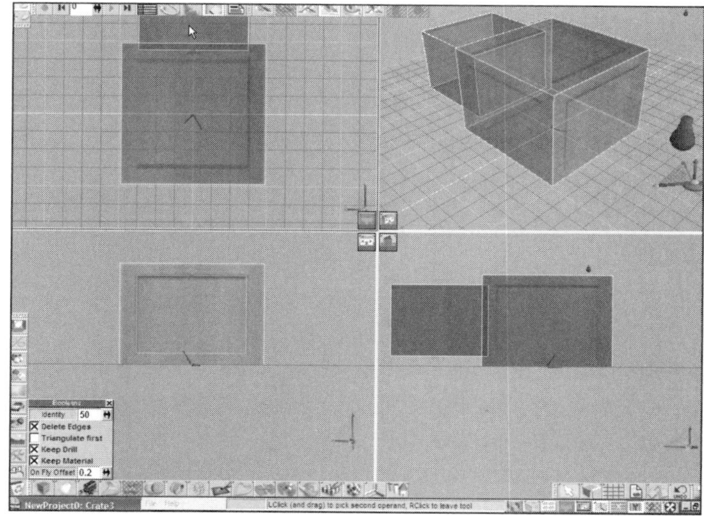

Figure 7.31
With movement disabled in the X axis, it is easy to slide the drill cube perfectly into position.

Reselect the crate object and then activate the Object Subtraction tool. Click on the Object Subtraction tool to cut away the next inset. See Figure 7.32.

Drag the drill cube back down to its original position at the center of the crate as in Figure 7.33.

Press the A key to enable movement along the X axis, and then press the S key to disable movement along the Y axis.

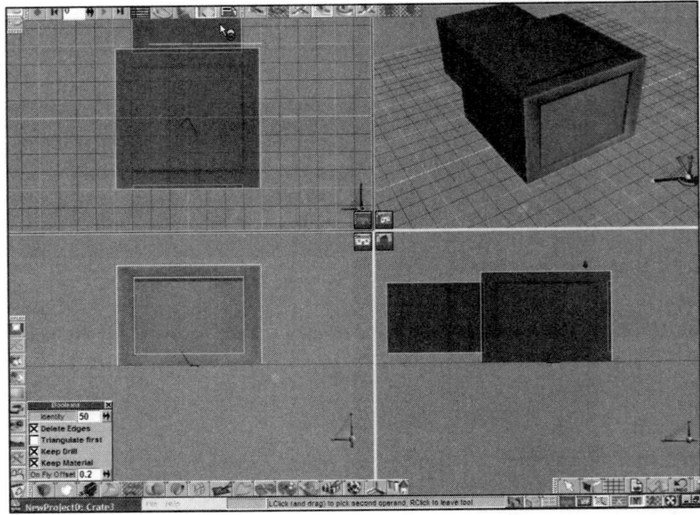

Figure 7.32
Use the Object Subtraction tool to subtract the drill cube from the crate.

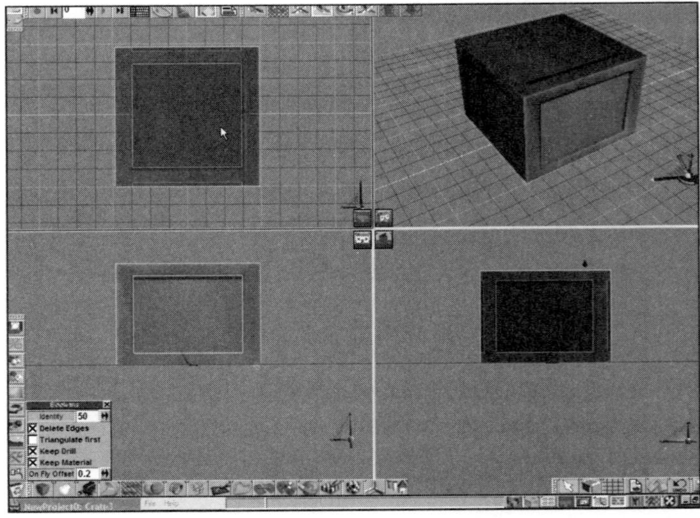

Figure 7.33
Reposition the drill cube near the center of the crate.

Slide the drill cube left in the top view until it slightly overlaps the left side of the crate object. See Figure 7.34.

Reselect the crate object, and then activate the Object Subtraction tool. Click on the drill cube once again, as shown in Figure 7.35.

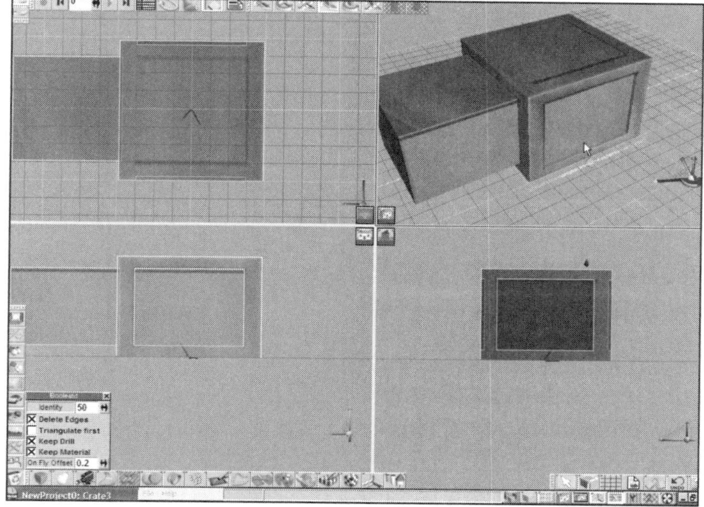

Figure 7.34
With movement disabled along the Y axis, it is easy to slide the drill cube precisely to the left.

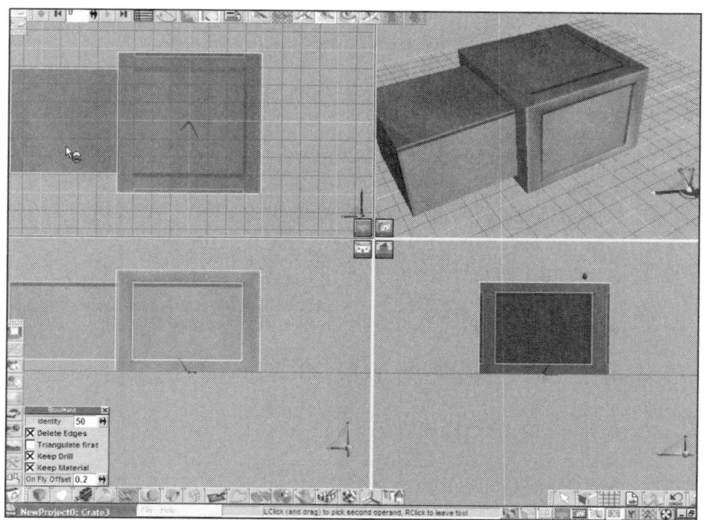

Figure 7.35
Use the Object Subtraction tool to cut away the drill cube again.

Use the Object tool to slide the drill cube so that it overlaps the right side of the crate object. Click on the drill cube to cut away another inset. See Figure 7.36.

Use the Object tool to slide the drill cube back to the center of the crate object.

Press the A key to disable movement along the X axis. Press the S key to enable movement along the Y axis.

Use the front view to slide the drill cube up to the top of the crate object. Be sure to leave a slight overlap, as seen in Figure 7.37.

Select the drill cube, and press the Delete key to remove it from the scene.

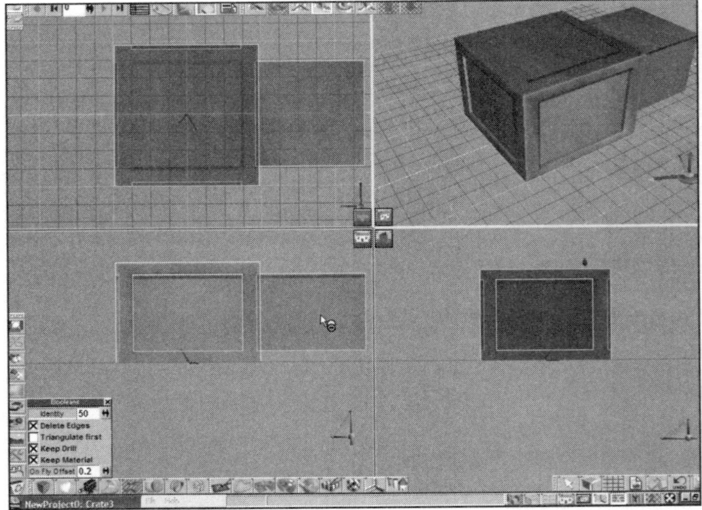

Figure 7.36
Carve a hole in the fourth side of the crate.

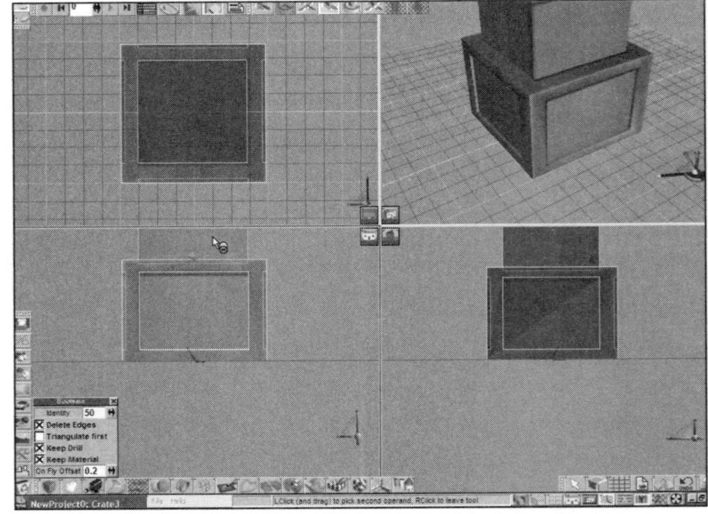

Figure 7.37
Use the Object Subtraction tool to carve out the inset in the top of the crate object.

Figure 7.38 shows the crate object with all five insets carved out. You could carve out the bottom inset as well, but the bottom will never be seen in the game. Carving it out would needlessly create more vertices and faces.

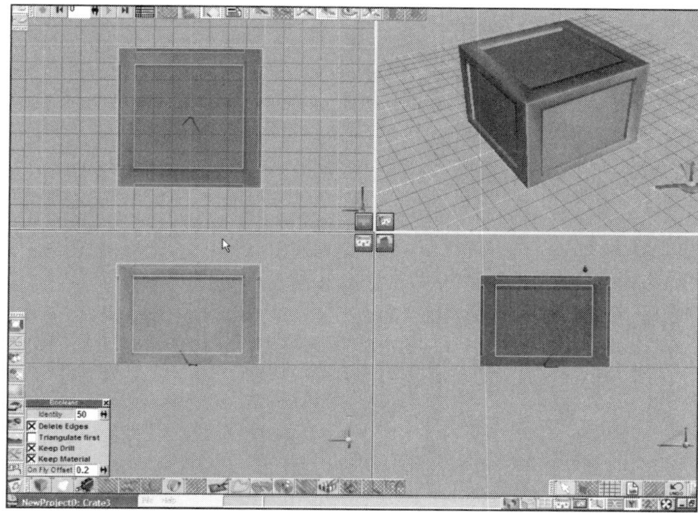

Figure 7.38
The crate now has five inset sides.

The Object Info Pane shown in Figure 7.39 shows that the new crate object has 48 vertices and 31 faces. The new carved crate has considerably more polygons than the 6 faces of the original version, but 31 faces is still very reasonable.

Save the scene by selecting File > Save > Scene.

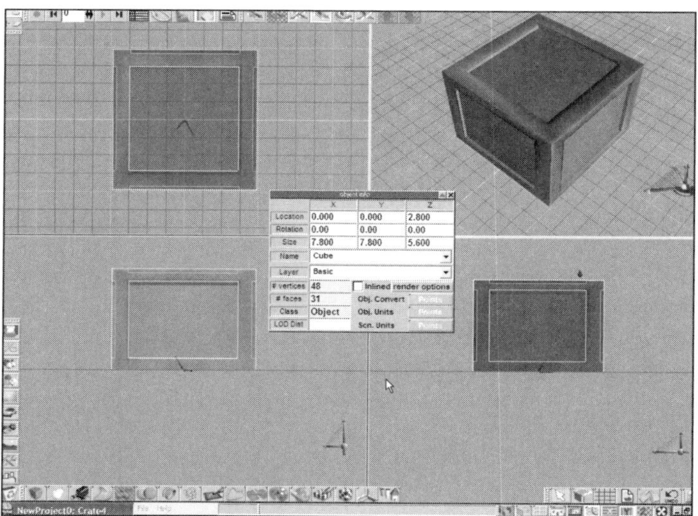

Figure 7.39
The Object Info Pane reveals the crate's poly count.

A Custom Paint Job

In the last few chapters, you have used several methods to apply a material to an object. Rarely do real objects look the same from every side. Before you export the finished crate model into Adventure Explorer, use the Material Editor to give the crate a custom paint job. Begin by setting up a material.

Open the Material Library and double-click the Caligari material, as shown in Figure 7.40.

Expand the Material Editor to reveal the Color panel. Click the large button that displays the name CALIGARI. See Figure 7.41.

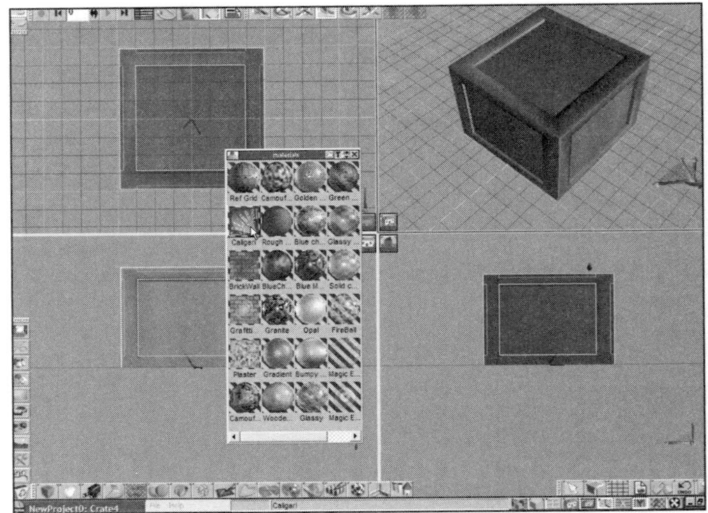

Figure 7.40
Double-click the Caligari material in the Material Library.

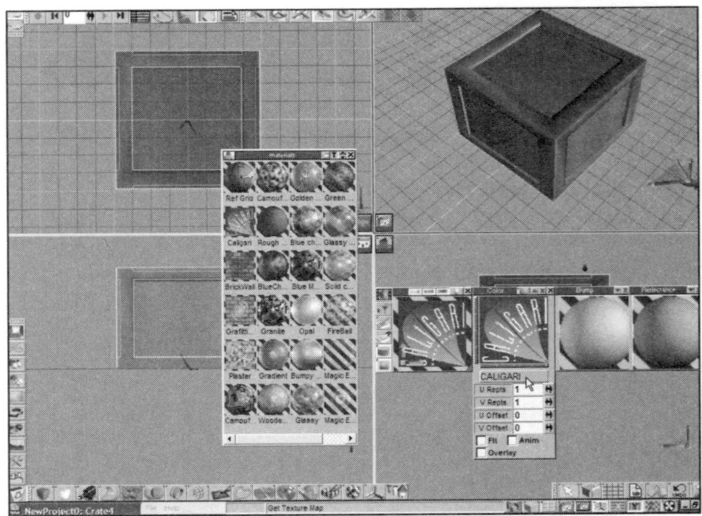

Figure 7.41
Click the CALIGARI button.

Choose the Crate3.jpg file, which is in the Textures folder on the companion CD. Crate3.jpg is a variation of the original crate texture, with the words "THIS END UP" painted diagonally across it. See Figure 7.42.

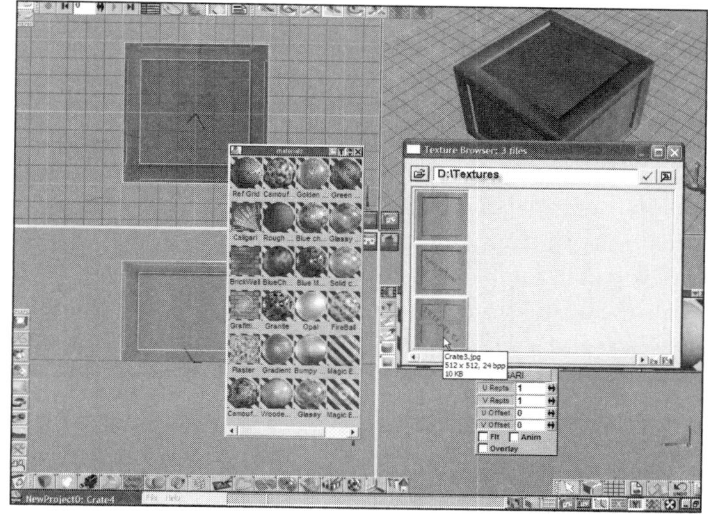

Figure 7.42
Choose Crate3.jpg from the Texture folder of the companion CD.

Activate the Paint Face tool, which is found in the third slot down on the small vertical toolbar at the far left side of the Material Editor. See Figure 7.43.

When the Paint Face tool is active, the mouse pointer becomes a small paintbrush.

Use the paintbrush to click near the center of the crate's top inset surface. See Figure 7.44.

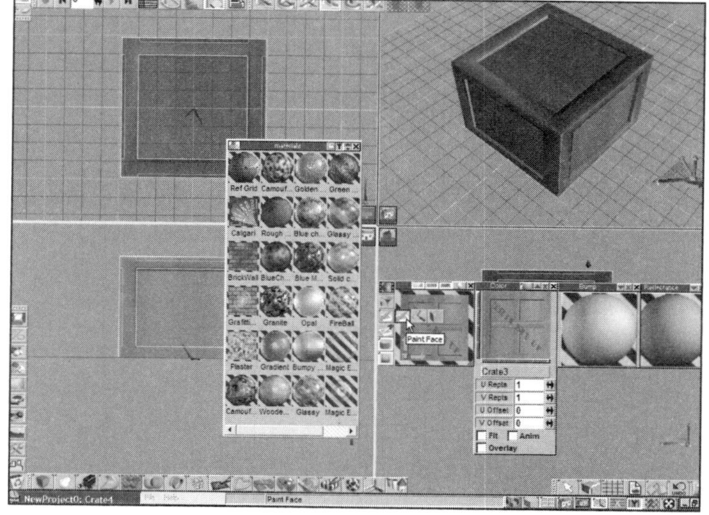

Figure 7.43
The Paint Face tool applies a material to individual surfaces of an object.

Notice that the new texture image does not quite line up with the existing texture and the crate's geometry.

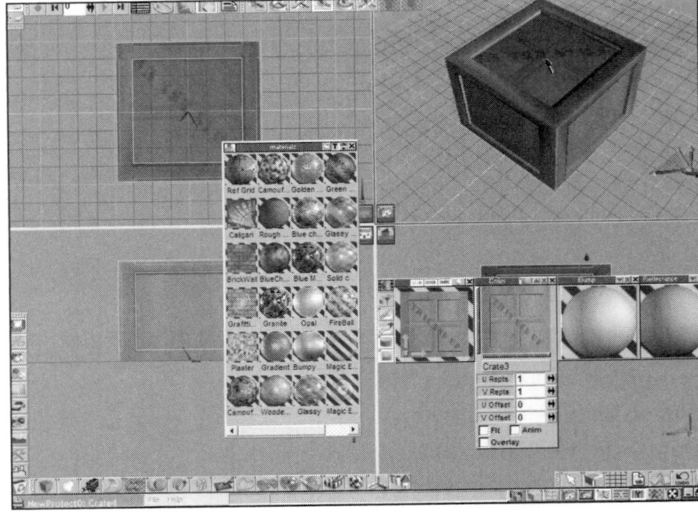

Figure 7.44
Use the paintbrush to paint the current material onto the crate's top face.

The U Repts and V Repts fields, beneath the image selection button on the Color panel, can be used to scale the texture image. The U Offset and V Offset fields allow you to precisely position the texture on the surface.

Remember that the letter U represents the horizontal placement of a texture, and the letter V is used to represent the vertical placement. Repts is an abbreviation for *repeats*. The more times a texture repeats, the smaller it must be scaled. The fewer times a texture repeats, the larger it must be scaled. A high U Repts value actually squeezes the texture so that it can repeat more times in the horizontal direction.

tip

Whenever the U Repts and V Repts are very different from each other, you are distorting the texture. This is called changing the aspect ratio of the image. If the texture image is a picture of a marble surface or a cloudy sky, it may not matter if you change the aspect ratio. If the texture is a picture of a face, an extreme aspect ratio could look weird.

Try adjusting the U Repts and V Repts and reapplying the texture to the top of the crate. Remember that when you change settings in the Material Editor, the changes do not affect any object until you reapply the material. See Figure 7.45.

Once the scale seems correct, try repositioning the texture image by adjusting the U Offset and V Offset, as in Figure 7.46.

Puzzles and Stairs

Save the scene by selecting File > Save > Scene, and then save the crate as a DirectX .x file, using File > Save As > Object.

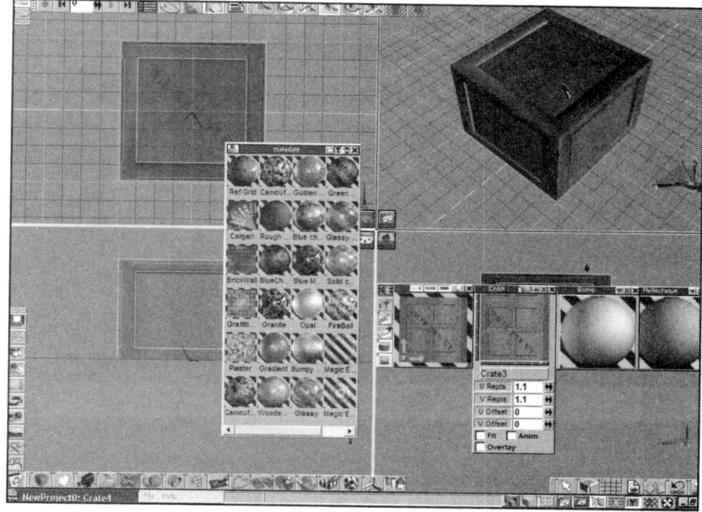

Figure 7.45
Adjust the scale of the texture image and reapply the material.

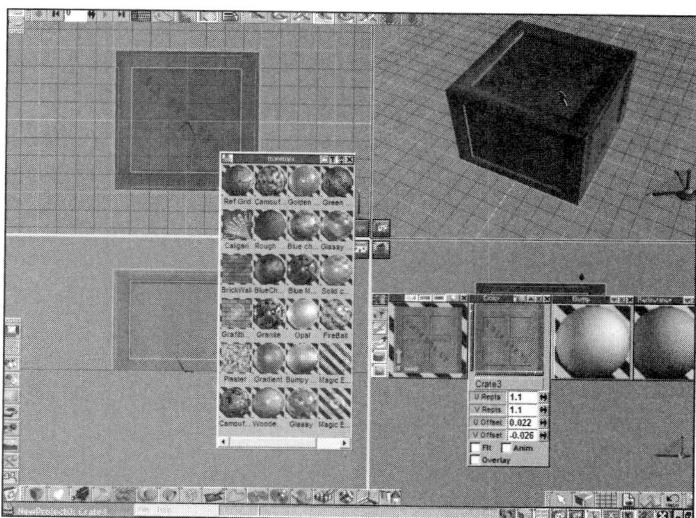

Figure 7.46
Adjust the offset of the texture image and reapply the material.

Close gameSpace and launch ObjectImporter. Use ObjectImporter to replace Object 2 with the final crate .x file. Close ObjectImporter and play the game, as in Figure 7.47.

Figure 7.47
Press the spacebar to jump onto the crates.

Slide the crates around the far shore of the river. Try to arrange the crates so that you can easily jump from one crate to the next. If you arrange the crates correctly, you should be able to climb all the way up to the door to the treasure room, as shown in Figure 7.48.

Figure 7.48
The challenge is to arrange the crates in the proper order.

This only works if you scaled the crates correctly. If the crates are too large or too small, you could have a problem. If necessary, adjust the scale of the crate object in gameSpace, save it as an object file, and use ObjectImporter to bring the updated model into the game.

Summary

In this chapter, you should have learned the following concepts:

- Architects and level designers have different goals and philosophies.
- Architects think about utility, organization, circulation, and statement.
- Level designers think about challenge, confusion, defense, motivation, emotion, and containment.
- Architectural storytelling emphasizes emotion, illusion, motivation, and psychological manipulation.
- The six key ingredients to environmental simulation are Layout, Important features, Forms, Textures, Environment, and Dressings.
- The Caligari material in the Material Library can be used to apply any bitmap image onto an object.
- Many level designers and game artists create a small set of base textures and expand them into a much larger set of variations on the base textures.
- Lines or images that appear in a texture image can be applied as a material and used as guidelines to help make more precise object models.
- Programmers often build backdoors or secret shortcuts into their games to assist the development team time throughout the development process.
- The Magic Ring controls allow you to adjust various parameters of a new primitive by clicking and dragging over each individually colored segment.
- Boolean subtraction is a mathematical operation in which the entirety of one solid object is removed or drilled away from another solid object.
- gameSpace's Object Subtraction tool is used to perform Boolean subtraction on two objects.
- The order of object selection can drastically change the results of a Boolean subtraction.
- Any solid object can be used as a drill by the Object Subtraction tool.
- Right-click on the Object Subtraction tool to display the Boolean panel.
- The Keep Drill option allows you to reuse the same object as a drill in multiple subtraction operations.
- The Paint Face tool applies the current texture to any individual surface of an object.
- You can select the level of transparency for any individual viewport.
- Adjust the U Rept and V Rept fields to change the scale of a texture image.
- Adjust the U Offset and V Offset fields to reposition a texture image.

- Changing the value of only one of the two texture scaling fields (U Rept or V Rept) changes the aspect ratio of the texture image.

Questions and Answers

Q: How do you select a new bitmap file for the current material's texture image?

A: Click the large button on the Color panel that displays the name of the current bitmap file.

Q: What is the standard shape of the drill used to carve an object with gameSpace's Object Subtraction tool?

A: There is no standard shape; any solid object can be used as a drill.

Q: What is controlled by clicking and dragging on the green band of the Magic Ring control?

A: The green band of the Magic Ring control adjusts the height of a primitive.

Q: What would be the result of increasing the value of a texture image's U Rept and V Rept fields before applying it to an object?

A: The texture image would appear smaller when applied to an object.

Q: How can you apply a different material to each side of a pyramid?

A: Use the Paint Face tool, which is found in the Material Editor.

Q: If Box A is completely inside Box B, what would happen to box B if you use the Object Subtraction tool to subtract Box A from Box B?

A: Box B would become hollow.

Q: If Box A is completely inside Box B, what would happen to Box A if you Boolean subtract Box B from Box A?

A: Box A would be completely removed.

Q: I use the acronym LIFTED to represent the key ingredients in simulating an environment. What are the six key ingredients in a successful environmental simulation?

A:

- Layout
- Important features
- Forms
- Textures
- Environment
- Dressings

Discussion Questions

1. How do the goals of an architect differ from the goals of a level designer?
2. Describe three objects that could be easily modeled using Boolean subtraction.
3. Take a scene from any western, period, or science fiction movie. "Lift" or analyze the scene using the six key ingredients in environmental simulation.
4. Describe an example of architectural storytelling.
5. Describe as many textures as possible that would be adversely affected by a significant change in aspect ratio.
6. Pick any real-world setting and describe the base textures that you would need to build a level based on that setting. Describe at least four possible variations you might then create for each base texture.

Exercises

Use the image in Figure 7.49 to answer the following questions.

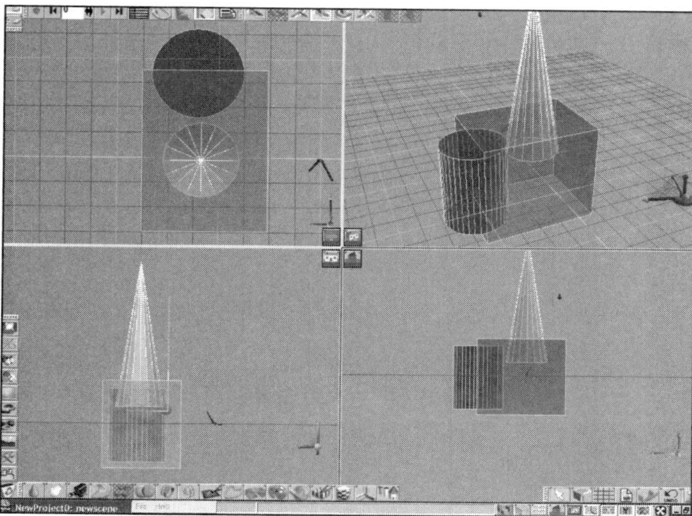

Figure 7.49
Use these three objects to answer the following questions.

1. Describe what would happen if you used the Object Subtraction tool to subtract the cube from the cylinder.
2. Describe what would happen if you used the Objection Subtraction tool to subtract the cube from the cone.

3. Describe what would happen if you used Boolean subtraction to subtract the cone from the cube.
4. You are asked to create a game level based on a pirate ship.
   A. List at least four base textures you would need to create the objects in that level.
   B. Describe at least four variations of each of these textures.
5. Describe an example of how architecture can be used to tell a story in a game.
6. Describe an example of how architecture can be used to enhance the game play of a game.
7. Start with a sphere primitive. Use the Object Subtraction tool to carve three finger holes in the sphere to make a model of a bowling ball.
8. The Texture folder on the companion CD contains several variations on the crate texture. Use the Paint Face tool to apply a different variation of the texture to each side of the crate object.
9. Use primitives and Boolean subtraction to carve a pumpkin face out of a sphere. Use the red segment of the Magic Ring control to create a small peak at the top of the pumpkin's head. Flatten the base of the pumpkin by subtracting a cube from the bottom of the sphere. Hint: Figure 7.50 shows an example, along with all the drill objects I used to carve it.

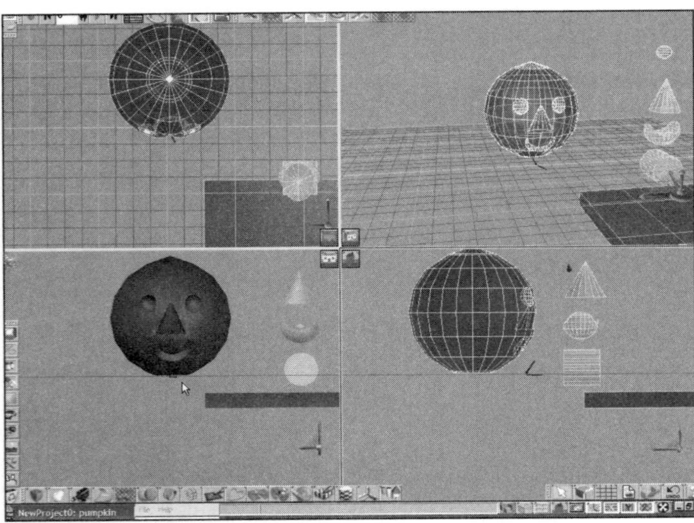

Figure 7.50
Happy Halloween!

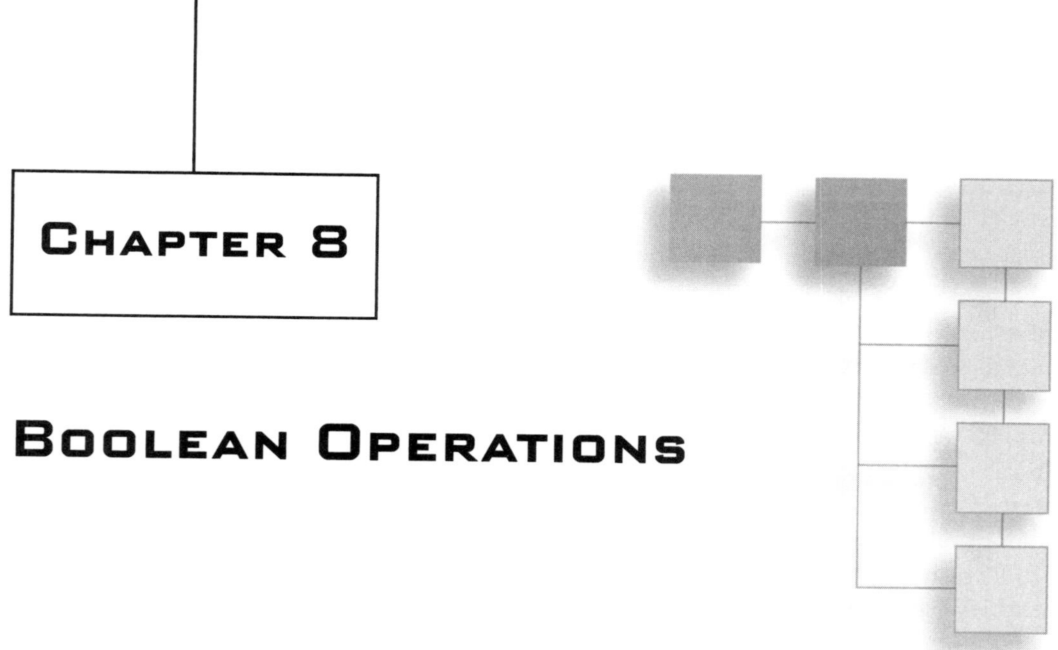

Chapter 8

Boolean Operations

In the last chapter, you used Boolean subtraction to cut away sections of a crate. This chapter introduces the rest of the Boolean family.

Introduction

Boolean operators are named for their inventor, George Boole. Mr. Boole was an educator, a philosopher, a writer, and a mathematician. He lived in England during the mid-1800s. He probably never imagined that his innovative linkage of mathematics and philosophy would someday enable game artists to create incredible three-dimensional worlds.

> Though he never plugged in a computer, George Boole is considered one of the founding fathers of computer science. Boole's writings focus on the use of symbols to represent statements and the use of simple mathematics to determine validity and probability.
>
> Boole developed and popularized the language of modern symbolic logic. He devised a method of analyzing arguments by assigning every statement a truth value of either true or false. Boole used the Boolean operators as a means to combine, group, separate, or compare these various statements. He employed a simplified variation of algebra to manipulate, isolate, and prove these statements. This technique is now referred to as Boolean algebra.
>
> Because digital circuits can only be turned on or off (true or false), Boole's operators, which include And, Or, and Not, are the fundamental building blocks of all electronic circuits.

For a game artist who is trying to understand the use of Boolean operators in 3-D modeling, it is not necessary to study or comprehend their philosophical and mathematical origins. If you are interested in game programming, however, a clear understanding of Boolean algebra and set theory is highly recommended.

Unions

A union is formed when any number of individual pieces come together and become one. In terms of 3-D modeling, a union is the operation of merging two or more separate pieces into a single unified whole.

When 13 independent colonies joined together as a nation, they made a union. When thousands of angry employees band together to fight their employers, they also form a union. What do revolutionary states and frustrated workers have in common? They are both collections of individual entities (states or workers) who have fused together to become a single entity.

Figure 8.1 shows two objects, a cube and sphere. The sphere overlaps the cube and protrudes from its side.

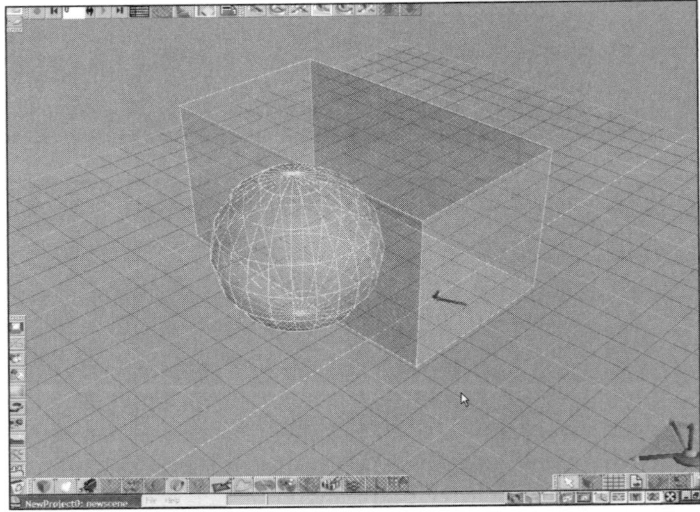

Figure 8.1
A cube and a sphere

Figure 8.2 shows the results of a Boolean union operation applied to the two objects. The cube and the sphere have been merged into a single solid object. Notice that all of the faces of the sphere that were previously embedded in the cube have been eliminated.

Unlike gameSpace's glue tools, a Boolean union does not create a hierarchy or collection of separate objects. The result of a Boolean union is a single new object that occupies the space of all of its original components. The order of object selection is irrelevant to a Boolean union operation.

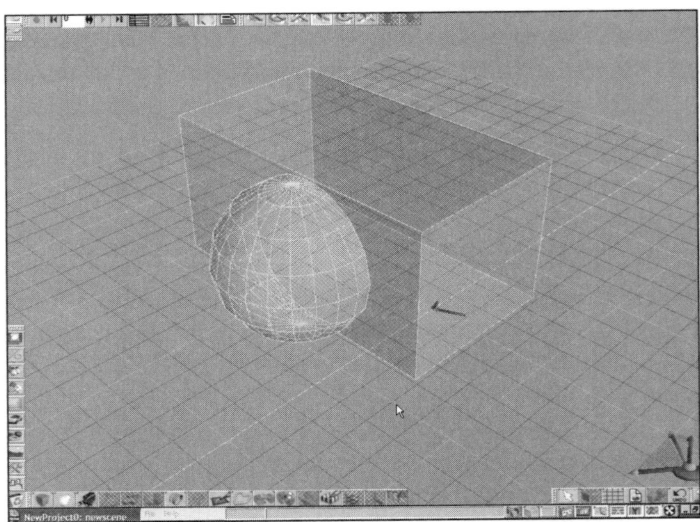

Figure 8.2
A union operation has been applied to the cube and the sphere.

It is not necessary for the objects in a Boolean union to intersect. Though it is somewhat unusual, two objects that do not connect in any way can still be grouped together as a single object. Alaska and Hawaii do not touch the contiguous United States, but they are still part of the Union.

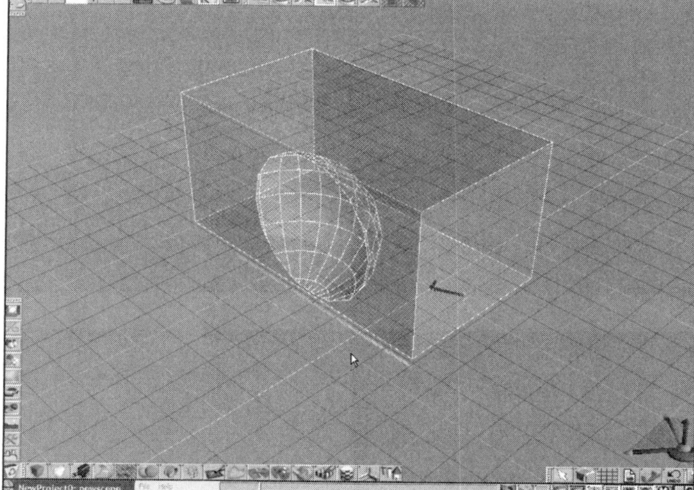

Figure 8.3
The sphere has been subtracted from the cube.

Subtraction

If you think of a union operation as adding two or more geometric objects, then the opposite operation is obviously subtraction. In the last chapter, you used Boolean subtraction to carve the insets out of your crate model.

Figure 8.3 shows the result of subtracting the sphere from the cube.

If the order of object selection is reversed, the cube would cut away one side of the sphere. The order of object selection is critical in a subtraction operation.

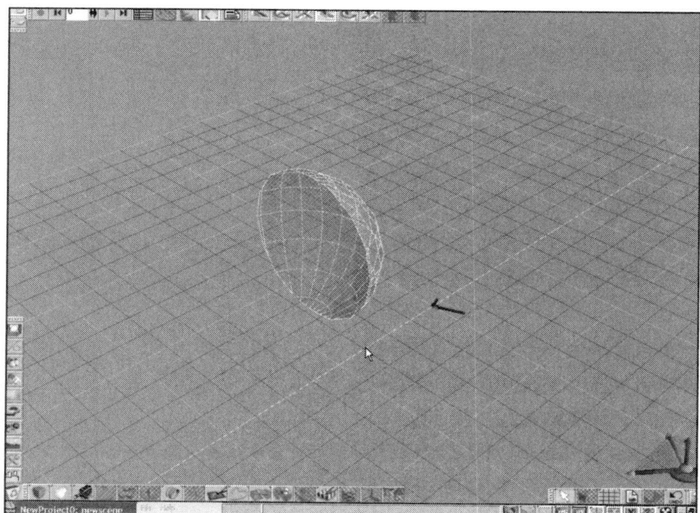

Figure 8.4
This is the intersection of the sphere and the cube.

Intersections

Wherever two streets, cross you have an intersection. The Department of Motor Vehicles defines an intersection as any piece of roadway that is shared by two or more streets.

Figure 8.4 shows the intersection of the sphere and the cube. The order of object selection is irrelevant when performing a Boolean intersection operation. When you drive through Hollywood, the intersection of Hollywood and Vine is exactly the same place as the intersection of Vine and Hollywood.

In 3-D modeling terms, Boolean intersection is the operation of creating a new object that consists of only those portions of any two objects in which the two objects occupy the same space.

During an intersection operation, a new object is created. The new object occupies any space in which the two original objects overlap.

An unusual situation occurs when the two objects intersect each other in multiple disconnected locations. Figure 8.5 shows an irregularly shaped object that overlaps a cube in two separate regions.

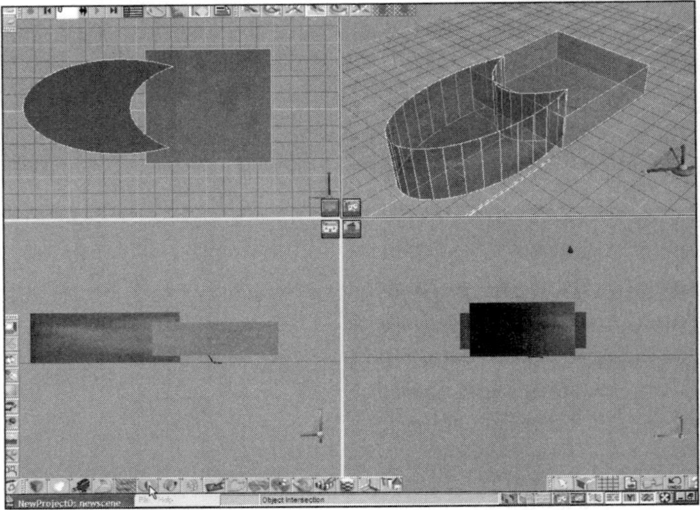

Figure 8.5
The crescent-shaped object overlaps the cube object in two disconnected regions.

Both pointed ends of the crescent-shaped object overlap the cube, but the rest of the crescent sits outside of the cube. When a Boolean intersection is performed on these two objects, a single new object is produced. The new object, which appears in Figure 8.6, has two disconnected pieces, but behaves in all other ways like a single solid object.

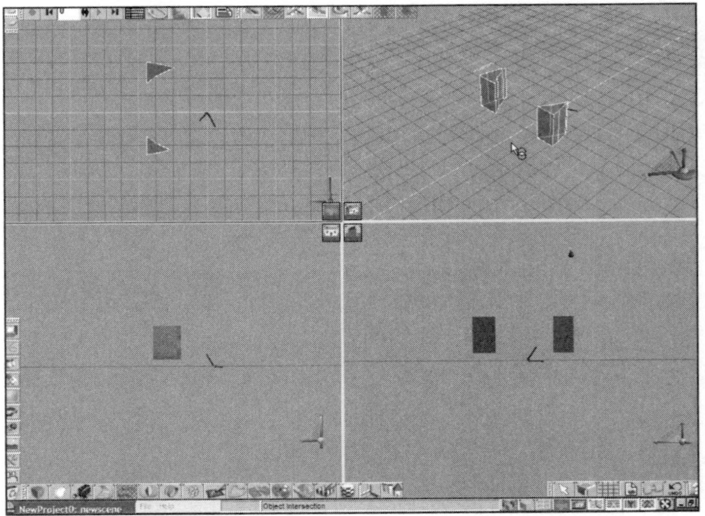

Figure 8.6
The intersection produces a single object with two separate parts.

If you are building models to export into other 3-D modeling programs or game engines, use caution when creating such an odd object. Some 3-D engines have trouble handling this type of split geometry.

Shells

There is no traditional Boolean shell operation. The developers of gameSpace chose to extend gameSpace's selection of Boolean operations by adding a fourth option to the Boolean tools' slot. The Shell tool creates a hollow shell in the shape of a single selected object.

Figure 8.7 shows a simple solid sphere. In Figure 8.8, that sphere has been encased in a hollow shell. The shell looks much like the original sphere, until you use Boolean subtraction to cut a hole in it, as in Figure 8.9.

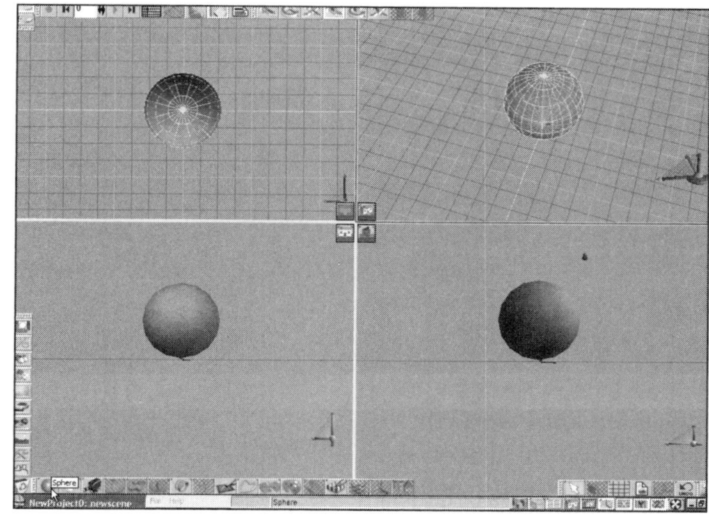

Figure 8.7
This a solid sphere.

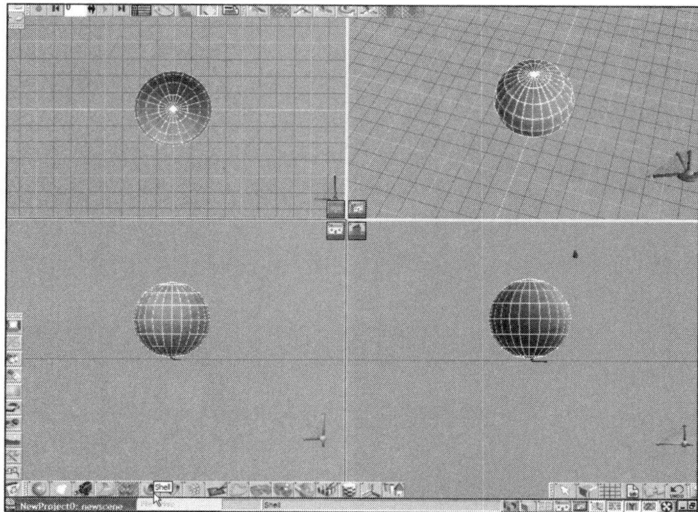

Figure 8.8
This is the same sphere wrapped in a hollow shell.

Compare the resulting objects shown in Figure 8.10. The first sphere is a hollow shell. Looking into the hole, you can see deep into the empty shell. The second sphere is solid. The hole in its top is only as deep as the section that was cut away.

Unlike the Boolean tools, the Shell tool works on a single object. Select the object before activating the Shell tool. Like the Boolean tools, the Shell tool offers a variety of options to control its operation. Right-click the Shell icon to reveal these options.

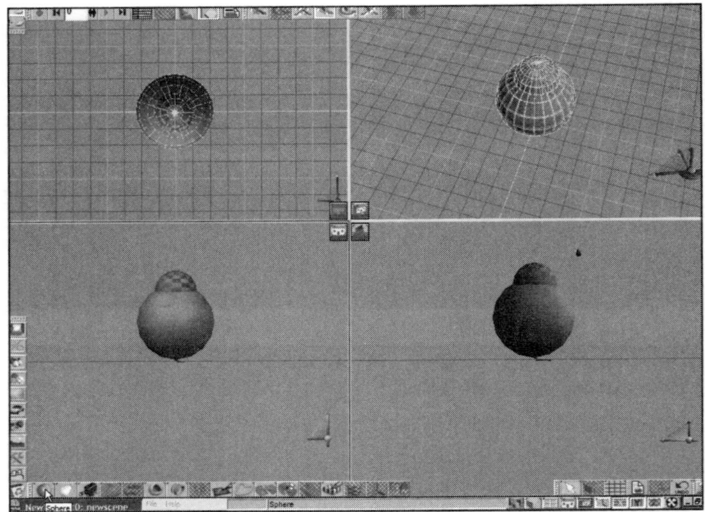

Figure 8.9
The small sphere is subtracted from both the solid sphere and the shell of a sphere.

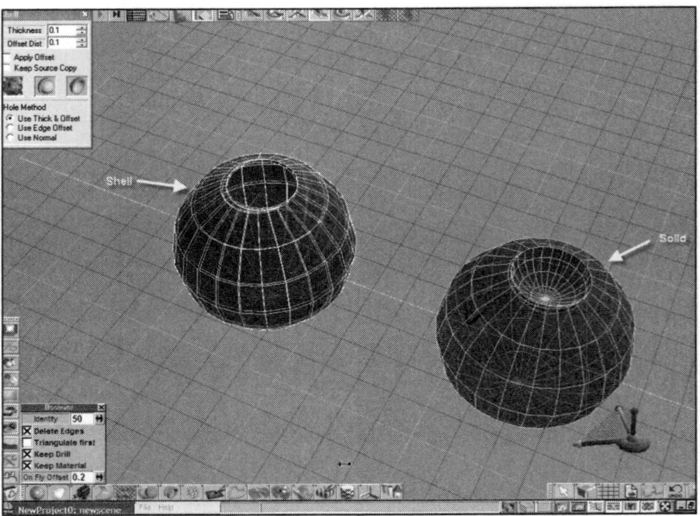

Figure 8.10
Look inside the shell and the solid.

Boolean Treasures

Back in Adventure Explorer, you have reached the secret treasure vault. You crossed the river, arranged the crates, and climbed up the wall to get here. Your heart beats with anticipation as you rush toward the only artifact in the room, a worthless empty crate. See Figure 8.11.

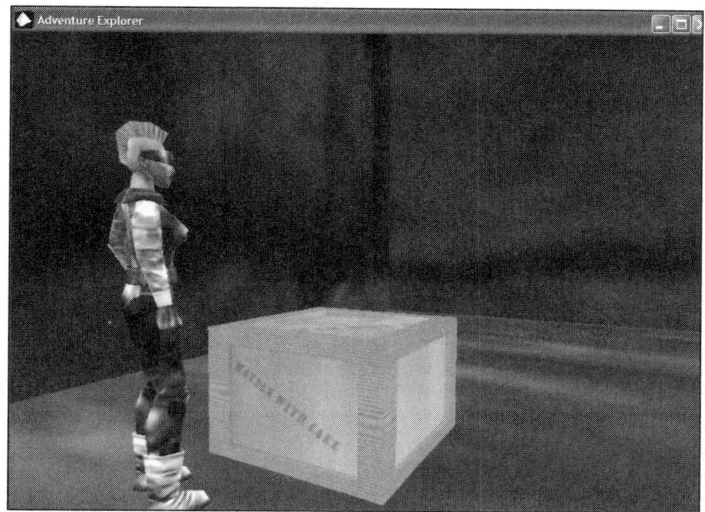

Figure 8.11
This is not the treasure of an epic adventure.

If this is a treasure vault, it appears that the treasure has already been looted. In this section, you will use Boolean intersection to create a magic gem, and then you will replace the crate with a much more impressive pedestal to hold the magic gem.

Creating a Magic Gem

Begin with a blank canvas by selecting File > New > Scene from the File menu.

Choose the Geosphere primitive tool. The Geosphere primitive tool looks like a faceted sphere and shares a toolbar slot with the Sphere primitive tool, as you can see in Figure 8.12.

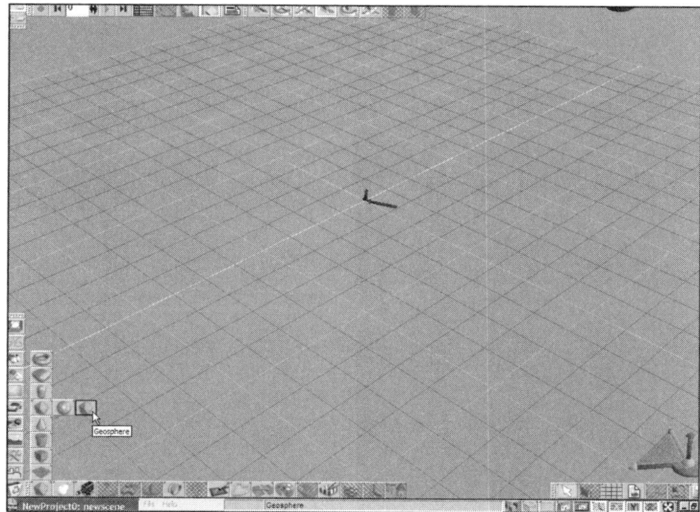

Figure 8.12
Select the Geosphere primitive tool.

Right-click on the Geosphere icon to open its options panel, as in Figure 8.13.

The only option on the Geosphere option panel is Resolution. The higher the resolution, the more vertices and faces are included in the geosphere. Figure 8.14 shows five geospheres. Each geosphere is labeled to indicate the resolution setting that was used to produce it.

Click and drag on the spin control (the left and right arrow) to raise or lower the value in the Resolution field. Set the Resolution value to 2.

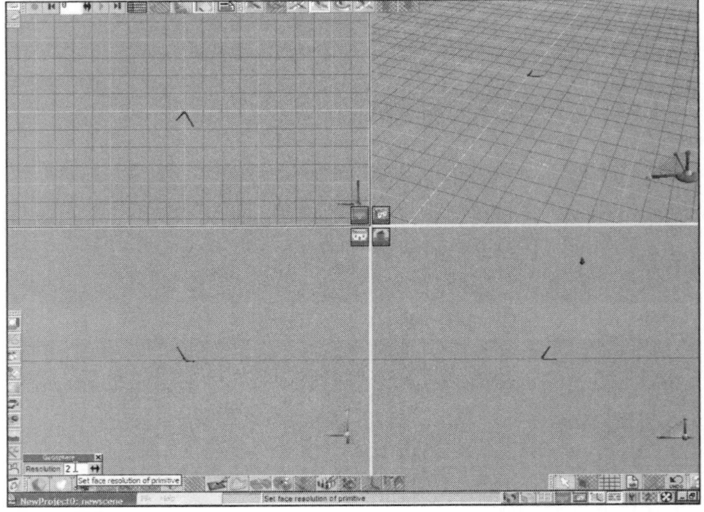

Figure 8.13
The Geosphere option panel has only one option.

Figure 8.14
These geospheres were created with a resolution setting of 1, 2, 3, 4, and 5, respectively.

Using the Geosphere primitive tool, use the grid lines to position the first sphere as shown in Figure 8.15. Click and drag to create the geosphere and continue dragging the mouse to enlarge the geosphere until it looks like the geosphere shown in Figure 8.16.

Figure 8.15
Start the first geosphere here.

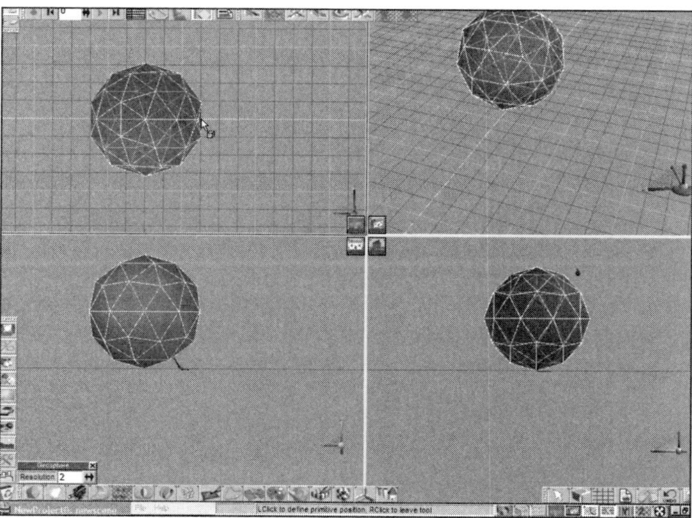

Figure 8.16
Continue enlarging the geosphere's radius until it appears as shown here.

Select the new geosphere and activate the Copy tool, as shown in Figure 8.17.

Use the axis enable buttons to disable movement along the Y and Z axes. Use the Object Move tool to slide the geosphere along the X axis. Position the new geosphere as shown in Figure 8.18.

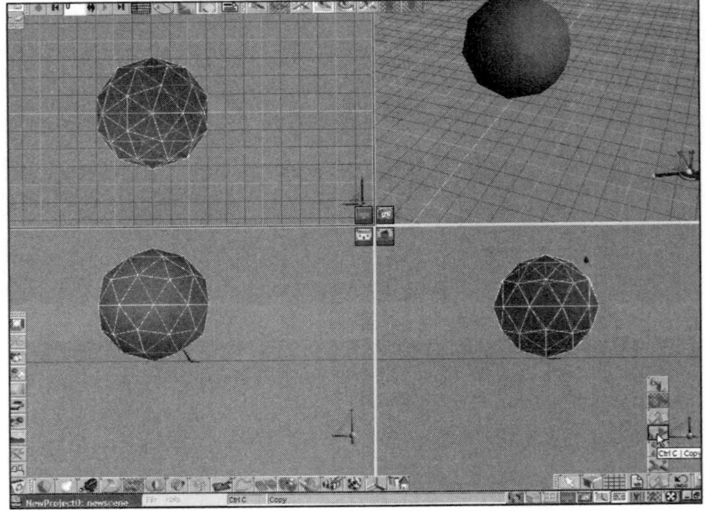

Figure 8.17
Duplicate the geosphere.

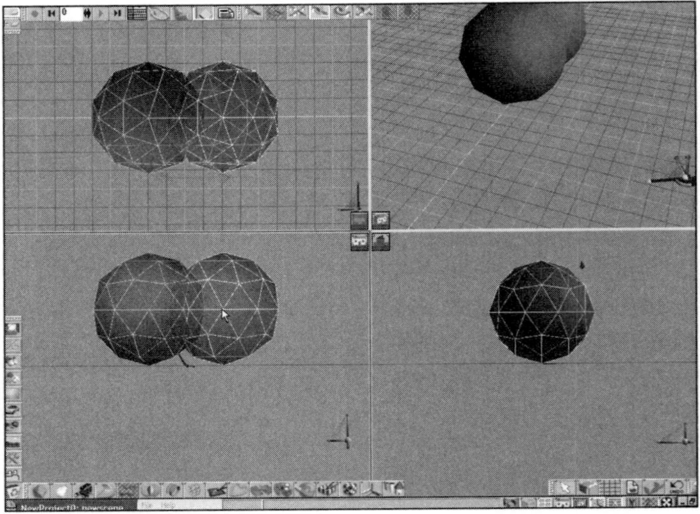

Figure 8.18
Move the duplicate geosphere so that it overlaps the first.

Activate the Object Intersection tool. See Figure 8.19.

When you perform the Boolean intersection operation, you will want gameSpace to remove the original geospheres. Right-click on the Object Intersection icon to open the Boolean options panel. If the Keep Drill option is checked, uncheck it by clicking on its check box. See Figure 8.20.

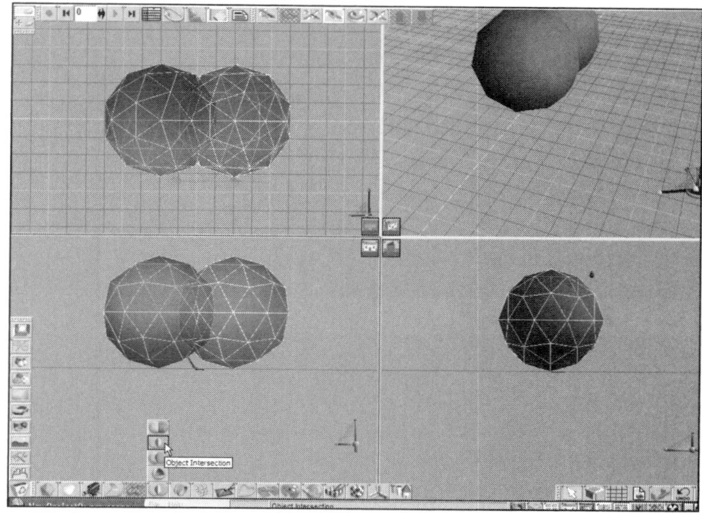

Figure 8.19
Activate the Object Intersection tool.

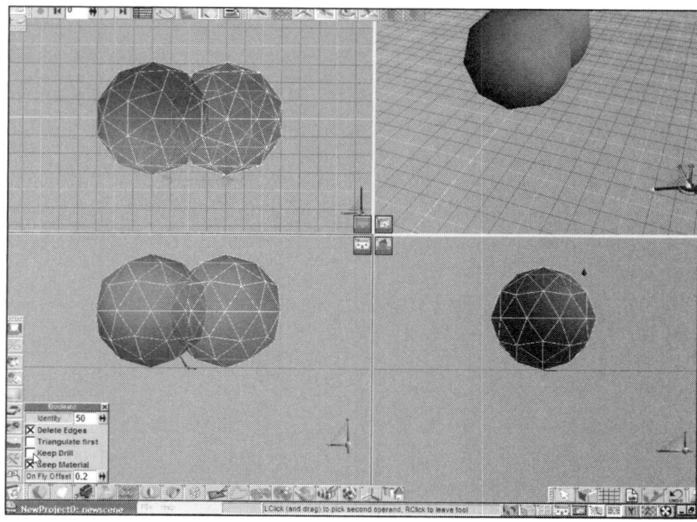

Figure 8.20
Uncheck the Keep Drill option.

With one of the geospheres selected, activate the Object Intersection tool and click on the other geosphere. See Figures 8.21 and 8.22.

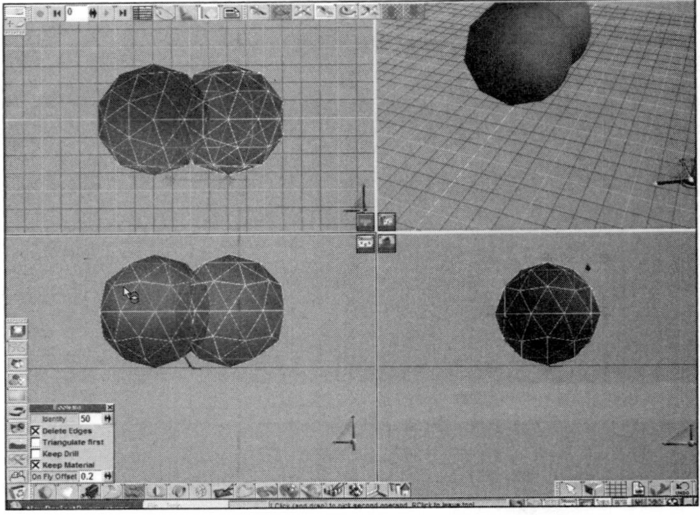

Figure 8.21
Use the Object Intersection tool to perform a Boolean intersection operation.

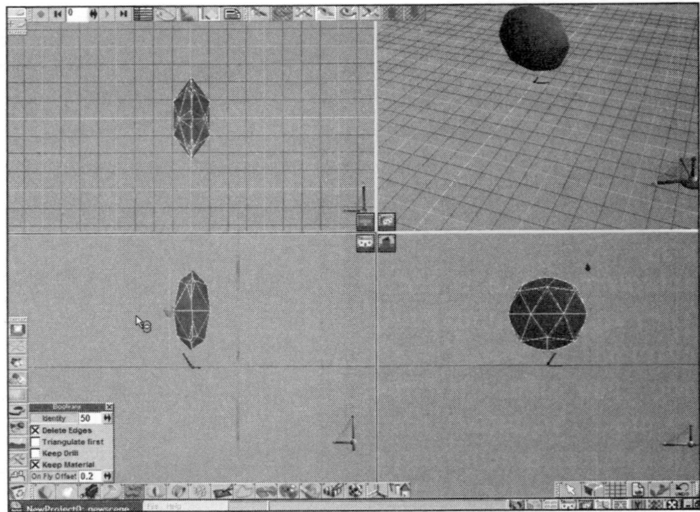

Figure 8.22
This is the result of the Boolean intersection.

Composite Materials

Open the Material Library and double-click the Opal material. See Figure 8.23.

Expand the Material Editor by clicking the black expansion triangle, as shown in Figure 8.24.

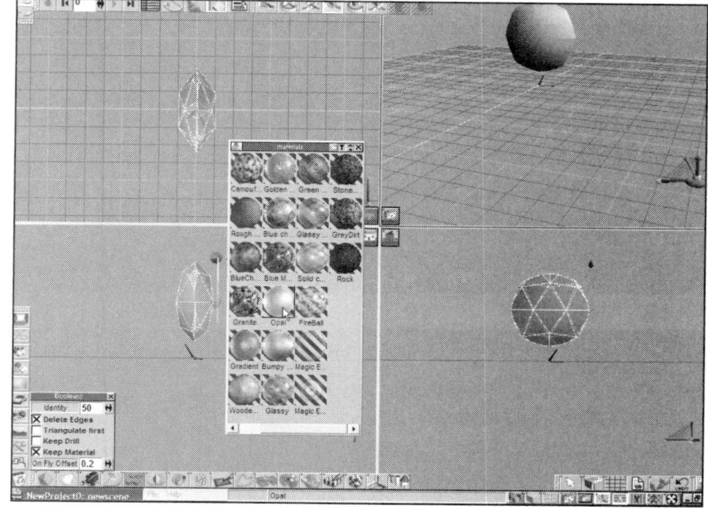

Figure 8.23
Select the Opal material from the Material Library.

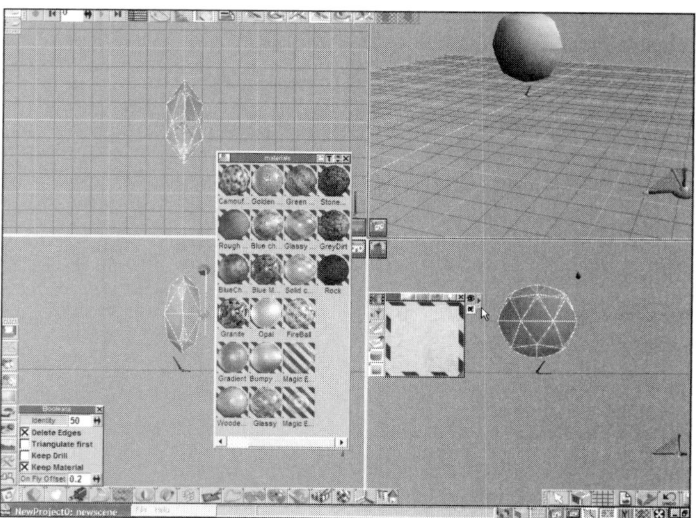

Figure 8.24
Expand the Material Editor to show all of its panels.

The Opal material consists of two separate layers. Each material layer can have its own set of shaders. The two eye icons, which cling to the right-hand side of the Material Editor preview window, indicate that there are two distinct layers in the current material. See Figure 8.25.

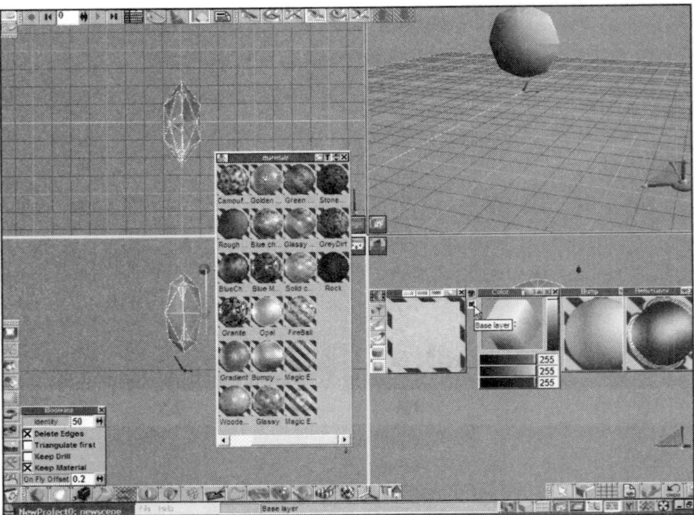

Figure 8.25
Use these eye icons to select between layers of the material.

Click either eye icon to choose between the two layers. Notice that the Color, Bump, and Reflectance panels all change to match the selected layer. The layer with the lowest eye icon is applied first, and then the layers above it are applied in order from the lowest to the highest.

tip

A material can contain any number of layers. To add a layer to a material, right-click on the Material Editor's preview window and select either Add new layer or Duplicate layer. An existing layer can be removed by right-clicking on the Material Editor's preview window and selecting Destroy layer.

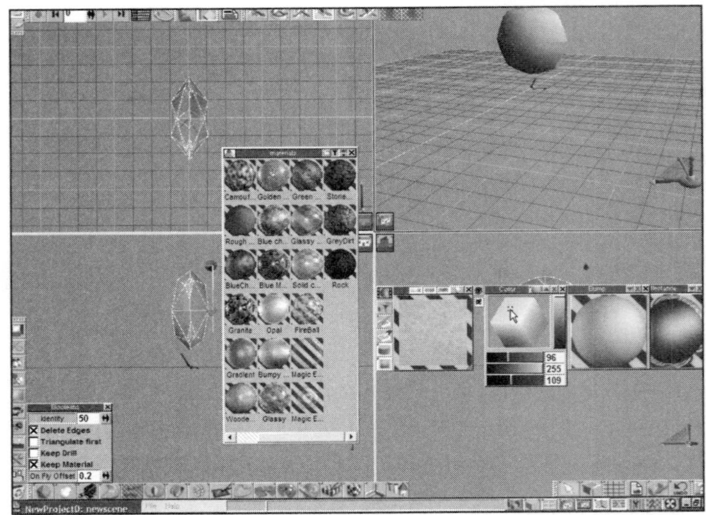

Figure 8.26
Use the color picker to select a new color for this layer's plain color shader.

Click the eye icon for the base layer. The base layer uses a plain color shader.

The Material Editor's Color pane shows a single color picker. See Figure 8.26.

A gameSpace color picker allows you to choose a color in a number of ways. The four sections of the gameSpace color picker are labeled in Figure 8.27.

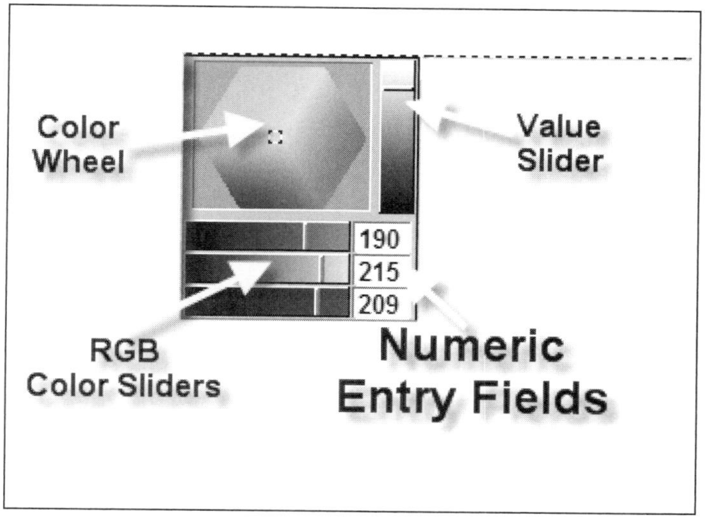

Figure 8.27
The gameSpace color picker offers several ways to select a color.

Colors can be selected by clicking anywhere on the color wheel. The value slider to the right of the color wheel is used to increase or decrease the brightness of all of the colors available on the color wheel. With the color wheel and the value slider, you can select any possible color.

gameSpace allows you to individually enter or adjust the red, green, and blue components of the selected color. Every displayable color is composed of some combination of red, green, and blue light. The RGB color sliders allow you to increase or decrease the amount of any of these three colors, which combine to create the final color. If you need more control, you can manually enter a number for the red, green, or blue components using the three numeric entry fields.

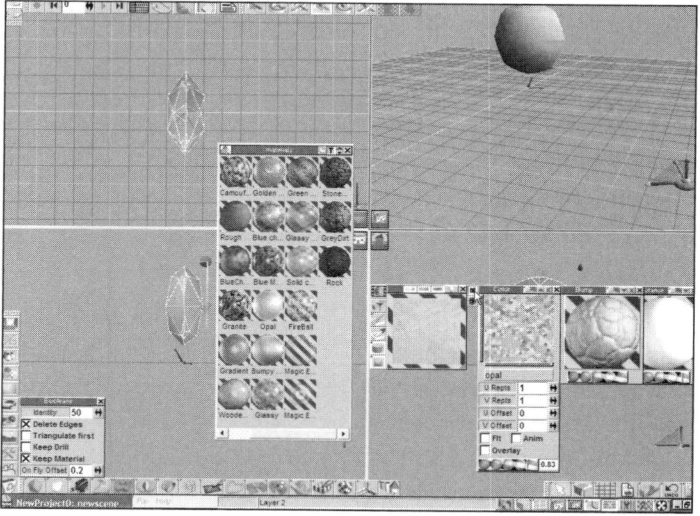

Figure 8.28
Select the second material layer.

Adjust the Color pane's color picker until it is close to the settings shown in Figure 8.26. Once you have adjusted the base layer's color, use the other eye icon to select the material's Layer 2. See Figure 8.28.

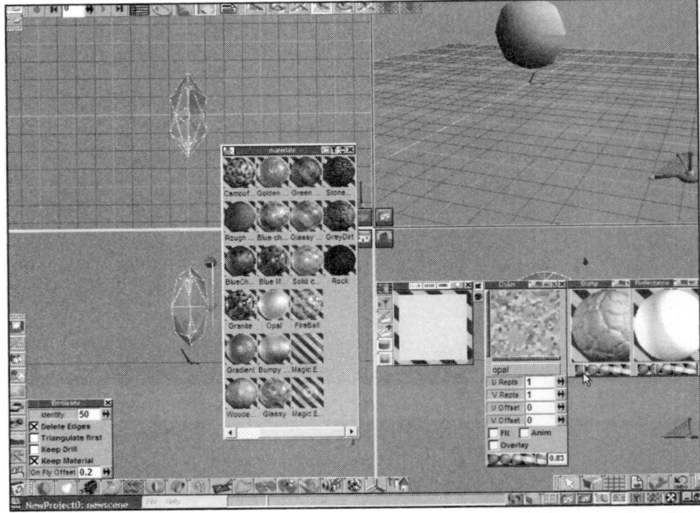

Figure 8.29
Set the transparency sliders as shown.

Because this is being added on top of the base layer, there is an extra slider at the bottom of every pane. The sliders near the bottom of the Color, Bump, and Reflectance panes show a series of five spheres. The spheres appear more transparent as they progress from left to right. These spheres and the numeric entry field attached to them control the amount of influence that each shader in the layer has on the final material.

It is possible to set up a layer so that it affects only the color, only the reflectance, or only the bumpiness of the overall material. A layer can affect all of these components of a material, or any combination thereof.

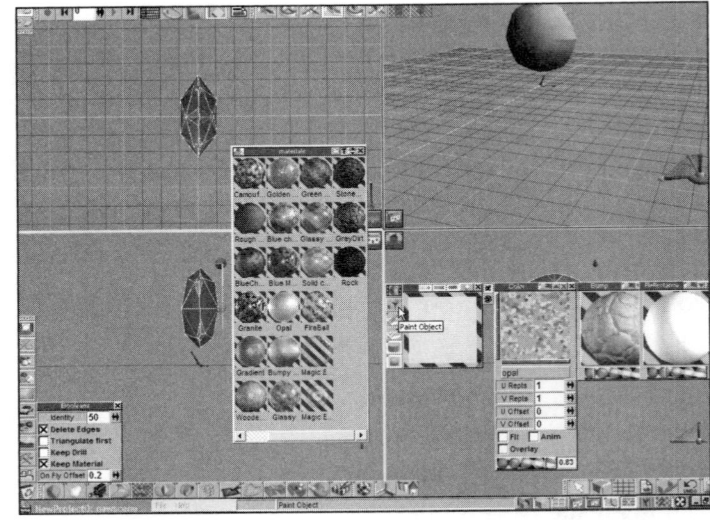

Figure 8.30
Apply the new material to the gem.

The number in the attached entry field is a representation of the layer's transparency. The transparency value must be a number between 0 and 1. A value of 0 indicates no transparency, which allows the current layer to completely replace the previous layers' effects. A value of 1 represents complete transparency, where the current layer is effectively invisible.

Adjust the transparency sliders so they match Figure 8.29.

Use the Paint Object tool to apply the new material to your gem. See Figure 8.30.

Shrink Wrap UV Computation

The gem is an odd-shaped object. You could apply a standard spherical UV projection or cubic UV projection, but the texture patterns would not precisely follow the shape of the gem. If your goal was to produce a smoothed or organic look, this might be acceptable, but a faceted gem should have a clearly faceted texture.

gameSpace offers a powerful tool that can automatically fit UV coordinates to any object. Shrink Wrap UV Computation is easy to use and fun to watch.

Select the Shrink Wrap UV Computation tool from the UV projections toolbar slot as in Figure 8.31, and watch what happens. Figures 8.32 and 8.33 show snapshots of the shrink-wrap process.

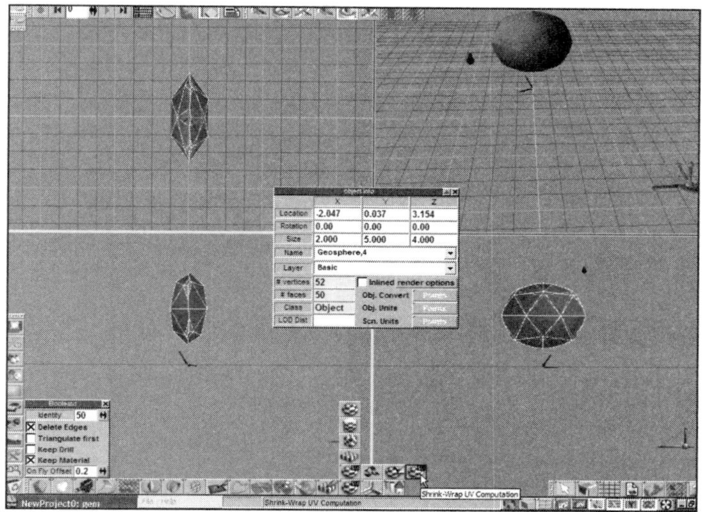

Figure 8.31
Activate the Shrink Wrap UV Computation tool.

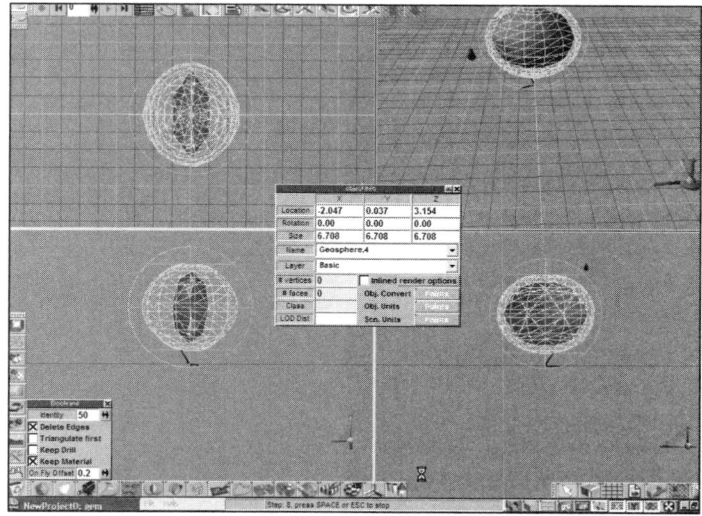

Figure 8.32
The shrink-wrap process is under way.

During the shrink-wrap process, a large white sphere appears around the selected object. The sphere slowly shrinks until it settles into a precise fit around the object's geometry. Depending upon the complexity of the selected object, this can be a slow process.

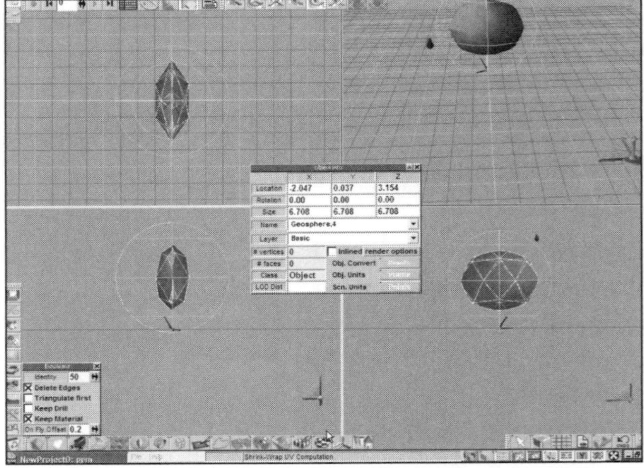

Figure 8.33
The shrink-wrap process has nearly completed.

Table 8.1 Gem Object Parameters

	X	Y	Z
Location	0.0	0.0	0.0
Rotation	0	0	0
Scale	2	5	4

All units and screen units are set in Points.

Precision Placement

Open the Object Info Pane by right-clicking on the Object icon. Set the gem's parameters as described in Table 8.1 and in Figure 8.34.

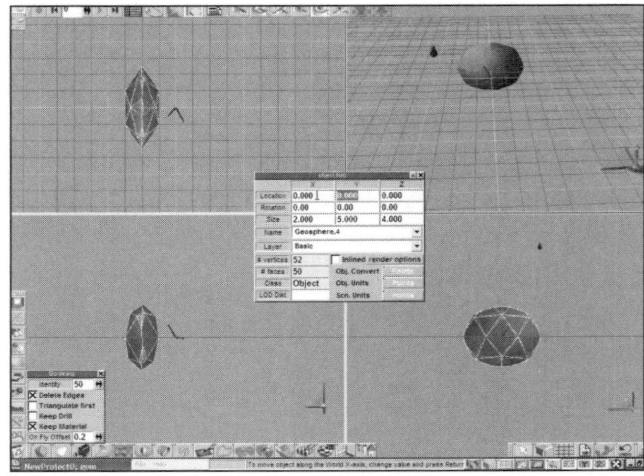

Figure 8.34
Use the Object Info Pane to adjust the gem's parameters.

The gem is now centered at the gameSpace origin, which is positioned at the X, Y, Z coordinates 0, 0, 0. The gem should appear exactly where the thin green and blue lines on the grid intersect each other.

If the gem is perfectly centered, why does it seem so far off center in the viewports? Another important factor can significantly affect the precise placement of objects. In order for gameSpace or a game engine to properly position a model, the internal coordinates of the vertices that define that model must be positioned appropriately around their own internal point of origin.

Just as every object in gameSpace is positioned in relation to a central origin, each object also has its own internal axes. An object's axes are typically placed at the center or center of mass of an object. This origin can be manually repositioned to satisfy a variety of needs. An object's internal axes can also be changed as a result of geometry changes and modeling operations. This is what happened to the gem.

There are many times when an object's internal axes have to be offset in a particular way. A model of a door, for instance, is usually positioned with its internal axes aligned with the door's hinges. The door's access defines its pivot point, about which it will swing, when it is rotated in a game level.

gameSpace gives you several tools to adjust the placement of an object's origin. These tools are located in the toolbar slot that is immediately to the right of the UV Projection tools.

Activate the "Move axes to center of object" tool, shown in Figure 8.35.

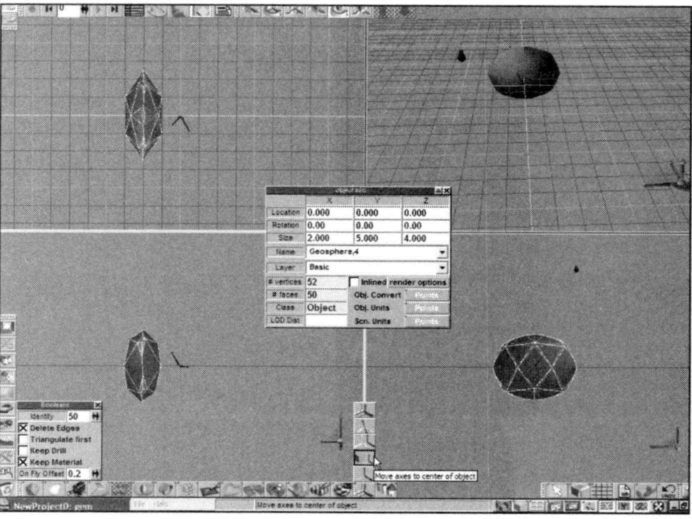

Figure 8.35
Center the object's internal axes.

The gem should now appear properly centered. See Figure 8.36. Use the Object Info Pane to be sure it is located at the precisely 0, 0, 0 on the X, Y, and Z axes.

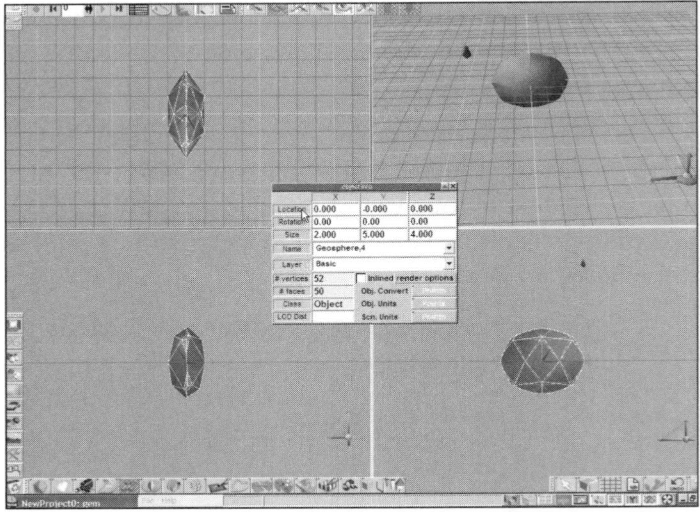

Figure 8.36
The object is now centered on its origin.

The gem is now centered perfectly on its own origin. It is also still centered perfectly on the world origin, so it appears directly above the origin lines on the gameSpace grid.

Use the Object tool to reselect the gem, and then save the scene by selecting File > Save As > Scene from the File menu.

Select File > Save As > Object to save the gem as a DirectX .x file in its own folder. See Figure 8.37.

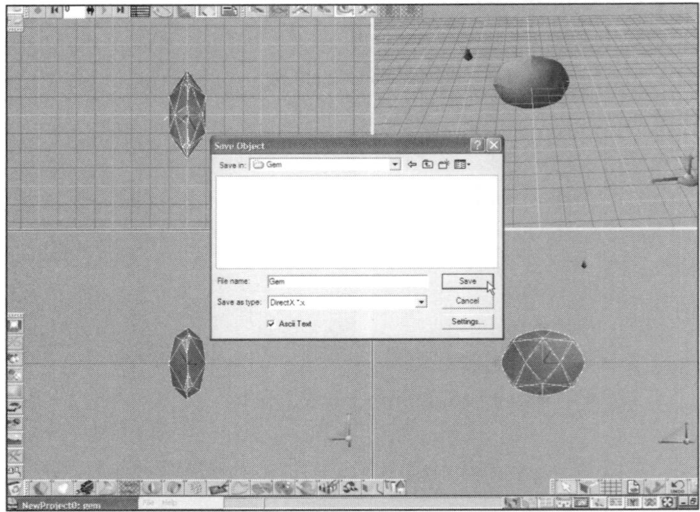

Figure 8.37
Save the gem in its own folder.

Close gameSpace, and use ObjectImporter to choose your new gem model as Game Object 3.

Launch AdventureExplorer. Cross the river, arrange and climb the crates, and climb the stairs to enter the treasure vault. If this is too much work, simply hold down the Shift key and press the right-bracket (]) key. This is a backdoor shortcut to jump into the treasure vault.

Figure 8.38 shows the new gem, atop the crate in the treasure vault.

Figure 8.38
The gem sits on a crate.

Regardless of how shiny or polished the gem may appear, it is hardly impressive sitting on a crate. Every setting tells a story, and the story this setting tells is that someone dropped a rock on a box and then left it in a corner. This is hardly the story of an epic quest.

Sculpting a Pedestal

Exit AdventureExplorer and launch gameSpace. Create a new scene by selecting File > New > Scene from the File menu.

Select the Cylinder primitive tool to bring it into the toolbar slot. See Figure 8.39. Right-click in any viewport to deactivate the Cylinder primitive tool, and then right-click the Cylinder primitive icon. The Cylinder options panel appears, as shown in Figure 8.39.

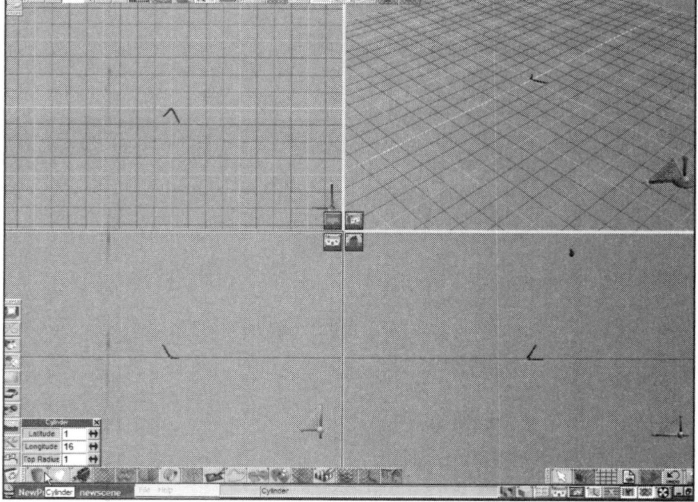
Figure 8.39
Right-click the Cylinder primitive tool to display the Cylinder options panel.

The Latitude parameter controls the number or density of the faces from the top to the bottom of the cylinder. Figure 8.40 shows a series of cylinders with increasing Latitude values.

The Longitude parameter controls the number or density of the faces that make up the curved surface of the cylinder. Figure 8.41 shows a series of cylinders with increasing Longitude values.

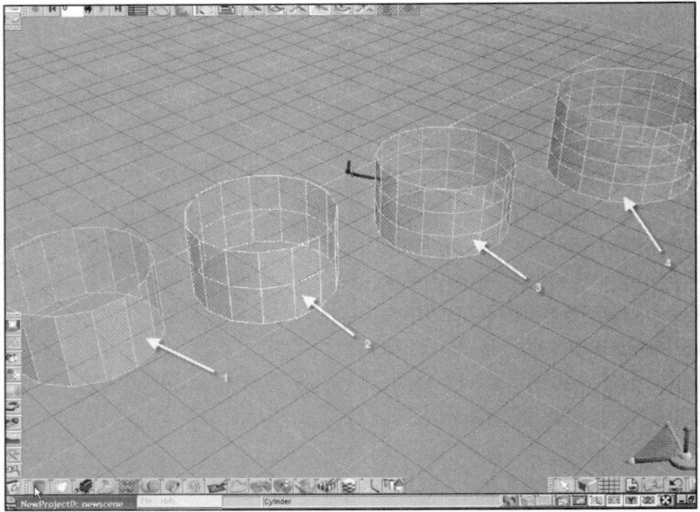

Figure 8.40
Each of these cylinders has a different Latitude value.

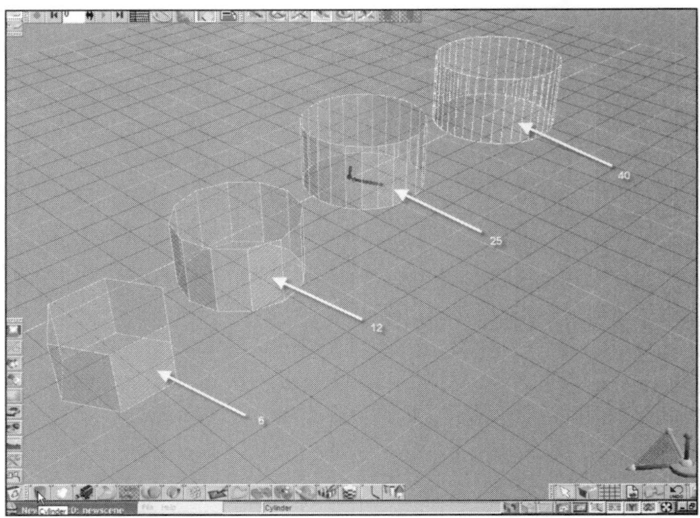

Figure 8.41
Each of these cylinders has a different Longitude value.

The Top Radius parameter represents the ratio between the size of the top of the cylinder and the size of the bottom of the cylinder. Figure 8.42 illustrates the impact of the Top Radius parameter.

Set the parameters in the Cylinder options window as indicated in Table 8.2 and in Figure 8.43.

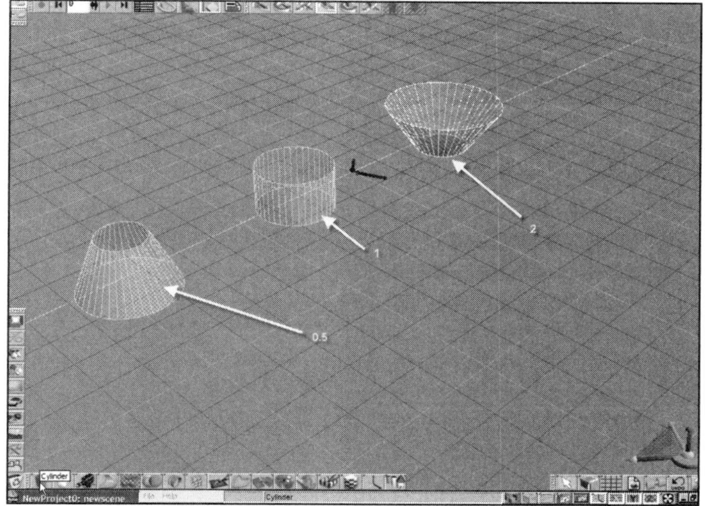

Figure 8.42
Each of these cylinders has a different Top Radius value.

Table 8.2 Cylinder Parameters

Latitude	1
Longitude	8
Top Radius	1

Use the Cylinder primitive tool to create a cylinder. Right-click on the Object tool to display the Object Info Pane. Adjust the new cylinder in accordance with Table 8.3 on the next page.

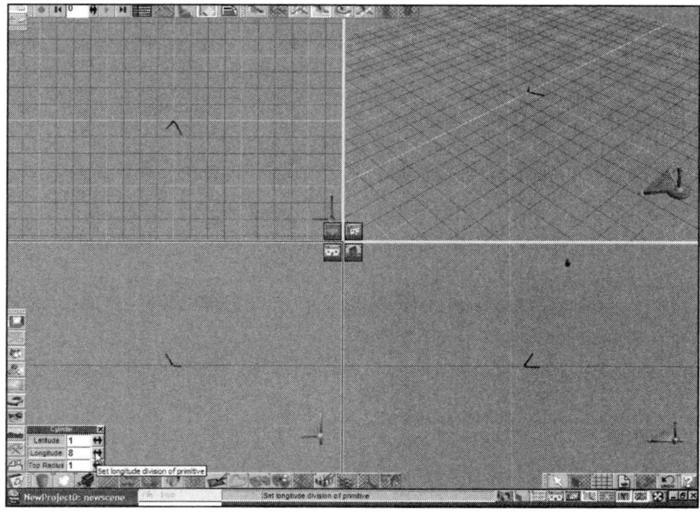

Figure 8.43
Set the Longitude to 8.

Table 8.3 Cylinder Object Parameters

	X	Y	Z
Location	0	0	2
Rotation	0	0	0
Scale	2	2	4

All units and screen units are set in Points.

For the top of the pedestal, you will create an elaborately tapered cylinder.

Reactivate the Cylinder primitive tool, and then right-click the Cylinder primitive icon. Two panels appear above the primitive tools slot. The Primitive parameters and Primitive shape panels appear whenever you right-click a primitive tool's icon once that tool is already activated.

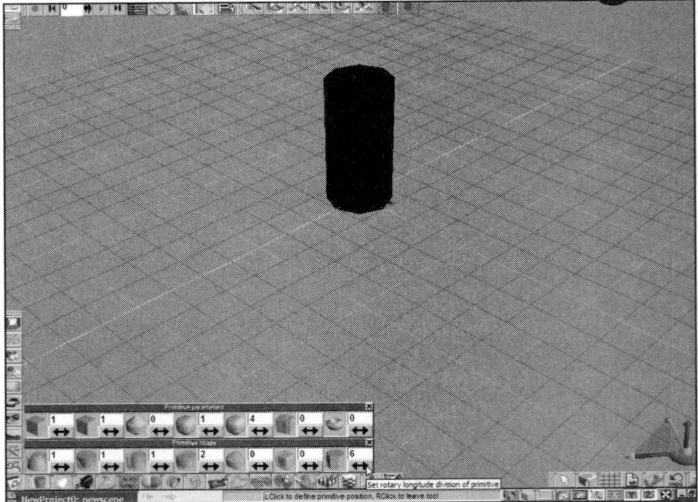

Figure 8.44
This cylinder will be the vertical support element of the pedestal.

tip

Each primitive tool has its own unique option panel that appears if you right-click that tool's icon when it is not currently activated. The Primitive parameters and Primitive shape panels appear when you right-click on any primitive tool that is already activated.

The Primitive parameters panel controls the density and complexity of the mesh created for a new primitive. These parameters allow you to precisely adjust the level of detail in the new object.

The Primitive shape panel controls the size, angles, and aspect ratios of the various components of a new primitive. The controls on this panel allow you to adjust the overall form of the new object.

Use the Primitive shape panel to set the rotary bottom radius to 0.8. This makes the bottom of the cylinder 20 percent smaller than the top of the cylinder. See Figure 8.45.

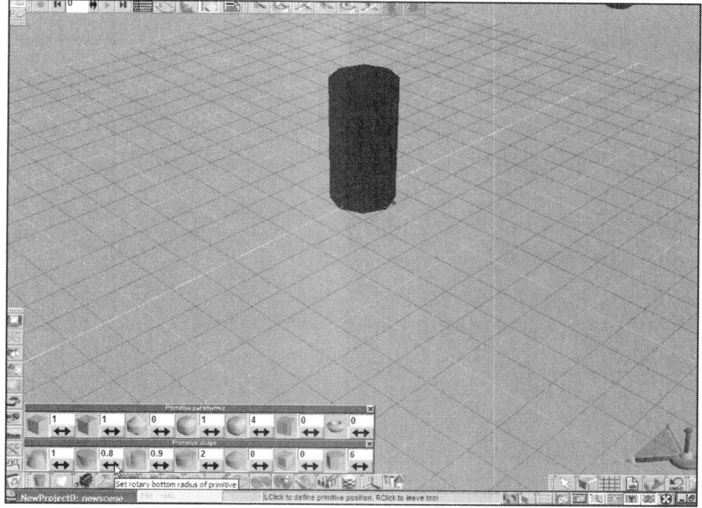

Figure 8.45
The bottom of the next cylinder should taper in slightly.

tip

After you create a new primitive, the Primitive parameters and Primitive shape panels can be used to adjust that primitive interactively as long as the Magic Ring controls remain visible.

Use the Primitive parameters panel to set the conic latitude to 4. This divides the top and bottom of the cylinder into four rings of faces. See Figure 8.46.

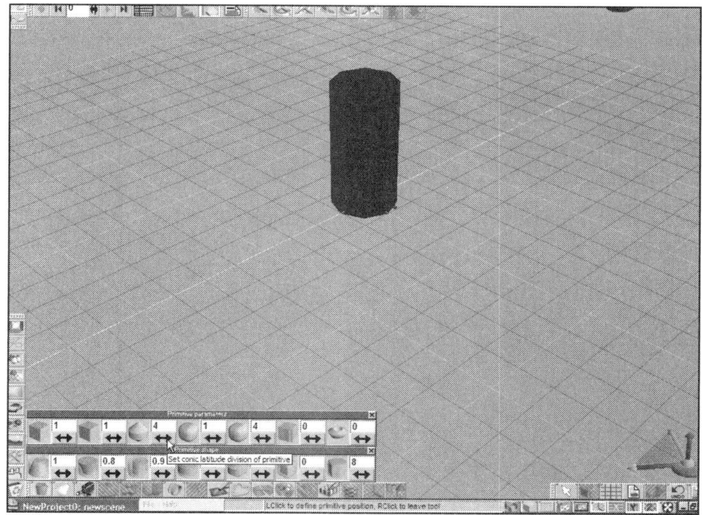

Figure 8.46
The two end-caps of the cylinder should be divided into four rings of faces.

Use the Cylinder primitive tool to create a new cylinder. See Figure 8.47.

Use the Magic Ring control to create a depression in the top of the cylinder. Click and drag the red segment of the Magic Ring control, as shown in Figure 8.48.

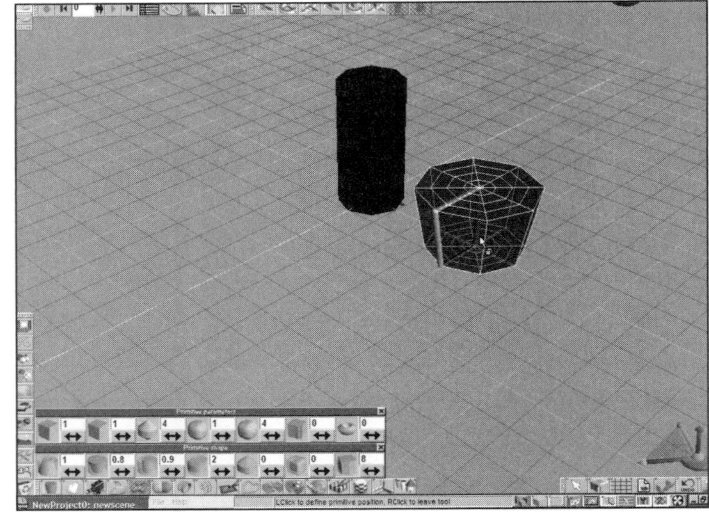

Figure 8.47
This cylinder will be the top of the pedestal.

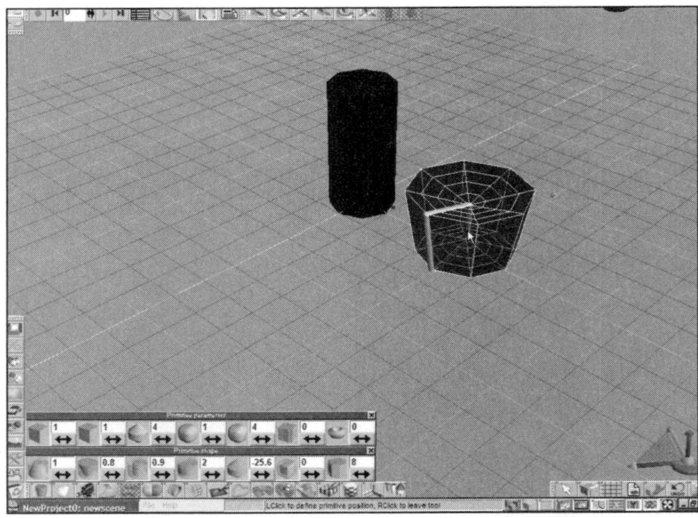

Figure 8.48
Drag downward over the red segment of the Magic Ring control.

Use the green segment of the Magic Ring control to reduce the height of the cylinder. The completed cylinder should appear as shown in Figure 8.49.

Use the Object Info Pane to position and scale the new cylinder as indicated in Table 8.4 below and in Figure 8.50 on the next page.

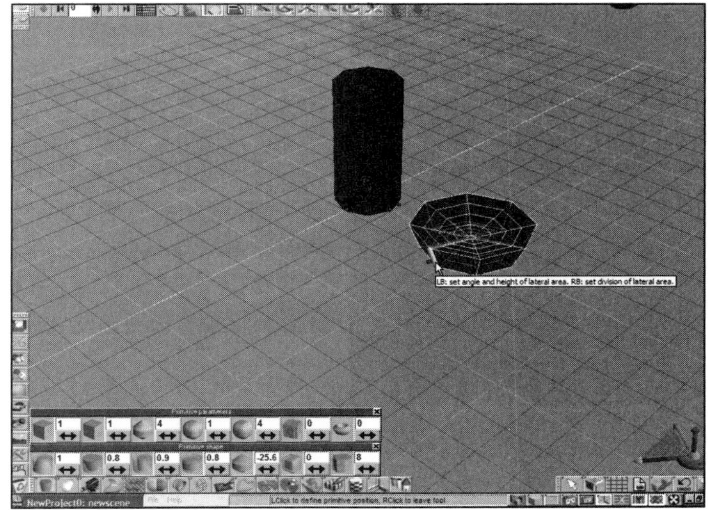

Figure 8.49
Drag downward over the green segment of the Magic Ring control.

Table 8.4 Cylinder Object Parameters

	X	Y	Z
Location	0	0	0
Rotation	0	0	0
Scale	3.5	3.5	7.8

All units and screen units are set in Points.

Set the axes enable buttons to disable movement along the X axis. Using the Object Move tool, drag the gem upward in the front view until it appears as shown in Figure 8.51.

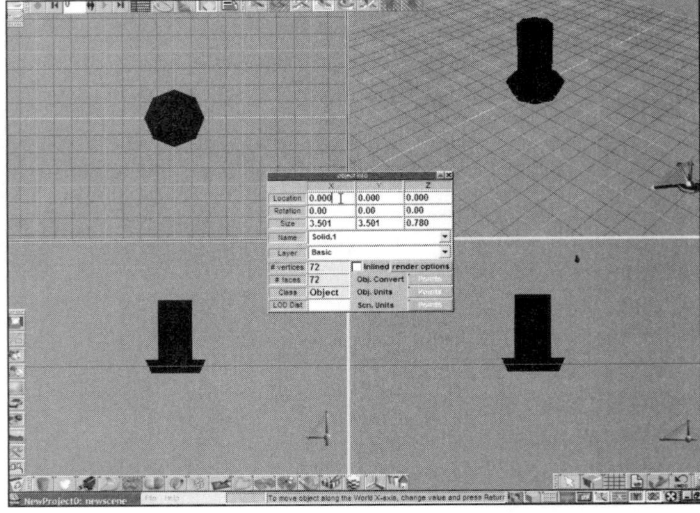

Figure 8.50
Use the Object Info Pane to position and scale the new cylinder.

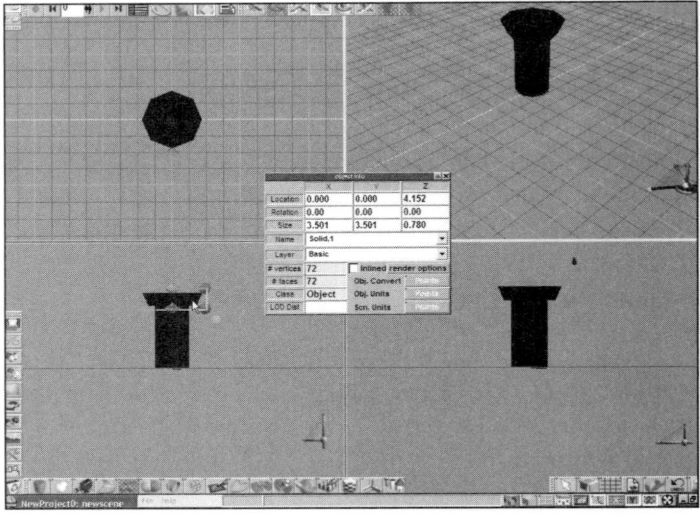

Figure 8.51
Move the new cylinder to the top of the pedestal.

Using the Primitive shape panel set the rotary longitude value to 6. See Figure 8.52.

Adjust the rest of the parameters in the Primitive shape panel, as shown in Figure 8.53.

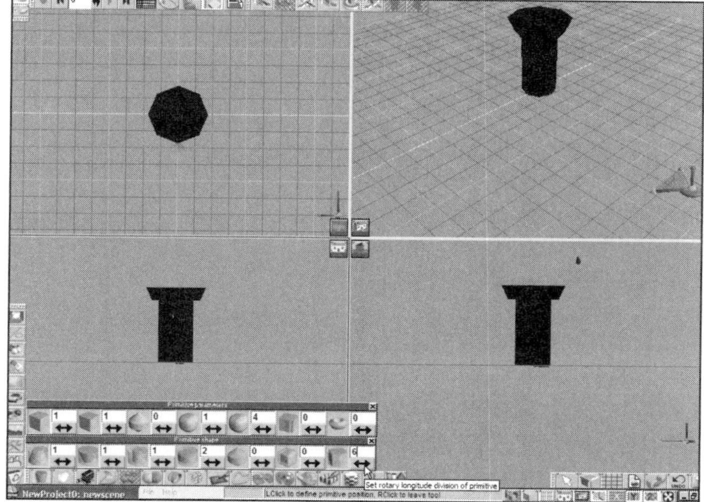

Figure 8.52
Set the rotary longitude to 6.

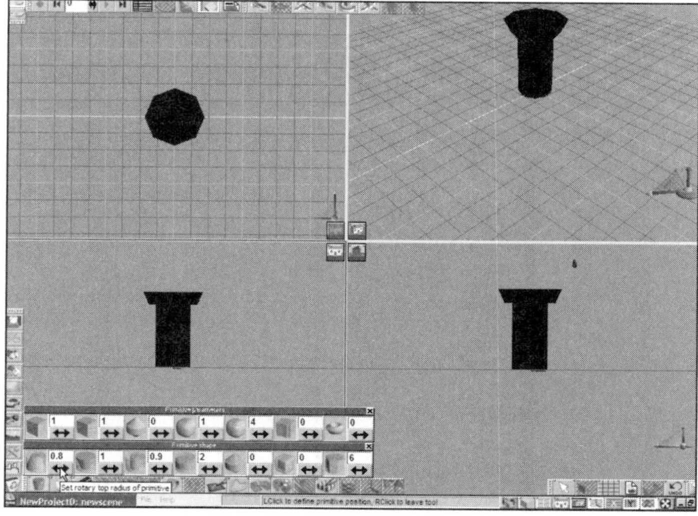

Figure 8.53
The next cylinder tapers in toward the top.

Use the Cylinder primitive tool to create a new cylinder, as shown in Figure 8.54.

Use the green segment of the Magic Ring control to adjust the height of the new cylinder, until it appears as shown in Figure 8.55.

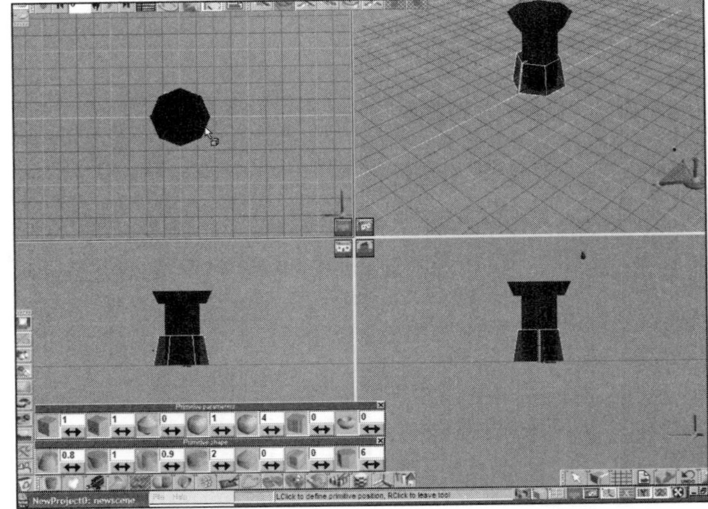

Figure 8.54
Click and drag to create a new cylinder.

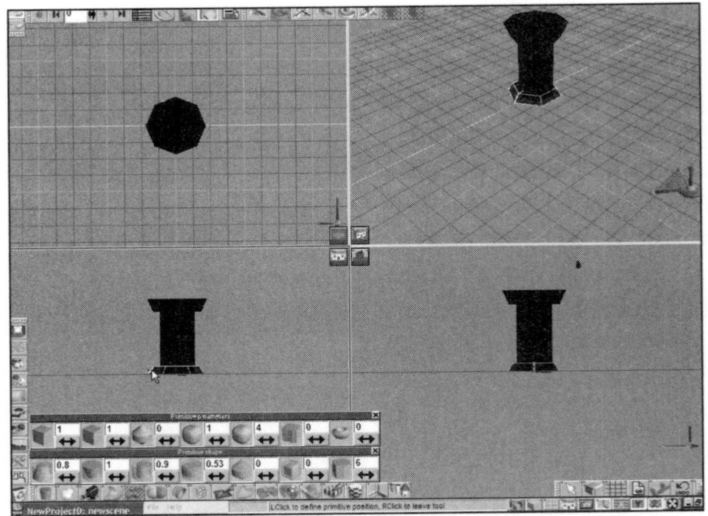

Figure 8.55
Use the Object Info Pane to position and scale the new cylinder.

Select the first cylinder, the vertical support section of the pedestal, and activate the Object Union tool. See Figure 8.56.

Use the Object Union tool to click on the top cylinder. See Figure 8.57.

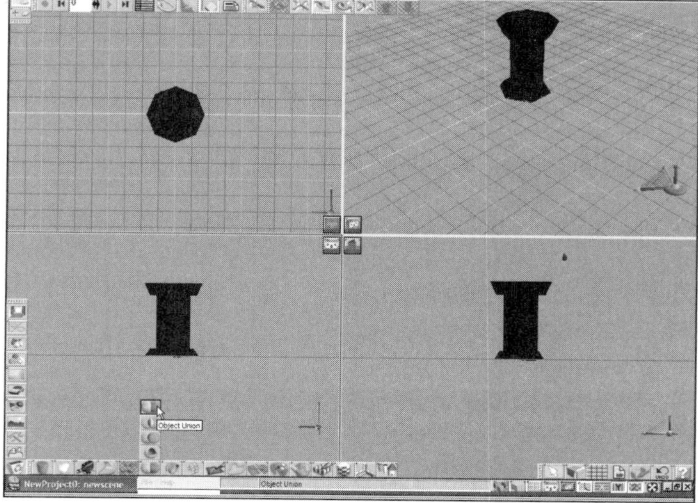

Figure 8.56
Activate the Object Union tool.

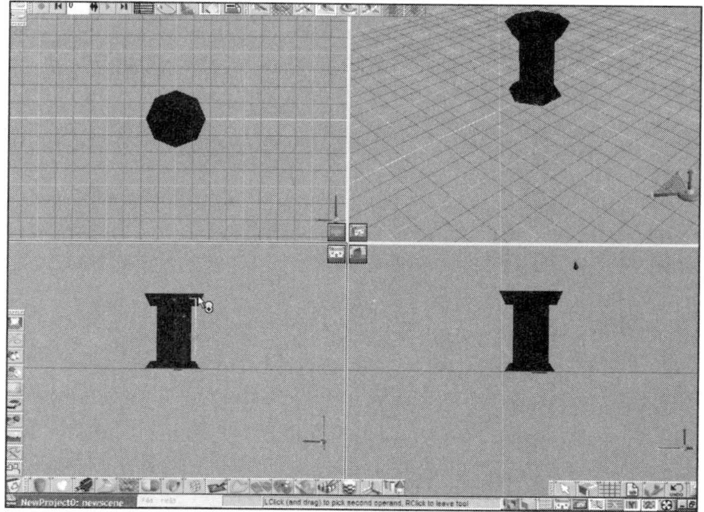

Figure 8.57
Perform a Boolean union operation to combine the pedestal with its top.

Continue using the Object Union tool to click on the bottom cylinder. See Figure 8.58.

Open the Material Editor, and double-click on the Blue Marble material. See Figure 8.59.

The Blue Marble material is a composite of two layers. The base layer uses a Granite shader, which automatically generates a rocklike pattern. The second layer uses a Solid Clouds shader.

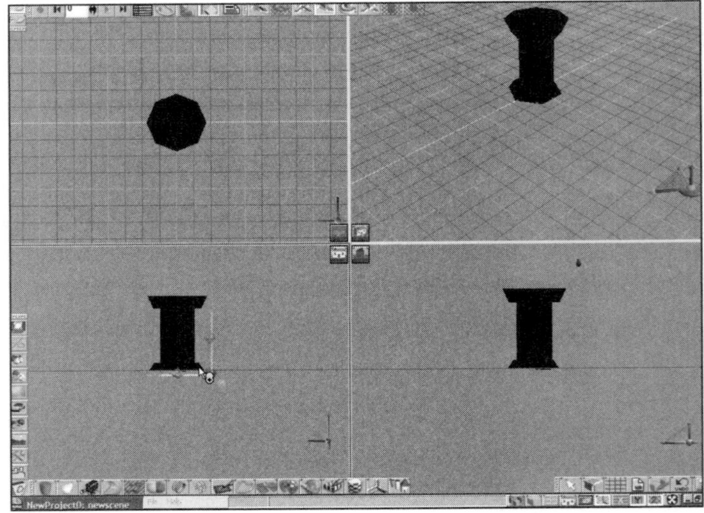

Figure 8.58
Perform a Boolean union operation to combine the pedestal with its base.

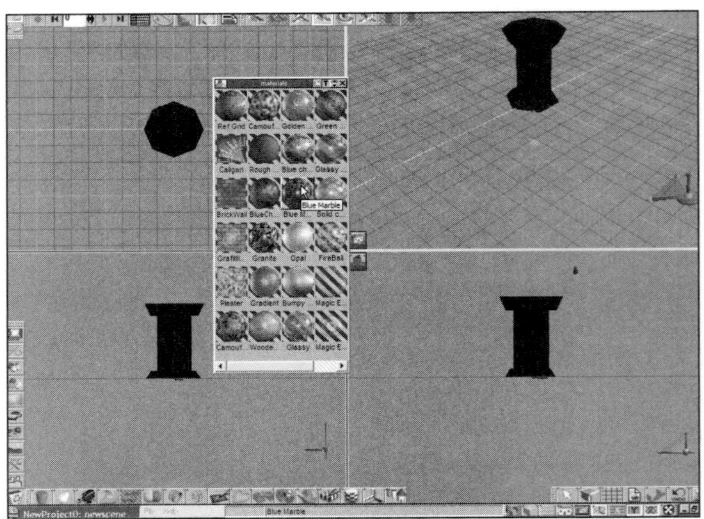

Figure 8.59
Choose the Blue Marble material.

Expand the Material Editor, and select Layer 2. See Figure 8.60.

The Solid Clouds shader uses a foreground color and a background color to generate a cloud pattern. Click the blue color swatch labeled Back Color, as shown in Figure 8.61.

Figure 8.60
Select Layer 2 using the eye icons in the Material Editor.

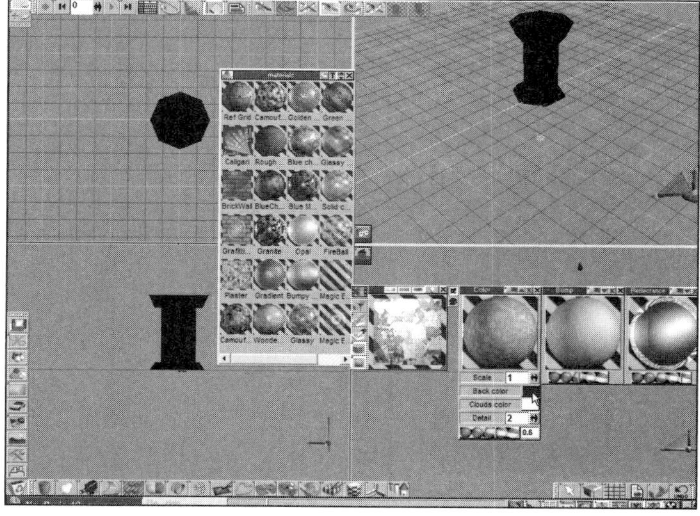

Figure 8.61
Click the Back Color swatch.

The Background Color picker appears. Select a new color for this layer. I chose a light green color for the cloudy background. See Figure 8.62.

Use the Paint Object tool to apply the material to the pedestal. See Figure 8.63.

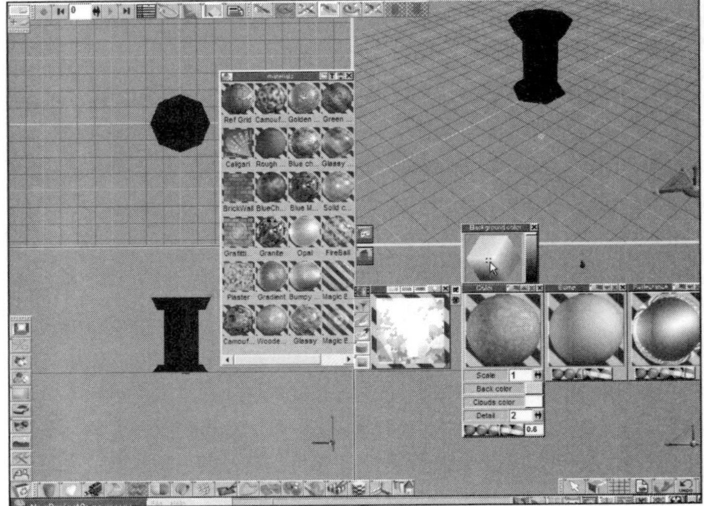

Figure 8.62
Use the Background Color picker to change the color.

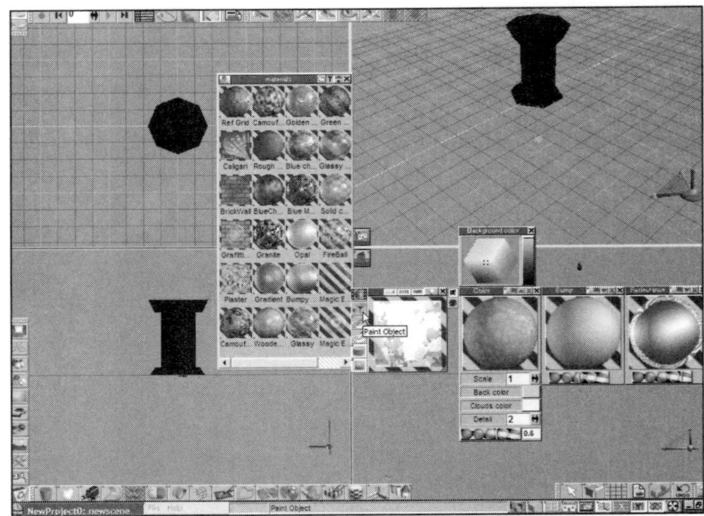

Figure 8.63
Apply the material to the pedestal.

Table 8.5 Pedestal Object Parameters

	X	Y	Z
Location	0	0	5
Rotation	0	0	0
Scale	8	8	12

All units and screen units are set in Points.

Use the Object Info Pane to adjust the scale as shown in Table 8.5 and in Figure 8.64.

The pedestal should appear as shown in Figure 8.65.

Save the scene by selecting File > Save As > Scene, and then save the object as a DirectX .x file by selecting File > Save As > Object.

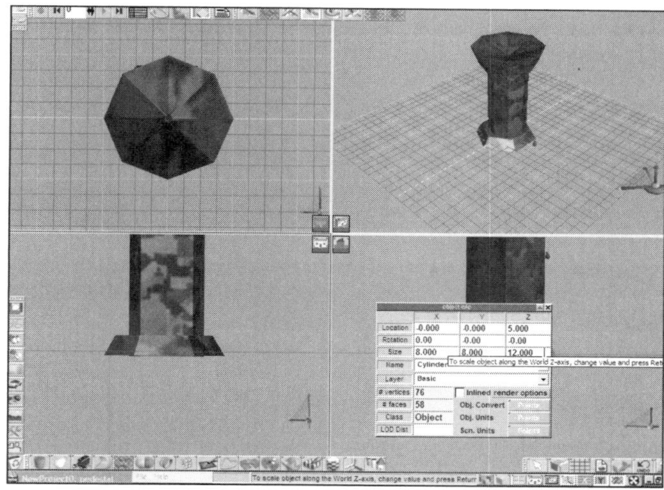

Figure 8.64
Use the Object Info Pane to stretch the height of the pedestal.

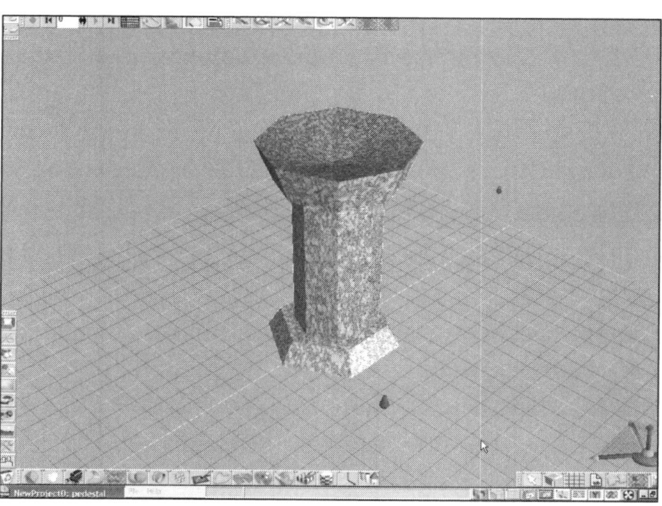

Figure 8.65
This is the textured pedestal.

Use ObjectImporter to choose the pedestal as Game Object 4. Close ObjectImporter and play the game. See Figure 8.66.

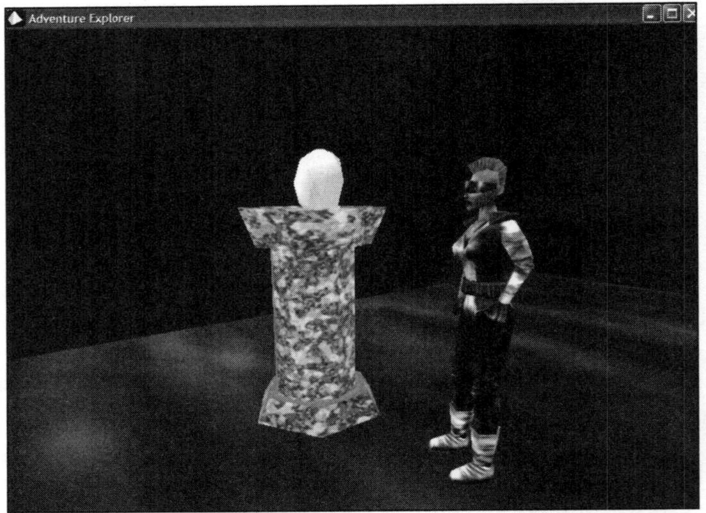

Figure 8.66
The gem looks much better on top of the pedestal.

Summary

In this chapter, you should have learned the following concepts:

- There are three Boolean geometry operations: union, subtraction, and intersection.
- The Boolean union operation merges two objects together.
- The Boolean subtraction operation subtracts one object from another.
- The Boolean intersection operation removes all sections of two objects that do not overlap.
- gameSpace provides three Boolean operation tools in the form of the Object Union, Object Subtraction, and Object Intersection tools.
- The Boolean operations each operate on two objects at a time.
- The Object Shell tool is used to create a hollow shell in the shape of a single existing object.
- Right-clicking the icon of any primitive tool while it is not activated opens that primitive's own options panel.
- Right-clicking the icon of any primitive tool while it is activated displays the Primitive shape and Primitive parameters panels.
- Materials can be composed of multiple layers.

- Each material layer has its own set of Color, Bump, and Reflectance shaders.
- The eye icons select between the layers that make up a material.
- The transparency of each layer's shaders can be set independently.
- Use the pop-up menu that appears when you right-click in the Material Editor's preview window to create or delete a material layer.
- The Shrink Wrap UV Projection tool automatically fits texture coordinates to the shape of an object.
- Every object has its own internal axes and origin.
- The "Move axes to center of object" tool aligns an object's axes to its center.

Questions and Answers

Q: The order of object selection is essential to which Boolean operations?

A: The order of object selection is only significant when performing Boolean subtraction.

Q: What is the Boolean operation that adds two objects' geometry to form a single object?

A: Boolean union is an operation that adds the geometry of two objects.

Q: If a material has several layers, how do you select one of those layers in the Material Editor?

A: Use the eye icons, which cling to the right of the Material Editor's preview window, to select any individual layer within the Material Editor.

Q: Where is the icon for the Shell tool found?

A: The Shell tool is grouped with the Object Union, Object Subtraction, and Object Intersection tools.

Q: How does a material's base layer differ from any other layers in the Material Editor?

A: The base layer is the first layer applied to the object, and all other layers are applied on top of it. Because it is the first layer, the base layer is the only layer that does not have a transparency control for each of its shaders.

Q: If Box A is completely inside Box B, what would happen if you use the Object Union tool on Box A and Box B?

A: Box A would be swallowed by Box B, and the result would be identical to Box B.

Q: If Box A is completely inside Box B, what would happen if you perform a Boolean intersection on Box A from Box B?

A: The portions of Box B that are outside of Box A would be removed, and the result would look exactly like Box A.

Discussion Questions

1. How does a Boolean union operation differ from the effects of the glue tool? Describe a situation where one solution would be better than the other.
2. Describe an object that could be easily modeled using Boolean union.
3. Describe an object that could be easily modeled using Boolean intersection.
4. Describe a use for the Shell tool.
5. Describe the effect of the Shrink Wrap UV Projection tool.
6. Describe how you would create three different but similar textures using a common material base layer.
7. Discuss how you would model a coffee mug using the Boolean operations.
8. Discuss how you would model the same coffee mug with the added help of the Shell tool.

Exercises

1. Create a scene in gameSpace consisting of a series of four spheres with a longitude parameter value of 8 and a latitude parameter value of 4, 8, 16, and 32, respectively.
2. Use appropriate primitive tool to create a perfect octagon. An octagon is a regular polygon with eight identical sides.
3. Create a single primitive using the Primitive shape and Primitive parameters panels in the shape of the object shown in Figure 8.67.

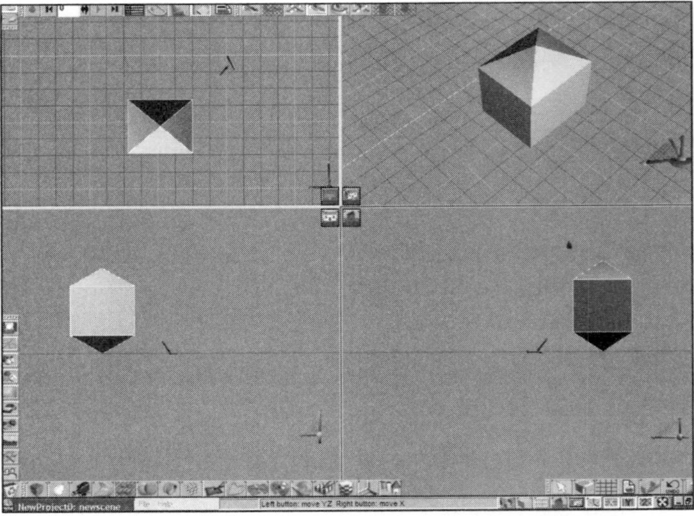

Figure 8.67
Create this shape using a single primitive.

4. Using the Shell tool, a cylinder, and Boolean subtraction, convert the object you built in Exercise 3 into the birdhouse shown in Figure 8.68.
5. Use the Material Editor to create a material that has three material layers.
6. Apply the material from Exercise 5 to a cube, change one material layer, and apply the altered material to three sides of the cube.
7. Use primitives and Boolean operations to model the snowman shown in Figure 8.69.

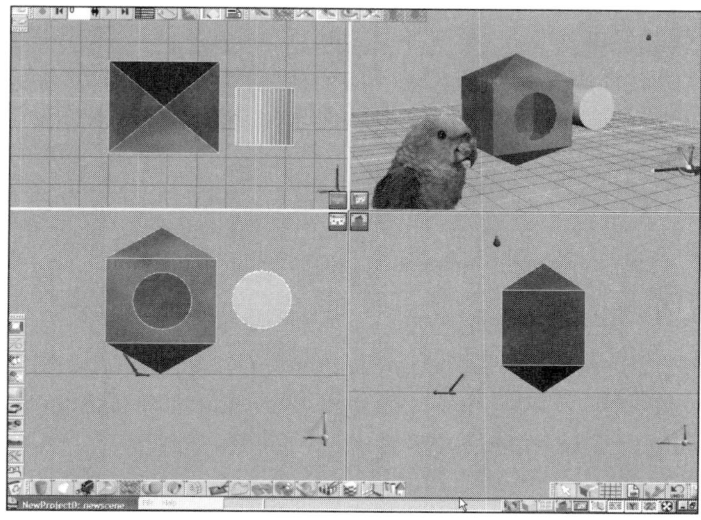

Figure 8.68
Create this birdhouse. Sherman, the bird, is only for extra credit.

Figure 8.69
Happy Holidays!

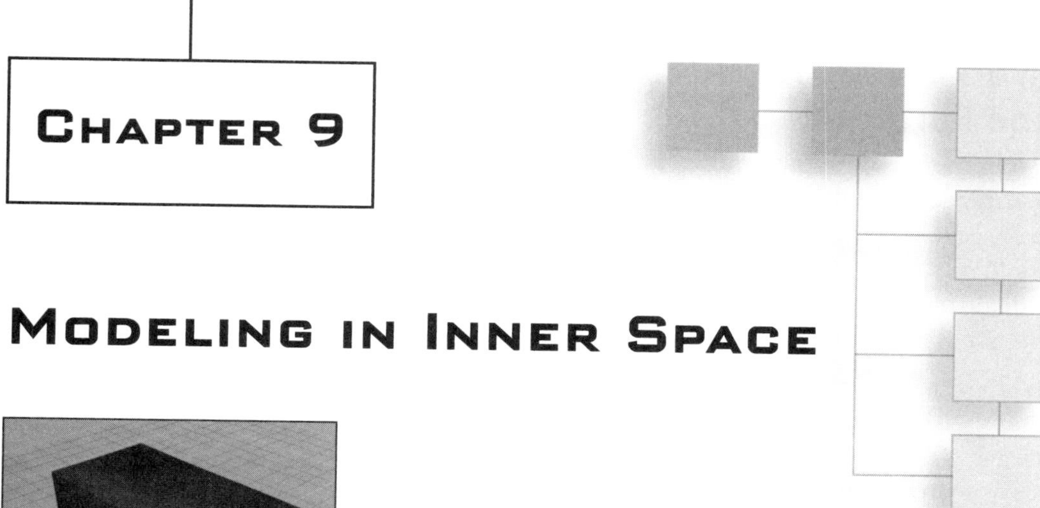

Chapter 9

Modeling in Inner Space

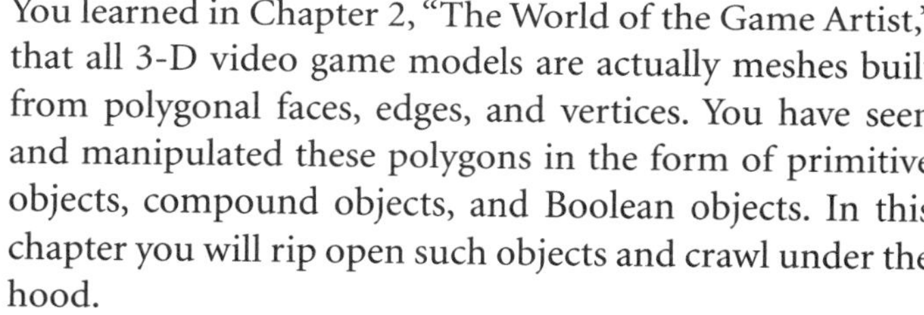

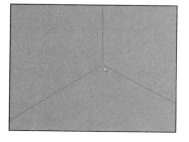

You learned in Chapter 2, "The World of the Game Artist," that all 3-D video game models are actually meshes built from polygonal faces, edges, and vertices. You have seen and manipulated these polygons in the form of primitive objects, compound objects, and Boolean objects. In this chapter you will rip open such objects and crawl under the hood.

Introduction

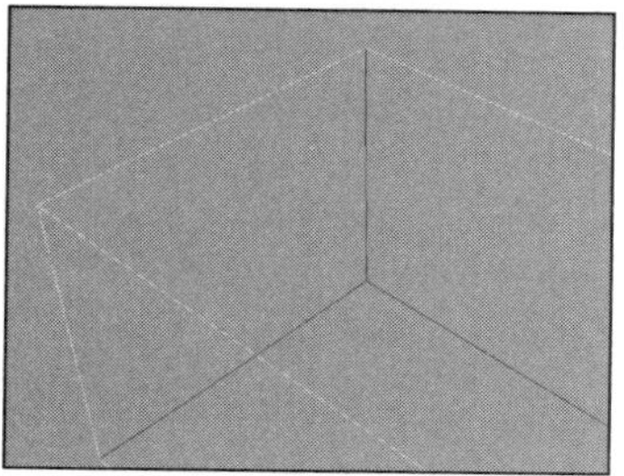

Through the mighty microscope you descend. The models around you grow larger and larger as you shrink into the vastness of virtual inner space. The solid cube that stood so massively before you begins to appear porous and hollow. Its walls are but ethereal holograms framed by thin wirelike edges. The edges are strung between vertices like narrow beams of light. From this microscopic vantage point, you can see the vertices, the individual dots that hold the edges firmly in place. Legends speak of a time when powerful sorcerers could manipulate individual vertices. They could shift, create, and destroy the very vertices and edges that gave an object its form and shape. They could mutate solid simple primitives into complex masterpieces of unspeakable beauty. They call these sorcerers game artists, and the powerful magic they used is as simple as a right-click.

Working Below the Surface

Begin a new scene in gameSpace. Use the Create new scene icon on the main toolbar toward the right side of the screen. See Figure 9.1.

It is not necessary, but you may wish to select the Draw as wire icon, as shown in Figure 9.2. A transparent wire-frame display mode will make the following demonstration easier to see.

Figure 9.1
Create a new scene.

Figure 9.2
Select the Draw as wire icon.

Create a simple cube primitive, and select it using the Object tool. See Figure 9.3.

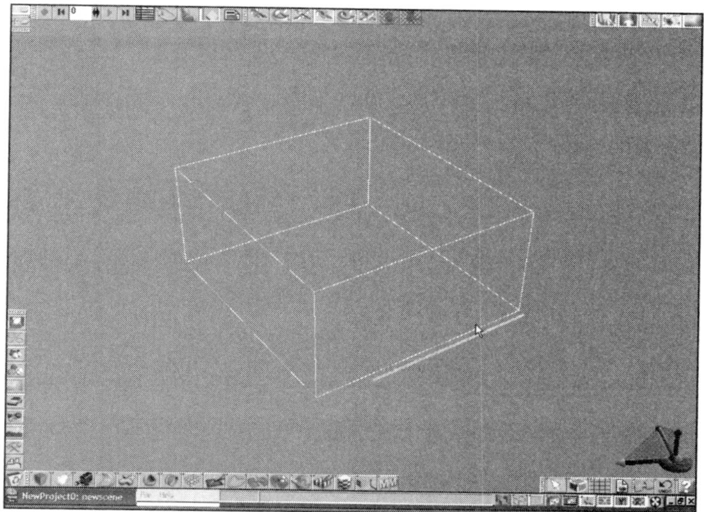

Figure 9.3
Create a cube and select it.

Point Edit Mode

To access the individual faces, edges, and vertices that define the cube, you will work in Point Edit mode. The easiest way to enter Point Edit mode is to right-click on the selected object. See Figure 9.4.

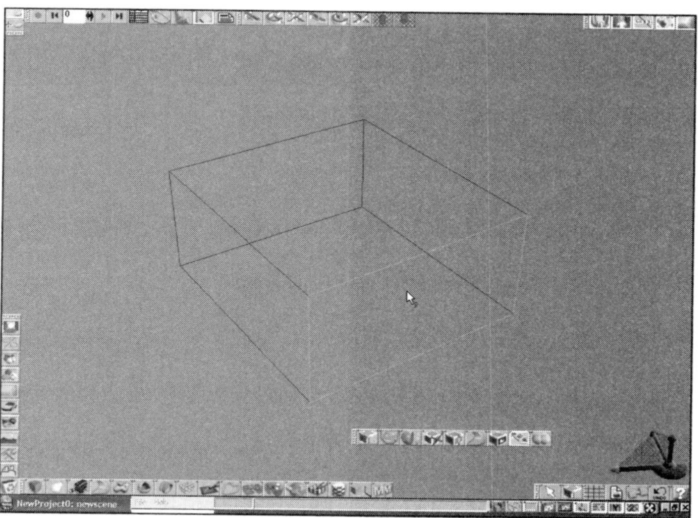

Figure 9.4
Right-click to enter Point Edit mode.

tip

It is easy to move or collapse the Point Edit mode's toolbar by clicking or dragging the black pin or the handle. The handle is the small silver strip at the far left of the toolbar. In its totally minimized state, the toolbar may be reduced to a very small silver cube. If you are in Point Edit mode and find you have lost or misplaced the toolbar, click the Reset Tool Bars Layout icon, as shown in Figure 9.5.

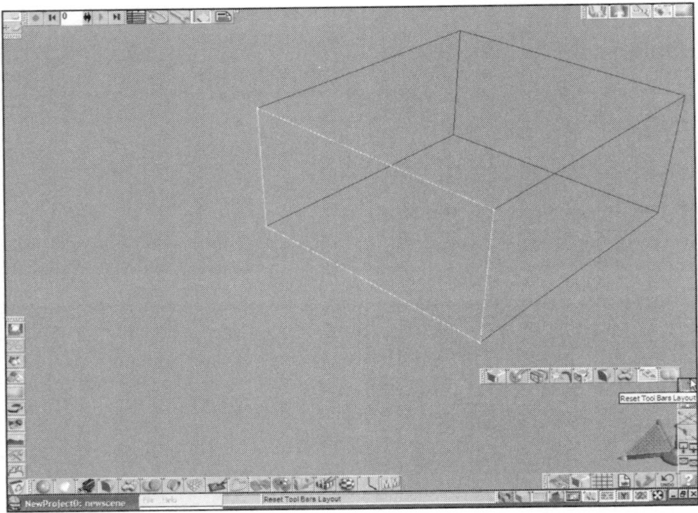

Figure 9.5
Use this icon to retrieve a misplaced toolbar.

tip

You can also select Point Edit mode by clicking the Point Edit icon in the toolbar slot to the right of the Object tool. See Figure 9.6 and 9.7.

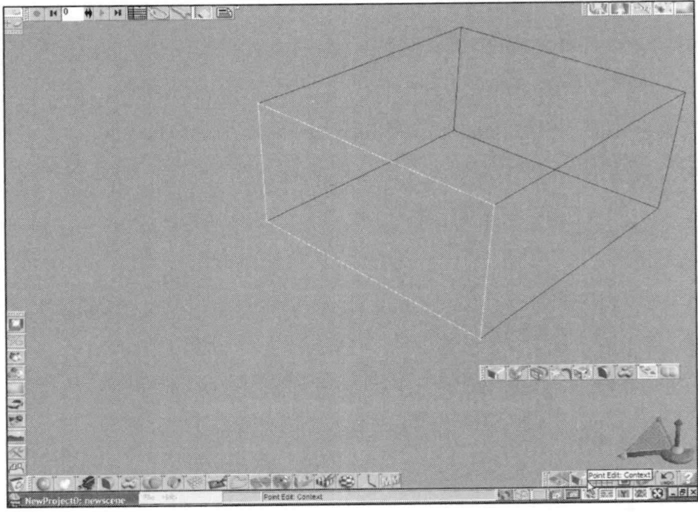

Figure 9.6
This icon selects Point Edit mode.

Use Point Edit: Faces mode to select the side face of the cube. Select the Point Move tool as shown in Figure 9.8. The Point Move tool is just like the Object Move tool, only it applies to selected faces, edges, or vertices.

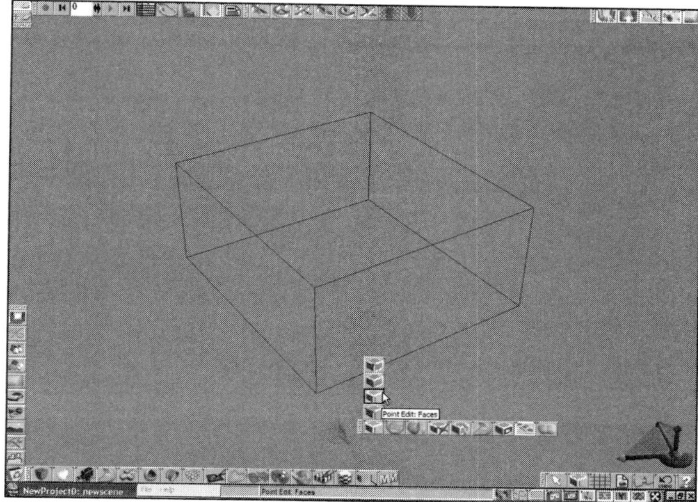

Figure 9.7
The Point Edit: Faces mode allows you to select and edit only the faces in an object.

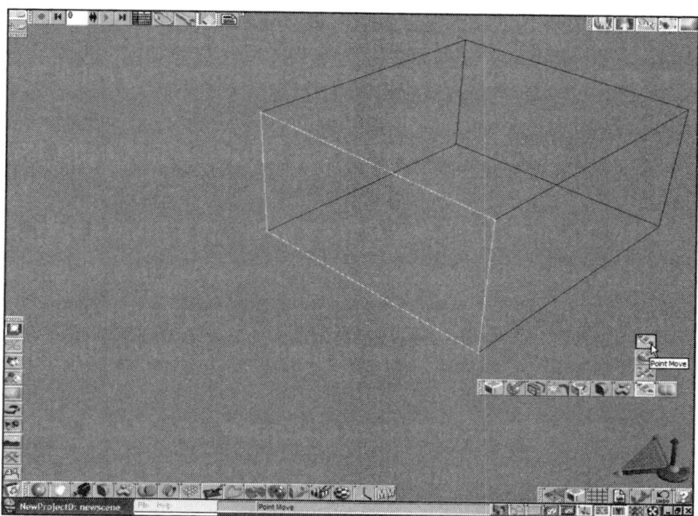

Figure 9.8
Choose the Point Move tool.

If you are working in a single viewport configuration, use the icon shown in Figure 9.9 to change to a multiple viewport configuration.

Disable movement along the Y axis. Use the Point Move tool to drag the selected face of the cube in the top view until it appears similar to Figure 9.10.

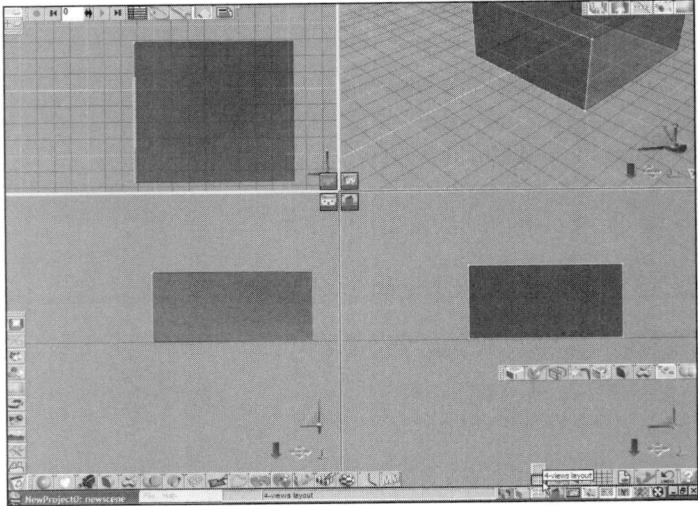

Figure 9.9
Select the multiple viewport screen configuration.

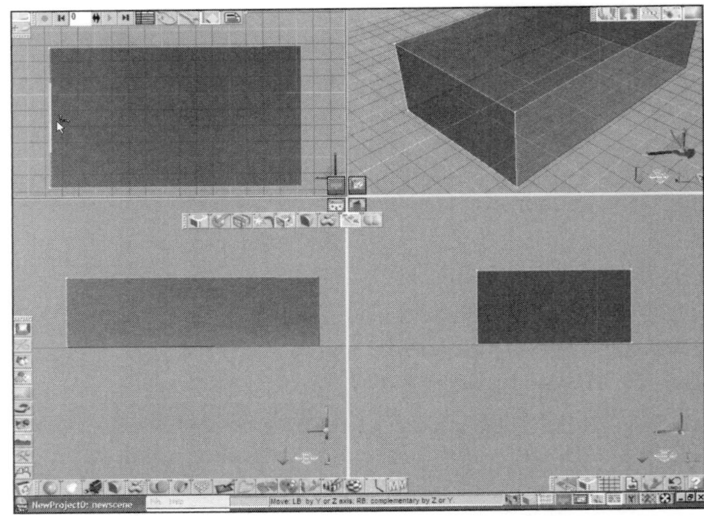

Figure 9.10
Use the Point Move tool to adjust the selected face.

Notice how the shape of the cube changes in the perspective viewport. Select the Point Scale tool shown in Figure 9.11.

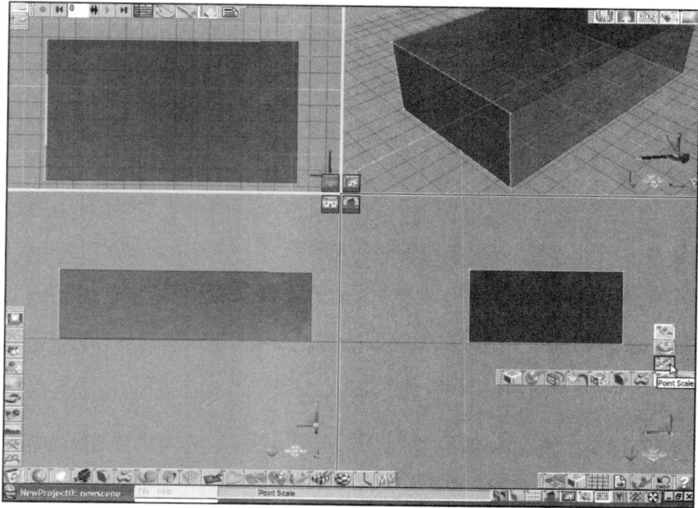

Figure 9.11
Select the Point Scale tool.

Click and drag in the side viewport to shrink the selected face. The face is only scaled along the viewport's X axis, because the Y axis is still disabled. Watch the perspective viewport as you drag in the side viewport. See Figure 9.12.

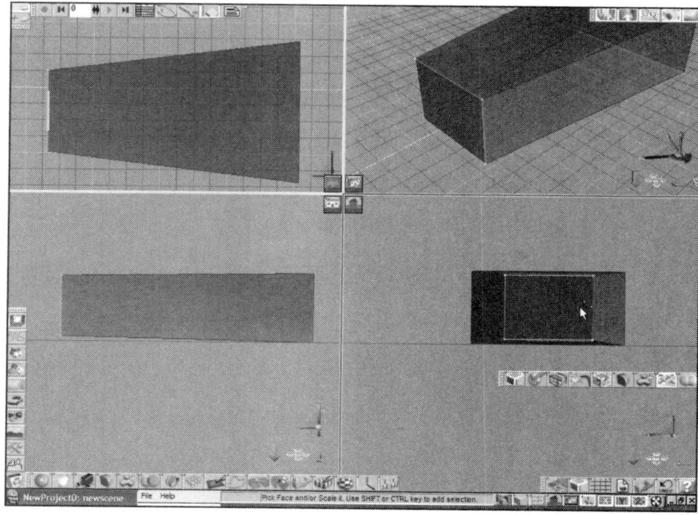

Figure 9.12
Scale down the selected face.

Now that you have seen how to manipulate a face, switch to the Point Edit: Vertices mode, as shown in Figure 9.13.

Select the vertex that is the top left corner of the face you just edited. Use the perspective viewport, as shown in Figure 9.14.

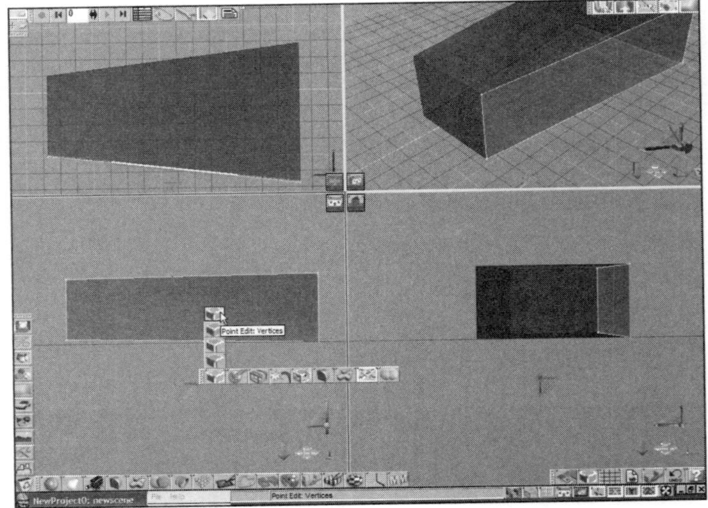

Figure 9.13
Select the Point Edit: Vertices mode.

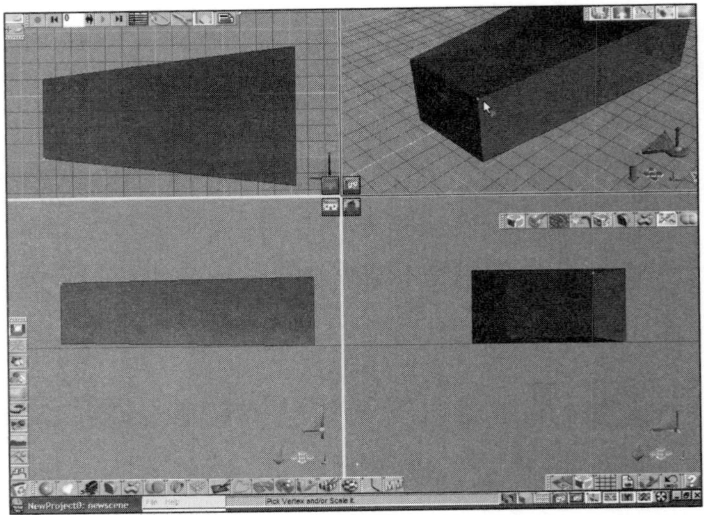

Figure 9.14
Select this vertex.

Disable movement along the X axis and enable movement along the Y axis. Select the Point Move tool as shown in Figure 9.15.

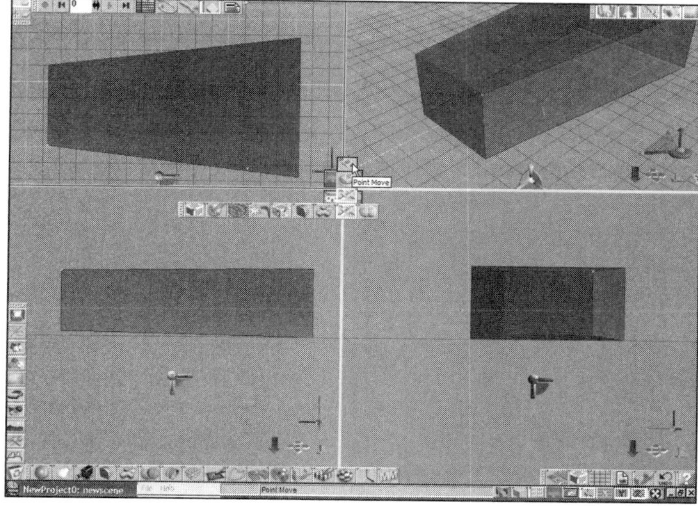

Figure 9.15
Reselect the Point Move tool.

Click and drag downward in the front or side viewports until the vertex moves into the position shown in Figure 9.16.

The cube is no longer recognizable as a cube. Using Point Edit mode, you can move, scale and rotate any vertex, edge or face, or any group of vertices, edges or faces. This gives you incredible control of an object's form.

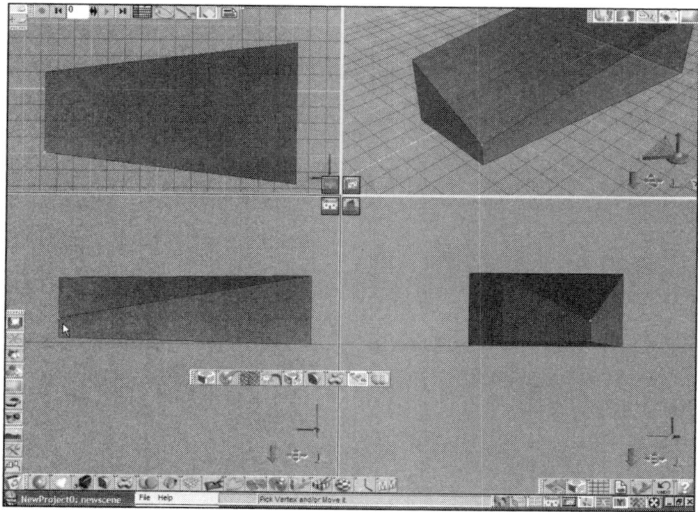

Figure 9.16
Use the Point Move tool to reposition the vertex.

Conjuring Geometry

I'll roll up my sleeves to demonstrate that there is nothing in my hands. I place a small silk scarf in the palm of my right hand, and with the left hand, I slowly gesture as if tugging on an imaginary string. The square silk begins to grow and rise out of my hand, draping into the form of a large silky cube. This is the magic of extrusion.

Extrusion is the process of manufacturing an object by pushing it through or thrusting it out of another object.

Extrusion is not always a magical process. Many real-world products are manufactured by squeezing compressed plastic or liquid metal through a precisely shaped opening. A simple demonstration of extrusion occurs whenever you squeeze an open tube of toothpaste. The toothpaste comes out as a long cylinder, in the precise shape of the round hole through which it passes.

As a student at California State University Northridge, I attended a class entitled Manufacturing Processes and Materials. I was given the assignment to arrange a field trip for the class to any place that manufactured a product using the process of extrusion. I spent weeks trying to find an example of extrusion in the Los Angeles area. Strict manufacturing regulations had driven most extruders out of the area, and the ones that remained were either unwilling or unable to accommodate our class. I finally found one willing extruder and arranged a visit for the class.

A few days after the field trip, I met my mom for dinner at an Olive Garden restaurant. As we waited in the lobby, I could not help but notice a large shiny machine with an enormous stainless steel funnel on the top and a seemingly endless strand of spaghetti flowing out the front.

It had never occurred to me that my favorite food, pasta, was a product of extrusion. After all my weeks of searching, I suddenly realized that I could have saved myself weeks of stress and simply taken the class to a nice Italian lunch.

In gameSpace, any face or group of faces can be selected as the shape for an extrusion. The Sweep tool extrudes a new group of faces out of these existing faces, much like the silk described earlier.

Reselect the Point Edit: Faces mode, as shown in Figure 9.17.

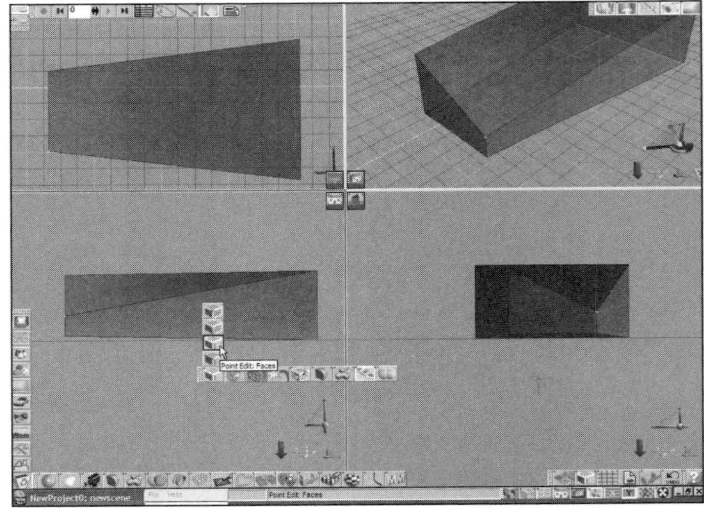

Figure 9.17
Reselect the Point Edit: Faces mode.

Select the same face you edited before. See Figure 9.18.

With the face selected, activate the Sweep tool, as shown in Figure 9.19.

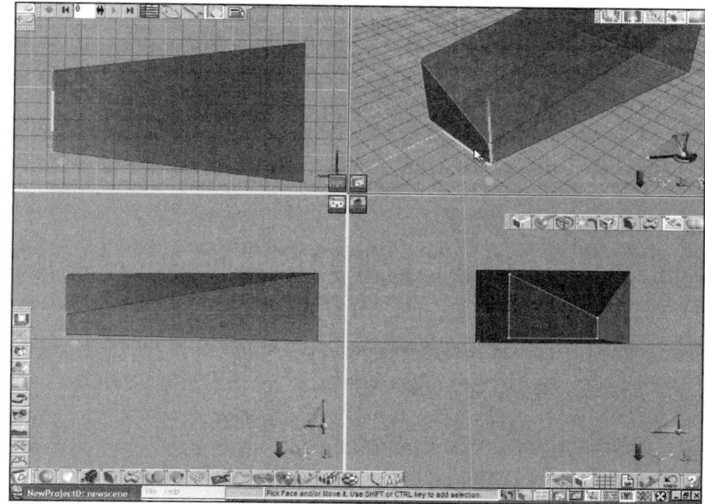

Figure 9.18
Select the face you have originally edited.

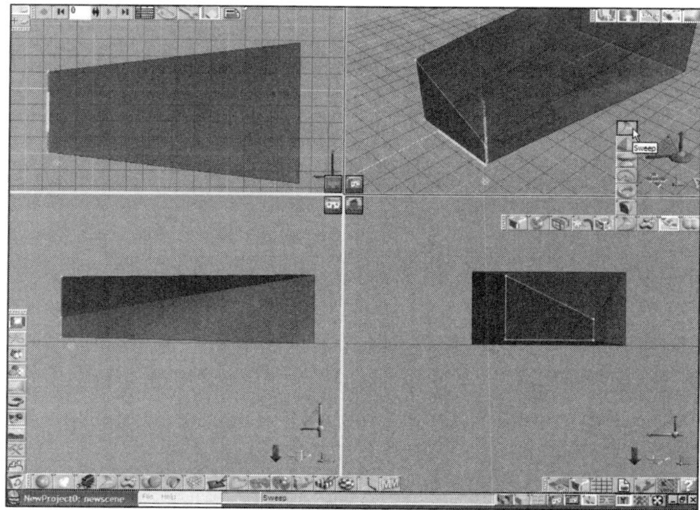

Figure 9.19
Activate the Sweep tool.

The Sweep tool extrudes the selected face and produces a whole new segment of the object. See Figure 9.20.

The face at the end of the new extruded section is now selected so that you can easily adjust the shape and size of the newly extruded section. Enable movement along only the X axis, and use the Point Move tool to extend the newly extruded segment, as shown in Figure 9.21.

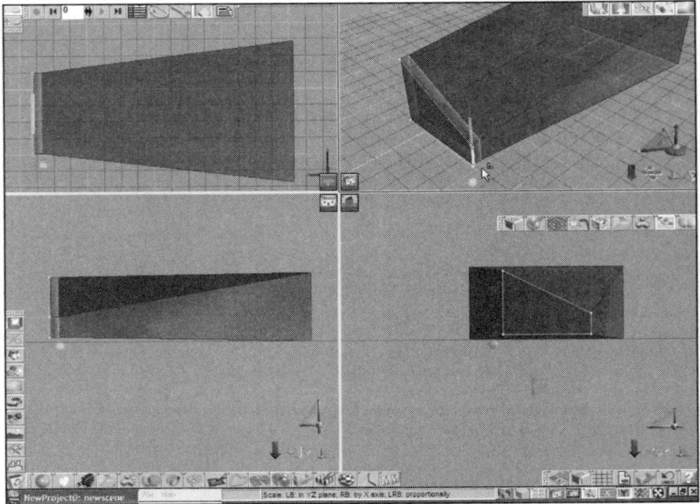

Figure 9.20
The selected face has been extruded.

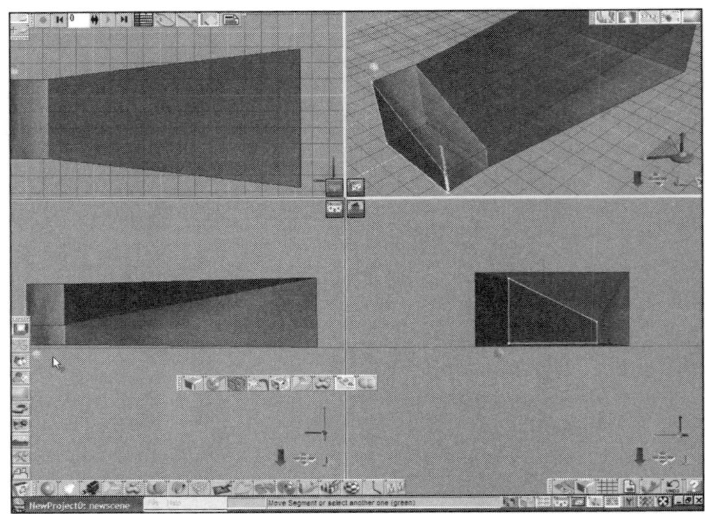

Figure 9.21
Use the Point Move tool to enlarge the extruded segment.

Activate the Point Scale tool and shrink the end of the newly extruded section, as shown in Figure 9.22.

Activate the Sweep tool again and watch what happens. The Sweep tool repeats the extrusion, and also attempts to repeat all of the additional adjustments you made to the last extrusion. See Figure 9.23.

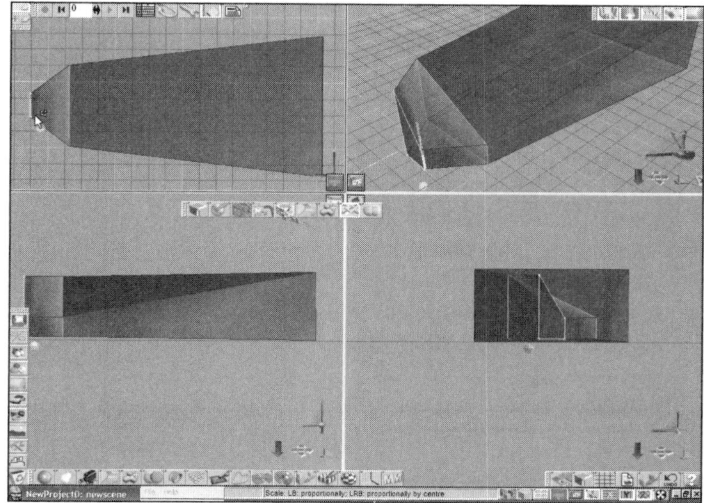

Figure 9.22
Use the Point Scale tool to taper the end of the newly extruded segment.

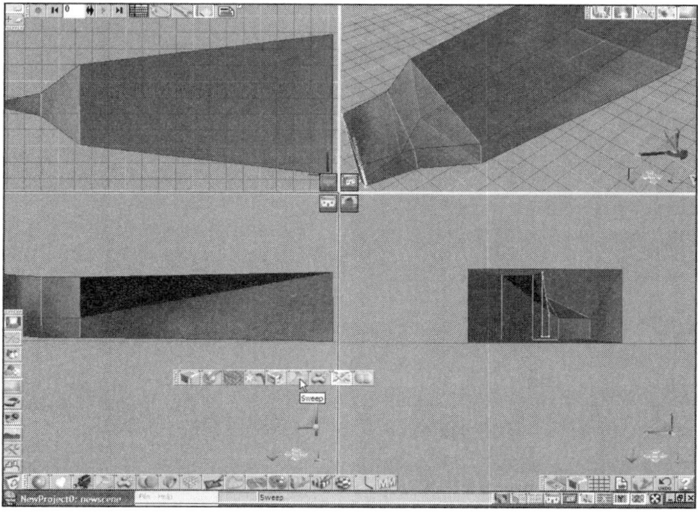

Figure 9.23
Reactivating the Sweep tool repeats all of the steps performed following the last extrusion.

tip

It can be very helpful to have the Sweep tool exactly repeat the last extrusion, but many times it is not. If you want to continue the extrusion without repeating the previous adjustments, select any other face before reselecting the face you wish to extrude. See Figures 9.24 through 9.26.

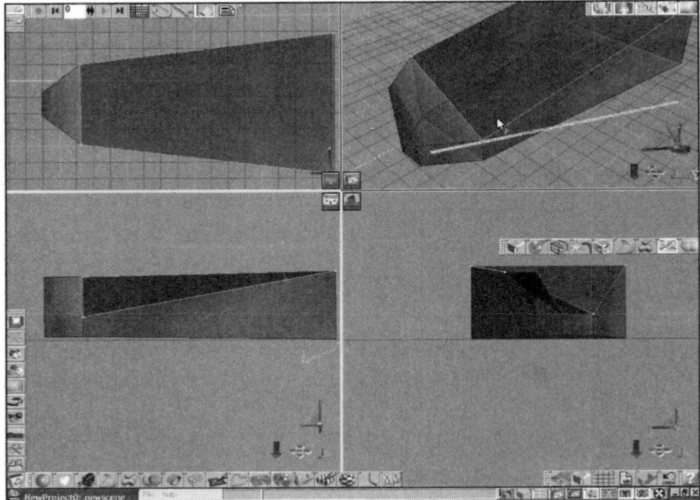

Figure 9.24
Select any other face.

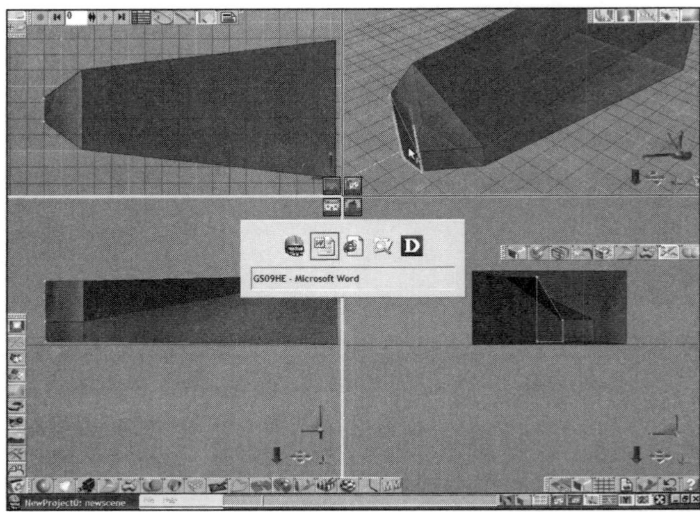

Figure 9.25
Reselect the face you wish to extrude.

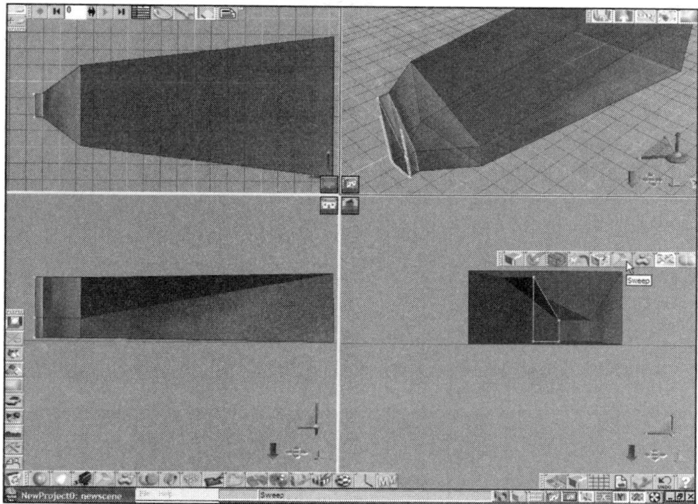

Figure 9.26
Activate the Sweep tool to begin a fresh sweep.

Sweeping into Action

The Sweep tool is one of the most useful tools in gameSpace. A vast number of real-world objects can be easily modeled by sweeping.

In Chapter 8, "Boolean Operations," you could have used the Sweep tool to create a pedestal for the gem. In this section, you will use the Sweep tool to make some columns to decorate the treasure vault.

Begin a new scene and create a cylinder with eight sides. Change the cylinder's name to "Column," and adjust its location, rotation, and scale as shown below in Table 9.1 and in Figure 9.27.

Table 9.1 Cylinder Object Parameters

	X	Y	Z
Location	0.0	0.0	0.0
Rotation	0	0	0
Scale	1	1	0.7

All units and screen units are set in points.

Select the column and right-click on it to enter Point Edit mode. Right-click on the second icon from the left in the Point Edit mode's toolbar. This is the slot immediately left of the Point Edit mode icons. See Figure 9.28. These icons are used to control the way in which faces, edges, or vertices are selected.

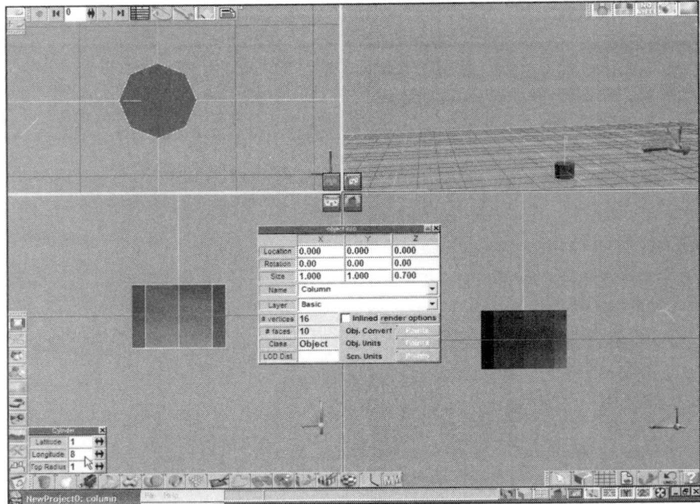

Figure 9.27
Create the base of the column.

Right-clicking whichever icon is visible in this slot opens the Selection panel. The Highlight box on the Selection panel determines whether or not the selected face, edge, or vertex should be highlighted in the viewports. It is usually wise to keep this box checked.

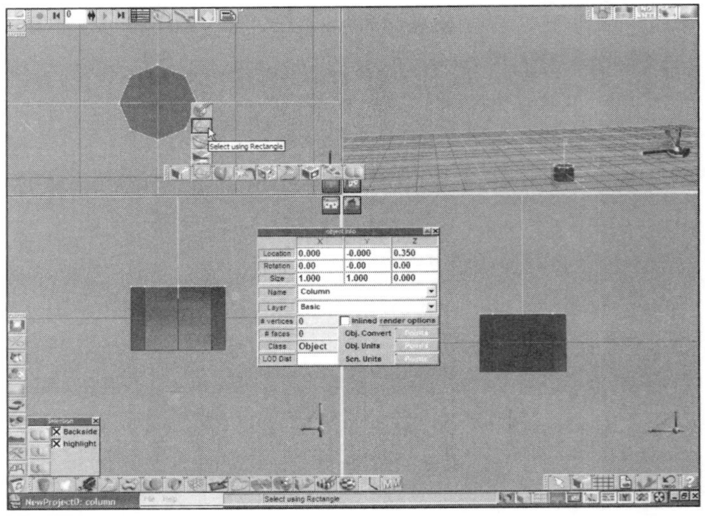

Figure 9.28
Select the Backside option and then activate the Select using Rectangle tool.

When you click on an edge, face, or vertex in a viewport, these is a very good chance that the mouse will actually be on top of more than one single edge, face, or vertex. The Backside box controls whether selecting a visible edge, face, or vertex will choose just that single edge, face, or vertex, or all of the edges, faces, and vertices that may be hidden behind it. To see how this works, check the Backside box, and activate the Select using Rectangle tool as shown in Figure 9.28. This tool allows you to select entities by dragging a rectangular fence around them.

In the top viewport, drag a rectangle completely around the cylinder. See Figure 9.29.

Figure 9.30 shows that all of the faces have been selected.

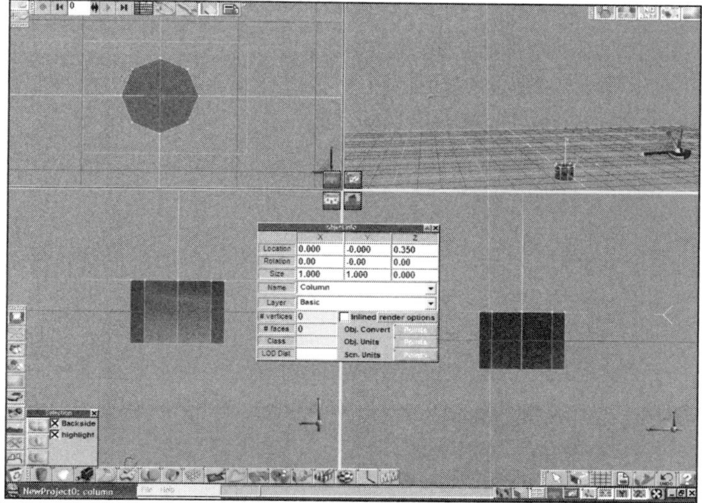

Figure 9.29
Drag a rectangle around the cylinder.

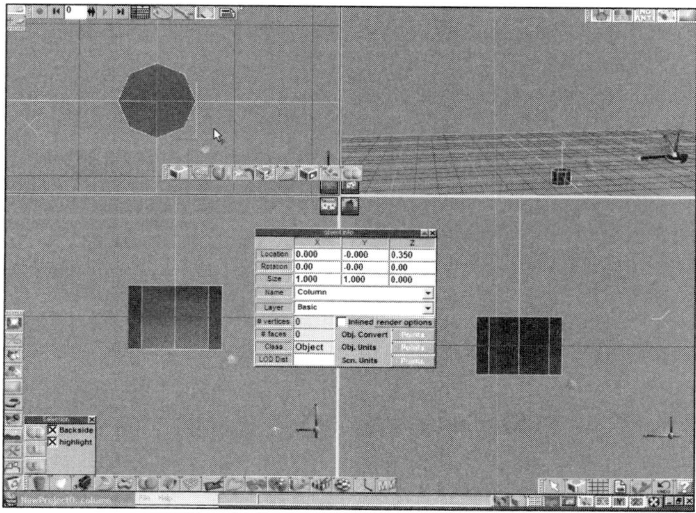

Figure 9.30
Because the Backside option was checked, all of the faces within the rectangle were selected.

Uncheck the Backside option, and once again drag the Select using Rectangle tool completely around the cylinder. See Figure 9.31.

Figure 9.32 shows that only the top face is selected this time. This is because the Backside option is not checked.

tip

Forgetting to check or uncheck the Backside option is a very common mistake and can lead to a great deal of confusion. I generally keep the Selection panel open whenever I am modeling in the Point Edit modes.

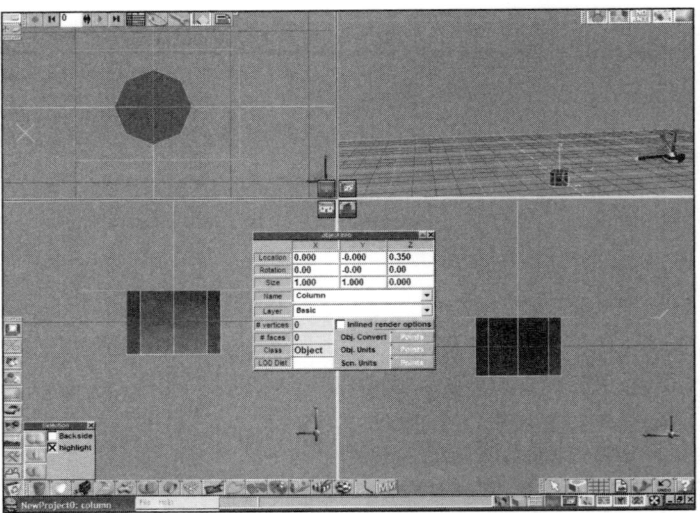

Figure 9.31
Reselect the faces without the Backside option selected.

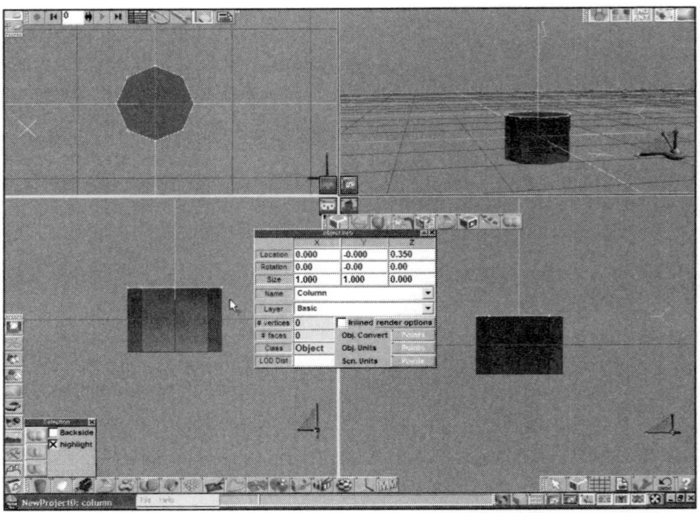

Figure 9.32
Only the top face is selected.

With only the top face selected, activate the Sweep tool, as shown in Figure 9.33.

Disable movement along the X axis, and enable movement along Y axis. Activate the Point Move tool, and drag downward in the front view to move the selected face down. Reduce the height of the extrusion until it appears similar to Figure 9.34.

tip

Notice the numbers in the Object Info Pane that appear throughout the following figures. Many of these numbers adjust to correspond with the specific faces being adjusted in the screenshots. Matching these numbers will help you precisely replicate this version of the model. Of course, you can certainly feel free to exercise your own creativity if you so choose.

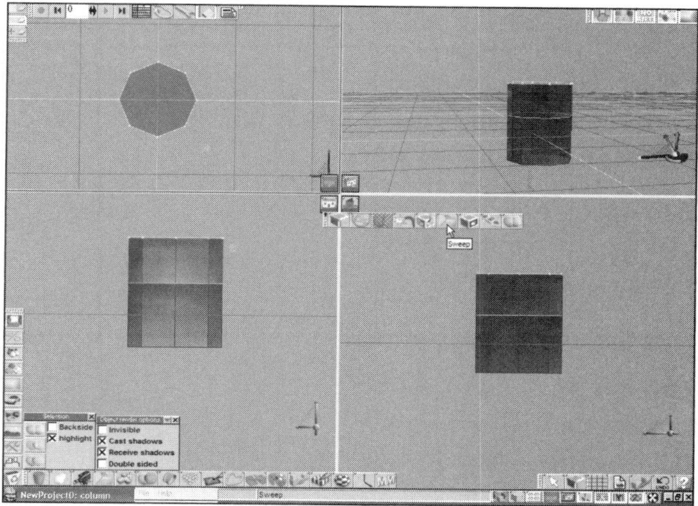

Figure 9.33
Activate the Sweep tool.

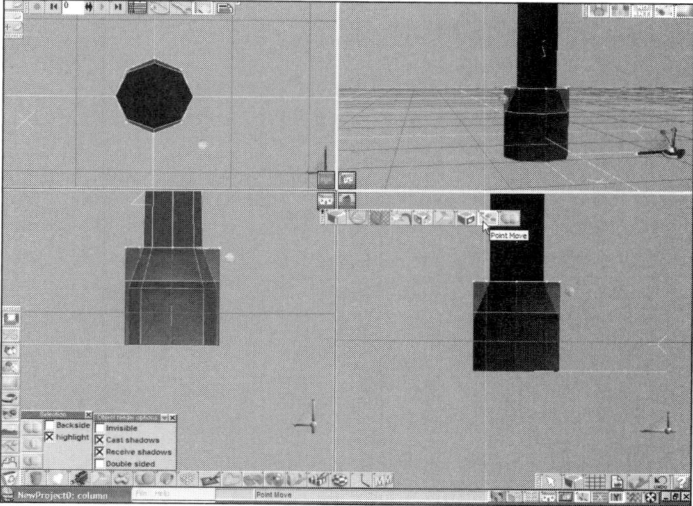

Figure 9.34
Use the Point Move tool to reduce the size of the height of the extrusion.

Enable movement along the X and Y axes, and then activate the Point Scale tool, as shown in Figure 9.35.

Scale the top of the extrusion down until it looks similar to Figure 9.36.

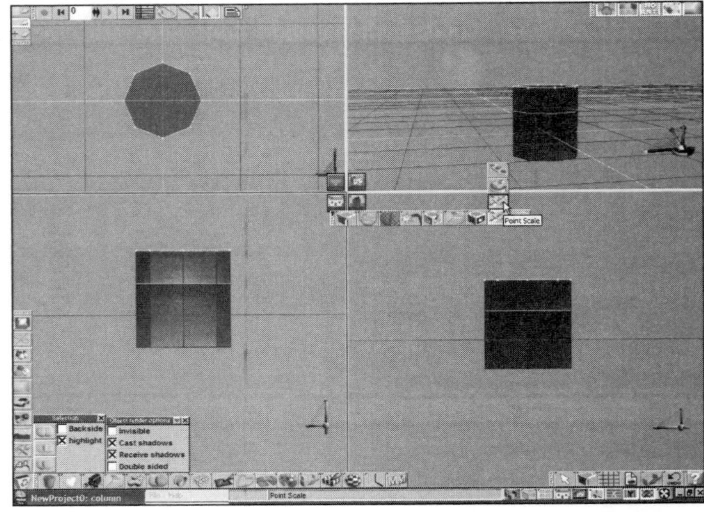

Figure 9.35
Activate the Point Scale tool.

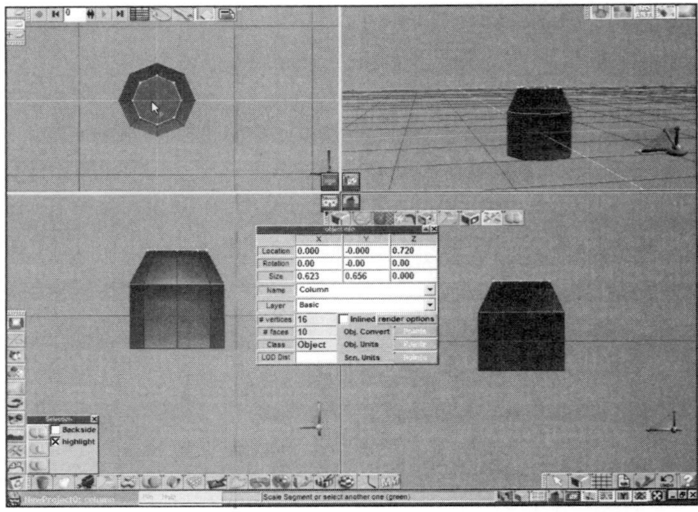

Figure 9.36
Use the Point Scale tool to taper the top of the extrusion.

You want to continue extruding the column upward, but if you activate the Sweep tool now, it will continue to taper the column inward. You don't want this to happen, so use the Point Edit: Faces mode to select any other face in the column. See Figure 9.37.

Reselect the face at the end of the latest extrusion, as shown in Figure 9.38.

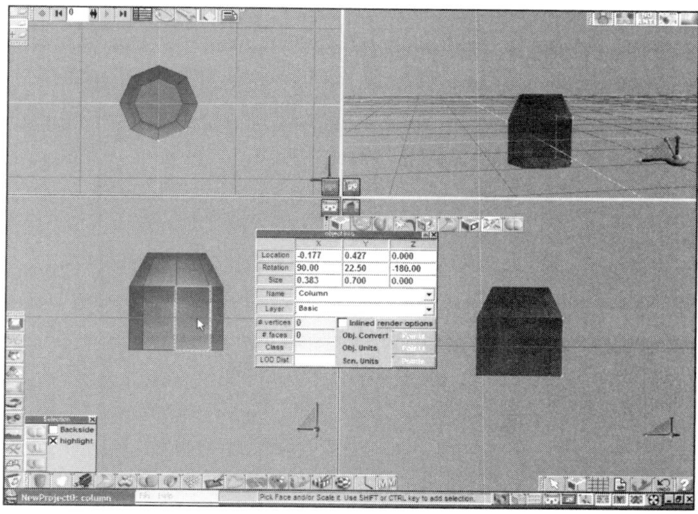

Figure 9.37
Select any other face.

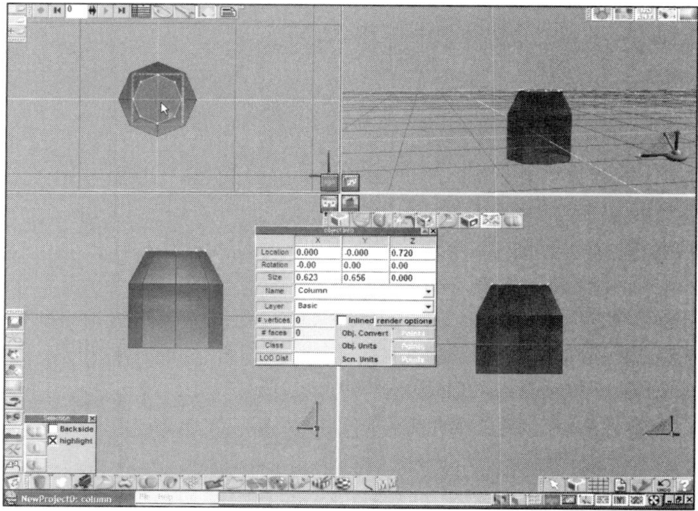

Figure 9.38
Select the top face, where you wish to continue the extrusion.

Activate the Sweep tool to begin another sweep. See Figure 9.39.

Select the Point Move tool, as shown in Figure 9.40.

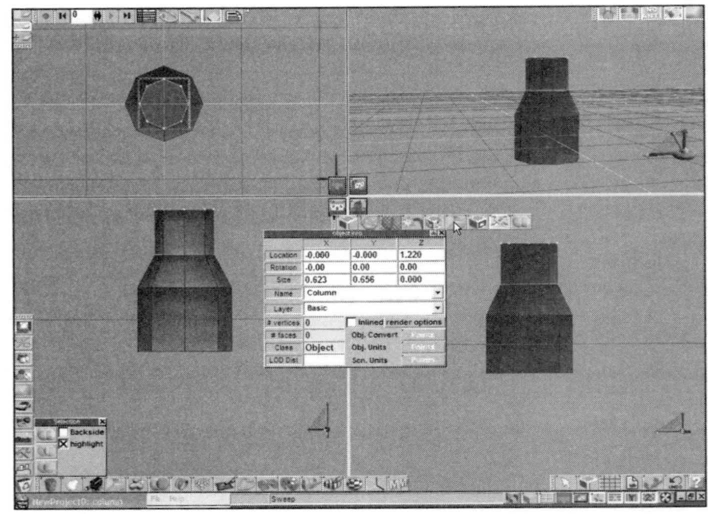

Figure 9.39
Activate the Sweep tool.

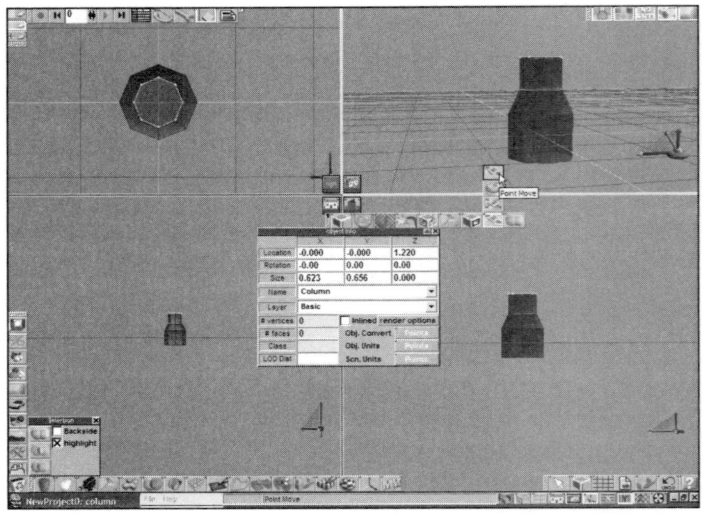

Figure 9.40
Activate the Point Move tool.

Disable movement along the X axis, and drag the mouse up in the front viewport until the new extrusion appears similar to Figure 9.41.

Enable movement along the X and Y axes. Activate the Point Scale tool, and click and drag in the top viewport to taper the column inward as shown in Figure 9.42.

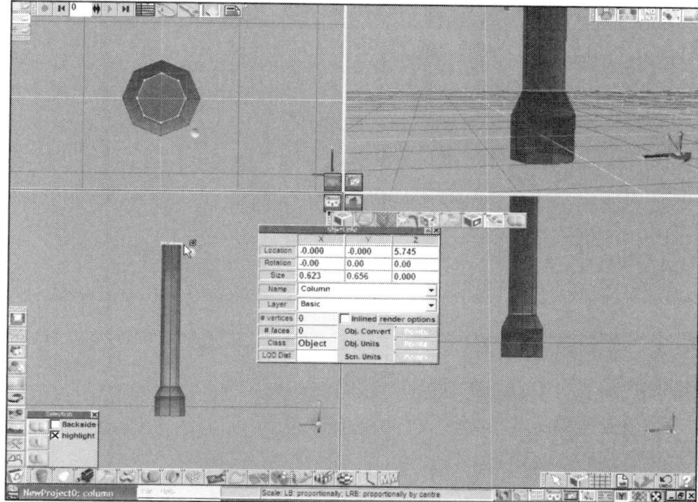

Figure 9.41
Use the Point Move tool to drag the top face of the extrusion upward.

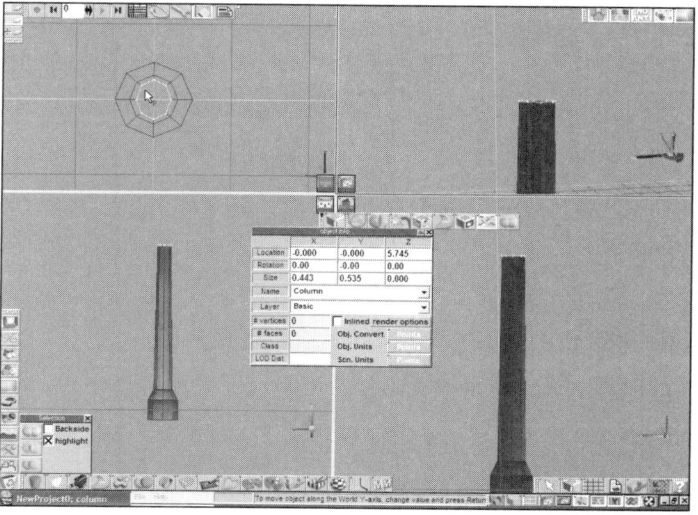

Figure 9.42
Use the Point Scale tool to taper the top of the column inward.

Disengage the Sweep tool by using the Point Edit: Faces mode to select another face. Then reselect the top face and continue extruding by reactivating the Sweep tool. See Figures 9.43 through 9.45.

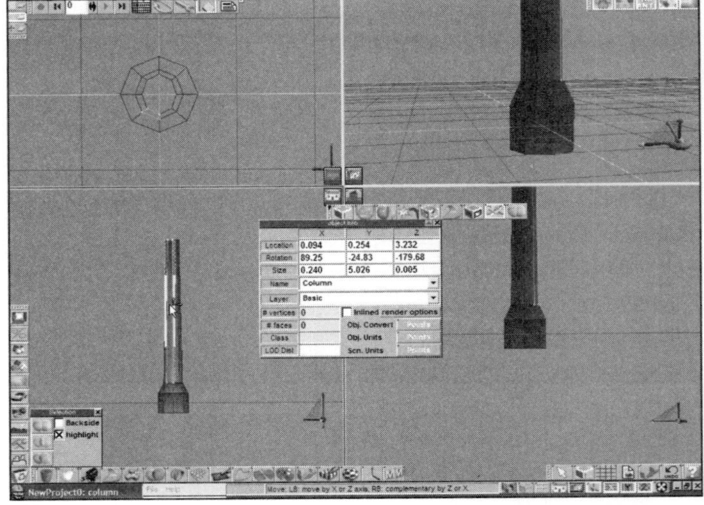

Figure 9.43
Select any other face.

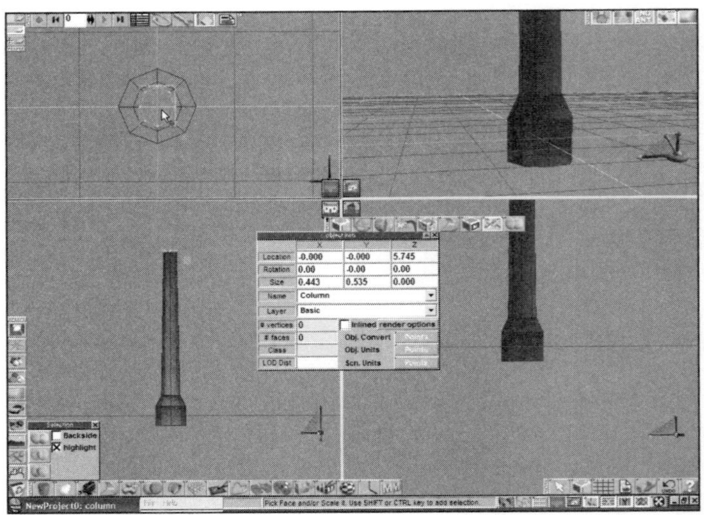

Figure 9.44
Select the top face, where you wish to continue the extrusion.

With movement enabled along the X and Y axes, use the Point Scale tool to scale up the new top face until it appears as shown in Figure 9.46.

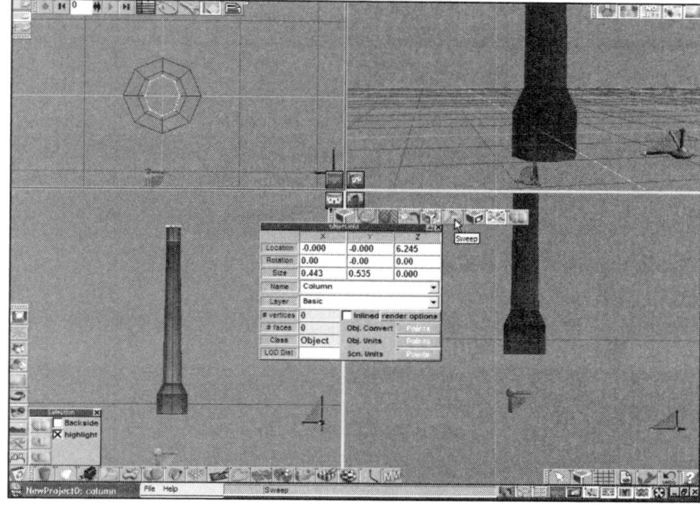

Figure 9.45
Activate the Sweep tool.

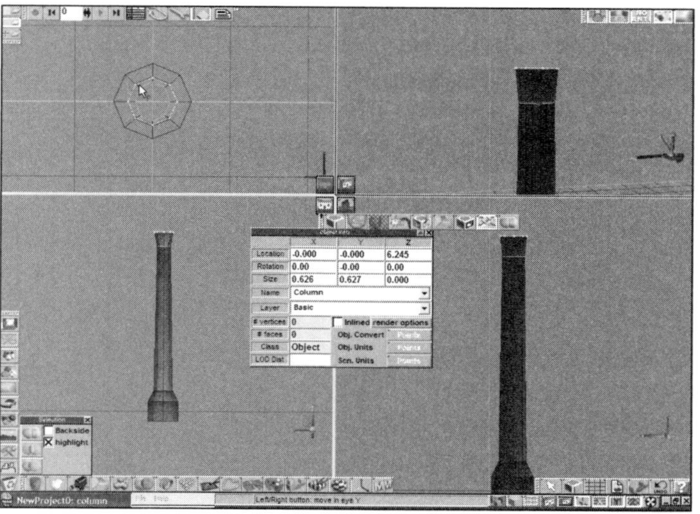

Figure 9.46
Use the Point Scale tool to enlarge the top face of the column.

Without deselecting and reselecting anything, just reactivate the Sweep tool. This time you want the Sweep tool to repeat the last sweep, as shown in Figure 9.47.

To add a bit more curvature to the top of the column, use the Point Scale tool to slightly enlarge the top face even more. See Figure 9.48.

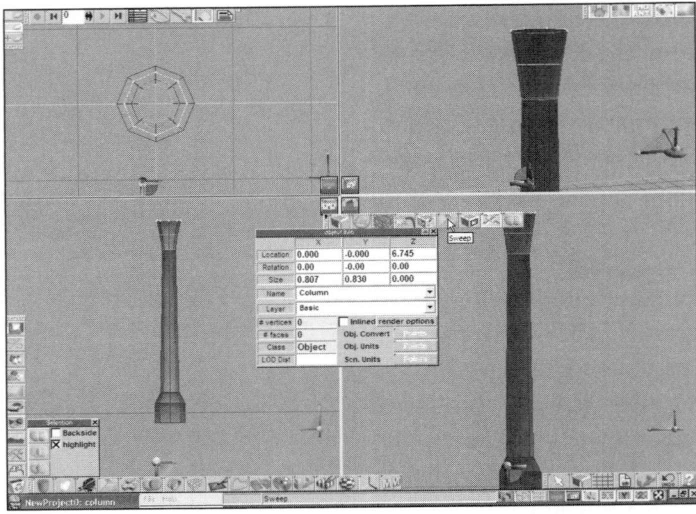

Figure 9.47
Use the Sweep tool to repeat the last sweep.

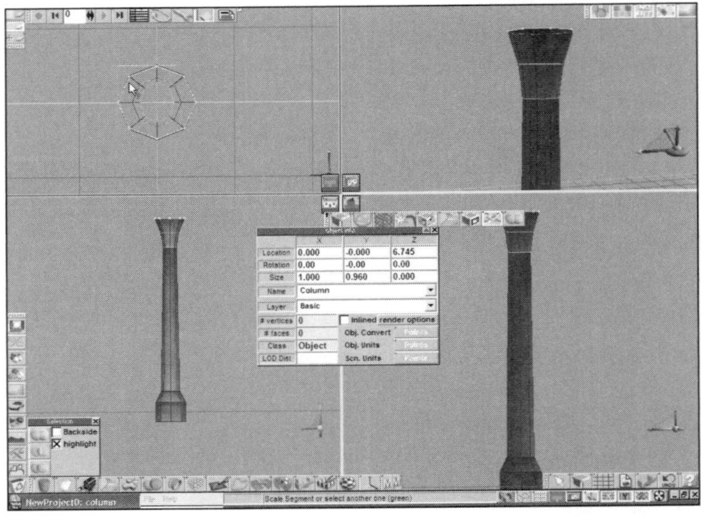

Figure 9.48
Use the Point Scale tool to further enlarge the top of the column.

The column is nearly complete. Select the Object tool, and use the Object Move tool to lift the column slightly so that it is completely above the origin line. In other words, no part of the column should be below 0 on the Z axis. This will keep the column from disappearing into the ground. See Figure 9.49.

Use the Object Info Pane to verify that the column's dimensions are similar to those shown in the Table 9.2.

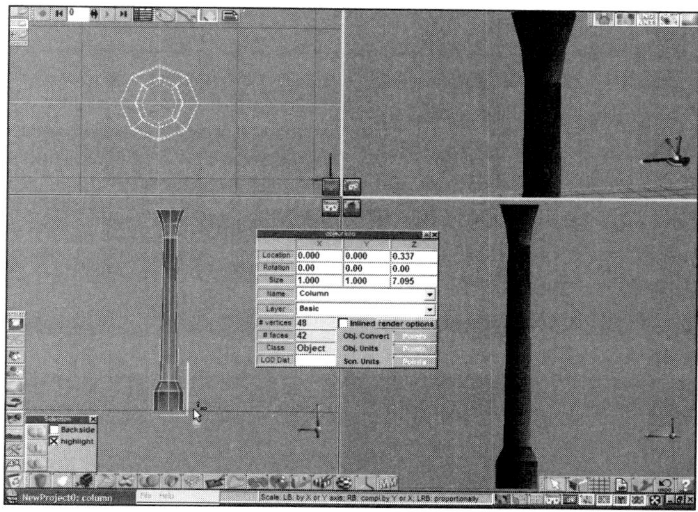

Figure 9.49
Use the Object Move tool to position the column above the Z axis.

Table 9.2 Column Object Parameters

	X	Y	Z
Location	0.0	0.0	0.337
Rotation	0	0	0
Scale	1	1	7.095

All units and screen units are set in points.

Use the Materials Editor to create a suitable texture for the column, and apply Cylindrical UV Mapping.

When you are satisfied with your column, save the scene, and save the completed object as a DirectX .x file. Exit gameSpace, and use ObjectImporter to choose the new object file as Game Object 8.

Launch Adventure Ex-plorer and climb up to the treasure vault. Four of your columns should stand in the room. Figure 9.50 shows the columns in position around the pedestal and gem.

Figure 9.50
The columns add a sense of grandeur to the treasure vault.

Sweeping Profiles

The columns help, but the treasure vault still seems pretty empty. In the following demonstration, you will add even more décor to the magnificent treasure vault.

Begin a new scene in gameSpace. You are going to build an archway using extrusion, but this time, you will not extrude a surface from an existing primitive.

Begin by drawing a profile. A profile is a cross-section of one piece of the archway. Imagine cutting a small slice out of the archway. That slice is the section you must draw.

Using NURBS in gameSpace is much easier than describing them.

Begin by opening a DrawPanel.

NURBS is an acronym for Non-Uniform Rational B-Splines. This marvel of mathematical techno-babble simply means the curves are defined by control points and handles. The control points are like pins or nails that hold a wire in place. Two handles adjust the tension or gravitational pull that affects the wire on either side of each nail. The handles can be positioned in a variety of ways to control the angle and curvature of each segment of line.

A DrawPanel is a windowlike surface floating in three-dimensional space on which you can draw curves in gameSpace. Think of a DrawPanel as an endlessly stretchable sheet of glass that you can float anywhere in a room and upon which you can paint lines and shapes.

Figure 9.51 shows a typical DrawPanel with each of its controls labeled.

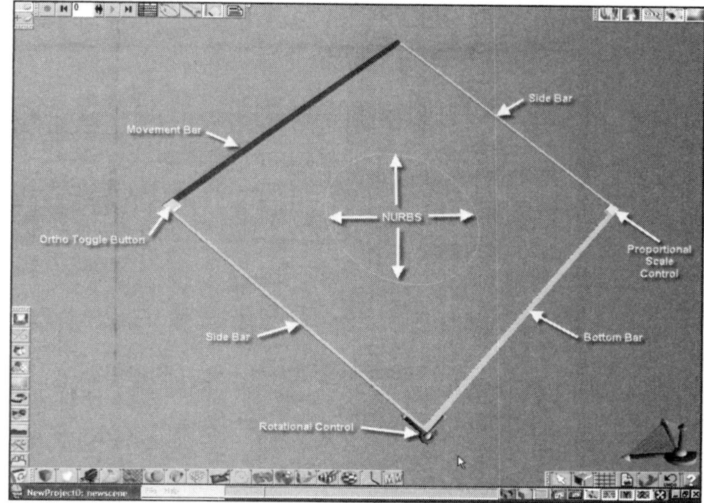

Figure 9.51
A DrawPanel's controls

- The blue Movement Bar at the top of the DrawPanel is used to reposition the DrawPanel in any viewport.
- Click and drag on the Side Bars and Bottom Bar to adjust the size of the DrawPanel's work area.
- Click and drag on the Proportional Scale Control in the bottom corner of the DrawPanel to expand or contract the DrawPanel's work area evenly in both the horizontal and vertical directions. This control scales the DrawPanel without changing its aspect ratio.
- Drag the various segments of the Rotational Control to change the orientation of the DrawPanel in 3-D space. The various segments of this control perform similarly to the view navigation controls, which are used to adjust the orientation of a viewport.
- The Ortho Toggle Control in the upper left corner is extremely useful. Click this control once to view the DrawPanel from directly above. This provides optimal viewing of the work area without any perspective distortion. Click this control again to return the DrawPanel to its proper three-dimensional orientation.

The circle shown in the center of the work area is made up of curves. Each section of a curve is called a spline. Each spline has two control points that tug at it to control its curvature and shape. Each control point has an adjustable handle that determines its affect on the spline and its relative degree of influence.

By rotating or moving a DrawPanel, you can reorient or reposition all of the individual curves that are contained in that DrawPanel. This is just like drawing a bunch of shapes on a piece of paper, and then moving or rotating the paper to move all the shapes it contains.

tip

Creating a DrawPanel is easy, but there is a trick to creating it in the proper orientation. The initial orientation of a DrawPanel is determined by the orientation of the viewport in which you click and drag the mouse.

By dragging the mouse in first one direction, and then back in another, you can switch the axes about which the DrawPanel is oriented. You can also rotate a DrawPanel once it is created by clicking and dragging on the red, green, and blue rotation controls located at one corner of the DrawPanel.

tip

You do not need to create a DrawPanel before you begin drawing curves in gameSpace. You can draw curves by selecting points directly in a viewport, and gameSpace automatically creates a DrawPanel when the curve is complete.

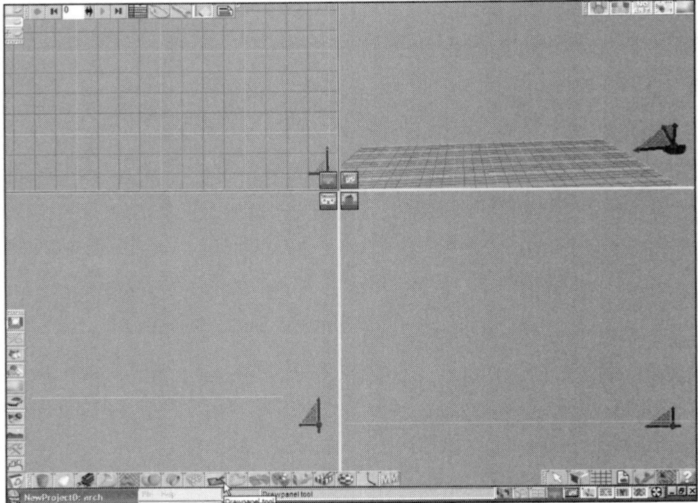

Figure 9.52
Activate the DrawPanel tool.

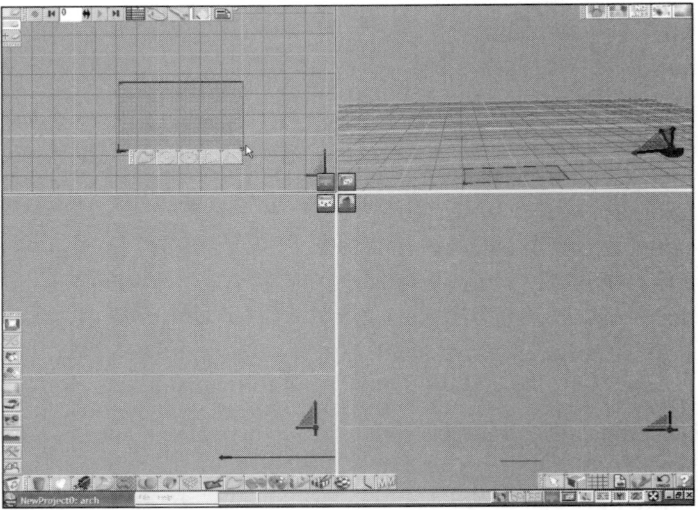

Figure 9.53
Click and drag to define the corners of the DrawPanel.

Activate the DrawPanel tool as shown in Figure 9.52.

Click and drag in the top viewport to create a DrawPanel, as shown in Figure 9.53.

The curve-edit context-sensitive toolbar appears when you right-click on the curve. Right-clicking on a curve brings you into curve edit mode. Activate the Add Curve tool to begin defining a curve. See Figure 9.54.

The Draw new curve point tool should appear activated, as shown in Figure 9.55. If it does not appear activated in this slot, activate it.

Figure 9.54
Activate the Add Curve tool.

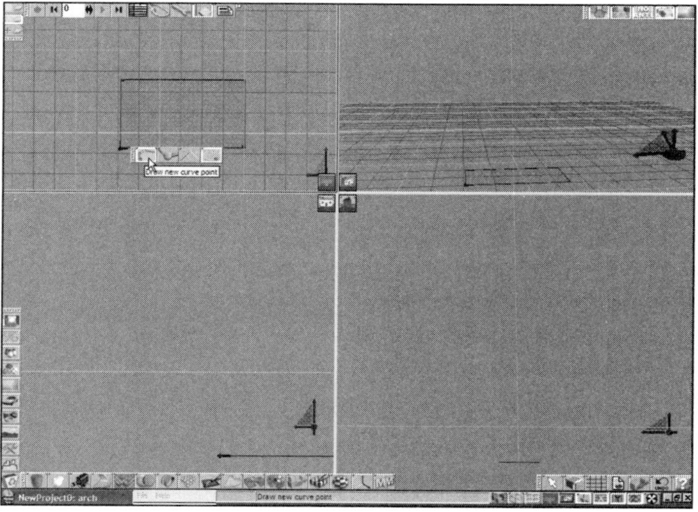

Figure 9.55
Activate the Draw new curve point tool.

Using the grid as a guide, click to place the first control point, as shown in Figure 9.56.

Without changing any tools, continue clicking to place the rest of the curve control points shown in Figures 9.57 through 9.63. Notice how gameSpace fits a flexible curve around your control points.

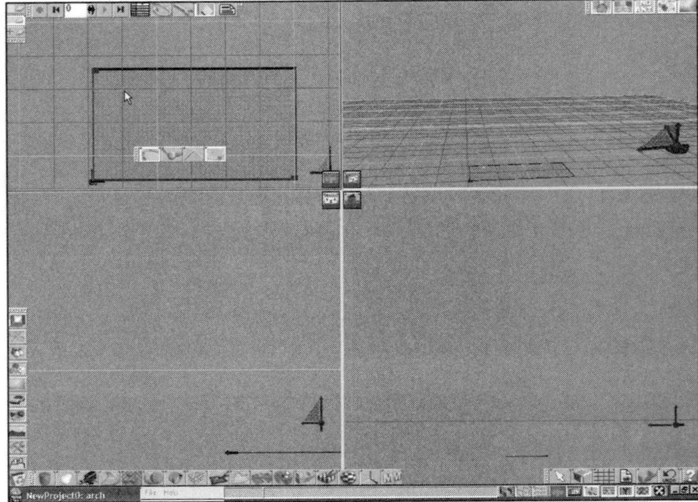

Figure 9.56
Place the first control point.

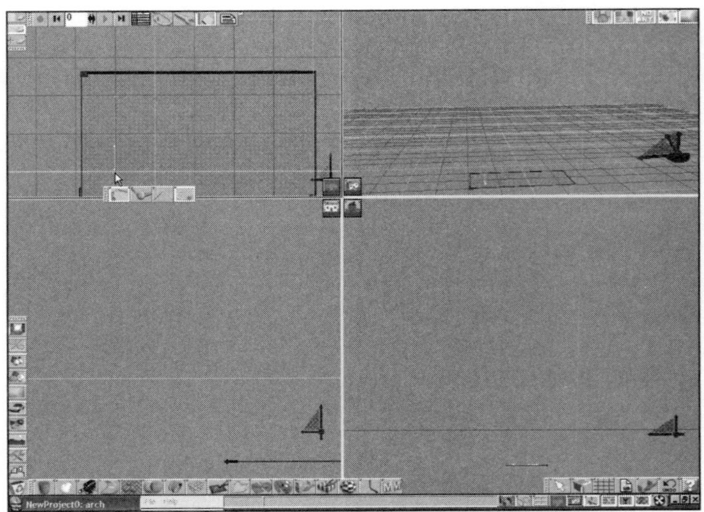

Figure 9.57
Place the second control point.

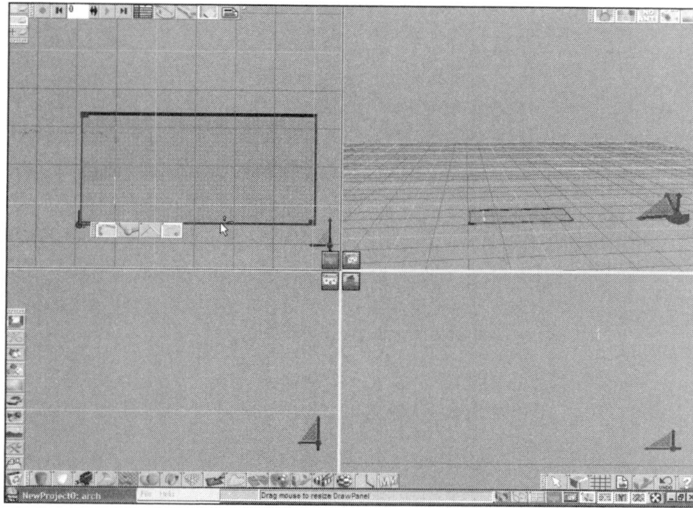

Figure 9.58
Place the third control point.

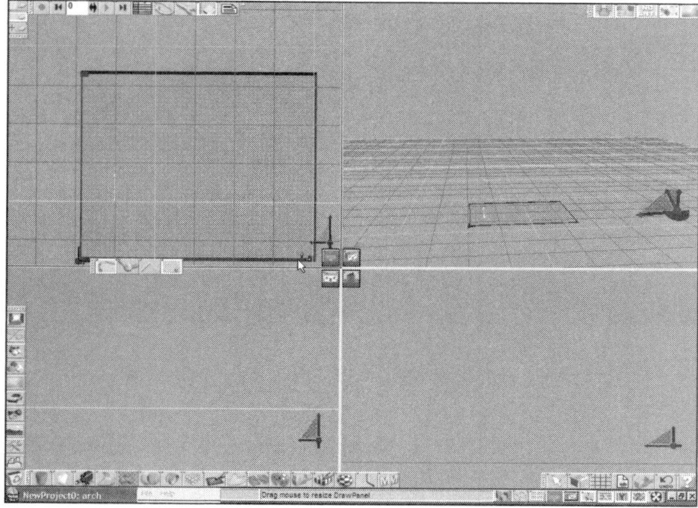

Figure 9.59
Place the fourth control point.

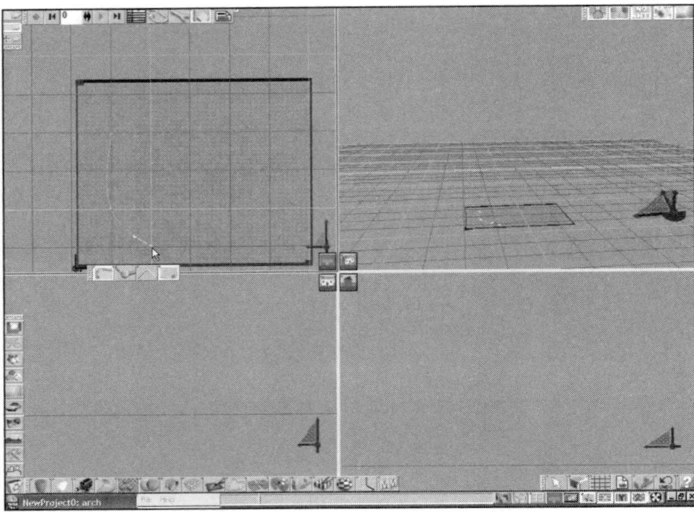

Figure 9.60
Place the fifth control point.

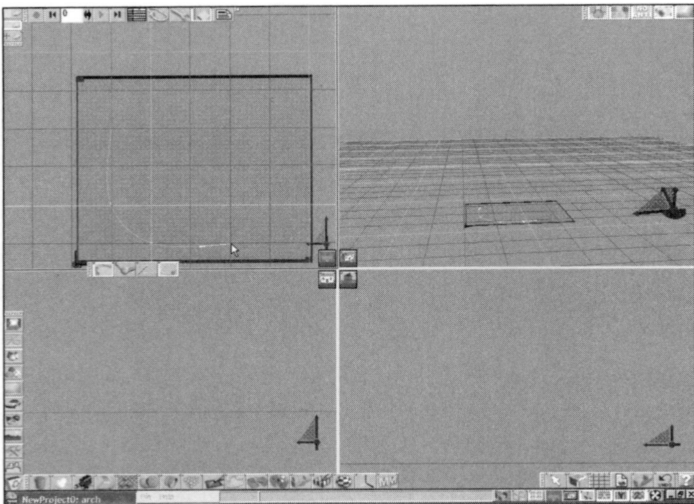

Figure 9.61
Place the sixth control point.

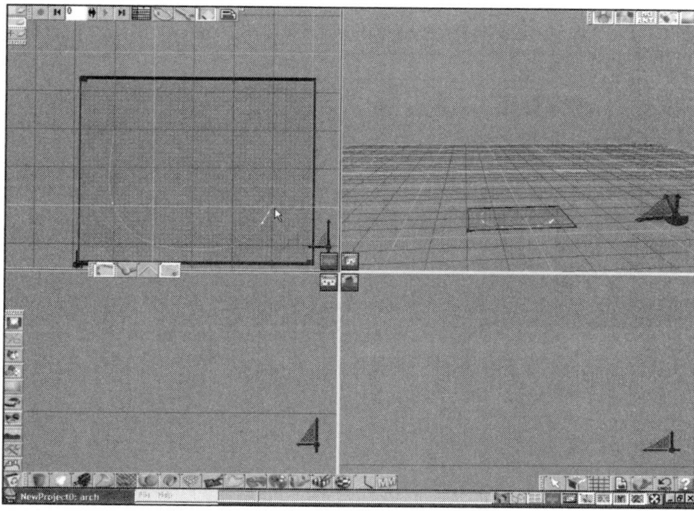

Figure 9.62
Place the seventh control point.

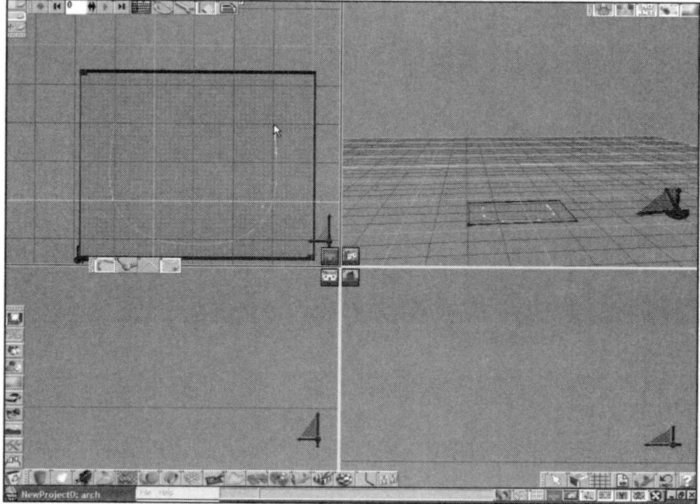

Figure 9.63
Place the eighth control point.

Do not click over the first control point to complete the shape. It is unlikely that you can precisely click on the exact starting position, and even if you could, gameSpace might not recognize that the shape is a complete closed curve.

To close the curve, activate the Close curve tool, as shown in Figure 9.64.

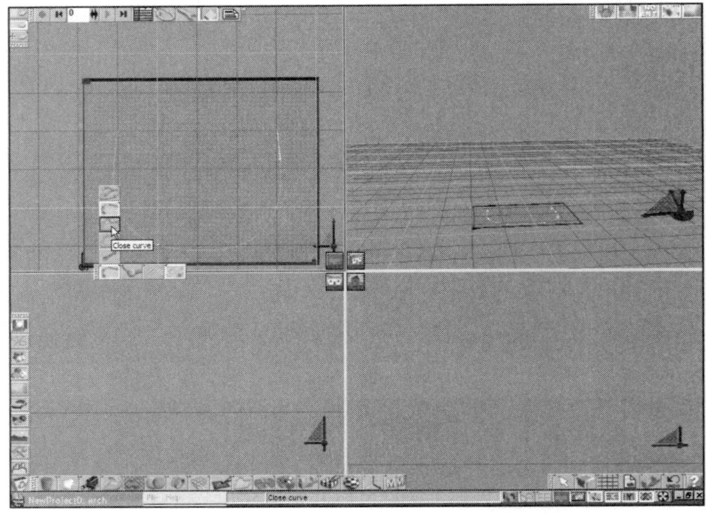

Figure 9.64
Complete the closed curve.

The front of this profile looks good, but you will be attaching more geometry to the back of the arch. The last segment of the profile curve should be a straight line. Straight lines in gameSpace are still technically curves with the handles set at right angles to the control point. You could adjust the curve handles of the last control points manually, but there is a much easier way to completely remove the curvature.

Select the first control point, which is also now the last control point. In the third slot of the curve-edit toolbar, activate the Curve: sharp corner tool. See Figure 9.65.

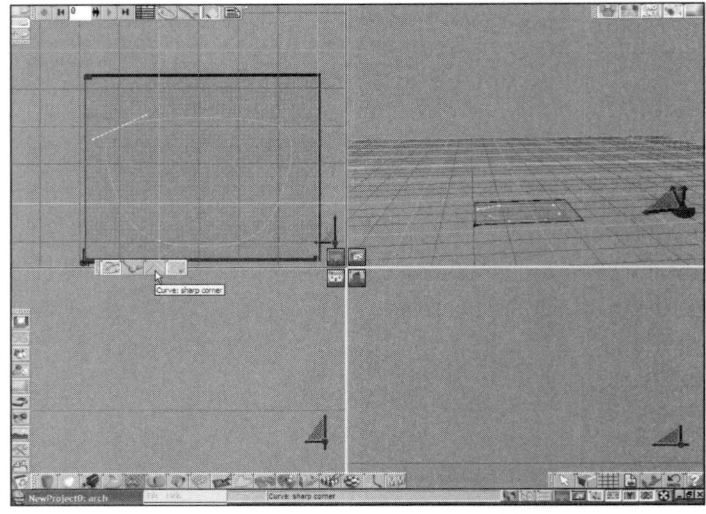

Figure 9.65
Activate the Curve: sharp corner tool.

This tool automatically sets the selected control point's handles in the proper position to create a sharp curve. Notice the effect on the overall curvature of the profile. See Figure 9.66.

Select the eighth control point in the profile, as shown in Figure 9.67.

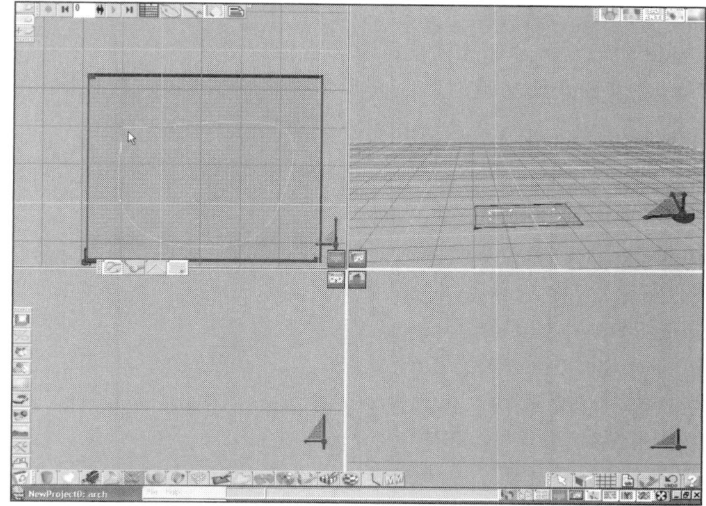

Figure 9.66
One corner has been sharpened.

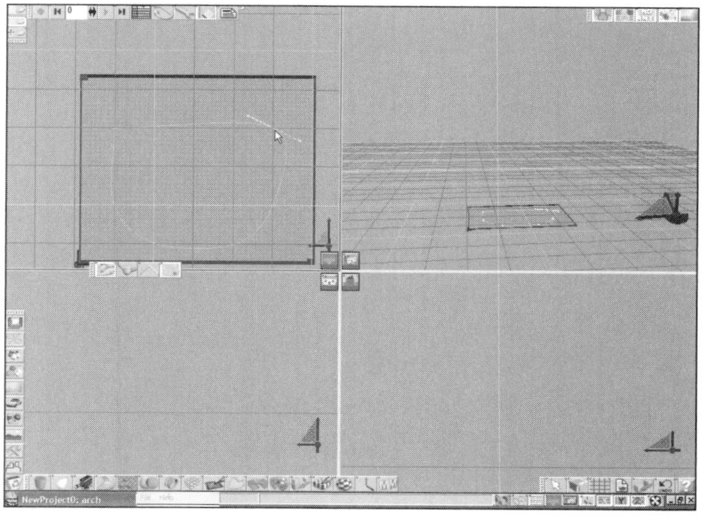

Figure 9.67
Select the eighth control point.

Activate the Curve: sharp corner tool once again, as shown in Figure 9.68.

The back profile should now be completely flat.

Sweeping the Arch

You will now perform an extrusion operation using the profile that you have created. Activate the Sweep tool, which can be found on the main toolbar. See Figure 9.69.

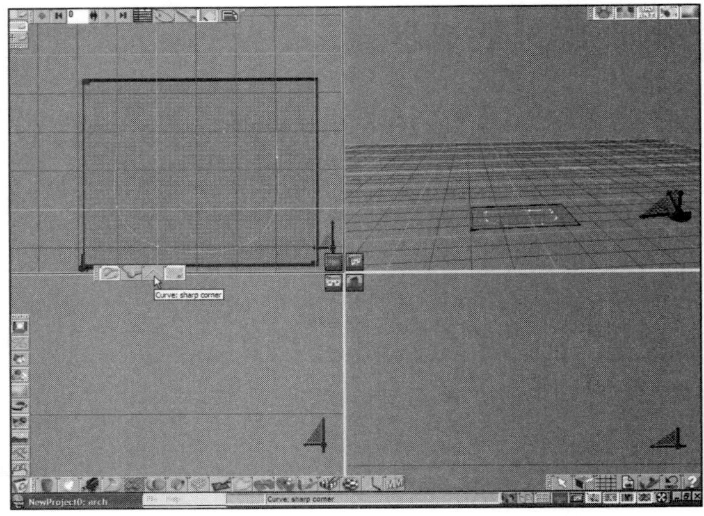

Figure 9.68
Activate the Curve: sharp corner tool again.

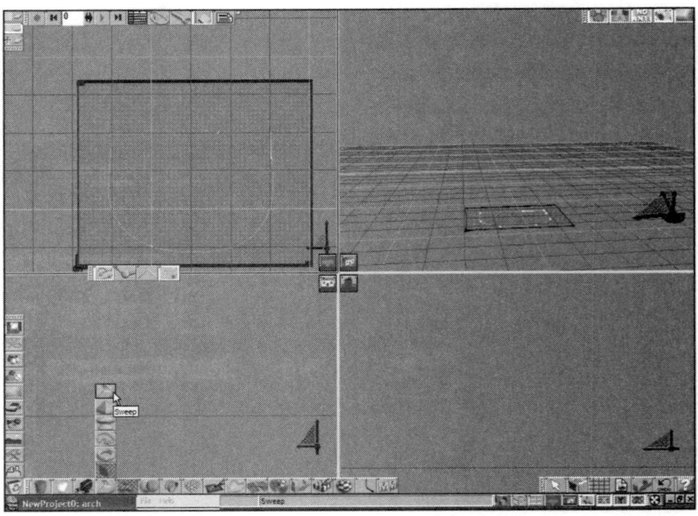

Figure 9.69
Activate the Sweep tool.

gameSpace converts the profile from a curve into a polyhedron, and then extrudes that polygon to create a three-dimensional object. After the sweep is complete, gameSpace enters Point Edit mode. See Figure 9.70.

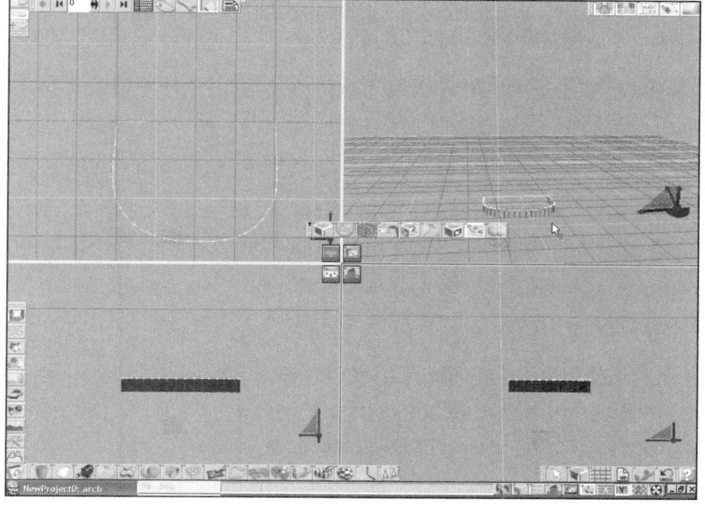

Figure 9.70
The profile has been extruded into a three-dimensional object.

You can select and adjust the faces, edges, and vertices of this new object exactly as you selected and adjusted the cylinder's faces, edges, and vertices before.

Right-click on the Object tool to open the Object Info Pane. Use the Object Info Pane to rename the new object "Archway," as shown in Figure 9.71.

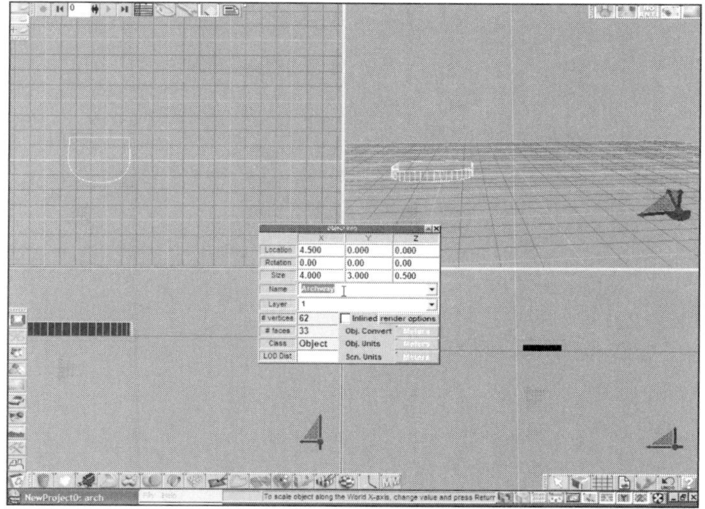

Figure 9.71
Rename the object.

Set the object's parameters as shown in Table 9.3.

Table 9.3 First Archway Segment Object Parameters

	X	Y	Z
Location	4.5	0.0	0.0
Rotation	0	0	0
Scale	4	3	0.5

All units and screen units are set in meters.

Right-click on the archway to re-enter Point Edit mode, and select the face on the top of the object. See Figure 9.72.

Disable movement along the X and Z axes, and use the Point Move tool to raise the top face of the archway to the position shown in Figure 9.73.

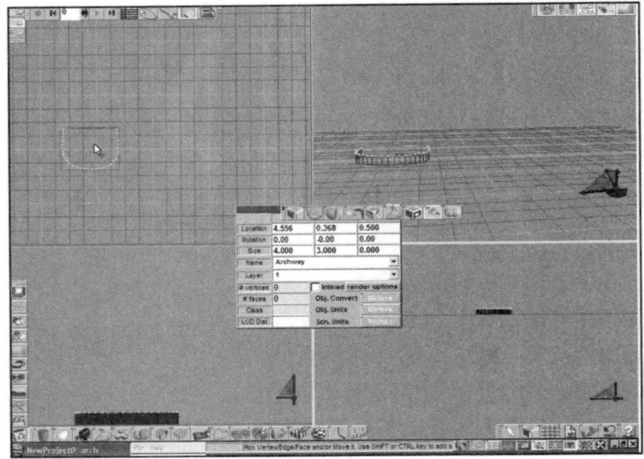

Figure 9.72
Return to Point Edit mode, and select the top face.

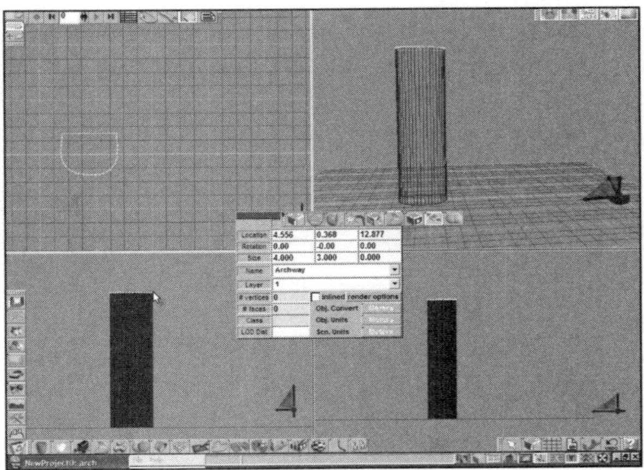

Figure 9.73
Use the Point Move tool to raise the top face.

Activate the Object tool and then immediately re-enter Point Edit mode. Select the topmost face. See Figures 9.74 and 9.75.

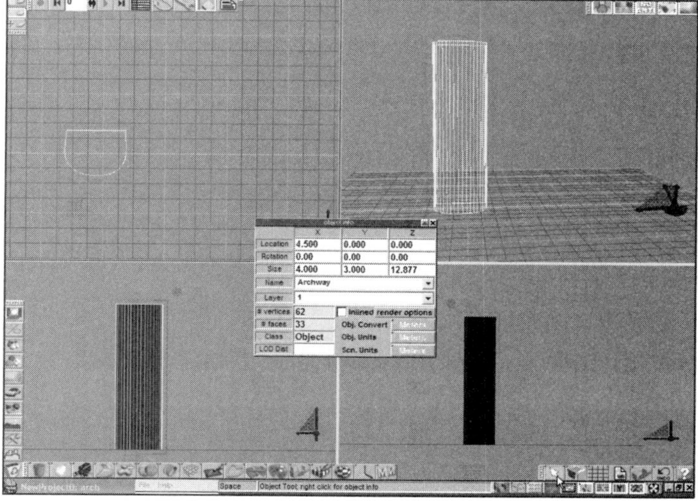

Figure 9.74
Reset the Sweep tool by clicking the Object tool.

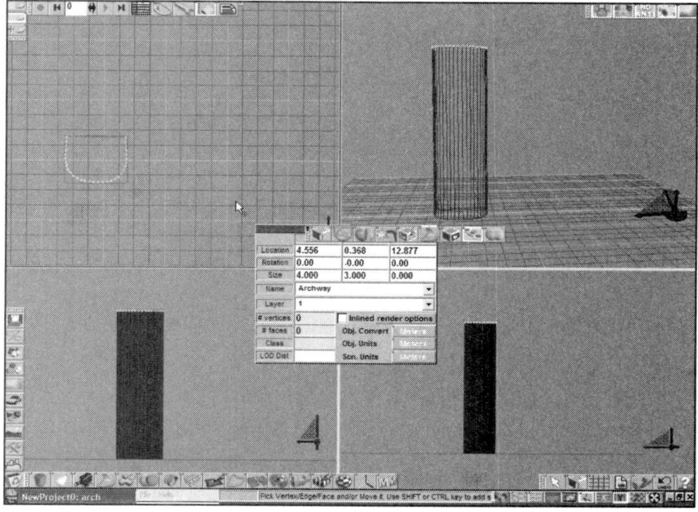

Figure 9.75
Return to Point Edit mode, and reselect the topmost face.

Activate the Sweep tool, as shown in Figure 9.76.

Use the Point Move tool to raise the top face. See Figure 9.77.

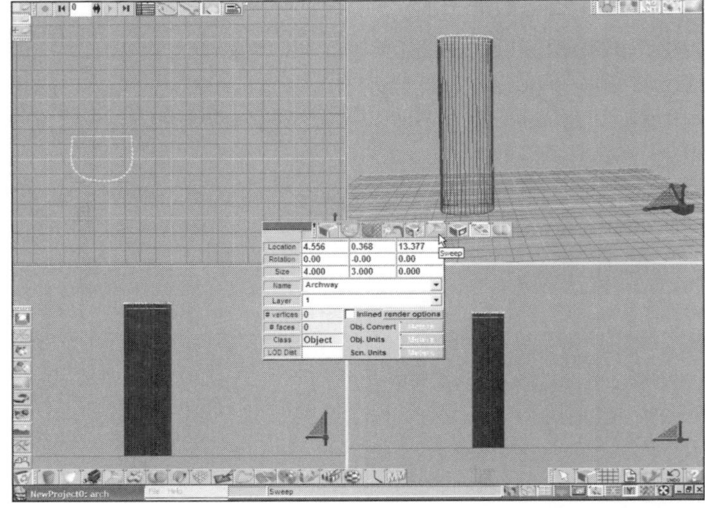

Figure 9.76
Activate the Sweep tool.

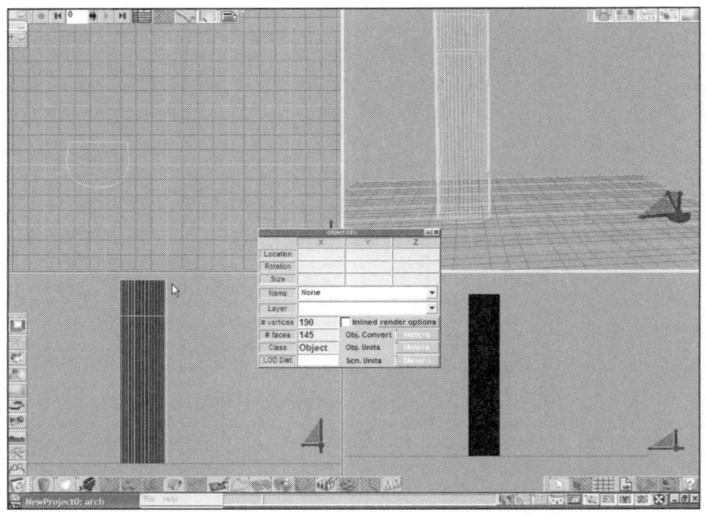

Figure 9.77
Raise the top face.

Disable movement along the Y axis and enable movement along the X axis. Click and drag in the top view to move the top face horizontally into the position shown in Figure 9.78.

Activate the Point Rotate tool, as shown in Figure 9.79.

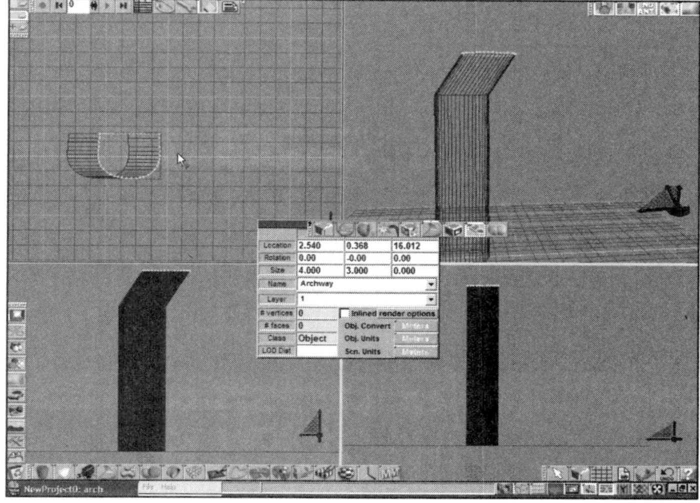

Figure 9.78
Slide the top face horizontally.

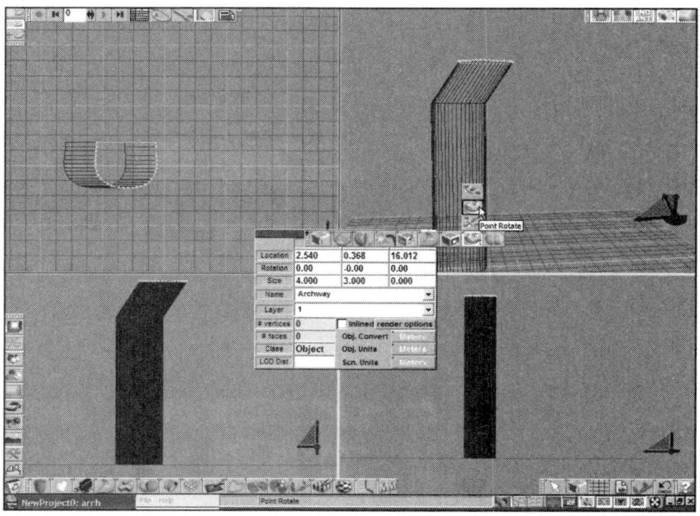

Figure 9.79
Activate the Point Rotate tool.

Like the Object Rotate tool, Point Rotate tool allows you to rotate the selected items around various axes. To perform the rotation shown in Figure 9.80, right-click and drag in the front view.

Once the rotation is correct, activate the Sweep tool, as shown in Figure 9.81.

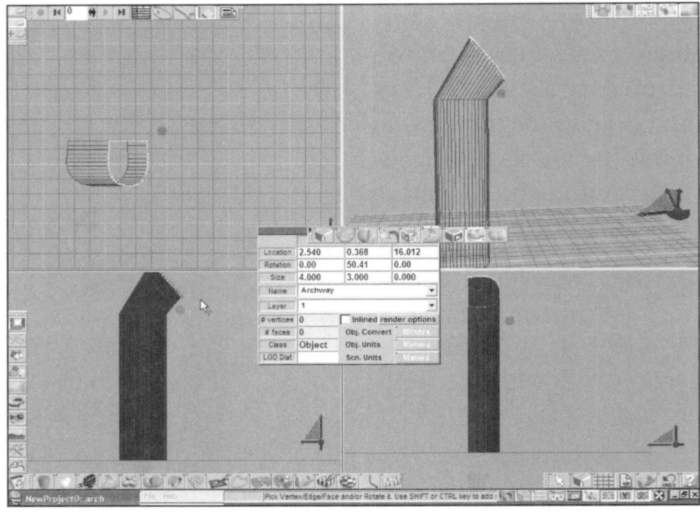

Figure 9.80
Rotate the face by right-clicking and dragging in the front view.

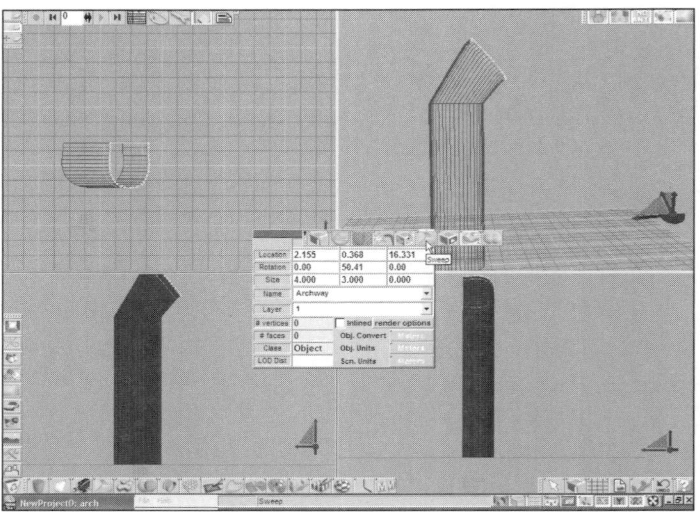

Figure 9.81
Activate the Sweep tool.

Again you will rotate the swept face, but this time you will use the Object Info Pane to directly enter the rotation information. It is essential that the selected face is rotated to an exact 90 degree angle around the Y axis. See Figure 9.82.

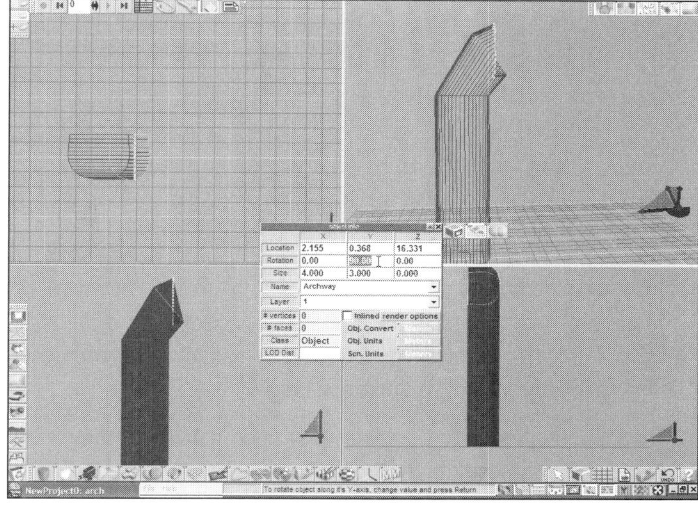

Figure 9.82
Set the Y Rotation value to exactly 90 degrees.

tip

You can also enter a math formula into the Object Info Panel. If rotation was at, say, 10 in x, you can type in "+80" after the 10 and hit Enter. You would now have the 90 degrees of rotation.

Use the Object Info Pane to position the face at exactly 0 on the X axis. See Figure 9.83.

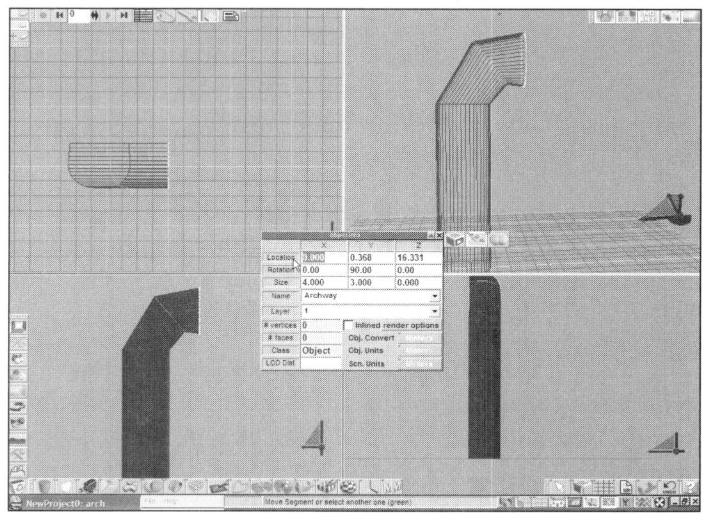

Figure 9.83
Set the X Location to 0.0.

Modeling with Mirrors

You've modeled one side of the archway. The other side should look exactly the same. It must be the mirror image of the side you have completed. Archways and many other real-world objects are symmetrical.

Symmetry refers to the condition of being precisely balanced in design. An object is symmetrical wherever one side of an object exactly mirrors or replicates the other side of that object.

> Many real-world objects are symmetrical. Faces are symmetrical. Bodies are symmetrical. Even many fabricated objects like automobiles and airplanes are generally symmetrical. Humans tend to find symmetry attractive and appealing.
>
> From the moment human babies first open their eyes, they learn to recognize symmetry as a welcome and uplifting trait. In the wilderness, warm living things tend to be symmetrical, while rock, clay, and ice tend to be asymmetrical (not symmetrical).

A common and noticeable mistake many novice game artists make is to fail to maintain the symmetry of symmetrical objects. This is especially dangerous with humanoid characters and faces. The viewers of your models are so adept and experienced at viewing people's faces that even the slightest lack of symmetry can trigger a disproportionate response. Occasionally, this response can be manipulated to make a character seem more interesting, unique, and memorable, but unless artfully implemented, it is more likely to send a message of sloppiness and incompetence.

The developers of gameSpace created a tool that makes it easy to produce perfect symmetry in a model. The theory behind this tool is similar to a sculptor sculpting a statue against a mirror. Whatever is placed on one side of the mirror is precisely reflected on the other side of the mirror.

The Mirror Modeling tool has an obvious advantage for game artists. When you can reflect half of your model in a mirror, you only need to build one side of your model. This means you can often build a character in about half of the time it would otherwise require.

Of course, in life, nothing is ever exactly symmetrical. Even the most perfect face has some subtle differences between one side and another. The Mirror Modeling tool solves this problem as well. When you use the Mirror Modeling tool, you create one side of your object. You select a surface to define the direction and orientation of a mirror for that object, and the object appears mirrored. Any changes you then make in the original object are perfectly reflected in the mirrored side. Once you are satisfied with the mirrored image, you weld the two sides together. When the sides are welded, you can proceed to adjust each side of the object individually.

If you were modeling Peter Pan's nemesis Captain Hook, you would create half of the captain's body and then create a mirror to reflect the other half. You could observe the mirrored image as you continue to fine-tune the details of both sides simultaneously. Captain Hook has a hook at the end of one arm and a hand at the end of the other. You would not model the hook or the hand in the reflected image because they are different on each side of the mirror.

Once the remainder of the character looked correct, you would weld the two sides together and then proceed to add the hand and the hook at the end of their respective wrists. Once the sides of the mirrored image were welded, the subsequent changes to each side would no longer be mirrored.

Two Sides That Behave as One

With the face at the end of the archway still selected, select the Mirror Modeler tool, as shown in Figure 9.84.

You may see a mirror image appear when you select the tool, but if a mirror image appears, click the undo icon to undo it. There is an important parameter you should check first.

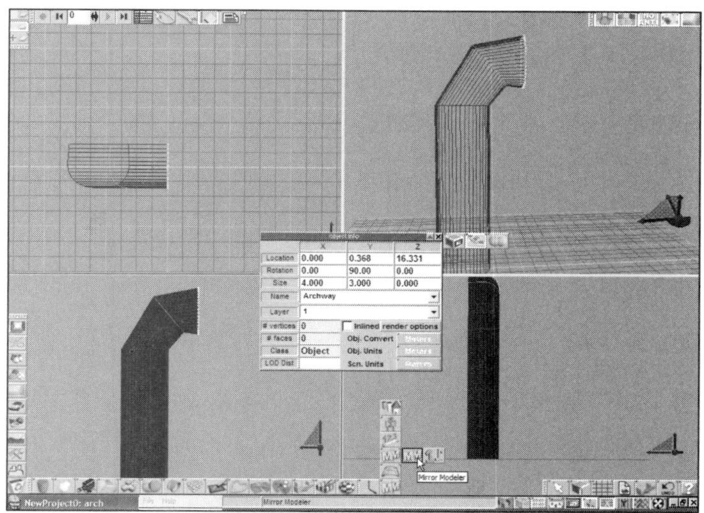

Figure 9.84
Select the Mirror Modeler tool.

Right-click the Mirror Modeler tool to display the Mirror options panel. On this panel, you should check Remove Interior Faces and uncheck the other check boxes, as shown in Figure 9.85.

It is especially important that Quick Weld is not checked. Quick Weld tells gameSpace to weld together the two sides immediately upon mirroring. Once this occurs, the changes you make on the original side of the mirror are no longer reflected on the other. It is usually better to weld the two sides manually later, which is exactly what you will do.

Once you have verified that the options settings are correct, activate the Mirror Modeling tool, as shown in Figure 9.86.

The archway appears mirrored and actually looks like a complete archway. At this point, the mirrored side of the archway is still just a phantom projection, and any changes you make to the original side of the archway are reflected.

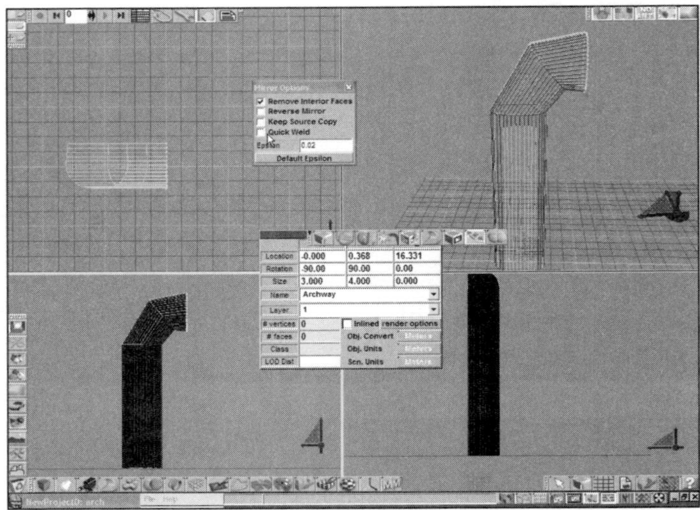

Figure 9.85
Set the check boxes as shown.

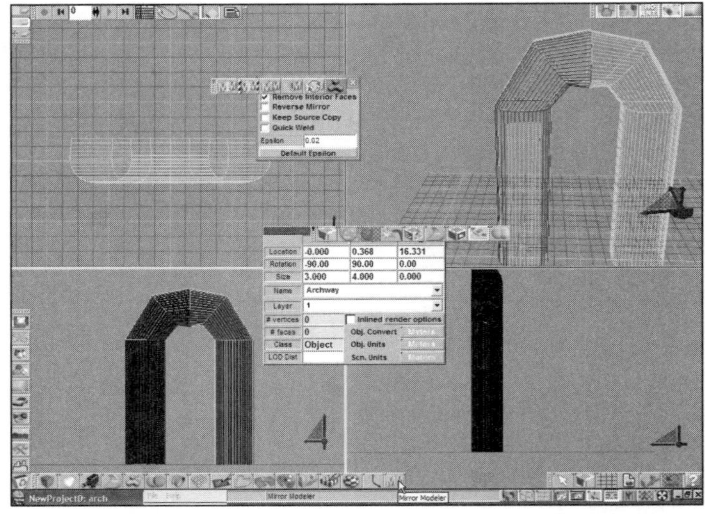

Figure 9.86
Activate the Mirror Modeling tool.

Use the perspective viewport's navigation control to revolve the perspective viewport's eye around the archway. See Figure 9.87. Continue to revolve the viewport's eye until you can easily select the back faces of the original side of the archway.

In the perspective viewport, use the Point Edit: Faces tool to select the back face of the lowest segment of the original side of the archway. See Figure 9.88.

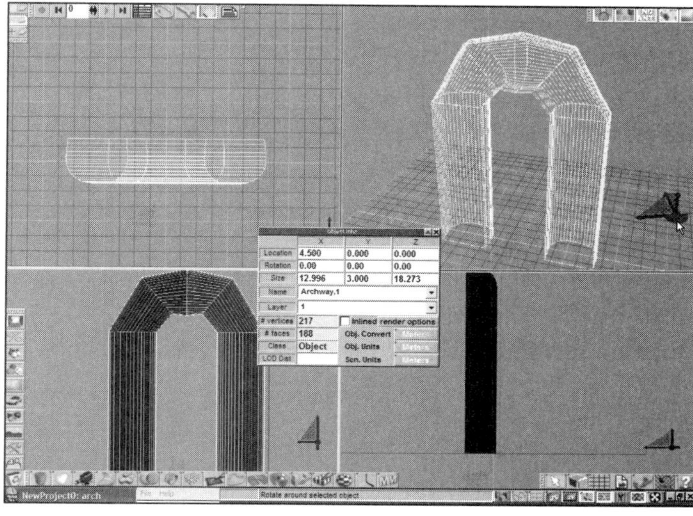

Figure 9.87
Use the navigation controls to view the back side of the archway.

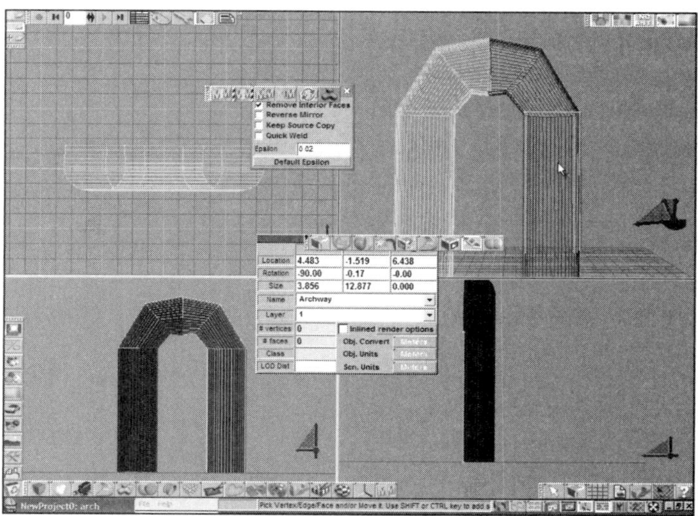

Figure 9.88
Select the back face of the first segment on the original side of the archway.

Hold down the Ctrl key, and select the back face of the second segment on the original side of the archway. See Figure 9.89. This will add this face to the original selection set. Now two faces are selected.

Hold down the Ctrl key and select the back face of the highest segment on the original side of the archway. See Figure 9.90.

Be sure the three back faces on the original side of the archway are selected. No faces on the mirrored side of the archway should be selected.

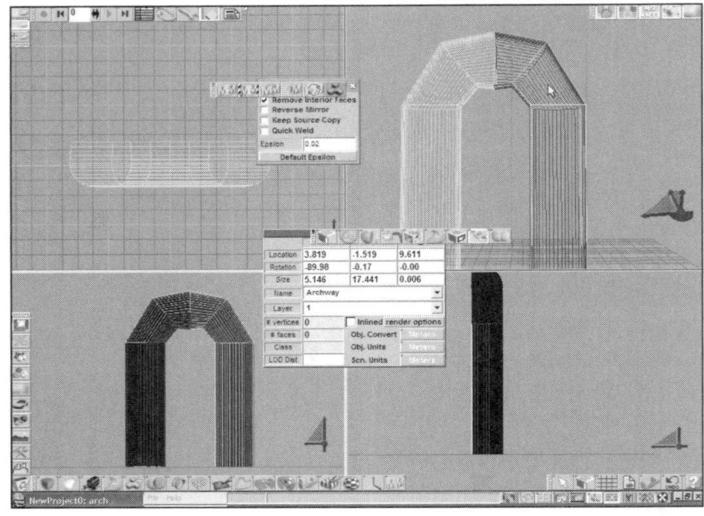

Figure 9.89
Ctrl-click to add another face to the selection set.

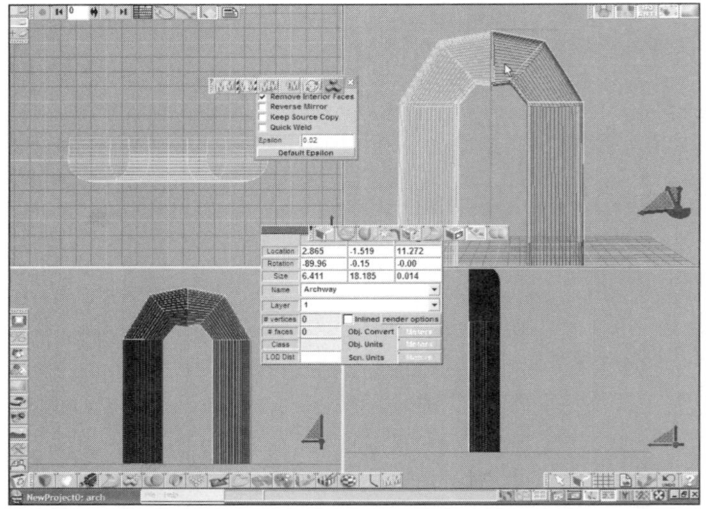

Figure 9.90
Ctrl-click to add the final face to the selection set.

Activate the Sweep tool to extrude the selected faces. See Figure 9.91.

Notice that the new extrusion appears on both sides of the mirror.

Activate the Point Scale tool, as shown in Figure 9.92.

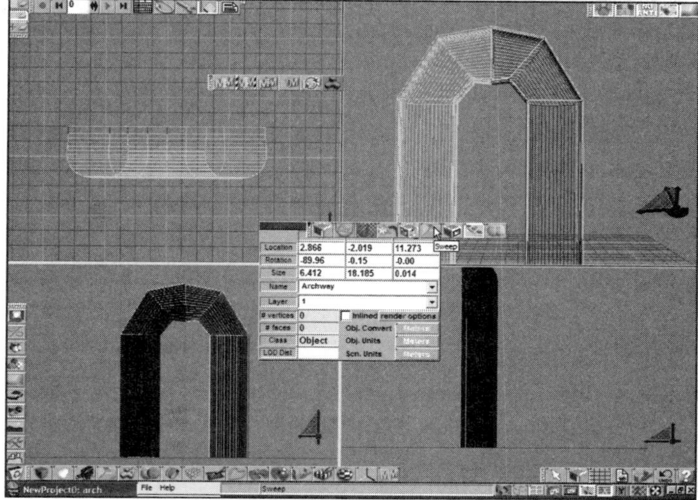

Figure 9.91
Activate the Sweep tool.

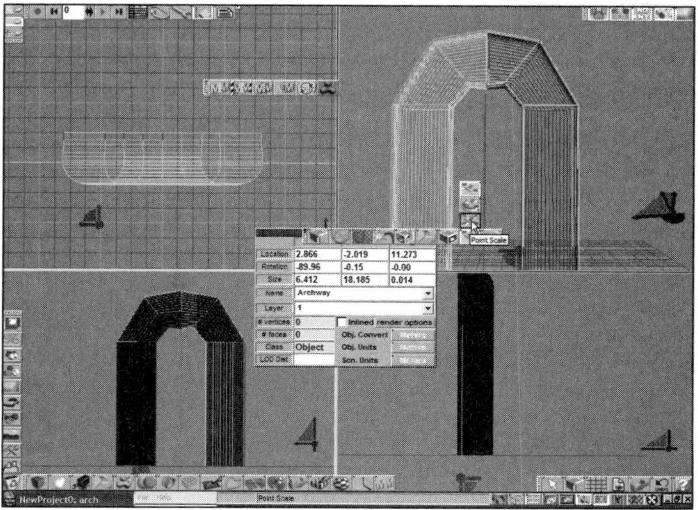

Figure 9.92
Activate the Point Scale tool.

Enable movement along the X and Z axes, but not the Y axis. Click and drag in the front viewport to stretch the back faces of the newly extruded segments. See Figure 9.93.

Activate the Create welded object tool from the Mirror Modeler's toolbar. See Figure 9.94.

You may wish to add a threshold or platform at the base of the archway. Use the Glue tools to glue together the pieces. Use the Material Editor to assign an appropriate material to the archway. I recommend a wood, stone, or precious metal material, but feel free to use your imagination.

Save the scene, save the object as a DirectX .x file, and close gameSpace.

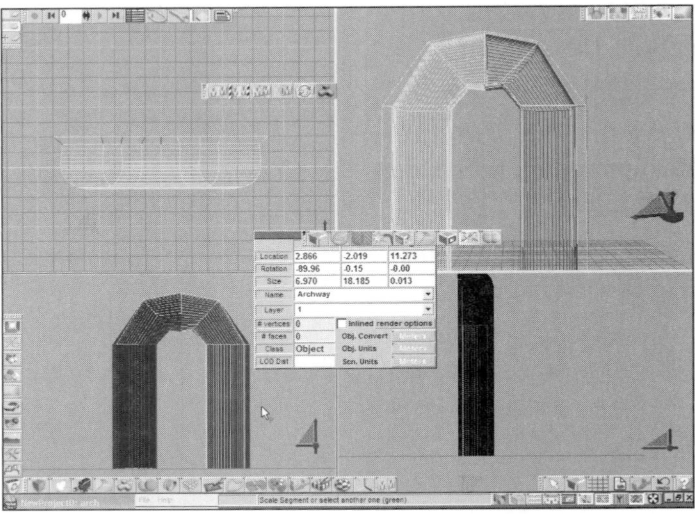

Figure 9.93
Scale up the back faces of the new extrusions.

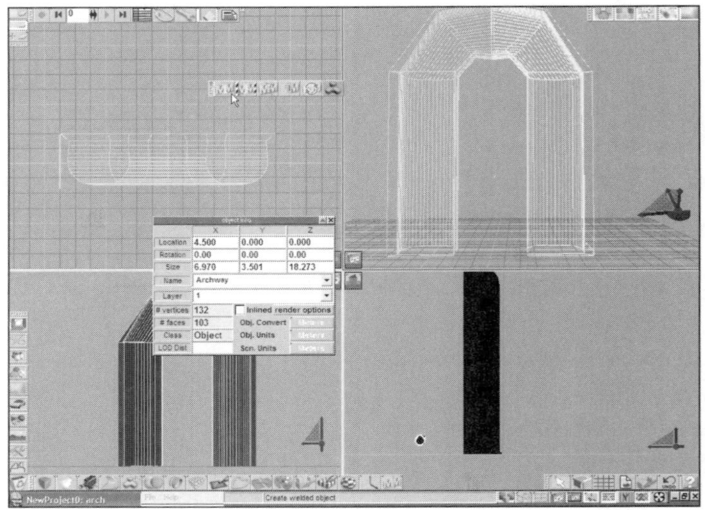

Figure 9.94
Weld the two sides of the archway together.

Use ObjectImporter to choose the Archway object as Game Object 9. Launch Adventure Explorer and climb back to the treasure vault. The new archway should appear on the far wall of the treasure vault. See Figure 9.95.

Figure 9.95
The archway model sits against the back wall of the treasure vault.

Summary

In this chapter, you should have learned the following concepts:

- The Point Edit modes allow you to select and modify the individual faces, edges, and vertices of an object.
- Right-click on a selected object or use the Point Edit icon to enter Point Edit mode.
- There are four submodes within Point Edit mode.
- Point Edit: Context mode selects faces, edges, or vertices, depending upon where you point the mouse.
- The Select using Rectangle tool selects all of the items within a rectangular window.
- Right-click on any selection tool on the Point Edit toolbar to open the Selection Panel.
- The Backside check box determines whether or not to select just the frontmost items within a selection area.
- Use the Point Move, Point Rotate, and Point Scale tools to adjust the selected faces, edges, and vertices.
- The Object Info Pane can be used to numerically monitor and control any selected face, edge, or vertex.

- The Sweep tool extrudes a face.
- Unless it is reset, the Sweep tool repeats the last sweep along with all of its subsequent adjustments.
- The Sweep tool can be reset by selecting any other object or face before reactivating the Sweep tool.
- DrawPanels are used to create two-dimensional shapes.
- NURBS are curves that are defined by control points and handles.
- Use the Close curve tool to complete a closed shape.
- A curve can be extruded into an object once it is converted to a polyhedron with the Sweep tool.
- A control point's handles can be automatically set with the Curve: sharp corner and Curve: smooth corner tools.
- Most living objects are symmetrical.
- The Mirror Modeler reflects the geometry from one side of a mirror plane onto the other side.
- You can choose any face to define the position and orientation of a mirror plane.
- Until you weld the two sides of a Mirror Modeler object, the mirrored side continues to reflect any changes to the original side.
- After you weld the two sides of Mirror Modeler object, you can adjust the two sides of the object independently.

Questions and Answers

Q: How can you select only the top face of an object?

A: Use the Point Edit: Faces mode and turn off the Backside option.

Q: How do you enter Point Edit mode?

A: Right-click on a selected object or use the Point Edit mode icons on the main toolbar.

Q: How can you extrude multiple faces at the same time?

A: Hold down the Ctrl key while you select each face, then perform the extrusion.

Q: What gameSpace tool is used to extrude faces?

A: The Sweep tool.

Q: You sweep a face and then move the new face up and to the right. If you immediately sweep the face again, what happens?

A: The new face is extruded up and to the right.

Q: You sweep a face and then move the new face down and to the left. If you move another face before returning to the newly extruded face and sweeping it once again, what happens?

A: The newly extruded face extrudes directly out and does not repeat the adjustments that occurred after the last sweep.

Q: Why would you not select the Quick Weld option when you use the Mirror Modeler to model a complex character?

A: The Quick Weld option forces the Mirror Modeler to immediately weld the two sides of the model. Once they are welded, changes you make to the original side are not reflected in the other.

Q: When would you want to use the Quick Weld option?

A: Use the Quick Weld option when you know there will be no need to adjust the two sides of the mirrored image simultaneously.

Discussion Questions

1. Describe a situation where you would want to select the Backside option before selecting vertices.
2. Describe an object that could be easily modeled using extrusion.
3. Describe a way to perform the same operation using both the Point Edit: Vertices mode and the Point Edit: Edges mode.
4. How would you use the Mirror Modeler to help model a face?
5. When you were modeling the archway, why was it important that the last sweep surface was positioned precisely?
6. When you were modeling the archway, why was it important that the last sweep surface was rotated precisely?
7. Describe how you would use the Sweep tool to model a computer monitor.
8. Describe how you would use a primitive and the Point Move, Point Rotate, and Point Scale tools to model a computer monitor.

Exercises

1. Draw a profile you would use to extrude a bowling pin.
2. Use a gameSpace DrawPanel to create the profile you drew in Exercise 1.
3. Use the Sweep tool to extrude the curves from Exercise 2 into a model of a bowling pin.

4. Use a DrawPanel, the Sweep tool, and the Point Edit mode to create a new object to replace the gem in Adventure Explorer. Use ObjectImporter to import your new gem as Game Object 3.
5. Use the Sweep tool and Point Edit mode to create a more elaborate decorative pedestal. Use ObjectImporter to import your new pedestal as Game Object 4.
6. Use the Sweep tool, Point Edit mode, and the Mirror Modeler to create a more elaborate decorative column for the treasure vault. Use ObjectImporter to import your new column as Game Object 8.

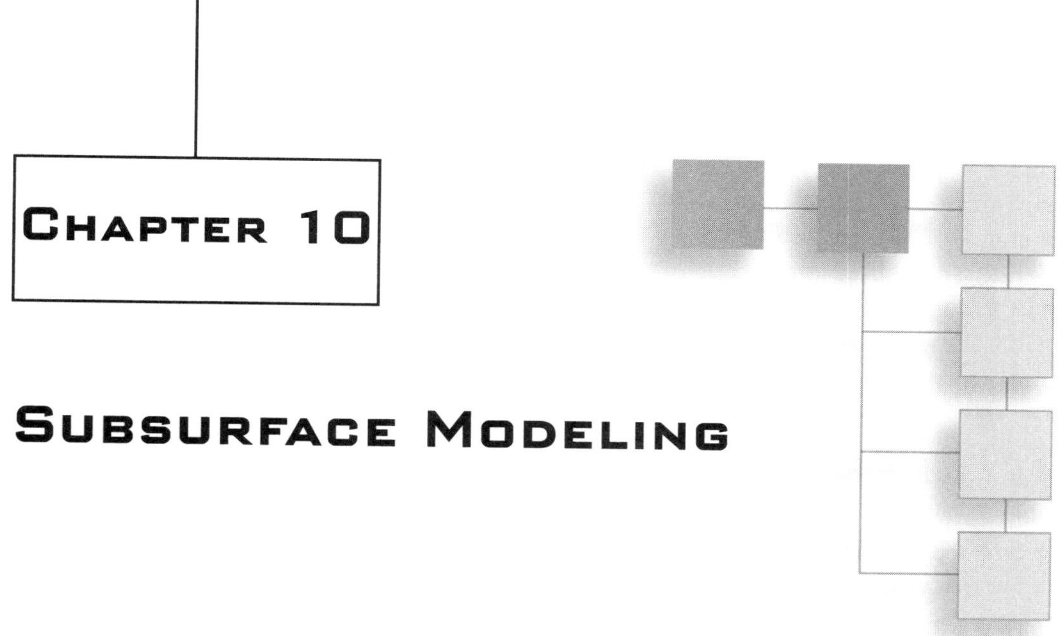

Chapter 10

Subsurface Modeling

Video-game graphics have always been an odd marriage of artistry, mathematics, and engineering. Sometimes this marriage results in the development of awkward tools and stilted creativity, but occasionally, engineers and mathematicians find a process or workflow that can produce magic in the hands of an artist. This chapter introduces several useful workflows.

A workflow is a process or a frequently repeated method of individual steps that an artist uses to create a specific type of result. A workflow defines the order of activities or individual processes that must be undertaken. Game artists often speak of their preferred workflows when describing the set of tools and methods they frequently employ to create a model.

Introduction

You have already seen a number of simple workflows. A game artist can model an object by simply gluing together a bunch of primitives. That is a simple workflow. Another game artist might model that same object using Boolean subtraction to carve the shape out of a solid block. That is another workflow.

By choosing the appropriate workflow for any object, game artists can substantially increase their work efficiency and their models' polygon efficiency. By choosing the wrong workflow, they can preordain disaster.

Traditional painters must also plan their workflows. A painter might start by penciling lines onto a canvas and then gradually cover the lines with opaque oil paints. The same painter might choose to sketch the next painting entirely with pastel crayons or airbrush images using thin acrylic paints.

Unlike a painter, a game artist must often think like an engineer when planning the ideal workflow for an object. Often the most efficient solutions come from modeling an object abstractly and then detailing the model with the appropriate refinements. There are many ways to accomplish this. The examples in this chapter demonstrate a few of them.

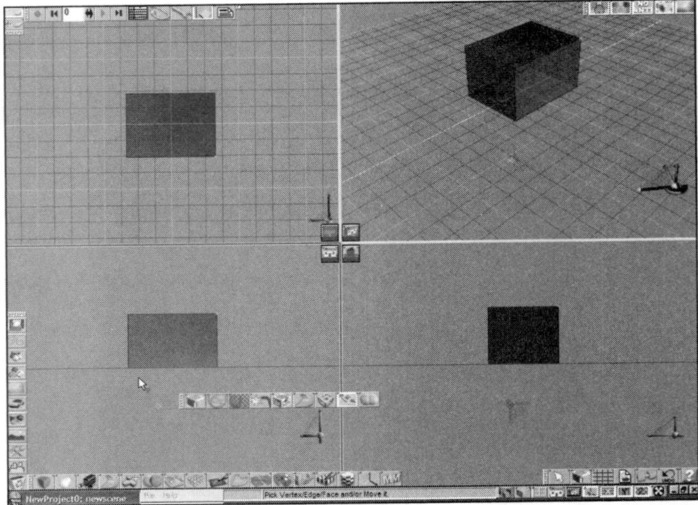

Figure 10.1
A cube has only six sides and eight vertices.

SubDivision Layers

In 3-D modeling, intricacy and detail come from adding faces to an object. The more faces an object has, the smoother and more complicated it can appear. Detail comes at a price, both in the final game and in the modeling process.

Figure 10.1 shows a simple six-sided cube.

You can easily reshape this cube by selecting one vertex and moving it out from the center of cube. See Figure 10.2.

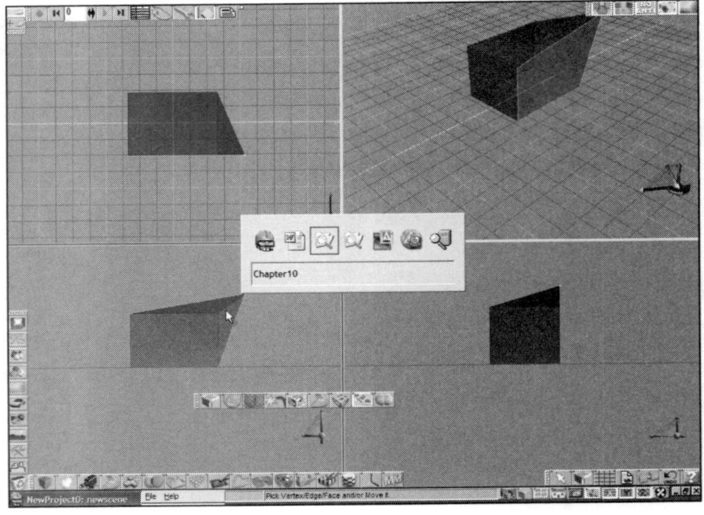

Figure 10.2
Moving just one vertex reshapes the cube.

With a simple cube, this is pretty easy, but what happens if you change the cube to a smooth sphere?

Figure 10.3 shows the result of moving just one of a sphere's vertices. How long would it take to reshape the sphere this way?

Clearly, it is much quicker to model a complex object out of cubes, but the object won't be smooth. The SubDivision Layer tools solve this problem. With the SubDivision Layer tools, you can sculpt an object using only the rudimentary geometry and then smooth the geometry to whatever level of detail is required.

If you were to apply the Add SubDivision Layer tool to the sphere in Figure 10.3, you would get the result shown in Figure 10.4.

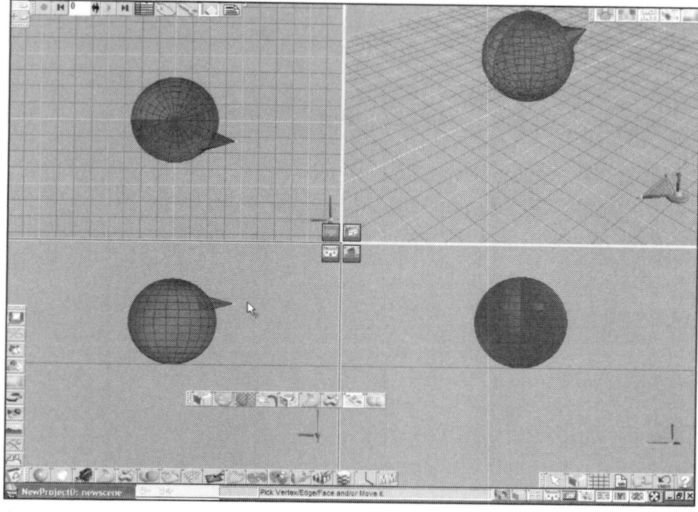

Figure 10.3
You would have to move a lot of vertices to reshape this sphere.

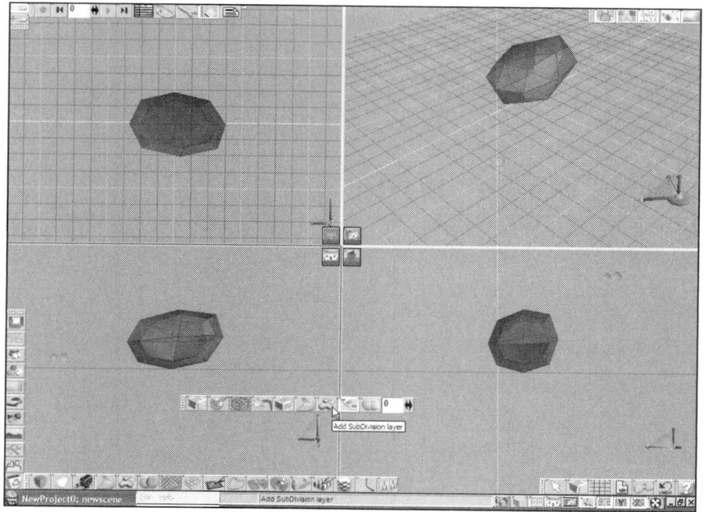

Figure 10.4
The cube's faces have been smoothly subdivided.

If you were to apply the Add SubDivision layer tool again, it would produce the result shown in Figure 10.5.

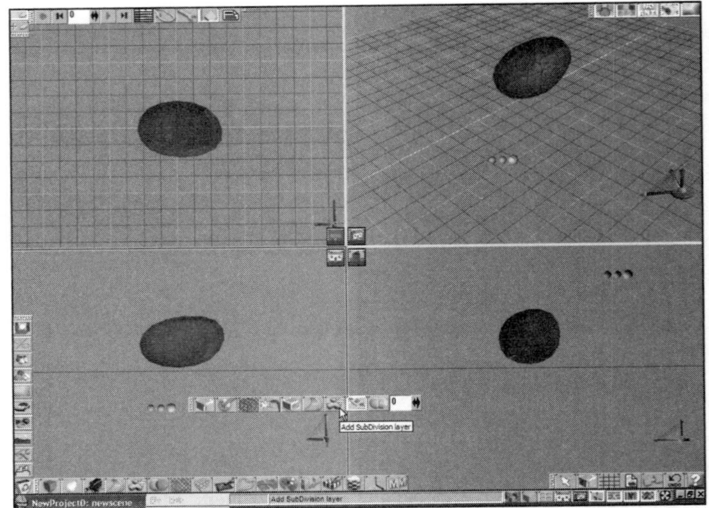

Figure 10.5
The Add SubDivision layer tool has been applied again.

Imagine how long it would have taken to adjust the vertices of a sphere to create this same form. Think how much longer it would take if you wanted to change it yet again.

With the SubDivision Layer tools, subsequent changes are easy. If your rounded object was not quite right, you can merely use the Delete SubDivision layer tool to reduce the level of subdivisions until you were left with the original simple geometry. You can then adjust the simple geometry as shown in Figure 10.6, and add several levels of subdivision to produce the result in Figure 10.7.

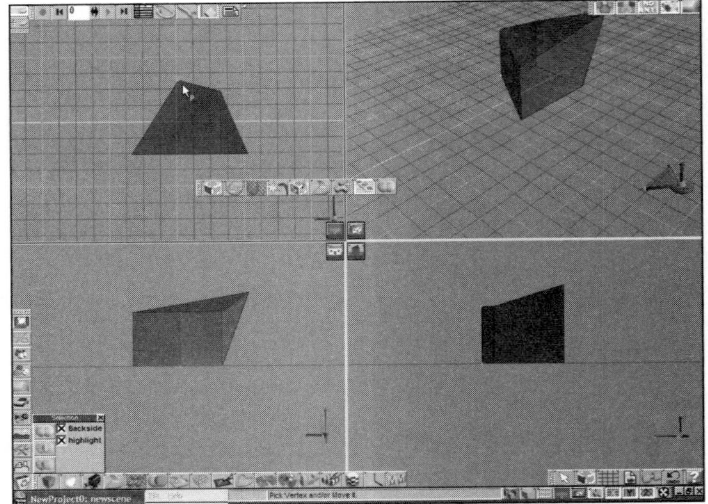

Figure 10.6
Remove the levels of subdivision to reshape the original cube again.

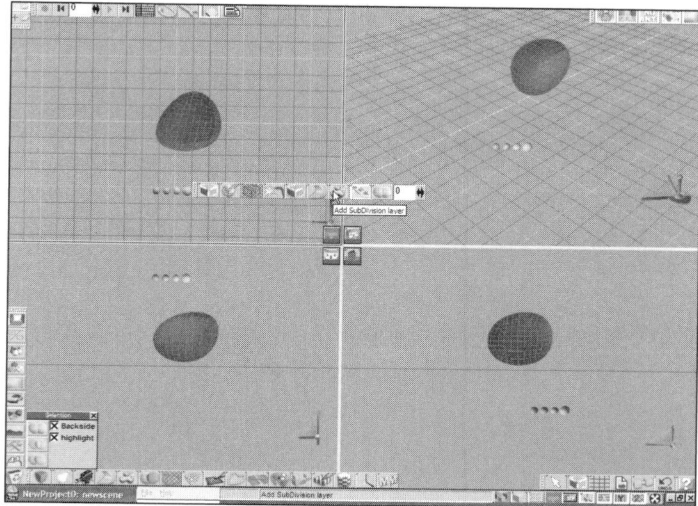

Figure 10.7
Reapply the levels of subdivision to produce a modified rounded object.

Recycling Models

Game artists must always look for ways to accelerate their projects and reduce their work. Nothing accelerates a workflow more than reusing preexisting objects. gameSpace offers a powerful library system that can organize, store, and retrieve any object you create.

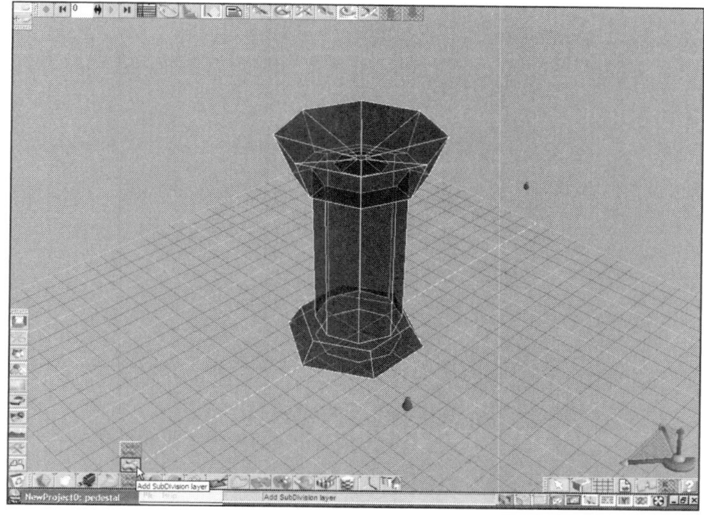

Figure 10.8
Activate the Add SubDivision layer tool.

In this demonstration, you will reuse your pedestal model from Chapter 8, "Boolean Operations." Reload the scene for the pedestal and use the Object tool to select the entire pedestal object.

Activate the Add SubDivision layer tool, as shown in Figure 10.8.

Add another layer of subdivisions by clicking the Add SubDivision layer icon again.

Applying Cylindrical UV Projection would make the pedestal appear even smoother. See Figure 10.9.

Figure 10.9
Proper texturing makes the object appear even smoother.

Extruding a Blade

Now that the pedestal is polished and smooth, you can scale it down and use it as the hilt of a sword or dagger. To accomplish this, you might employ a workflow based on successive sweeps with the Sweep tool. You will start with a profile curve and sweep it repeatedly, making minor adjustments with every sweep.

Activate the DrawPanel tool, as shown in Figure 10.10.

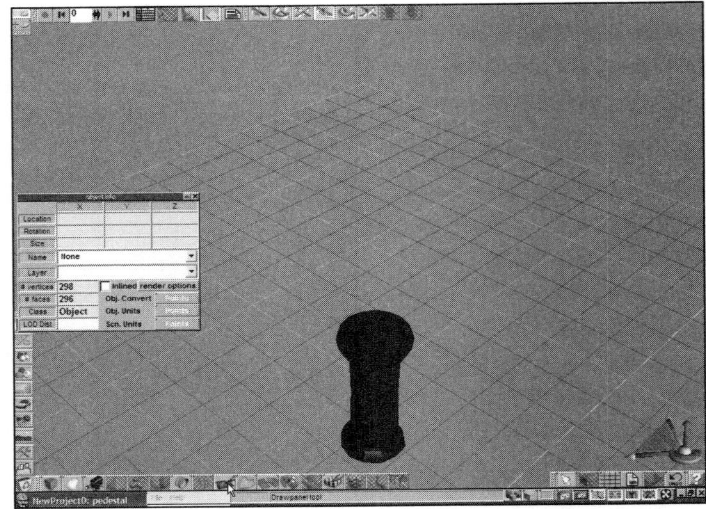

Figure 10.10
Activate the DrawPanel tool.

When you click and drag in the perspective viewport, a DrawPanel appears lying flat on the XY grid. See Figure 10.11.

Without releasing the mouse button, reverse directions and drag the mouse the opposite way. The DrawPanel should begin to collapse and then stand itself upright.

Delete the vertical DrawPanel, and create a DrawPanel that is flat against the XY grid, as shown in Figure 10.12.

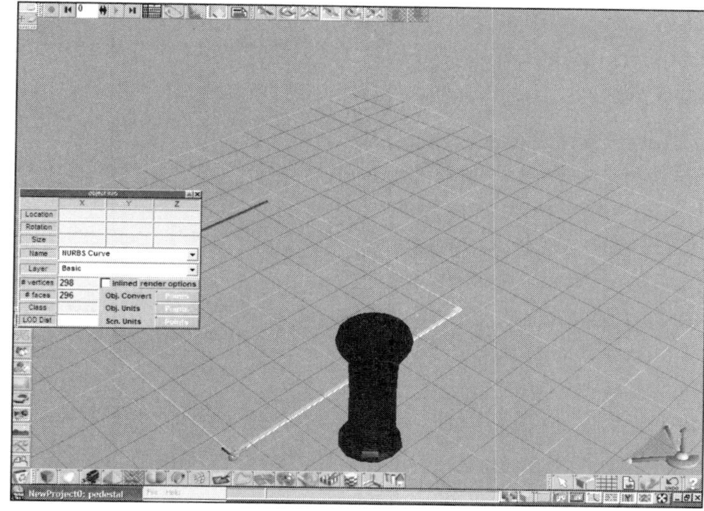

Figure 10.11
Drag in the perspective viewport.

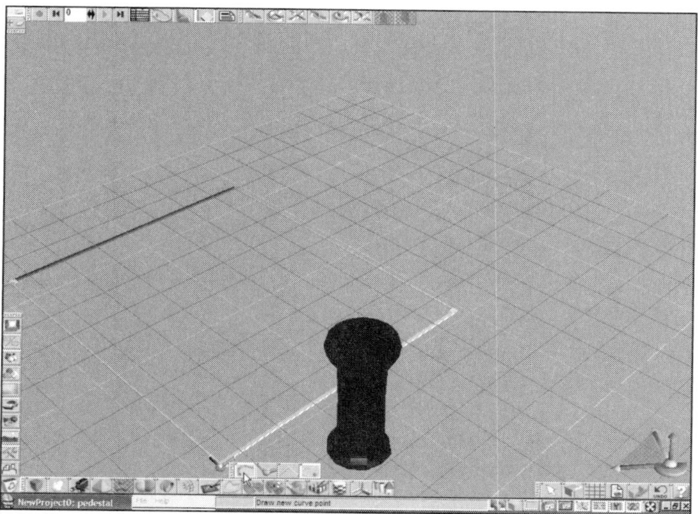

Figure 10.12
Create this DrawPanel.

Begin a new curve by following the steps in Figure 10.13.

Activate the Close Curve tool from the curve-editing toolbar to complete the curve, then activate the Sweep tool as shown in Figure 10.14.

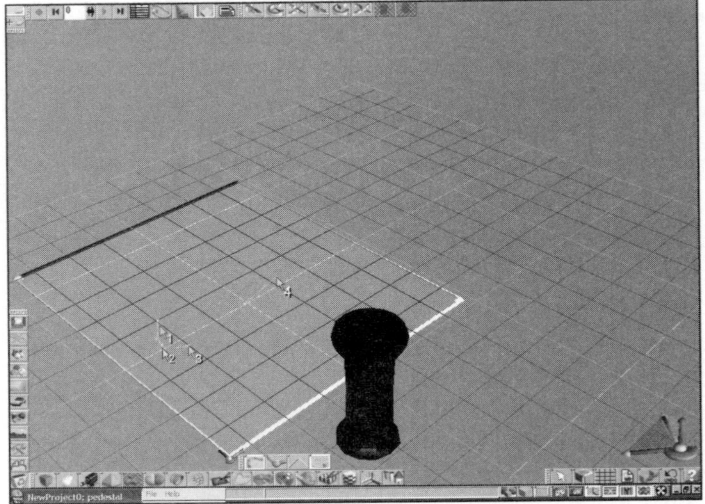

Figure 10.13
Add these curve points.

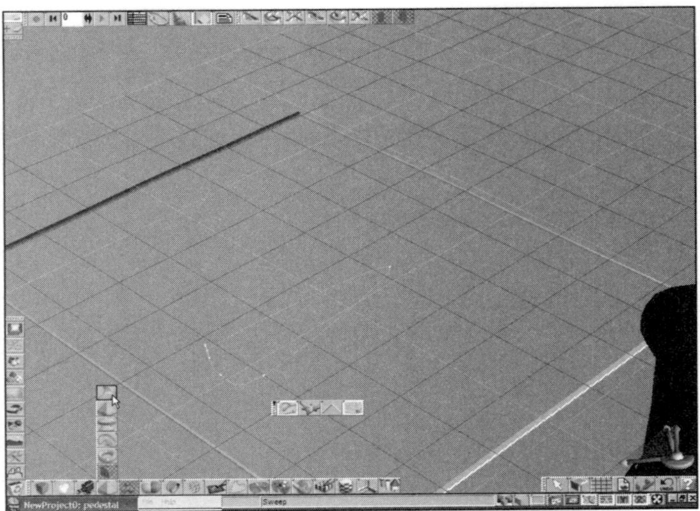

Figure 10.14
Sweep the closed curve.

The shape is extruded into a 3-D object, as shown in Figure 10.15.

Use the Point Move tool, and then right-click and drag to move the extrusion up along the Z axis. See Figure 10.16.

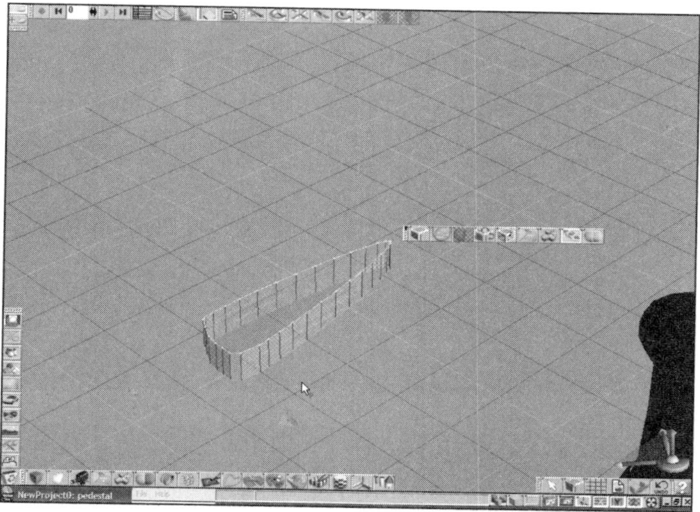

Figure 10.15
The shape has been extruded.

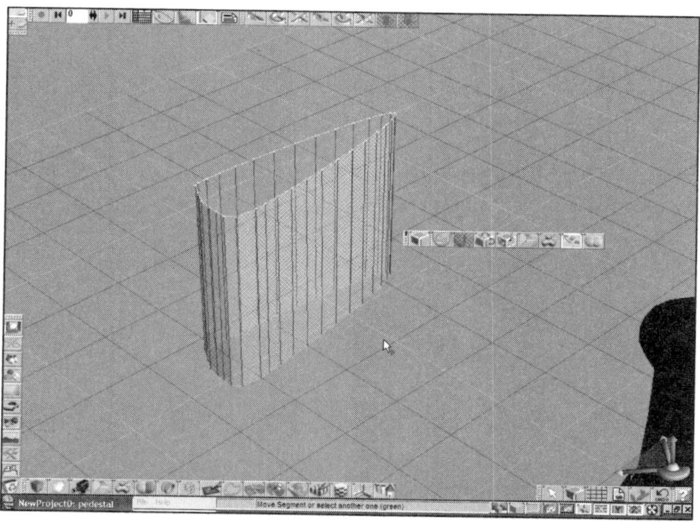

Figure 10.16
Extend the extruded object by moving the top face up.

Continue to sweep and adjust in small steps, until you have a curved blade similar to Figure 10.17.

For the point of the blade, you will use the Tip tool. The Tip tool is like the Sweep tool, but rather than just extruding a selected face to another similar face, the Tip tool attempts to extrude the face to a point. The Tip tool can be found in the same toolbar slot containing the Sweep tool. See Figure 10.18.

Figure 10.17
Continue smoothly bending and tapering the blade.

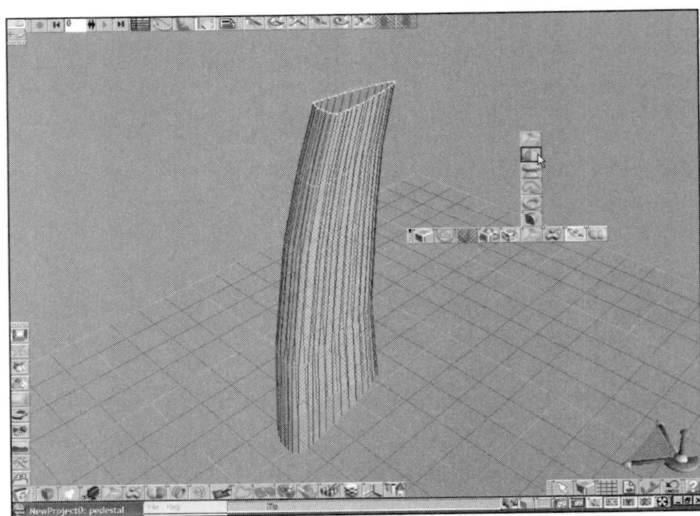

Figure 10.18
Activate the Tip tool.

Activate the Tip tool, and notice how it brings the blade to a single point. You can adjust this point using the Point Move tool to make the blade's end as sharp or dull as you please. See Figures 10.19 and 10.20.

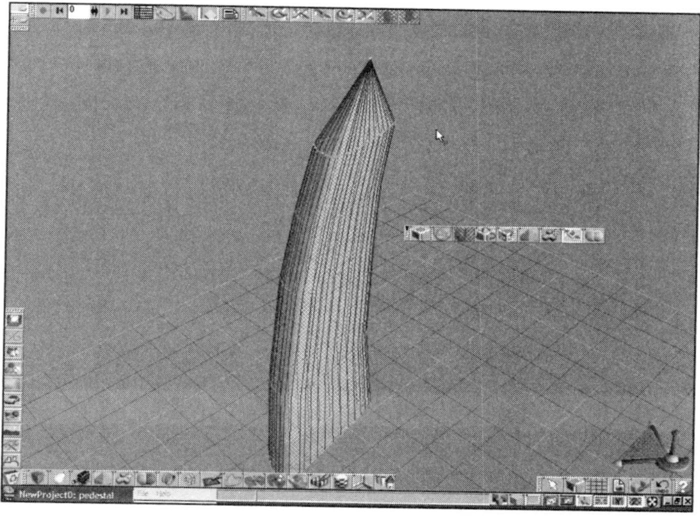

Figure 10.19
Use the Point Move tool to adjust the tip.

Use the Material Library to choose an appropriate texture for the blade, and then use the Object Move and Object Scale tools to position the blade on the hilt.

Save the scene.

The Problem with SubDivision Layers

The SubDivision Layer tools are extremely useful, but they do have a few drawbacks. Each additional layer of subdivision creates exponentially more faces and vertices. With a few clicks of the mouse, you can add so much detail in subdivision layers that your model drains the life out of your game engine.

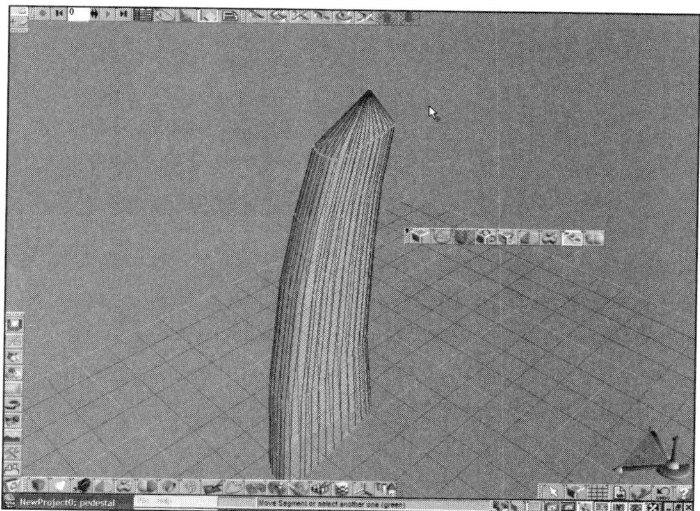

Figure 10.20
Move the tip point around to achieve a realistic look for the blade.

One solution is to apply the SubDivision Layer tool to only those pieces of your object that need the most detail. Another solution many experienced game artists prefer is to strategically implement their subdivision by hand.

Manual Subdivision

A typical workflow that is the favorite of many experienced game artists begins with the creation of very simple geometry. The artist proceeds to manually subdivide any faces necessary until the object has just the level of detail desired.

You will use such a workflow to create a much more majestic door for the side wall of the treasure vault.

Blocking Out the Door

Launch gameSpace, and begin a new scene. You will begin the door by creating a large, short cube primitive. Use the Object Info Pane to set the cube's parameters as indicated in Table 10.1 below.

Table 10.1 Cube Object Parameters

	X	Y	Z
Location	0.0	0.0	0.0
Rotation	0	0	0
Scale	5.9	9.1	0.2

This cube is the basic shape of your door. You could save it now and have a crude door, but instead, you will manually detail it, adding geometry wherever necessary to achieve a rich, majestic look.

Detailing the Door

Select the cube with Object tool, and right-click on the cube to enter Point Edit mode.

Using the top viewport, click near the center of the cube. This selects the top face of the cube, as shown in Figure 10.21.

Activate the Quad Divide tool, as shown in Figure 10.22.

The selected face is split in two directions. Where there was once a single face, there are now four separate faces. The face has split from top to bottom and from side to side.

With the four new faces still selected, click on the Quad Divide tool again.

The four selected faces each split apart to become four more individual faces. There are now 16 faces on this side of the cube.

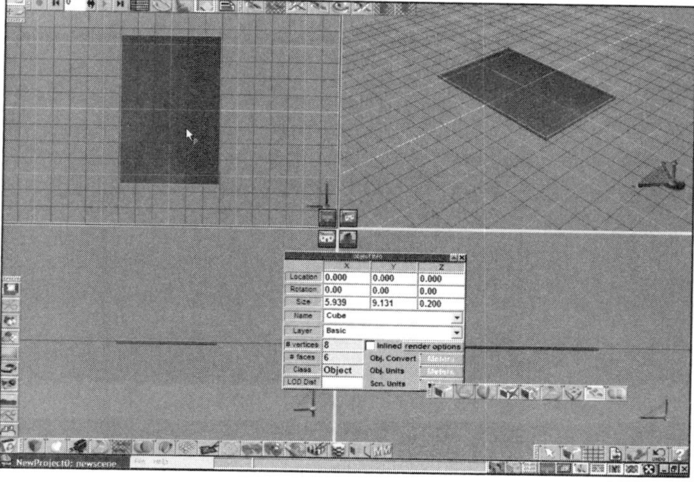

Figure 10.21
Select the top face of the cube.

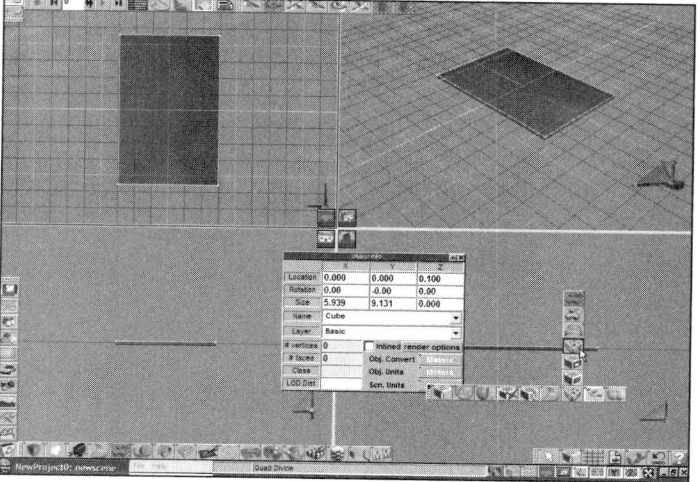

Figure 10.22
Quad Divide the selected face.

Use the Point Edit: Context mode or the Point Edit: Faces mode to select the bottom left face. It is labeled as face number 1, in the Figure 10.23.

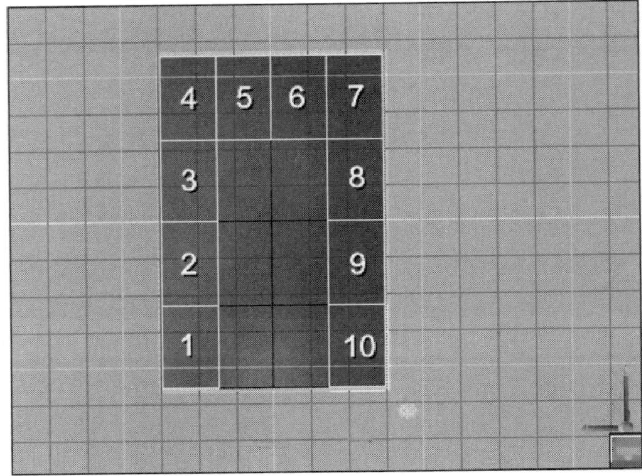

Figure 10.23
Select the numbered faces.

Hold the Ctrl key down while you click to add the faces numbered 2 through 10 in Figure 10.23.

Activate the Bevel tool, which is contained in the same toolbar slot as the Sweep and Tip tools. See Figure 10.24.

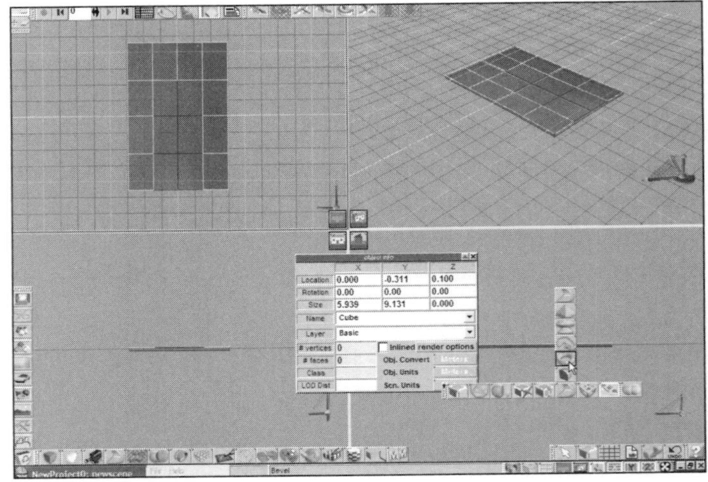

Figure 10.24
Activate the Bevel tool.

The Bevel tool works very much like the Sweep and Tip tools. You select a face or a set of faces and then activate the tool. Once an extrusion is created, the Bevel tool remains active, allowing you to interactively adjust the bevel it produces.

After you create a bevel with the Bevel tool, you can drag the mouse to pull the extruded surface away from or toward the original surface. As the Bevel tool lifts the extruded surface away, it shrinks the surface proportionally to form a bevel.

Drag the mouse upward in the top viewport to create a bevel in the shape of the selected faces. As you raise and lower the bevel, notice how the extruded faces are scaled in and out. If you are satisfied with the height (depth) of the bevel, activate the Point Scale tool to adjust the width of the beveled surface independently of the bevel's height. See Figure 10.25.

Adjust the bevel until it appears as shown in Figure 10.26.

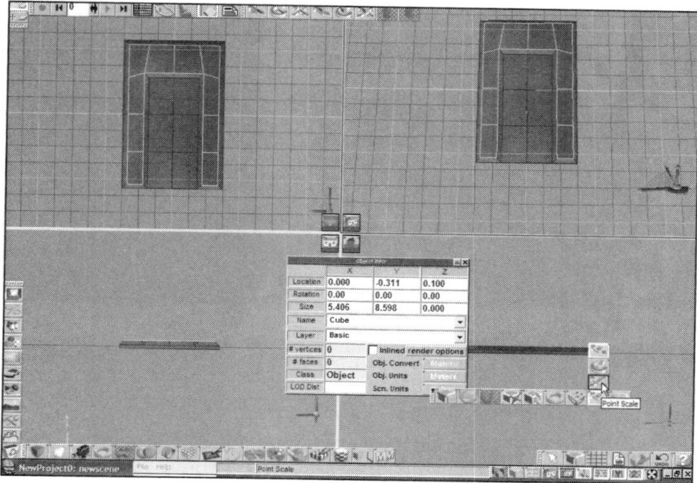

Figure 10.25
Adjust the depth and the width of the bevel.

Figure 10.26
This is the finished bevel.

Select Point Edit: Vertices mode, activate the Select using Rectangle tool.

Right-click the Select using Rectangle tool to open the Selection panel.

Make sure that both check boxes are checked.

Follow the steps illustrated in Figures 10.27 through 10.29.

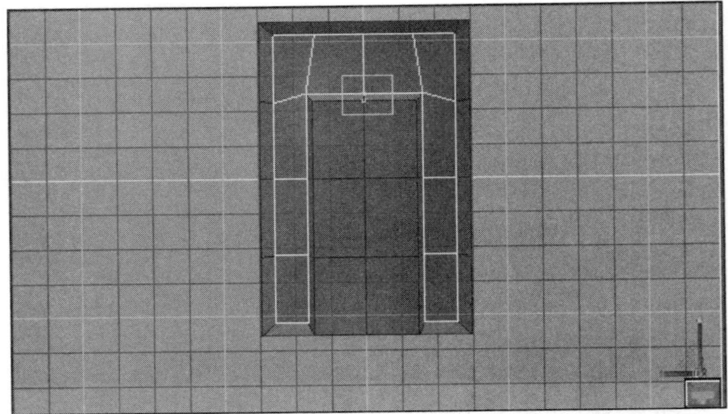

Figure 10.27
Use a rectangular window to select these vertices. Be sure to select the vertices on both sides of the beveled edge.

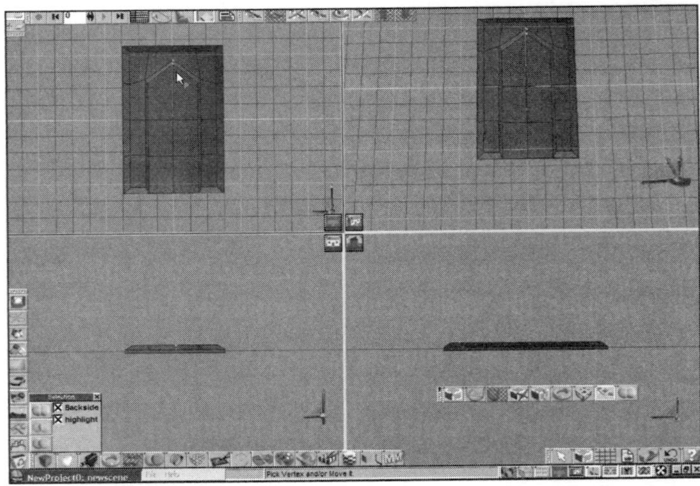

Figure 10.28
Activate the Point Move tool. With movement disabled in the X axis, drag the mouse upward in the top viewport.

Activate the Quad Divide tool. The selected faces each split four ways. Sixteen faces are now selected.

Use the Point Edit: Faces mode to select the numbered faces in Figure 10.30.

Activate the Sweep tool to extrude the selected faces.

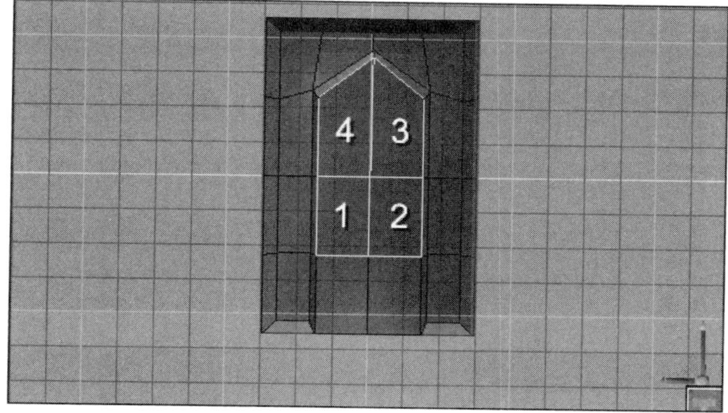

Figure 10.29
Use the Point Edit: Faces mode to select these faces. Select all of these faces.

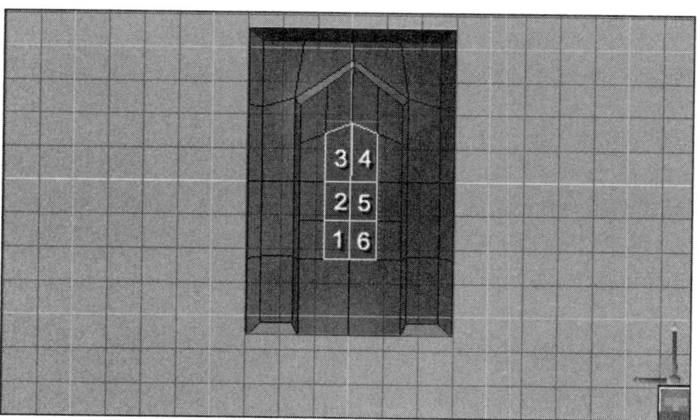

Figure 10.30
Select these six faces.

Enable movement along the X and Y axes, and activate the Point Scale tool. Scale the newly extruded faces until they appear as in Figure 10.31.

Complete the steps shown in Figures 10.31 and 10.32.

Disable movement along the X axis, and position the extruded surface as indicated in Figure 10.32.

Figure 10.31
Scale the new faces and then activate the Point Move tool.

Painting the Door

Open the Materials Library and double-click the Wooden Dolls texture.

Apply the Wooden Dolls material to the entire door, and then close the Material Library and Material Editor.

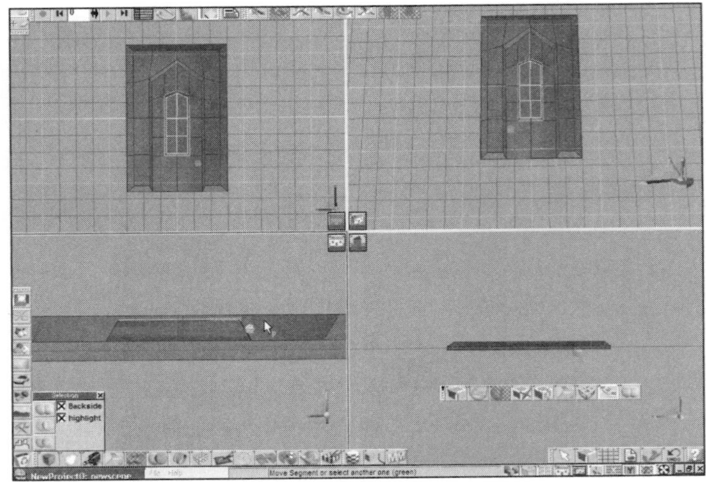

Figure 10.32
Move the extruded surfaces as indicated here.

Activate the cube primitive tool, and using the top viewport, begin to drag from the mouse location shown in Figure 10.33.

Release the mouse button when the new cube appears similar to the cube shown in Figure 10.34.

Figure 10.33
Begin creating a cube here.

Figure 10.34
Drag until the new cube looks like this.

With movement disabled in the X axis, use the front viewport to scale the new cube as shown in Figure 10.35. The cube must protrude above the rest of the door.

Figure 10.35
Scale the new cube.

Open the Material Library and double-click the Caligari material, as shown in Figure 10.36.

Open the Material Editor's Color panel, and click on the name Caligari to change the texture image. Browse the Texture directory from this book's accompanying CD and choose the DragonWood image.

Apply the DragonWood material to the new cube, and then activate the Planar UV Projection tool.

Figure 10.36
Select the Caligari material from the Material Library.

When you first apply the new material to the cube, you will see that the texture image is projected upside down. Use the Object Info Pane to rotate the object 180 degrees around the X axis.

Close the Object Info Pane, the Material Library, and the Material Editor. You would like the painted image to follow the contours of the door behind it, but there are not enough vertices to reshape the cube in that manner.

Right-click on the newly textured cube to enter Point Edit mode. Select the top face of the new cube.

Activate the Quad Divide tool.

Use the Select using Rectangle tool to make the selection shown in Figure 10.37.

Activate the Point Edit: Vertices mode. Using the front viewport, select the vertex shown in Figure 10.38.

Activate the Point Move tool.

Figure 10.37
Make this selection.

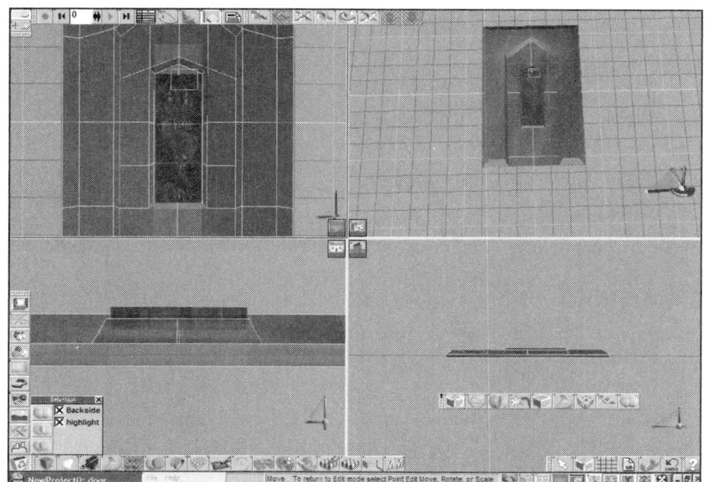

Figure 10.38
Using the front viewport, drag a rectangular window around the top center vertex of the painted cube.

Disable movement along the X axis, and drag the mouse upward in the front viewport. Continue to drag the vertices up and down until the painted cube appears as shown in Figure 10.39.

Figure 10.39
The top of the painted cube should match the design of the door behind it.

Use the Object tool to select the painted cube, and then activate the Glue as Child tool.

Use the Glue as Child tool to connect the two objects in the scene.

Positioning the Door

The door must stand vertically on end when it appears in the game. It must also be able to swing correctly, as if hinged to a wall in the level.

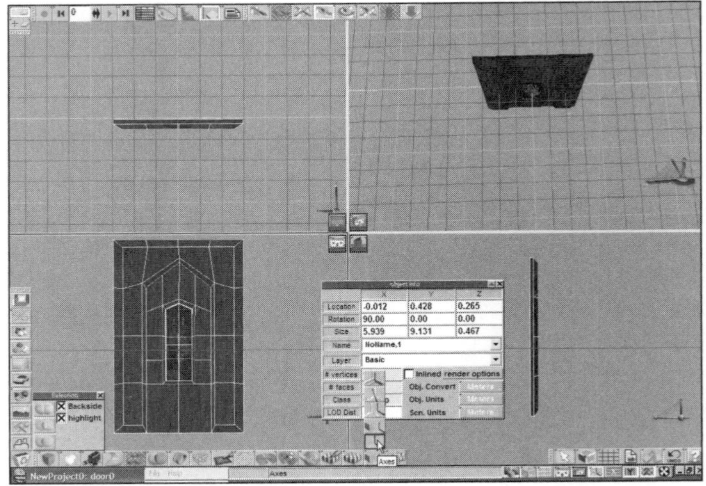

Figure 10.40
Activate the Axes tool.

The model of the door you've created is lying down, facing up toward the sky. If you were to open your door, it would spin around its center, because that is where its axes are placed. You should fix these problems before you import the door into the game.

Select the entire door object using the Object tool. Right-click on the Object tool to open the Object Info Pane and change the object's X Rotation value to 90 degrees. The first problem is already solved. The second problem's solution is almost as simple.

Activate the Axes tool by selecting its icon from the main toolbar, as shown in Figure 10.40.

Click in the top viewport and drag the door's axes to the left side of the door. See Figure 10.41.

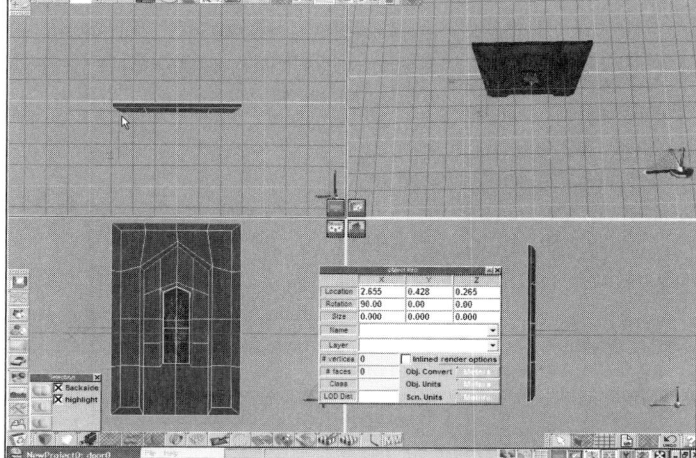

Figure 10.41
Move the door's axes to this position.

Activate the Object tool and select the door object itself. Use the Object Info Pane to set the door's properties as indicated in Table 10.2 below.

Table 10.2 Door Object Parameters

	X	Y	Z
Location	0.0	0.0	0.0
Rotation	90	0	0
Scale	5.9	9.1	0.46

Save the scene. Save the door as a DirectX .x file, and then close gameSpace.

Use ObjectImporter to choose the new door model as Game Object 5.

Launch Adventure Explorer, and climb to the treasure vault. The new door should appear against the wall, where the old door had previously stood. The new door is quite an improvement, but where does it lead?

Sculpting Vertices

No chapter on subsurface modeling would be complete without a mention of gameSpace's Deform Object and Sculpt Surface tools. Both are flexible tools for manipulating multiple vertices at a time, and they can be incredibly powerful additions to any modeling workflow.

The Sculpt Surface and Deform Object tools allow you to reach in and grab a vertex and push or pull it around like clay. When you use these tools to move a vertex, it drags its neighboring vertices along for the ride.

Imagine a piece of cloth lying on a table. See Figure 10.42.

When you pick up the center of the cloth, the center lifts and drags the rest of the cloth with it. If you can think of the cloth as being made up of thousands of threads, you could say that the farther any thread is from point at which the cloth is lifted, the less that particular thread will be affected. See Figure 10.43.

In Figure 10.43, the edges of the cloth are barely raised at all, but the center is pulled far off the table.

Figure 10.42
Imagine this is a piece of cloth on a table.

Figure 10.43
The cloth is lifted from its center.

You could use the Sculpt Surface tool to change the painted dragon on your door into a sculpted dragon. In Figure 10.44, you see the painted dragon object from the door model. I have hidden the rest of the door to make things easier to see.

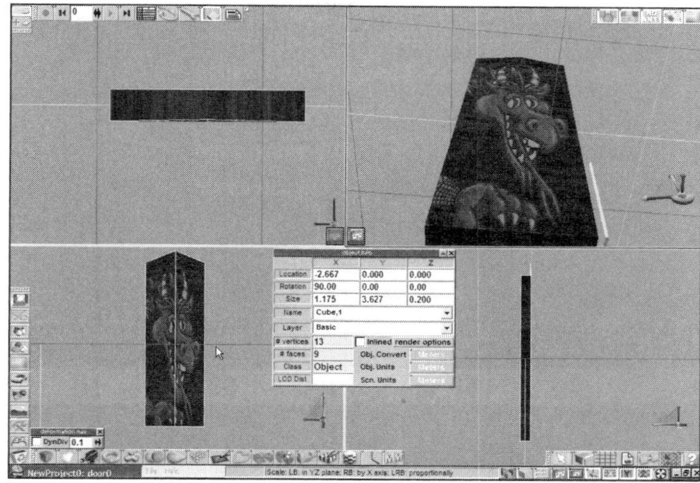

Figure 10.44
The painted dragon image is completely flat.

tip

> There are several ways to hide an object in gameSpace. One method involves placing the object to be hidden on another layer and hiding the layer. The simplest method is to check the Invisible check box on the Object render options panel. You display the Object render options panel by clicking the render options button on the Object Info Pane.

To sculpt the shape of the dragon, you should enter Point Edit mode and select the front faces of the painted dragon object.

Quad Divide the selected faces several times, as shown in Figure 10.45.

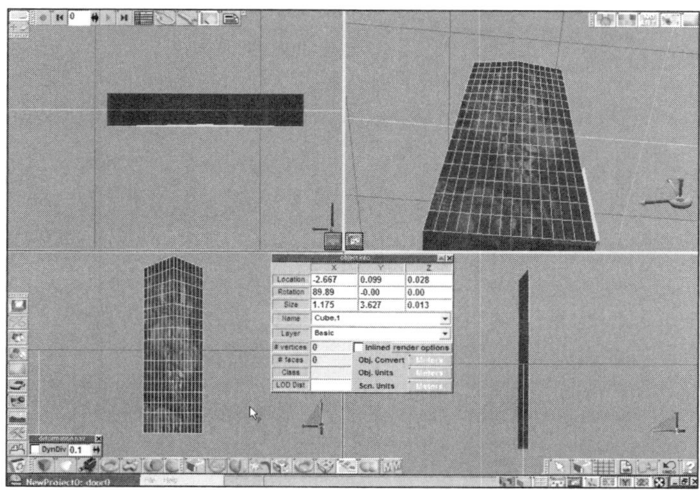

Figure 10.45
Prepare the faces for sculpting by Quad Dividing several times.

The more faces that you create, the smoother and more precise your sculpture will be. The Dyn Div (Dynamic Division) option automatically generates new faces as you sculpt, but I prefer to maintain control of my models' face count.

Activate the Sculpt Surface tool, as shown in Figure 10.46.

Click on any point in the geometry where you would like to begin sculpting. See Figure 10.47.

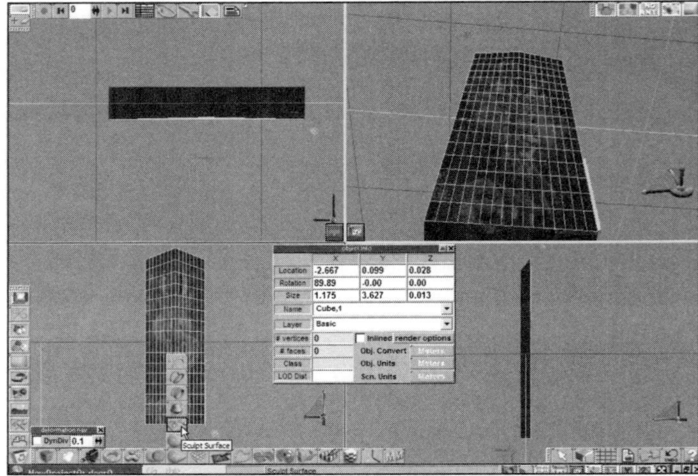

Figure 10.46
Activate the Sculpt Surface tool.

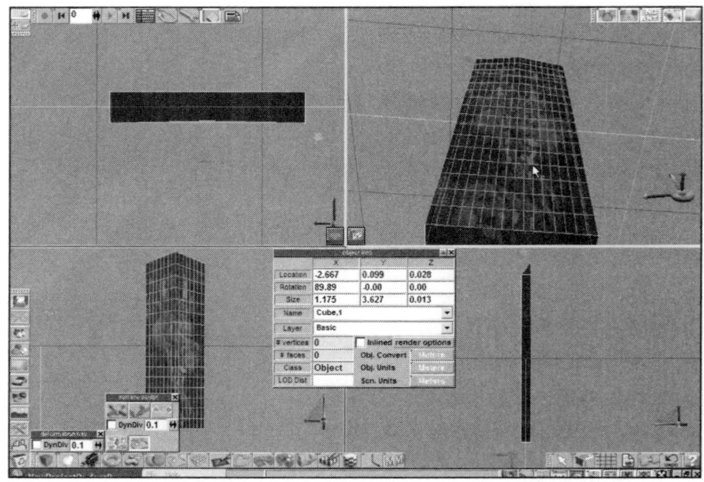

Figure 10.47
Click to begin sculpting.

Notice the deformation crosshairs that appear above the geometry you choose to sculpt. These crosshairs and the five dots that they connect are your primary sculpting tools when working with gameSpace's sculpting and deformation tools. See Figure 10.48.

Right-click and drag to pull the crosshairs away from the geometry and to gently pull the geometry up as well. Notice how the geometry now bulges out in the top view of Figure 10.49.

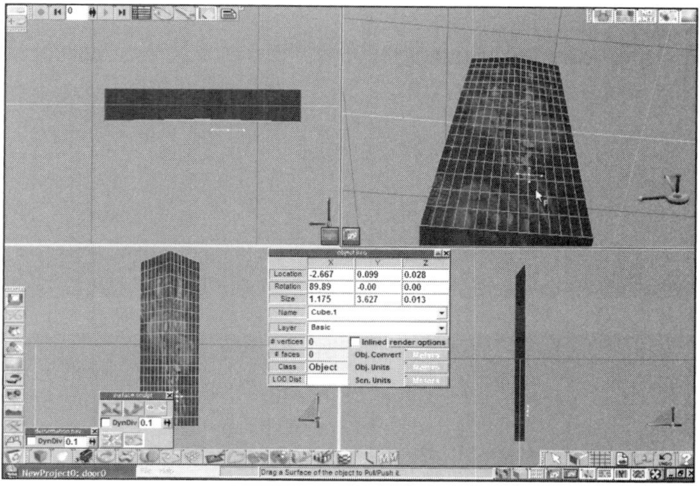

Figure 10.48
Use the crosshairs and the five dots they connect to sculpt and deform geometry.

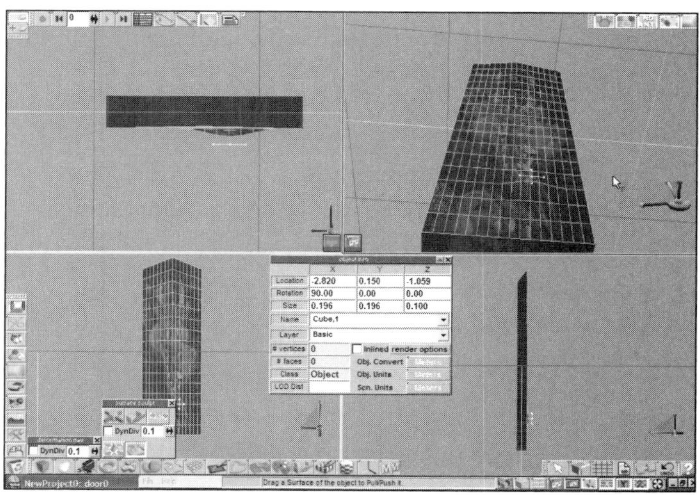

Figure 10.49
The geometry has been deformed.

Figure 10.50 shows the painted dragon object after numerous deformations.

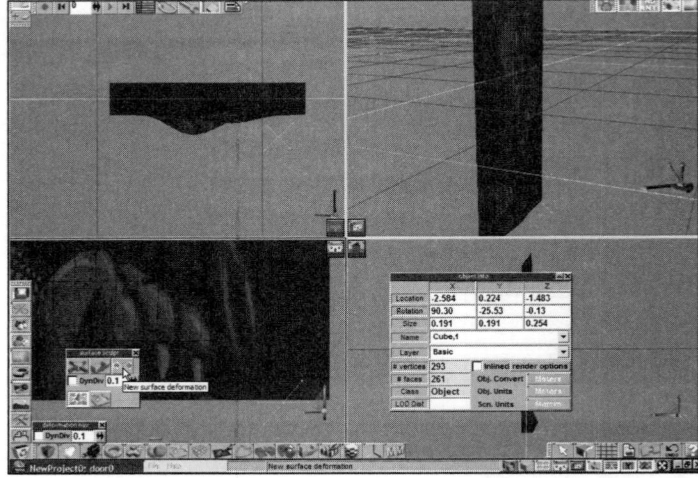

Figure 10.50
The dragon's face and hand have been sculpted out in relief.

Summary

In this chapter, you should have learned the following concepts:

- A workflow is a process or series of steps to used to produce a desired result.
- Often, many possible workflows produce the same result.
- By choosing the appropriate workflow for any object, a game artist can substantially increase work efficiency and a model's polygon efficiency.
- It is much easier to shape simple low-poly objects than it is to shape complex high-poly objects.
- Faces can be subdivided to create more geometric complexity.
- The SubDivision Layer tools add or subtract levels of smooth geometric detail to an object.
- The Quad Divide tool divides any selected faces horizontally and vertically.
- Each additional subdivision layer adds an exponentially increasing number of vertices and faces.
- The Tip tool extrudes a face or set of faces and tapers them into a single vertex.
- Use the Point Move tool to adjust the shape of the tip created with the Tip tool.
- The Bevel tool extrudes a face or set of faces and interactively scales them down as you increase the depth of the bevel.
- The Point Scale tool can be used after the Bevel tool to adjust the width of the bevel independently of the depth of the bevel.

- The Sculpt Surface tool is used to sculpt and deform subdivided surfaces.
- The Dyn Div option automatically creates new subdivisions as you sculpt.
- The deformation crosshairs and the five dots they connect are the handles to control gameSpace's sculpting and deformation processes.
- The Axes tool can be used to set the pivot point for a door.

Questions and Answers

Q: How many ways does the Quad Divide tool split a face?

A: The Quad Divide tool splits a selected face horizontally and vertically to produce four separate faces.

Q: If you Quad Divide two faces selected together, how many faces result?

A: Eight.

Q: If you select the face at the top of a cube and activate the Tip tool, how many new faces are created?

A: Four.

Q: How do you control the shape of an extrusion created with the Tip tool?

A: Use the Point Move tool to reposition the point at the tip.

Q: How does the Bevel tool differ from the Sweep tool?

A: Upon activation, the Bevel tool enters an interactive mode where the newly created faces are scaled to match the depth of the extrusion.

Q: Why is it rarely a good idea to apply several layers of subdivisions to a complicated game object?

A: Every subsequent layer of subdivisions generates exponentially more faces and vertices.

Discussion Questions

1. Describe an object that could be easily modeled with the SubDivision Layer tools.
2. Why is it important to know where the axes are located in a game model of a door?
3. How could you emulate the Bevel tool using the Sweep tool and Point Edit mode?
4. How could you approximate the effect of the Tip tool using the Sweep tool and Point Edit mode?
5. Describe a situation where you might need to use the Quad Divide tool.

6. Describe a type of common game object that could be easily modeled using the Sculpt Surface tool.
7. In the demonstration of the Sculpt Surface tool, why was it important to subdivide the original four faces?

Exercises

1. Use the Bevel tool to create a doghouse that looks similar to the doghouse shown in Figure 10.51.
2. Use the Quad Divide tool and the Sweep tool to add the lower walls and the opening to the doghouse, as shown in Figure 10.52.

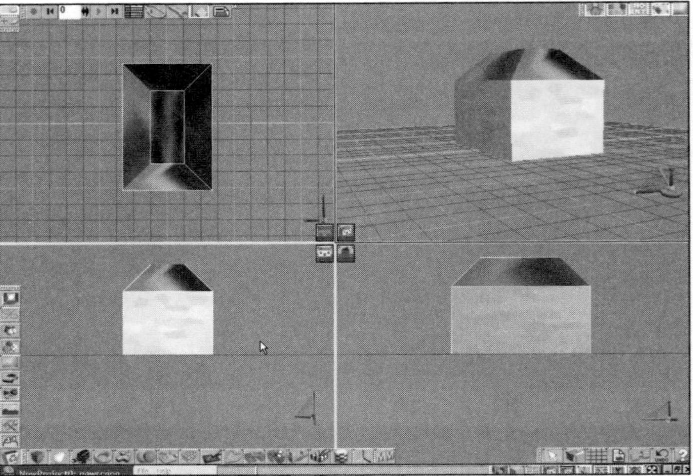

Figure 10.51
Use the Bevel tool to create this doghouse.

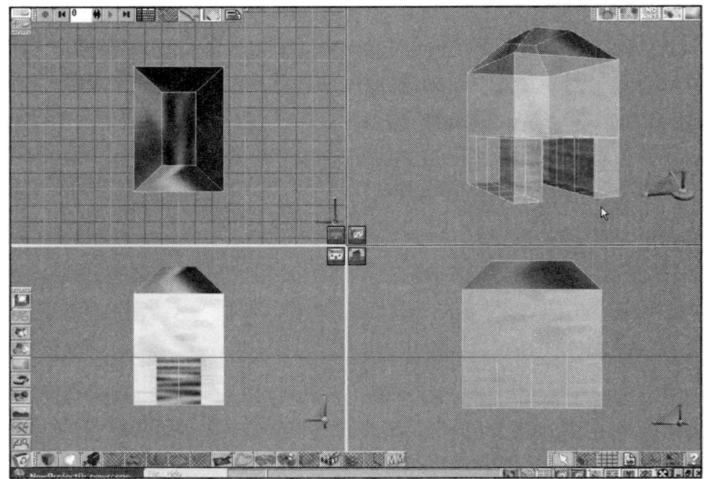

Figure 10.52
Add the lower wall and doggy door opening.

3. Add the cupola (the small structure on the roof) to your doghouse, as shown in Figure 10.53.
4. Use the Sweep tool to create a floor for the doghouse.
5. Use the Quad Divide and the Bevel tool to create a small step or threshold beneath the opening in the doghouse.
6. Create a snowman using a cube, the Sweep tool, and the Add SubDivision Layer tool.

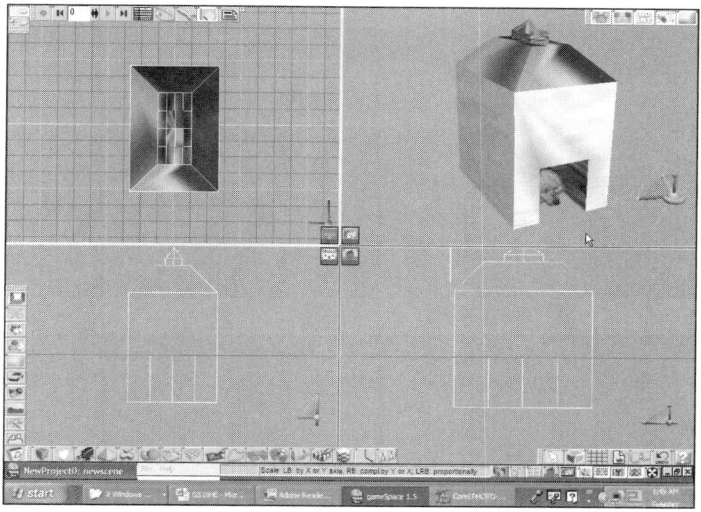

Figure 10.53
Add the cupola to the roof. Bizet, the dog, is extra credit!

7. Design a new look for the treasure vault by redesigning, modeling, and replacing the pedestal, the door, the column, and the archway. These are Game Objects 4, 5, 8, and 9, respectively. See the sidebar that follows.

> Can you create a cool new look for the treasure vault? If you create something fun, fresh, inspiring, and impressive, share it with us. Visit the book's companion Web site at **www.gamescapers.com/GameGraphics** for specific instructions and rules on how to share your creation with the world and enter the Adventure Explorer graphics design contest. Who knows? Maybe your original design will even make it into our next book.

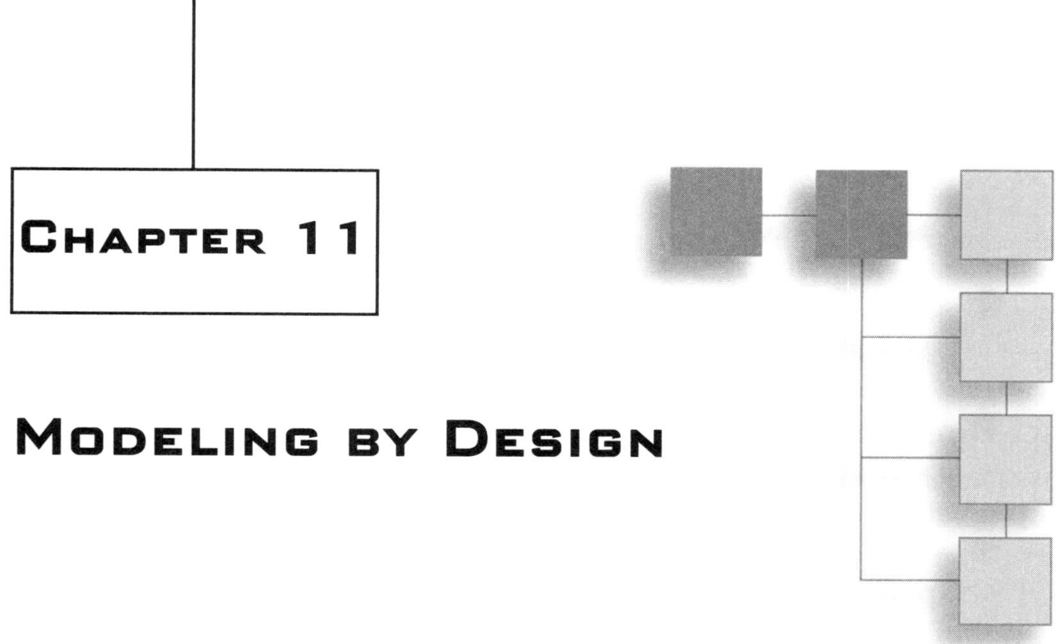

Chapter 11

Modeling by Design

Professional game companies spend millions of dollars developing every new game they release. Even more money is spent on the advertising, promotion, and marketing of a game.

When that kind of money is at stake, nothing can be left to chance. Every detail must be planned and designed with care. From the characters in a game to the vehicles the characters ride on, a blockbuster game is engineered to sell. Games should also be engineered to entertain, amuse, captivate, and tell a story, but if they don't sell, it really doesn't matter what else they can do. If a game doesn't sell, no one will ever play it.

Introduction

You make your way into the opulent treasure vault. Surrounded by the remains of a magnificent colonnade, a sparkling gem glistens through the darkness. You approach the gem, hypnotized by its beauty, but you cannot reach it. The gem sits on a pedestal, beckoning you from its marble perch. You wander around the room, entranced by the stone. The stone is said to guard secrets, but it is the gem's beauty alone that calls you to action.

You step back a pace and leap with all of your might. After several failed attempts, you land on the pedestal. The stone wobbles before you, stuck to its base by years of neglect, but you finally manage to pry it loose. A great rumbling nearly knocks you from the pedestal as a massive door begins to slowly swing open.

Beyond the door, you reach a ledge, which drops you into a long, steep corridor that leads to yet another massive room. In the center of this room, you see what can only be described as a gratuitous and useless special effect.

If you haven't already figured it out, this is exactly how you use the gem in Adventure Explorer to open the door leading out from the treasure vault. If you wander down the long steep corridor and reach the massive room, you will undoubtedly feel something is missing. Because this is your own game, you can choose to fill the gap with any object you imagine. But if you were a game artist working on a professional video game, you would probably have a discussion with the art director.

Art Direction

In professional game art departments, the art director is the captain of the ship. Art directors are generally responsible for setting the visual tone, quality, and style for the game. They are at least indirectly responsible for every object, texture, level, character, and effect that appears in a game. This is a profound responsibility.

A character is any person, creature, robot, or animal in a game. The players themselves are usually represented as characters in the game. Other NPCs (nonplayer characters) are scripted (programmed) to interact with the players' characters in various intelligent ways.

A good art director must consider how each character, prop, set, and location will look from any possible place in any level of the game. Even things like plants, trees, paving stones, cracks in the walls, and graffiti must be carefully designed to support the story, feel, and illusion of the game. Sometimes, the individual props and furnishings can be as crucial to the story as many of the characters the player encounters.

Scripting refers to the process of writing small specialized programs that control the actions and behavior of each character and prop in a game. In the past, game programmers were responsible for most game scripting, but with each passing year, more of this work is shifting to the level design team.

A prop is any object that a character can use, hold, take, or move in any manner.

A set or set piece is any static, nonmoving object or structure that a player or character might encounter, view, or inhabit during a game.

As in the real world, players make assumptions about the game's characters based on their apparent surroundings and personal environment. How a hobbit decorates a living room or what a detective keeps on the desk can tell you much about the character's personality, attitude, and situation.

Verisimilitude

> **Verisimilitude is the consistent appearance or illusion of reality and truth.**

The art director is largely responsible for maintaining the verisimilitude, the sense of reality, in a game.

Whether the game is set in modern times, the future, historical periods, or an imaginary world, an art director should strive to create the appearance of a credible consistent environment. Whenever possible, art directors research the genre, period, and location of their game. Books, libraries, films, the Internet, and other games can help them to better understand and visualize the cultural, scientific, and historical periods portrayed in their game. Remember though, that players' expectations can be even more important to a game's success than any true historical accuracy.

Artistic License

Artistic needs often conflict with accuracy. Many times, art directors make design decisions based on a sense of style or drama more than actual realism. They may select objects and design sets that are far from accurate but seem much more interesting, emotionally appropriate, and true to the spirit of the game.

As an example, the walls of the main picture hallway in Disneyland's Haunted Mansion do not just seem to converge on its guests, but actually angle sharply together in an extreme and claustrophobia-inducing manner. Another "hallway" in the Haunted Mansion winds this way and that like a confused snake, emphasizing the guests' feelings of oddness, confusion, mystery, and uncertainty.

Visual Psychology

Many art directors rely heavily on color, tone, and texture to help convey their visions and feelings toward a game's characters and settings. Often, the main characters and important set pieces are assigned color and texture palettes early in the design process. Sometimes these palettes substantially change throughout the course of a character's or place's progression or adaptation through the game.

A nonplayer character who appears helpful in the first level may appear dressed in bright warm colors on your first encounter. In a later level, you find him clothed in dark cool colors after you realize he has betrayed you and is now your enemy.

The trees on the heroes' home planet may appear forest green and softly lit when the game begins, but upon their return, the greens are faded and yellow, and stark contrast and shadows reflect the planet's fall into corrupt despotism and despair.

Texture is another essential tool of the art director. Just like the choice of color, the choice of materials can significantly alter the overall look and feel of a game. Think of the different feel of a room decorated with plush carpets and wooden paneling versus the same room lined with stark cold metal and riveted stainless steel wall plates.

Character Design

The design and costuming of the characters in a game are particularly important. In Chapter 1, "Fundamentals," you saw several ways that a character's appearance can greatly affect the player's enjoyment of a game.

Most video-game characters begin as sketches and rough illustrations. Dozens or hundreds of sketches may be produced before a suitable look is found.

Even after the design team has agreed on a look, the character is still not final. Most art directors insist on seeing their characters in 3-D. Only with a 3-D model can you really perceive the way a character will appear throughout a 3-D video game. Often small wood or clay sculptures called maquettes are created and placed in positions where they can be viewed from any angle.

Art directors often use their sculpted maquettes as guides to create a final set of blueprints or orthographic elevations. These elevations, or "As-Builts," become the definitive visual guide to the character.

Once a character is approved, the complete package of illustrations, renderings, elevations, color sheets, and As-Builts is added to the game's design document.

A maquette is a three-dimensional physical model used to visualize or test an artistic or architectural concept or design.

The term "As-Builts" refers to plans or elevations drawn to document a preexisting product, structure, prop, set, character, sculpture, or model.

A game design document, or game bible, refers to the collection of all the plans, designs, descriptions, rules, stories, and any other literary or illustrated concepts that have been accepted by the design team to become part of the game. These vitally important books are usually maintained by a single member of the design team and referenced by all of the other members throughout the entire development process.

Modeling from Plans

Professional game artists are often handed a set of plans or orthographic elevations to use as guides when creating the models for a game. The ability to create low-polygon models from a set of plans or elevations is perhaps the single most essential skill for a game artist looking to start a career in the video-game business.

In this chapter, you will model a large flaming tiki to sit beneath the gratuitous effect in the center of the large empty chamber. I have to express my thanks to Rolly Crump for providing the inspiration for this particular demonstration.

Tikis are traditional wooden, clay, or stone images of supernatural beings. They are commonly found throughout many African, Polynesian, Maori, and Indian cultures.

This is a rather complex model. In this modeling process, you will use many of the modeling tools that you have seen in the last few chapters. The fundamental difference in this project is that you will have a set of visual guides to keep the modeling process on track.

Setting Up Your Workspace

Launch gameSpace and begin a new scene.

Before you begin modeling, you need to arrange some things in your workspace. If you were a sculptor sculpting a large model or maquette in a studio, you might print or trace a set of elevations on the studio walls so you could see exactly how your model should look as you build it. You will do the same thing in gameSpace.

Like the sculptor in the studio, you need some walls on which to hang your elevations. Create a large plane primitive as shown in Figure 11.1.

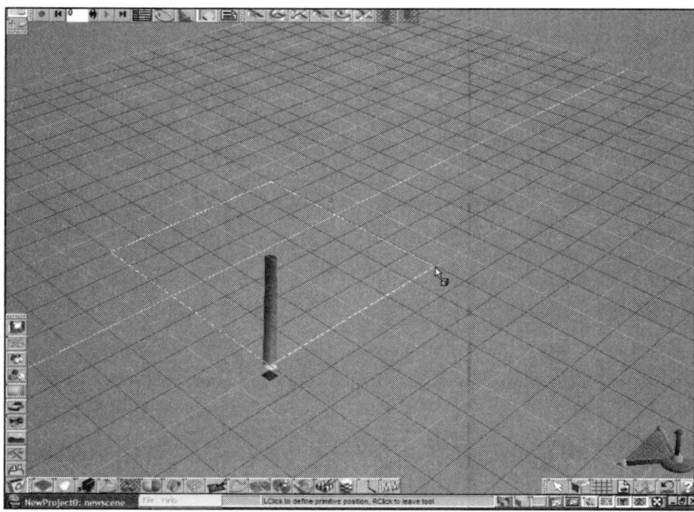

Figure 11.1
Create a large cube. Move one of the planes so that you can see both in the viewport.

Selecting the Elevation Images

Use the Object Move tool to slide the duplicate plane away from the original plane.

Open the Material Library and double-click the Caligari material.

Open the Color panel of the Material Editor, and click the large button on the Color panel that displays the name Caligari.

Use the Texture Browser to select the image file named TikiFront, which is included in the Textures folder on this book's accompanying CD. See Figure 11.2.

Apply the material from the Material Editor to the first of the two planes. See Figure 11.3.

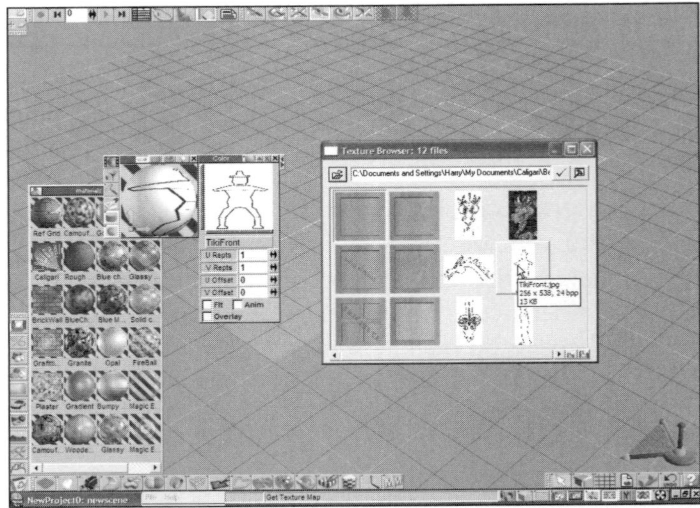

Figure 11.2
Select the TikiFront image.

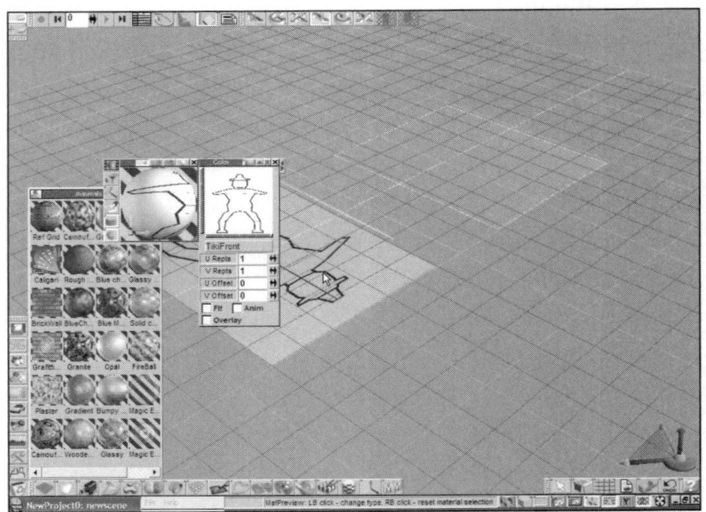

Figure 11.3
Apply the material to one of the planes.

Use the Texture Browser to select the image file named TikiSide, as shown in Figure 11.4.

Drag the TikiSide material from the Material Editor onto the second plane, as shown in Figure 11.5.

These two planes will serve as a visual reference for the rest of your modeling throughout this chapter.

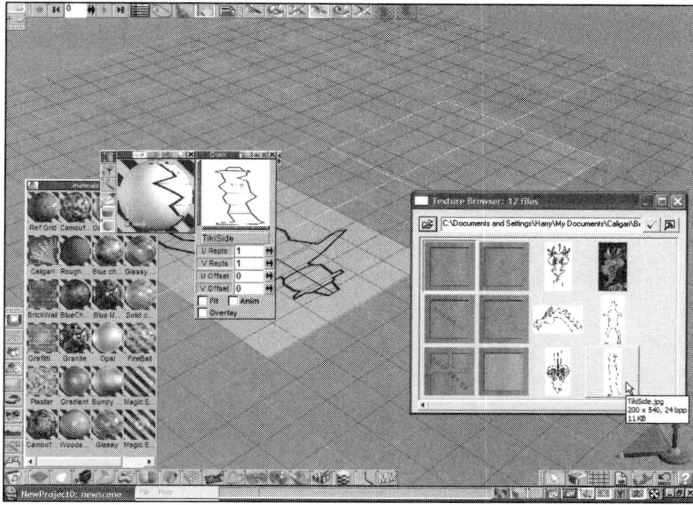

Figure 11.4
Select the TikiSide image.

Correcting the Aspect Ratio

Depending upon how you happened to create the planes, the elevation images that they now display are probably stretched out of proportion.

Select the plane displaying the front image. Right-click on the Object tool to open the Object Info Pane. The ratio of the X and Y Scale values indicated in the Object Info Pane is the exact aspect ratio of the plane.

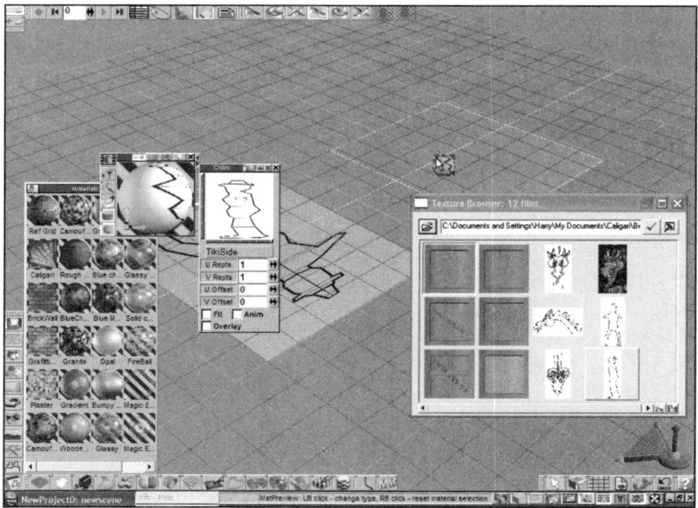

Figure 11.5
Drag the material with the side view onto the second plane.

To model the figure correctly, you must properly scale each of the planes to match the aspect ratio of the images they display. The Texture Browser offers a helpful feature that can assist you in setting the proper aspect ratio.

In Figure 11.6, you can see the information window that pops up when you move the mouse over any file in the Texture Browser.

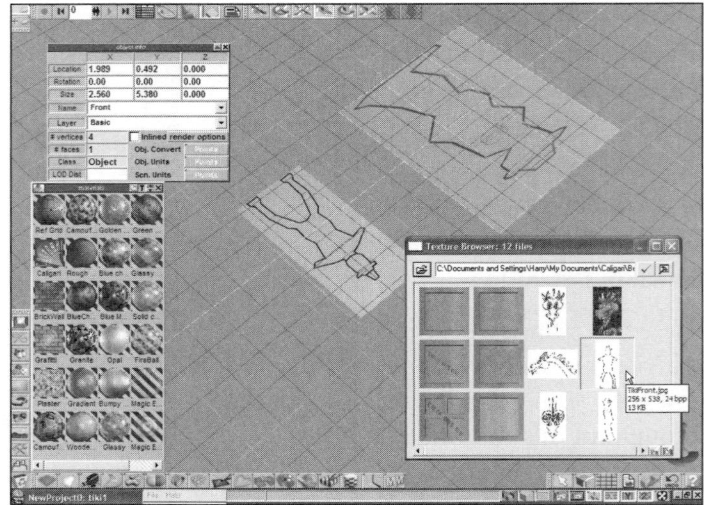

Figure 11.6
The Texture Browser displays a pop-up window with useful file information.

Notice the numbers 256 x 538. These numbers indicate the height and width of the image in pixels. The ratio of these two numbers is the exact aspect ratio of the original image. In order for the plane to properly display this image, it must be scaled to match some multiple of these numbers.

You could simply use the numbers 256 and 538 as the X and Y scale parameters for your plane, but the plane would be too large. If you divide each of these numbers by 100, you will have a reasonably sized plane with a perfect aspect ratio for the image. In Figure 11.7, you can see that I used the number 2.56 and 5.38 for the X and Y Size values. These numbers are derived by simply dividing 256 and 538 by 100.

Enter 2.56 and 5.38 in the Object Info Pane's X and Y Size fields, as shown in Figure 11.7. Select the plane displaying the side view, and repeat the process.

The TikiSide image is 200 pixels wide and 540 pixels high.

You should divide the second image's pixel counts by 100 and enter the numbers 2.0 and 5.4 in the X and Y Size fields for this plane.

Orienting the Elevation Planes

Now you will rotate the two planes into the proper orientation. The front view should face front, and the side view should face to the side.

Reselect the plane displaying the front image, and use the Object Info Pane to rotate it 90 degrees around the X axis. See Figure 11.7.

The front plane is now facing the right direction, but the tiki is standing on its head. Enter –180 in the Z Rotation field to stand the tiki on its feet. See Figure 11.8.

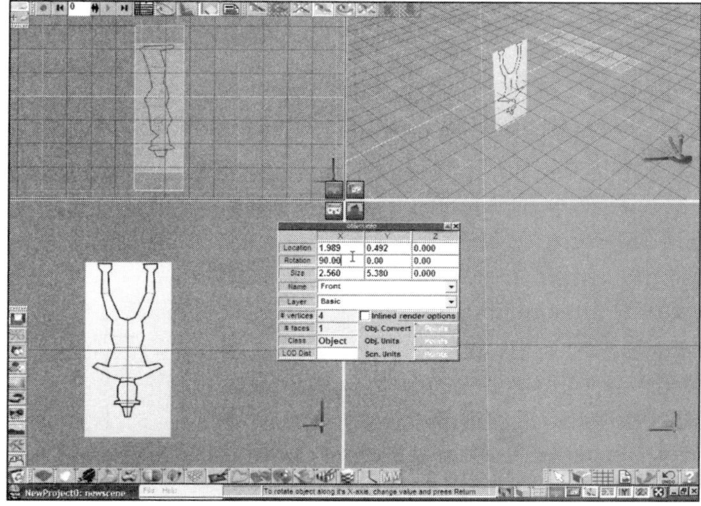

Figure 11.7
Stand the front image upright.

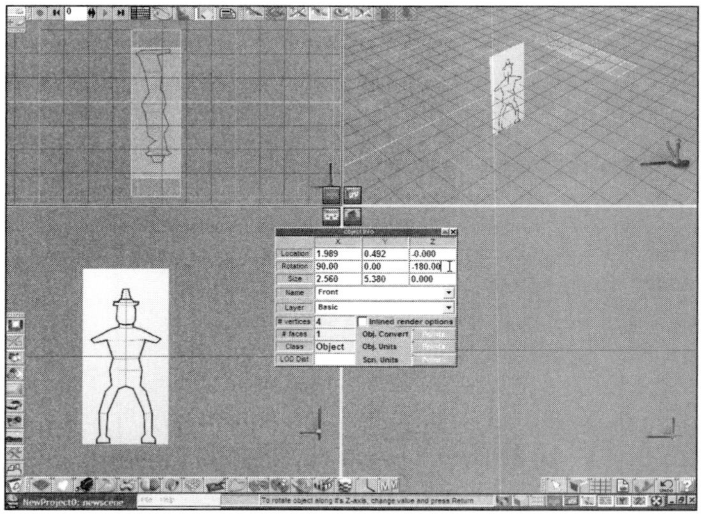

Figure 11.8
Stand the front view on its feet.

Select the plane displaying the side view, and use the Object Info Pane to rotate it –90 degrees around the X axis. See Figure 11.9.

The side view image also is upside down. To correct it, use the Object Info Pane to rotate the plane 90 degrees around its Y axis. See Figure 11.10.

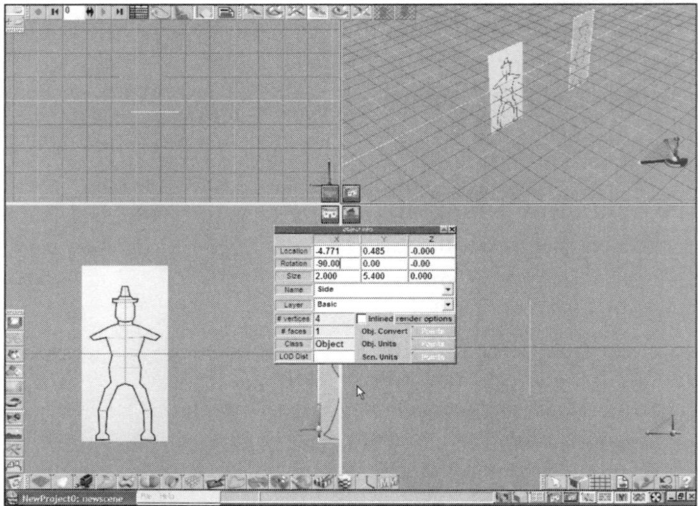

Figure 11.9
Stand the side view upright.

Positioning the Elevation Planes

Reselect the plane displaying the front view, and use the Object Info Pane to set its X, Y, and Z Location values all to 0.0.

Reselect the plane displaying the side view and the Object Info Pane to set its X, Y, and Z Location values all to 0.0.

In the perspective viewport, you can see how the two planes intersect. Revolving the perspective viewport, you can easily see the shape of the character defined by the two elevations.

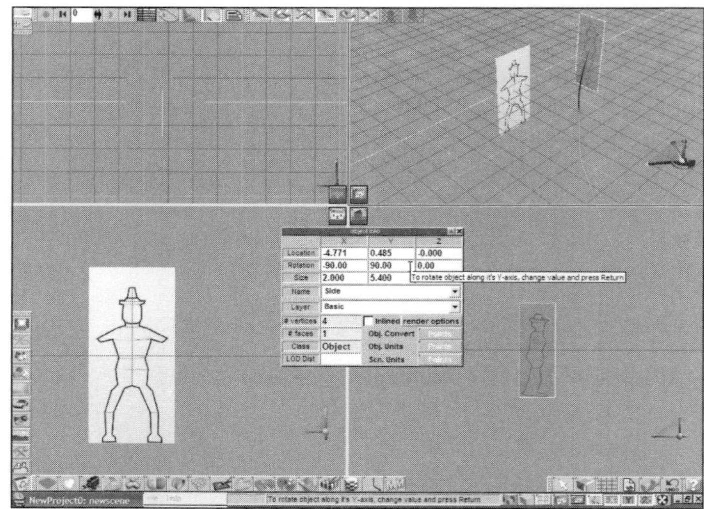

Figure 11.10
Stand the side view on its feet.

Adjusting the Focus

Depending upon gameSpace's current display settings, you might see a fuzzy depiction of the elevation images. See Figure 11.11.

To correct this problem, choose Display Options from the File menu, as shown in Figure 11.12.

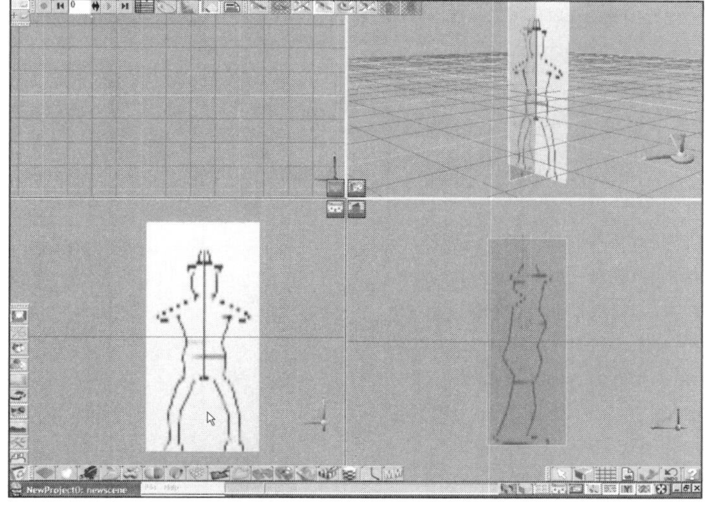

Figure 11.11
The elevation images are fuzzy and unclear.

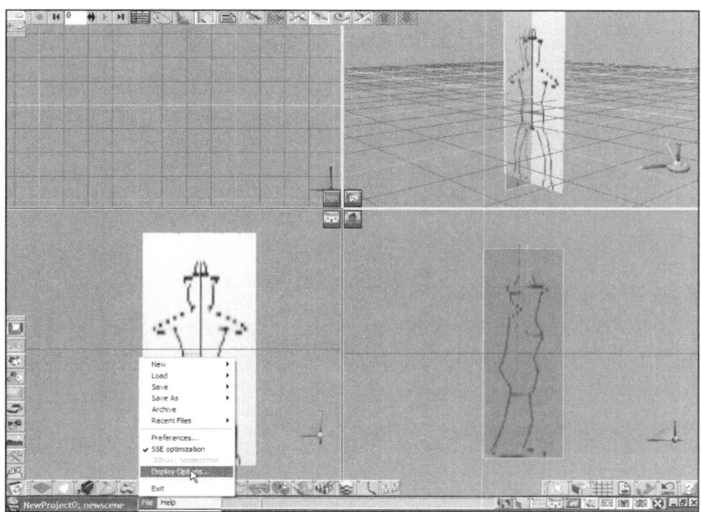

Figure 11.12
Adjust the Display Options to correct the image quality.

Near the center of the Display options panel, you will find a button labeled Txt res, displaying a set of numbers like 64 x 64. See Figure 11.13.

Txt res is an abbreviation of the words "texture resolution." The numbers displayed on the button indicate the number of pixels that gameSpace uses to display any texture images in the current viewport.

Click the Txt res button and select a higher texture resolution, as shown in Figure 11.14.

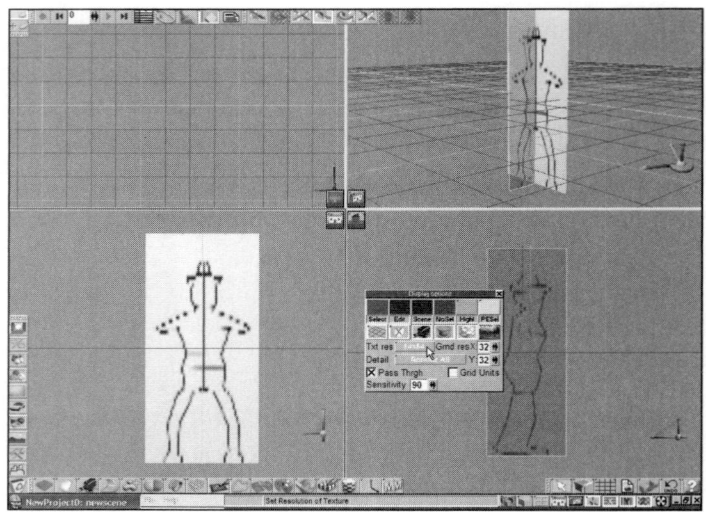

Figure 11.13
Adjust the texture resolution.

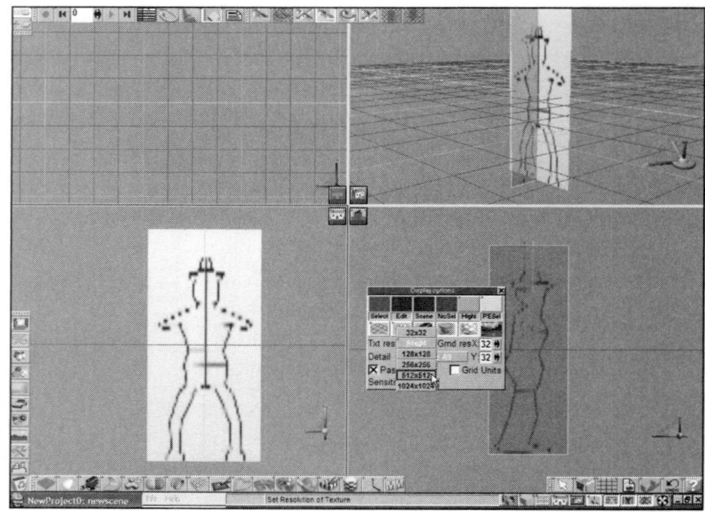

Figure 11.14
Choose a higher texture resolution.

Figure 11.15 shows the results of selecting a texture resolution of 512 x 512 pixels for the front viewport.

Click in each viewport on the screen and repeat the process.

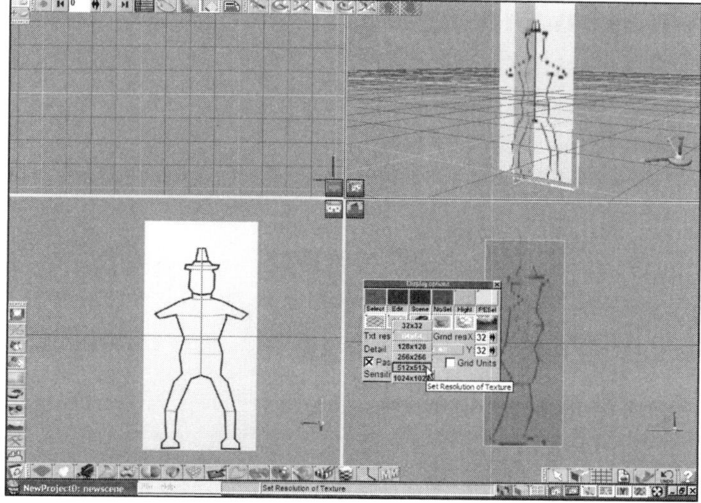

Figure 11.15
The textures in the front viewport are displayed at a resolution of 512 x 512 pixels.

Reset the Material Editor

If you were now to create a new primitive, the newly created primitive would be assigned the last texture you edited in the Material Editor. It would be confusing to see one of the elevation images projected on the model as you build it, so you should clear the material in the Material Editor.

Open the Material Editor by clicking the Material Editor icon on the main toolbar.

Clear the existing color shader by clicking the red x in the corner of the Color panel. See Figure 11.16.

Leave the Material Editor displaying a simple white color, and close the Material Editor.

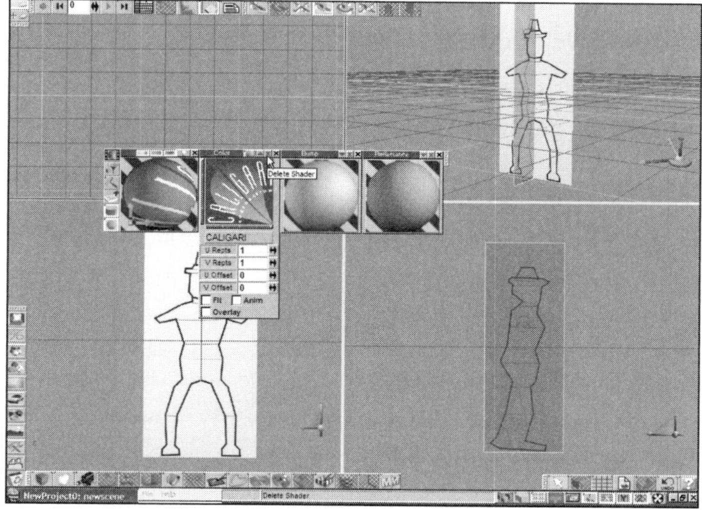

Figure 11.16
Delete the current color shader.

Modeling from the Ground Up

Activate the primitive Cube tool and draw a cube in the top viewport.

It doesn't really matter how large you make the cube as long as you can easily see it in every viewport. You will use the Object Move and Object Scale tools to position it more precisely later.

While the Magic Ring controls are still visible around your new cube, right-click on the Cube tool icon to open the Primitive parameters and Primitive shape panels. See Figure 11.17.

You will use the Primitive parameters panel to interactively subdivide the cube.

Place the mouse over the double-headed arrow beneath the first field on the Primitive parameters panel, then drag the mouse left or right to adjust the number of longitudinal divisions in the cube. Set this value to 3, as shown in Figure 11.18.

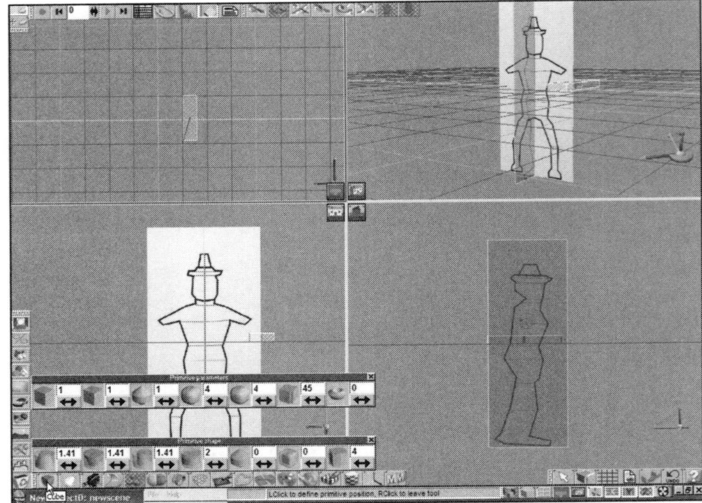

Figure 11.17
Right-click on the Cube tool icon.

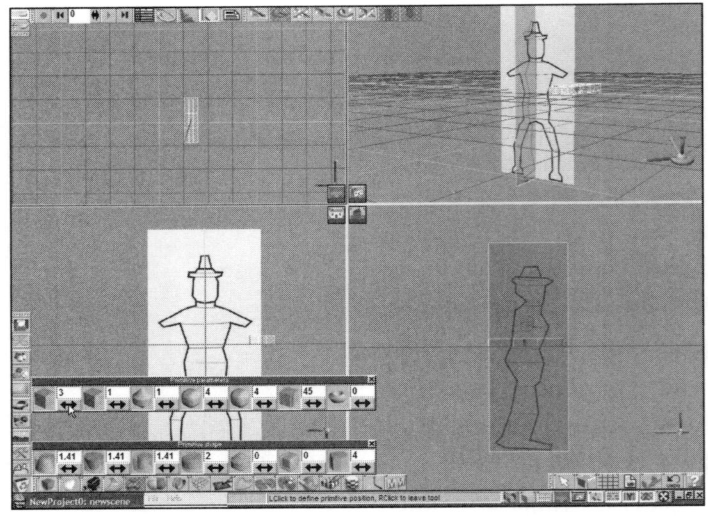

Figure 11.18
Divide the cube into three longitudinal sections.

Aligning the Geometry

Activate the Object tool. Move and scale the new cube in the front viewport so that it is aligned with the tiki's foot, as shown in Figure 11.19.

Once the cube is properly aligned in the front viewport, direct your attention to the side viewport and align the cube there as well. See Figure 11.20.

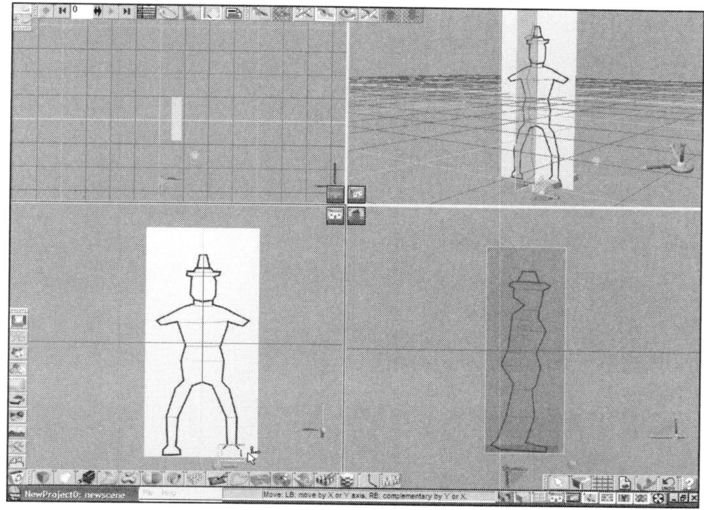

Figure 11.19
Align the cube with the tiki's front foot.

Shaping the Foot

Right-click on the cube to enter Point Edit mode.

Use the Point Edit toolbar to activate Point Edit: Edges mode, and the Select using Rectangle tool.

Right-click on the icon for the Select Using Rectangle tool to open the Selection panel. Verify that the Backside box is checked.

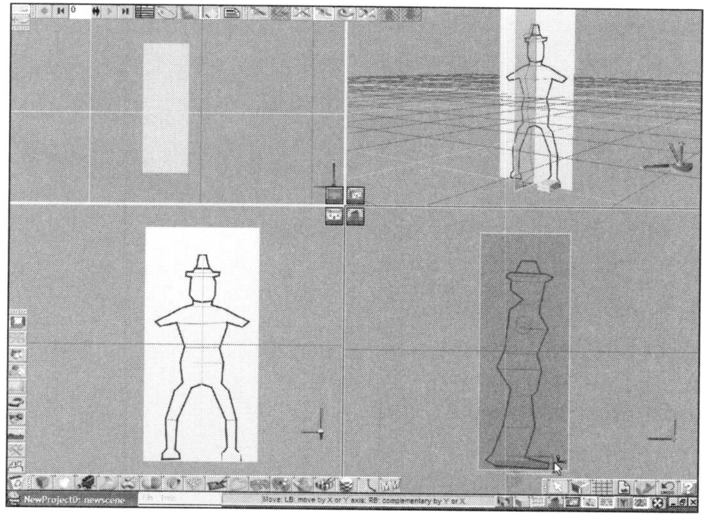

Figure 11.20
The cube must be aligned in the side viewport as well.

Shape the tiki's foot by following the steps indicated in Figures 11.21 through 11.34.

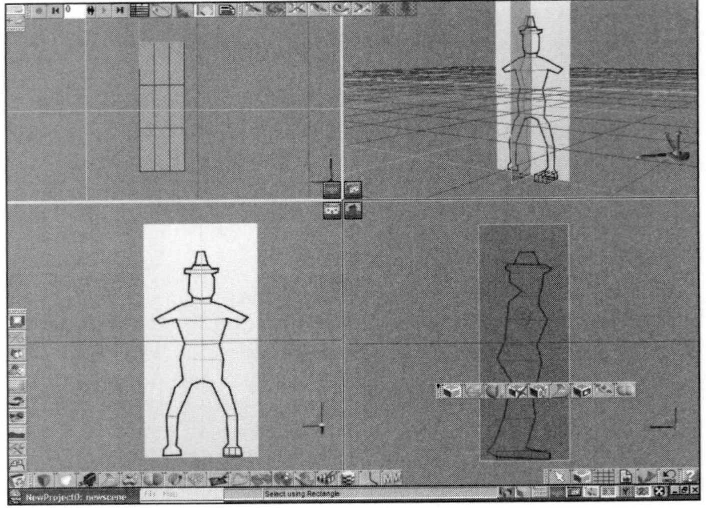

Figure 11.21
In the side viewport, drag a rectangle to select this edge.

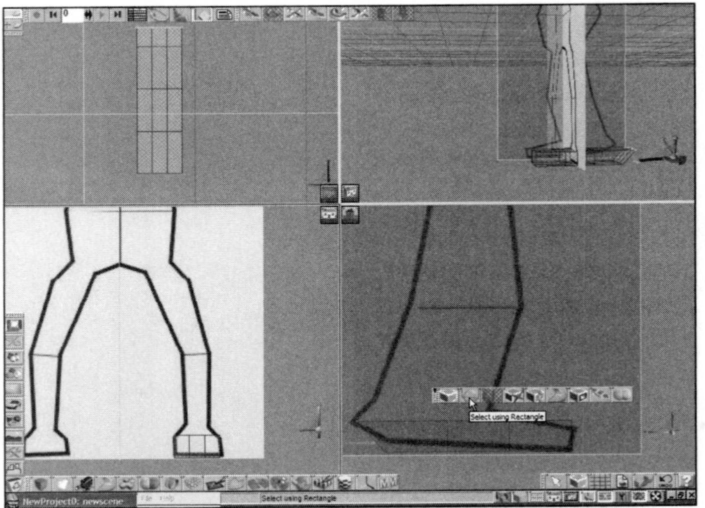

Figure 11.22
In the side viewport, use the Point Move tool to move the edge up and back to the rear of the ankle, then reactivate the Select using Rectangle tool.

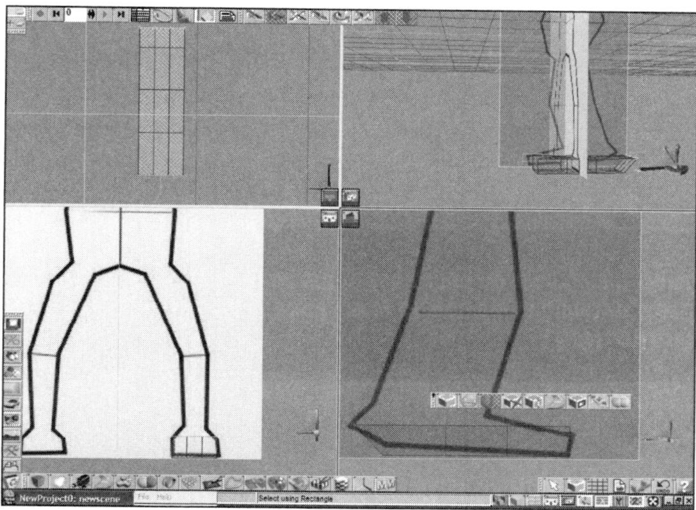

Figure 11.23
Draw a rectangle to select the top front edge.

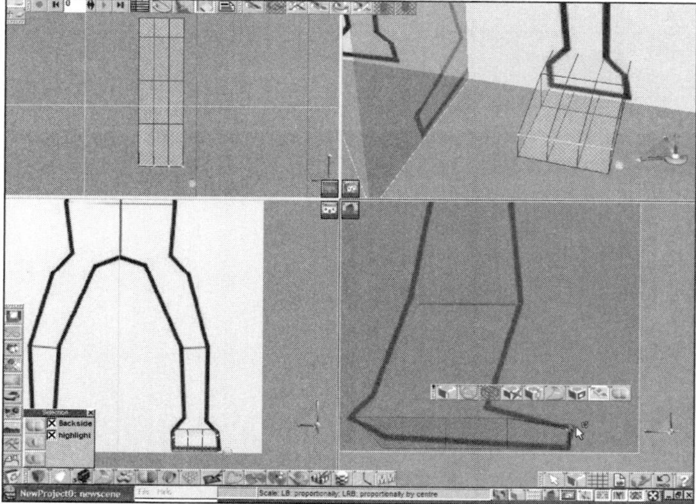

Figure 11.24
Activate the Point Move tool and align this edge with the front of the foot in the side elevation.

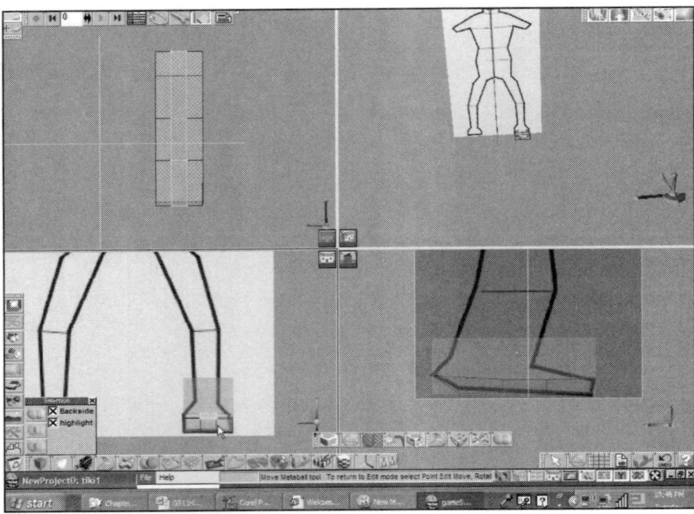

Figure 11.25
Using the front view, draw a rectangle to select the top center edges.

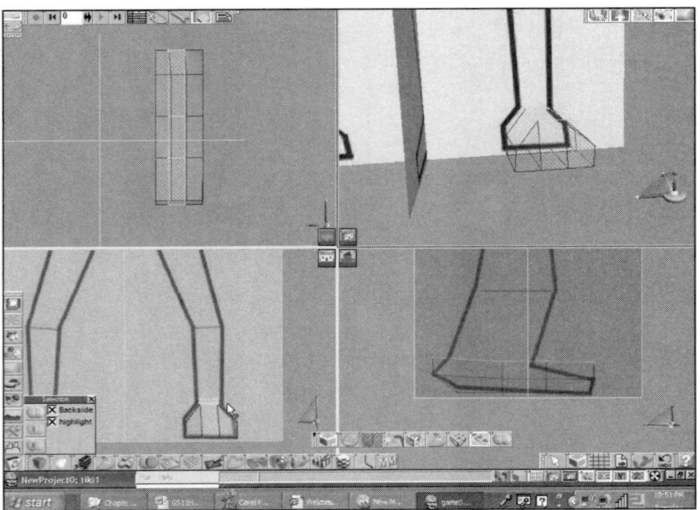

Figure 11.26
Use the Point Move tool to raise these faces until they are high enough to meet the tiki's leg.

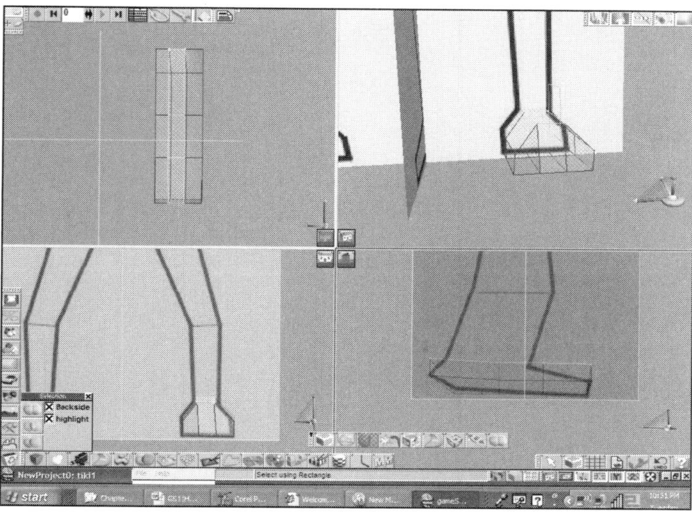

Figure 11.27
Draw a rectangle in the side viewport to select the front edge above the tiki's toes.

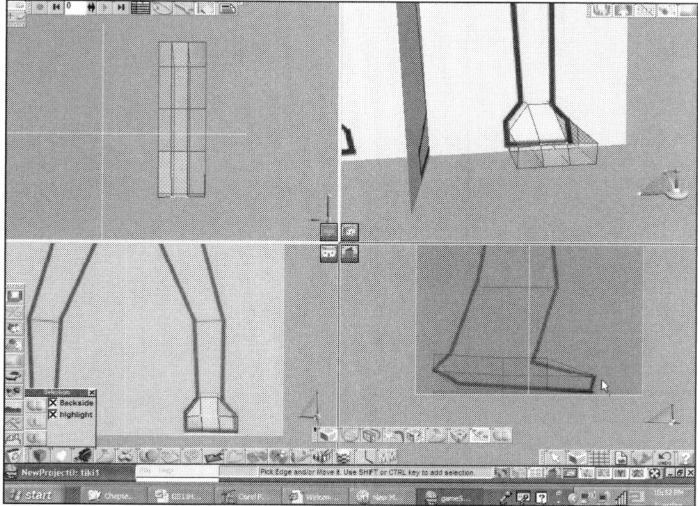

Figure 11.28
Use the Point Move tool to move this edge down into alignment with the elevation drawings.

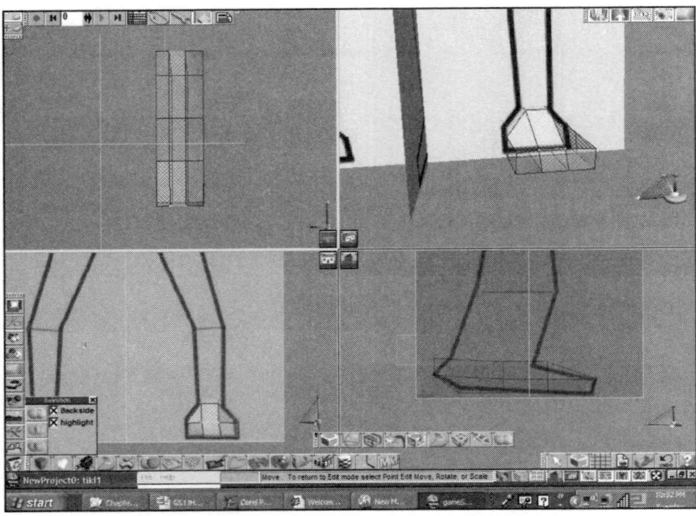

Figure 11.29
In the side viewport, select the edge above the tiki's ankle.

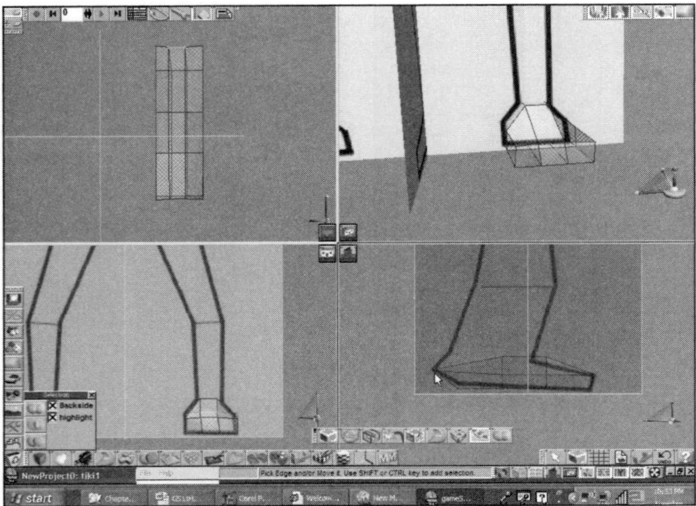

Figure 11.30
Use the Point Move tool to drag the ankle into alignment with the elevations.

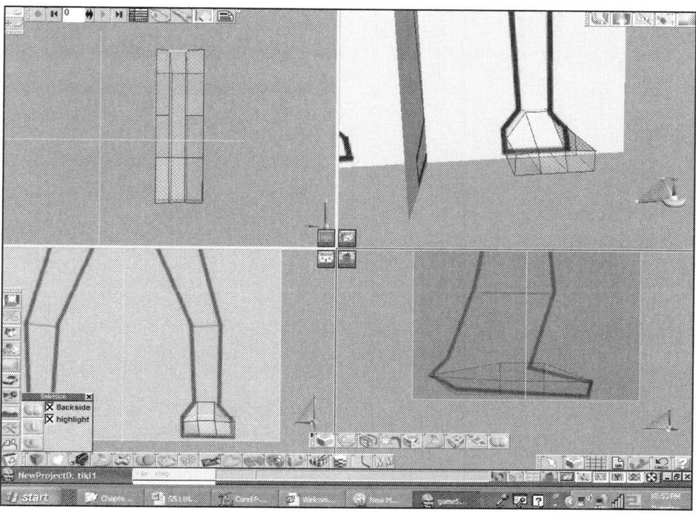

Figure 11.31
In the side viewport, select this edge.

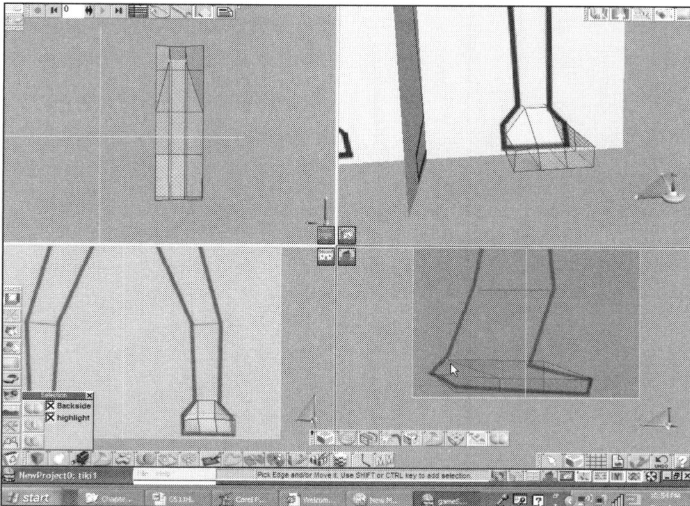

Figure 11.32
Use the Point Move tool to align it with the point where the ankle meets the leg.

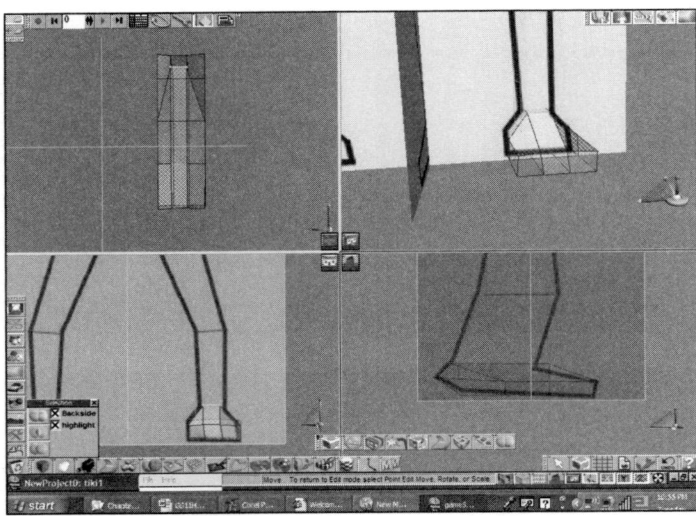

Figure 11.33
Select this edge at the top of the foot.

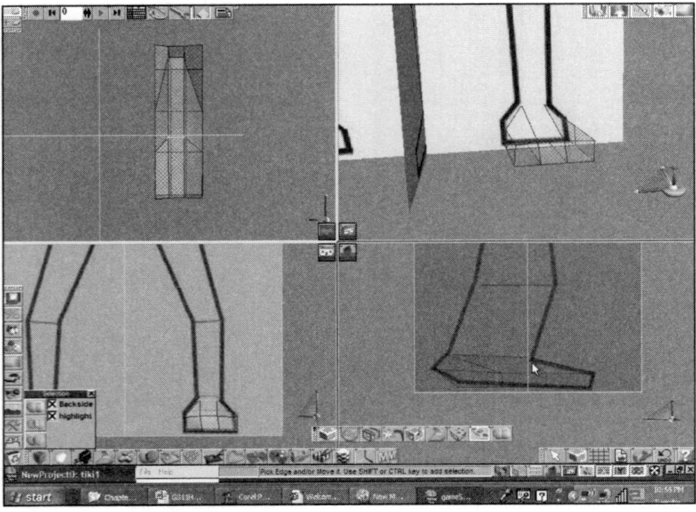

Figure 11.34
Use the Point Move tool to align it with the bottom front of the leg.

You have completed the shape for the foot using extremely few polygons.

Extruding a Leg

Now you must select a face from which you will extrude the leg. Follow the steps indicated in Figures 11.35 through 11.40.

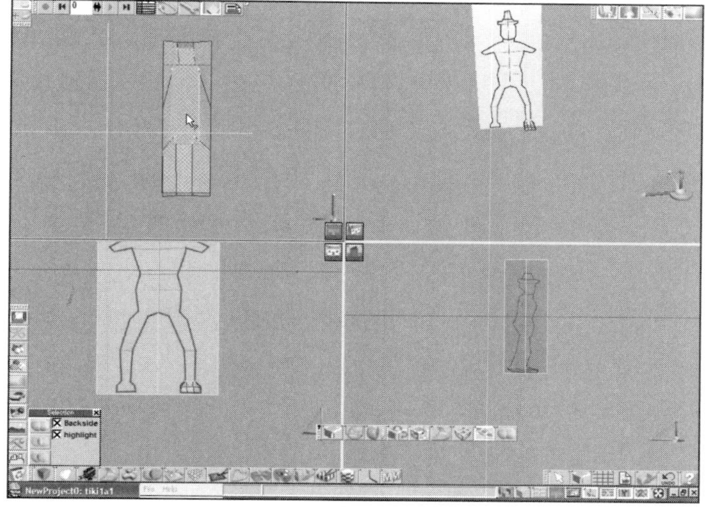

Figure 11.35
Activate the Point Edit: Faces tool, and select this face.

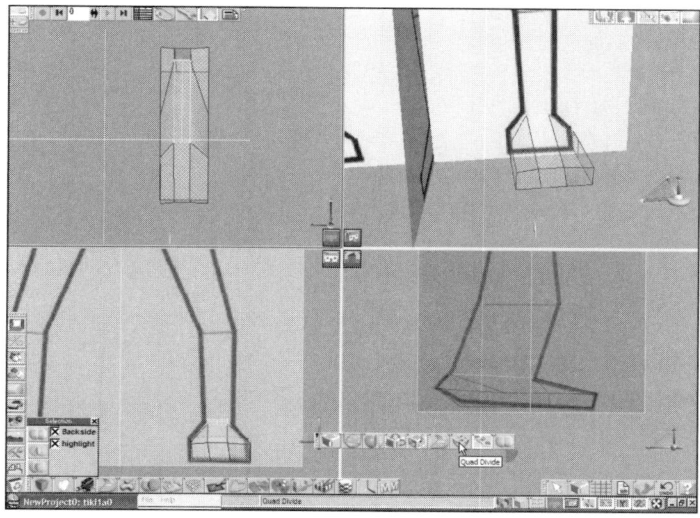

Figure 11.36
Activate the Quad Divide tool to add more detail to the leg.

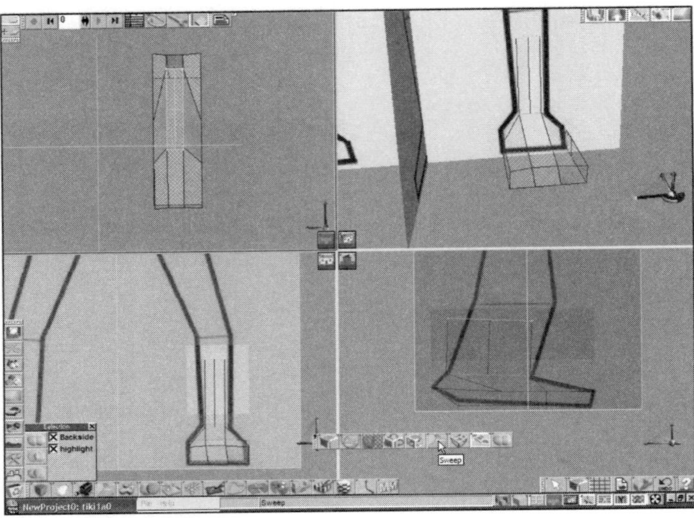

Figure 11.37
Activate the Sweep tool to extrude the face into a leg.

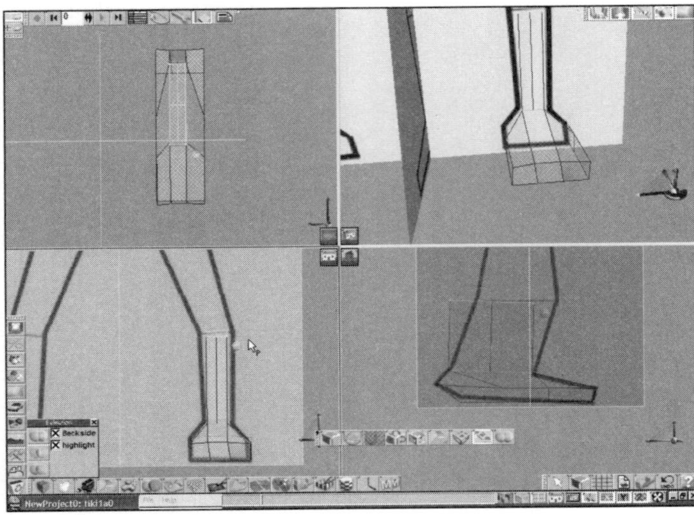

Figure 11.38
Working in the side viewport, use the Point Move tool to raise the top of the leg until it reaches the knee line, drawn on the side elevation.

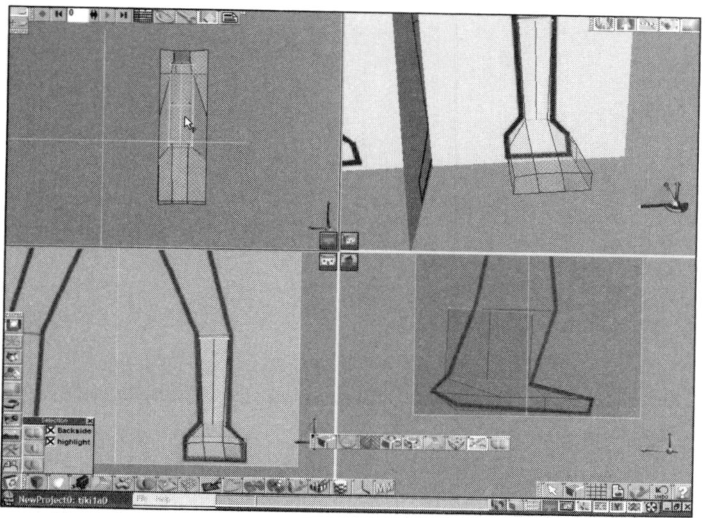

Figure 11.39
Use the Point Scale tool. Watch the front and side viewports as you drag in the top viewport to scale the top of the leg to match the elevations.

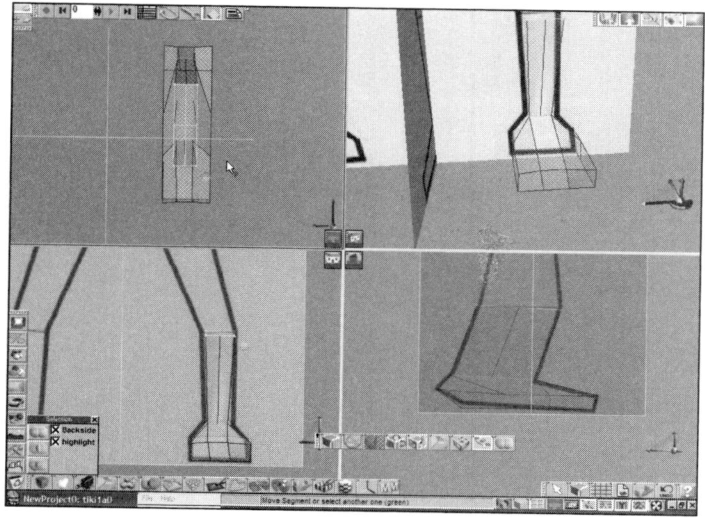

Figure 11.40
Use the Point Move tool. Watch the side viewport, as you drag horizontally in the top viewport to slide the top of the leg into alignment with the side elevation.

Uncheck the Backside box in the Selection panel.

Use the Point Edit: Vertices mode to select each vertex around the top of the newly extruded leg. Use the Point Move tool to move each vertex just enough to round out the knee. See Figure 11.41.

Extrude the upper portion of the leg by performing another sweep. Adjust the new extrusion so that it is aligned with the elevations. See Figure 11.42.

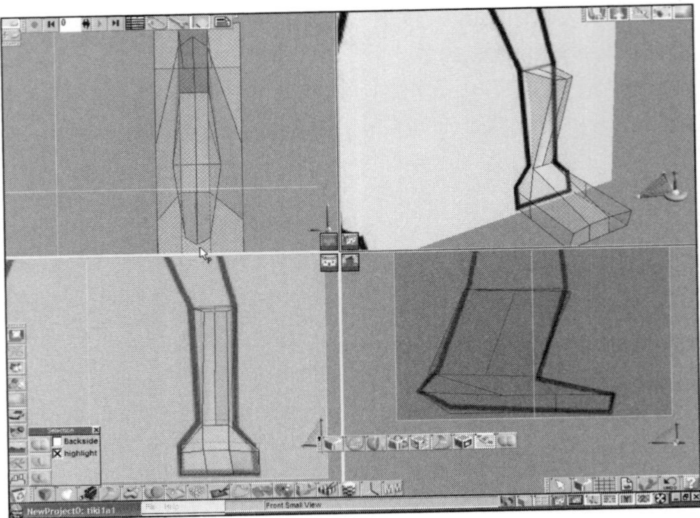

Figure 11.41
Working in the top viewport, use the Point Edit: Vertices mode and the Point Move tool to round out the knee.

Shaping the Hips

Modeling the hips is a bit trickier, because this is where the leg must expand to join the torso.

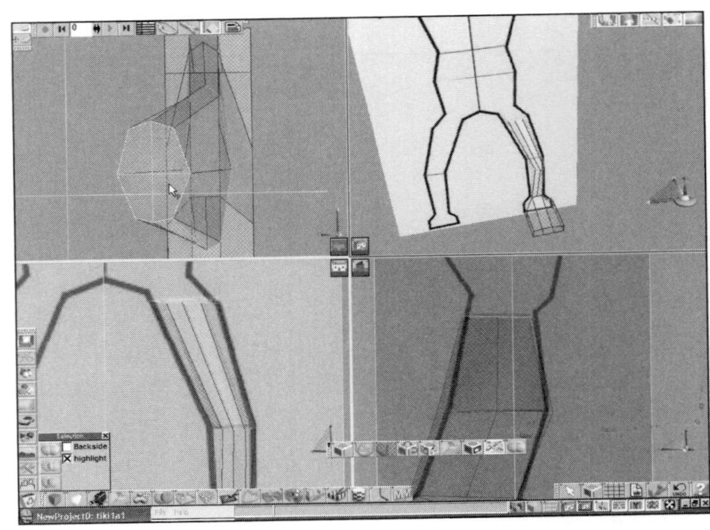

Figure 11.42
Use the Point Move, Point Rotate, and Point Scale tool to match the leg to the elevations.

Figures 11.43 through 11.46 illustrate the steps to complete the hips.

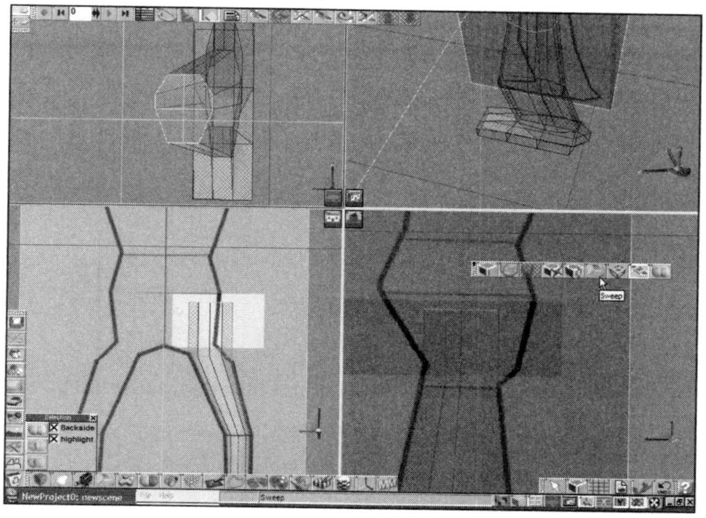

Figure 11.43
Select the four faces at the top of the leg.

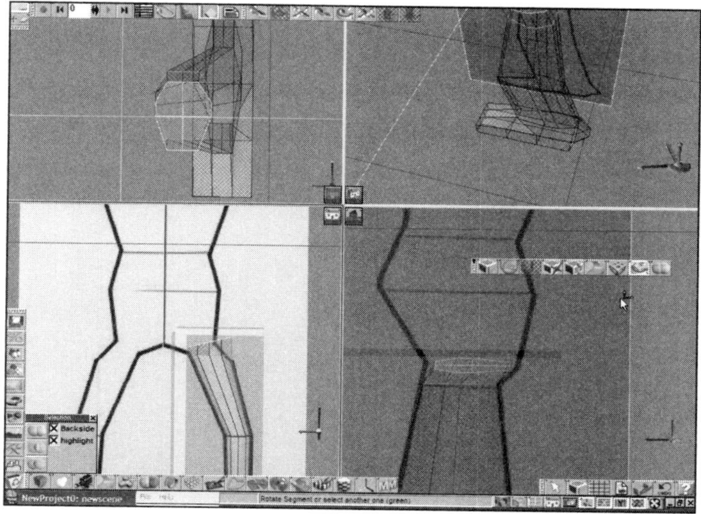

Figure 11.44
Activate the Sweep tool, then use the Point Rotate tool to turn the top inward.

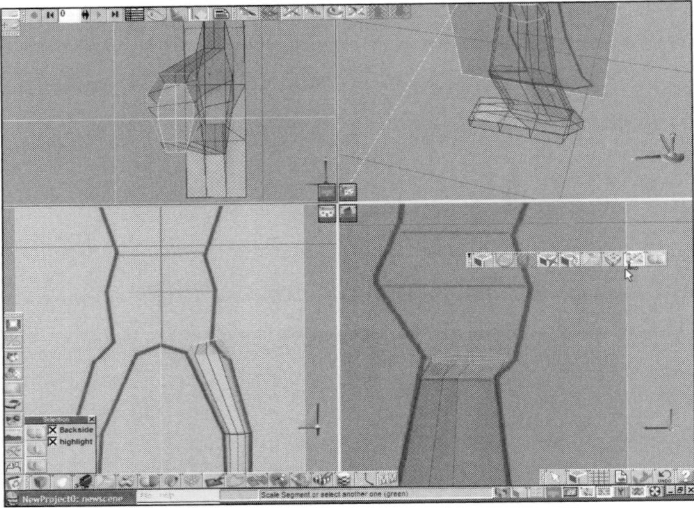

Figure 11.45
Use the Point Scale tool to match the shape of new extrusion to the elevations.

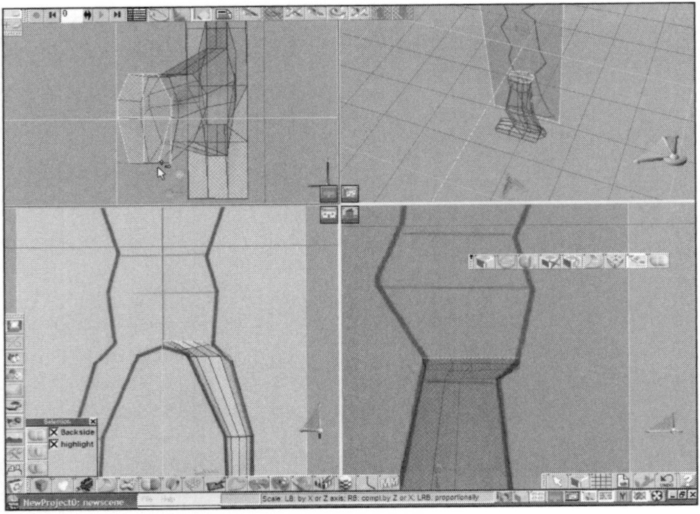

Figure 11.46
Activate the Sweep tool to continue the pelvis. If necessary use the Point Rotate tool to level off the top.

Shaping the Torso

Before you proceed, you will want to add a little more detail to help model the torso sections of the tiki. This time, you will use the Add Edges tool to split an existing face.

Figures 11.47 through 11.51 illustrate the procedure to follow.

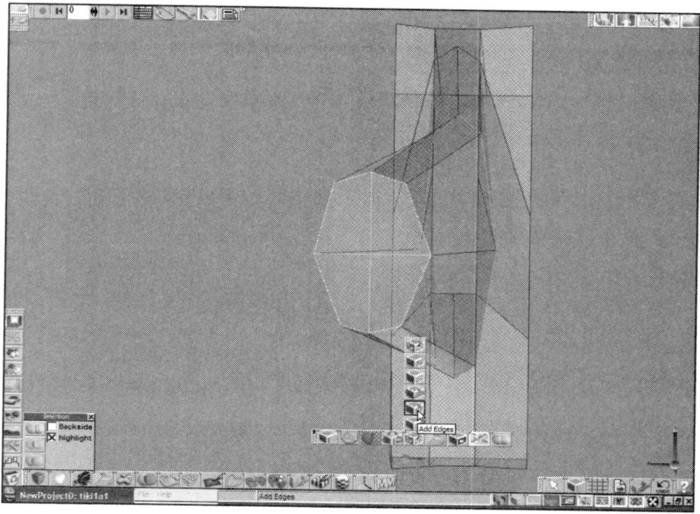

Figure 11.47
Activate the Add Edges tool.

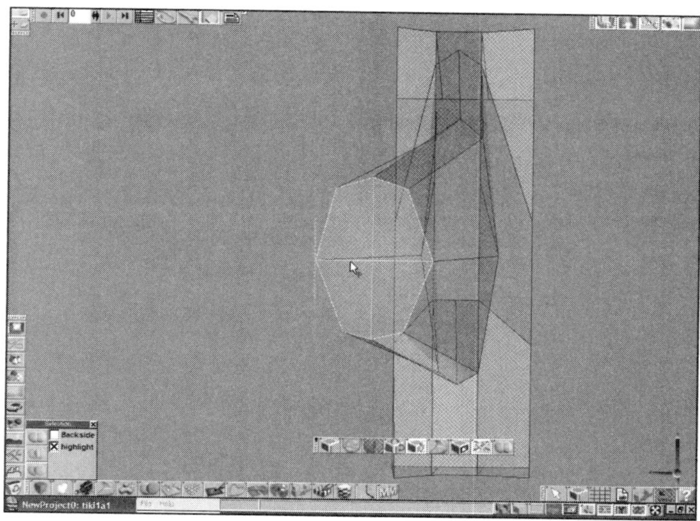

Figure 11.48
Using the top viewport, begin a new edge by clicking here.

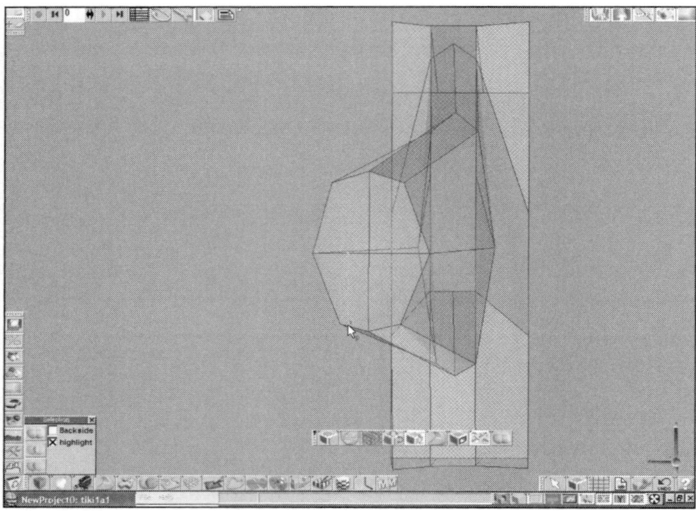

Figure 11.49
Click here to complete the new edge.

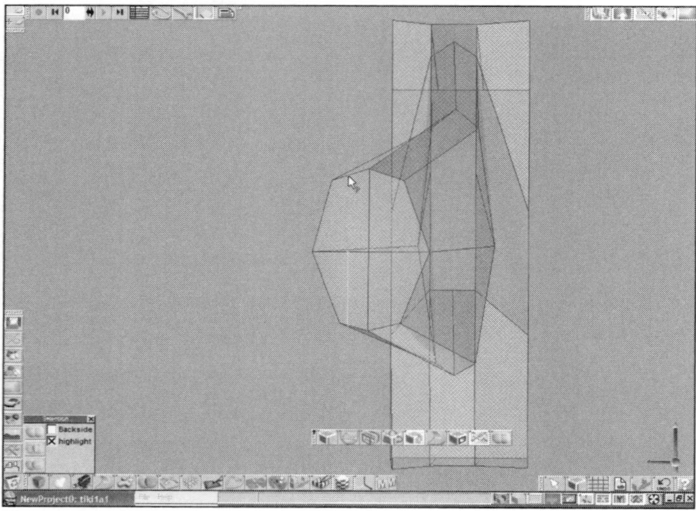

Figure 11.50
Begin another new edge by clicking here.

You are only concerned with modeling the left side of the tiki. Everything on the right side will be mirrored from the left.

Use Point Edit: Vertices mode and the Point Move tool to flatten out the right side of the last extrusion. Make sure the Backside box is not checked. See Figures 11.52 through 11.55.

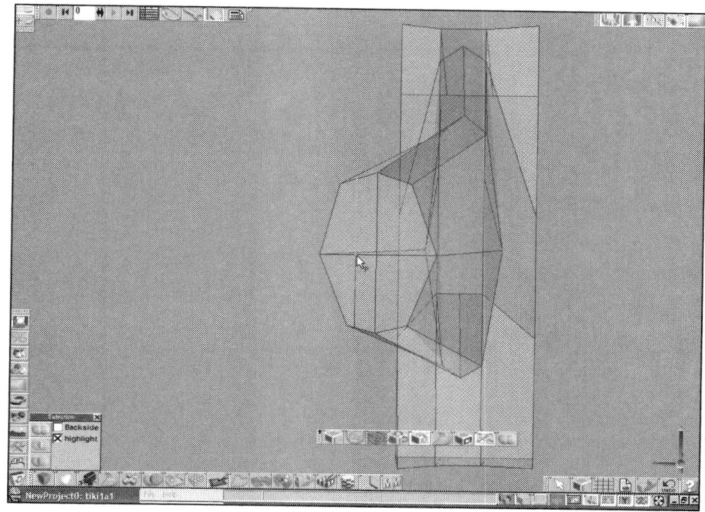

Figure 11.51
Click here to complete the edge.

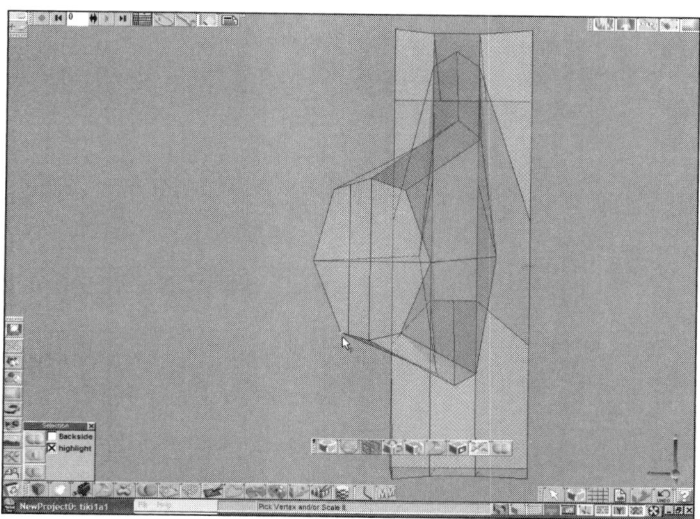

Figure 11.52
Select this vertex.

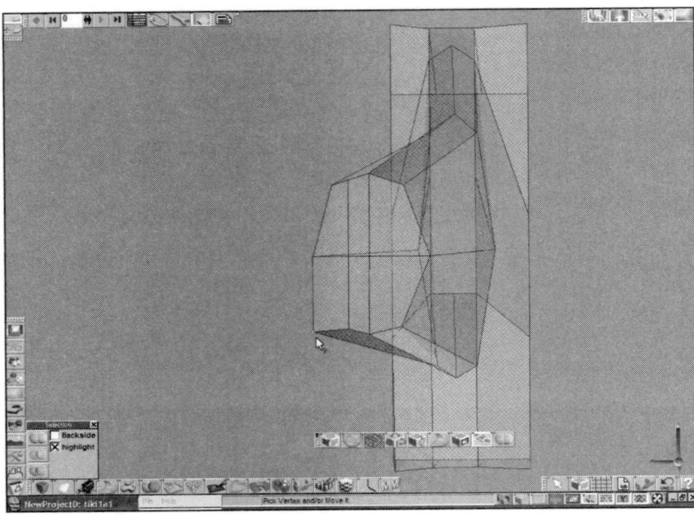

Figure 11.53
Use the Point Move tool to drag the vertex here.

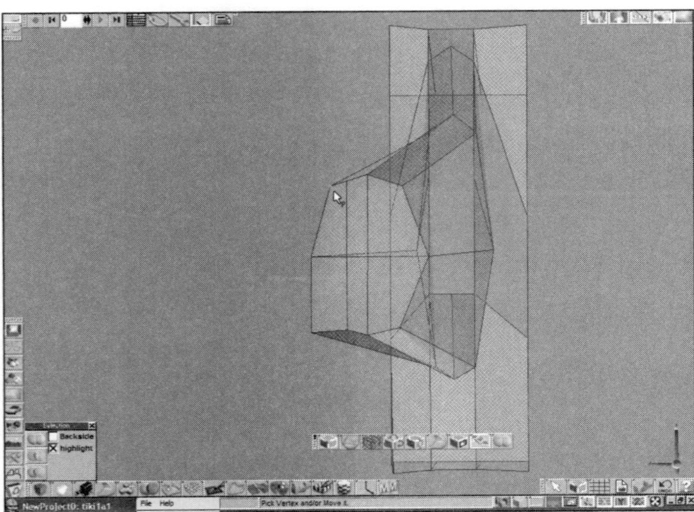

Figure 11.54
Select this vertex.

I will leave it to you to complete the tiki. After every extrusion, you simply adjust the appropriate edges, vertices, and faces until they appear to align with the images on the elevation. Then you select some or all of the top faces to be the base for your next sweep.

When you get to the hat, you might find it is easier to sweep the hat from a cylinder and then glue or use Boolean Union to attach it to the rest of the tiki.

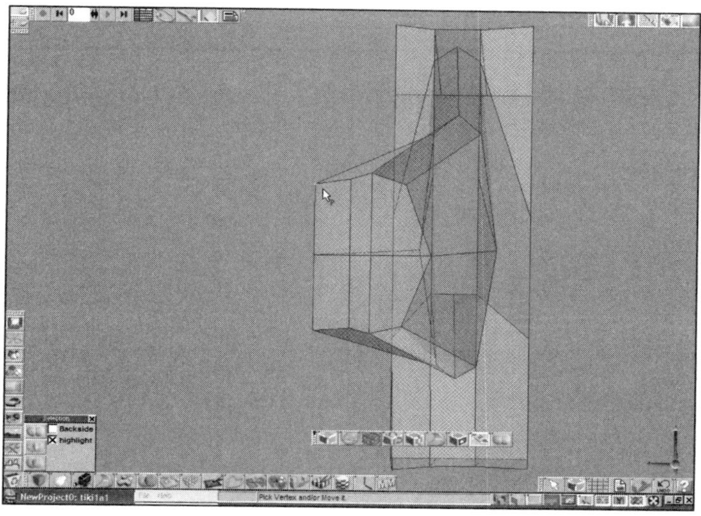

Figure 11.55
Use the Point Move tool to drag the vertex here.

Preparing for the Mirror

Remember, you are only modeling the left side of the character. Try to keep the right-hand side flat, but don't get overly concerned with it. There is a simple trick you can use to eliminate any irregularities along the mirror line.

Once your object is complete, but before you activate the Mirror Modeler, create a large cube that is taller and deeper than your model. See Figure 11.56.

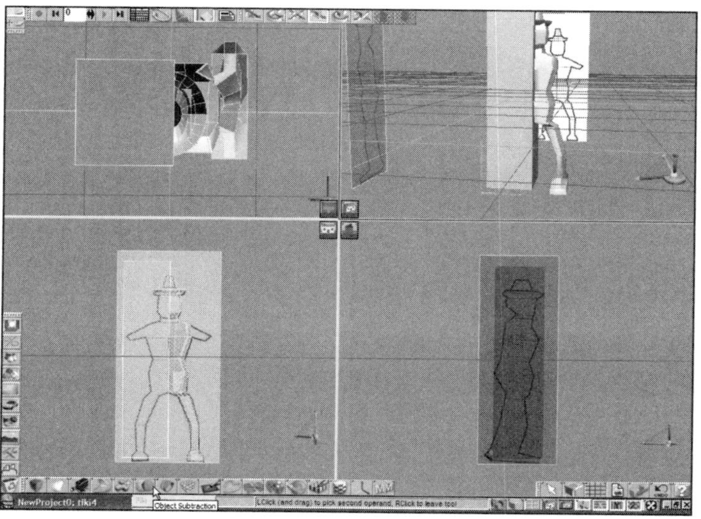

Figure 11.56
A large cube encases the far right side of the model.

Select the tiki model, and use the Object Subtraction tool to Boolean subtract the cube from the tiki. In Figures 11.57 and 11.58, you can see that the Boolean subtraction has left a perfectly clean edge for the Mirror Modeler to mirror across.

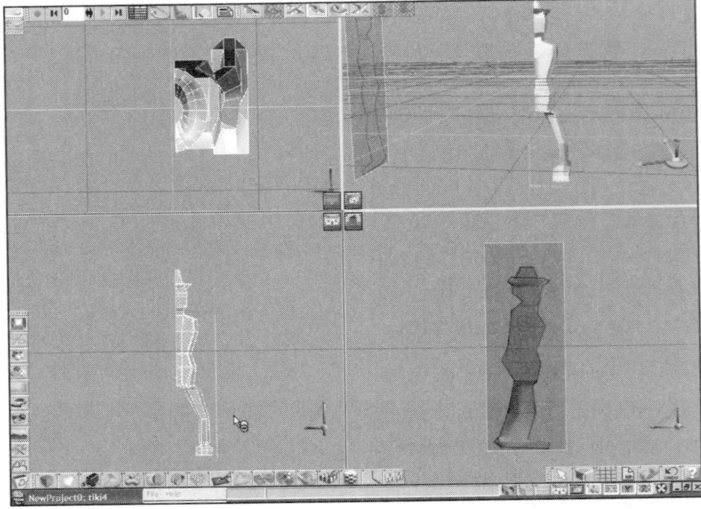

Figure 11.57
The tiki now has a perfectly flat edge on its right-hand side.

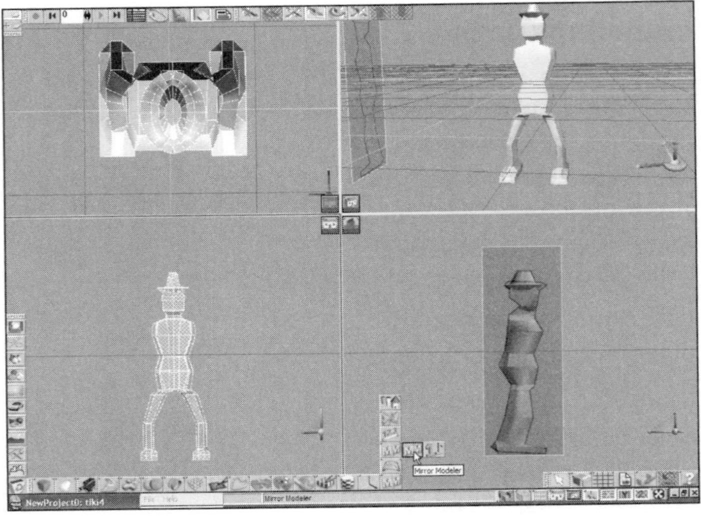

Figure 11.58
This is the result of mirroring across this edge.

When you have completed the tiki, position and scale it as indicated in Table 11.1.

Table 11.1 Tiki Object Parameters

	X	Y	Z
Location	0.0	0.0	0.0
Rotation	0	0	0
Scale	2	2	5

Use ObjectImporter to choose the tiki as Game Object 6, and look for it in the final room in the large room at the bottom of the long steep hall. See Figure 11.59.

Figure 11.59
Welcome to the lair of the great burning tiki.

The CD that accompanies this book contains a wonderful set of tutorials from 3D Buzz. One covers much of the material discussed in this chapter, and the other is an introduction to rigging characters with bones for animation. I am grateful to our friends at Caligari and 3D Buzz for allowing us to include them for you, and I recommend you watch them both.

Summary

In this chapter, you should have learned the following concepts:

- Art directors are at least indirectly responsible for every object, texture, level, character, and effect that appears in a game.
- A character is any person, creature, robot, or animal in a game.
- Scripting refers to the process of writing small specialized programs that control the actions and behavior of each character and prop in a game.

- A prop is any object that a character can use, hold, take, or move in any manner.
- Verisimilitude is the consistent appearance or illusion of reality and truth.
- A maquette is a three-dimensional physical model used to visualize or test an artistic or architectural concept or design.
- The term "As-Builts" refers to plans or elevations drawn to document a preexisting product, structure, prop, set, character, sculpture, or model.
- A game design document or game bible refers to the collection of all the plans, designs, descriptions, rules, stories, and any other literary or illustrated concepts that have been accepted by the design team to become part of the game.
- The Add Edges tool splits an existing face by creating a new edge from one selected point to another.
- Boolean subtraction can be used to create a smooth, flat edge for mirroring an object.
- Each viewport can be configured with its own texture resolution.
- Planes can be used to display elevations during the modeling process.

Questions and Answers

Q: What should be included in a character design package that is added to the game design document?

A: Illustrations, renderings, elevations, color sheets, and As-Builts.

Q: Who maintains the game design document?

A: Usually one member of the design team is charged with maintaining and updating the game design document.

Q: What are commonly presented to a game artist as a guide to model a character?

A: Elevations.

Q: Where can an art director research a game's genre, period, or locale?

A: Books, libraries, films, the Internet, other games, or practically anywhere else.

Q: How can you determine an image's original aspect ratio within gameSpace?

A: The file information pop-up window that appears whenever your mouse is over an image in the Texture Browser window displays the original image's precise aspect ratio.

Q: How can you adjust the aspect ratio of a plane primitive?

A: A plane primitive's X and Y Size values, which appear in the Object Info Pane, control the aspect ratio of that plane.

Discussion Questions

1. Discuss a way that an art director might use color to indicate a change in a character during a game.
2. Describe how an environment could be modified to create an increased sense of mystery or drama.
3. Describe a situation where an art director might draw a set of As-Builts from a maquette.
4. Why is it important that a game design team maintain an official game design document?
5. Why is it important that one member of a design team is assigned to maintain the official game design document?
6. What can an art director do to support the verisimilitude of a game?
7. What can an art director do that would hurt the verisimilitude of a game?
8. Is there ever a time when you would need more than two elevations to model a character? Why or why not?

Exercises

1. Draw a set of elevations or As-Builts for any item in your house.
2. Complete the tiki model begun in this chapter.
3. Add any form of arms and hands to the tiki model in this chapter.
4. Create a design package for a game character and include a set of elevations and color sheets describing the colors and materials to use with the character.
5. The Textures folder on the CD that accompanies this book includes a set of dragon elevations. Use these three elevations to create a dragon to replace the tiki as Game Object 6 in Adventure Explorer.
6. The Tutorials section of the CD that accompanies this book contains a set of video tutorials from 3D Buzz. Watch these tutorials and build the character model they discuss.

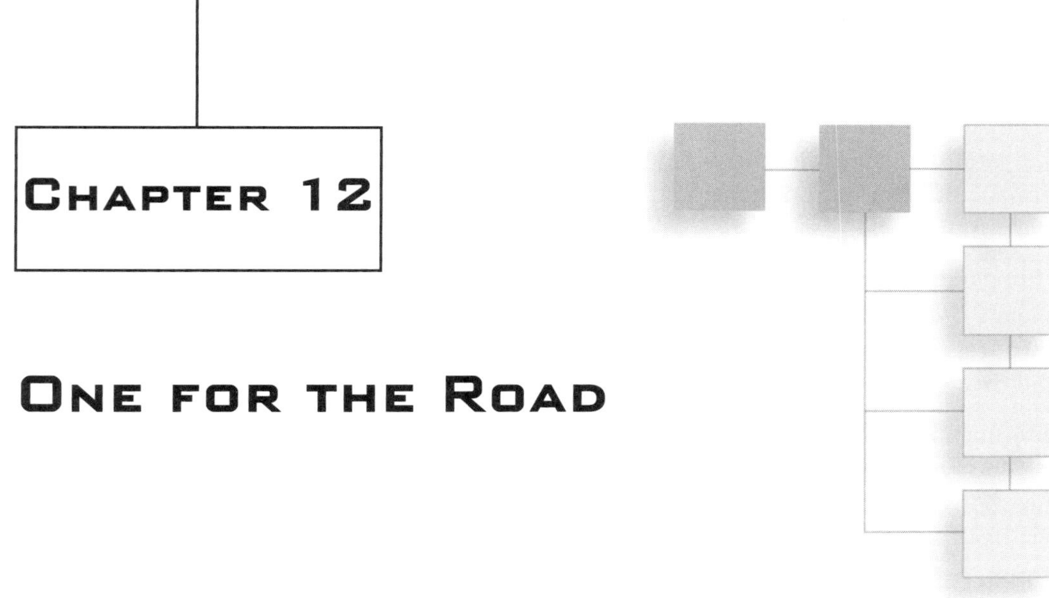

Chapter 12

One for the Road

Chapter 12 is a bonus chapter. In it you will learn how to make a mine car that you can actually ride in the Adventure Explorer game.

Finding the Bonus Chapter

You can find Chapter 12 online on the companion Web site. Along with this chapter, the Web site also hosts a vehicle gallery where you can post your own vehicle designs. There is also a section with vehicle design tips, and the Adventure Explorer racetrack may not be far behind. See Figure 12.1.

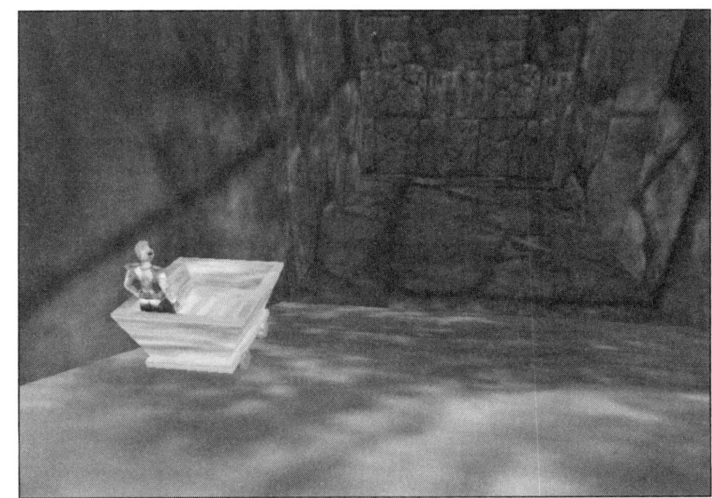

Figure 12.1
Enjoy the ride!

Next Steps

This book has covered the basics, and it has hopefully given you enough powerful tools to create some incredible game models. The tools available to you in gameSpace are far more powerful than anything that I imagined when I began making video games.

My own enthusiasm for game making has opened up many wonderful doors for me over the past 20 years. Along the way, I have met many incredible people and found vast collections of information, hope, and encouragement in the words and writings of a great many more.

I hope that you will find many innovative uses for the skills, thoughts, and ideas you have taken from this book. I hope they will, in some small manner, provide a springboard of encouragement to help launch you toward finding and pursuing your own unique visions and dreams.

As you continue your adventures in the video-game and interactive entertainment industry, you will find there are many wonderful books and resources available to assist you. I have posted a number of useful links on the companion site for this book, www.gamescapers.com/GameGraphics, and I will continue updating the site as new resources come to my attention.

If you have any thoughts or comments on this book, I would love to hear from you. My contact information is posted on the Web site www.gamescapers.com/GameGraphics. Please share any fun and innovative designs you might dream up for the various objects in Adventure Explorer.

Good luck, and best wishes on your lifelong adventure with video games.

INDEX

D

E

K

L

Q

R

T

U

V

W

X

Y

Z

License Agreement/Notice of Limited Warranty

By opening the sealed disc container in this book, you agree to the following terms and conditions. If, upon reading the following license agreement and notice of limited warranty, you cannot agree to the terms and conditions set forth, return the unused book with unopened disc to the place where you purchased it for a refund.

License:

The enclosed software is copyrighted by the copyright holder(s) indicated on the software disc. You are licensed to copy the software onto a single computer for use by a single user and to a backup disc. You may not reproduce, make copies, or distribute copies or rent or lease the software in whole or in part, except with written permission of the copyright holder(s). You may transfer the enclosed disc only together with this license, and only if you destroy all other copies of the software and the transferee agrees to the terms of the license. You may not decompile, reverse assemble, or reverse engineer the software.

Notice of Limited Warranty:

The enclosed disc is warranted by Thomson Course Technology PTR to be free of physical defects in materials and workmanship for a period of sixty (60) days from end user's purchase of the book/disc combination. During the sixty-day term of the limited warranty, Thomson Course Technology PTR will provide a replacement disc upon the return of a defective disc.

Limited Liability:

THE SOLE REMEDY FOR BREACH OF THIS LIMITED WARRANTY SHALL CONSIST ENTIRELY OF REPLACEMENT OF THE DEFECTIVE DISC. IN NO EVENT SHALL THOMSON COURSE TECHNOLOGY PTR OR THE AUTHOR BE LIABLE FOR ANY OTHER DAMAGES, INCLUDING LOSS OR CORRUPTION OF DATA, CHANGES IN THE FUNCTIONAL CHARACTERISTICS OF THE HARDWARE OR OPERATING SYSTEM, DELETERIOUS INTERACTION WITH OTHER SOFTWARE, OR ANY OTHER SPECIAL, INCIDENTAL, OR CONSEQUENTIAL DAMAGES THAT MAY ARISE, EVEN IF THOMSON COURSE TECHNOLOGY PTR AND/OR THE AUTHOR HAS PREVIOUSLY BEEN NOTIFIED THAT THE POSSIBILITY OF SUCH DAMAGES EXISTS.

Disclaimer of Warranties:

THOMSON COURSE TECHNOLOGY PTR AND THE AUTHOR SPECIFICALLY DISCLAIM ANY AND ALL OTHER WARRANTIES, EITHER EXPRESS OR IMPLIED, INCLUDING WARRANTIES OF MERCHANTABILITY, SUITABILITY TO A PARTICULAR TASK OR PURPOSE, OR FREEDOM FROM ERRORS. SOME STATES DO NOT ALLOW FOR EXCLUSION OF IMPLIED WARRANTIES OR LIMITATION OF INCIDENTAL OR CONSEQUENTIAL DAMAGES, SO THESE LIMITATIONS MIGHT NOT APPLY TO YOU.

Other:

This Agreement is governed by the laws of the State of Massachusetts without regard to choice of law principles. The United Convention of Contracts for the International Sale of Goods is specifically disclaimed. This Agreement constitutes the entire agreement between you and Thomson Course Technology PTR regarding use of the software.